ACKNOWLEDGMENTS

We thank Randi Gollin, Lynn Hazlewood, Rebecca Flint Marx, Bernard Onken and Miranda Van Gelder, as well as the following members of our staff: Caitlin Miehl (editor), Anna Hyclak (editor), Brian Albert, Sean Beachell, Maryanne Bertollo, Reni Chin, Larry Cohn, Nicole Diaz, Kelly Dobkin, Jeff Freier, Alison Gainor, Matthew Hamm, Justin Hartung, Marc Henson, Ryutaro Ishikane, Natalie Lebert, Mike Liao, Vivian Ma, James Mulcahy, Polina Paley, Josh Rogers, Amanda Spurlock, Chris Walsh, Jacqueline Wasilczyk, Sharon Yates, Anna Zappia and Kyle Zolner.

The reviews in this guide are based on public opinion surveys. The ratings reflect the average scores given by the survey participants who voted on each establishment. The text is based on quotes from, or paraphrasings of, the surveyors' comments. Phone numbers, addresses and other factual data were correct to the best of our knowledge when published in this guide.

Contents

About This Survey

This **2012/13 New York City Food Lover's Survey** is an update reflecting significant developments since our last Survey was published. It covers 1,537 establishments, including 70 important additions, plus 357 party sites and 98 online sources. To bring this guide up to the minute, we surveyed recent arrivals as well as last year's unrated properties, and also indicated new addresses, phone numbers and other major changes. Like all our guides, this one is based on input from avid local consumers – 6,909 all told. Our editors have synopsized this feedback, including representative comments (in quotation marks within each review).

ABOUT ZAGAT: In 1979, we started asking friends to rate and review restaurants purely for fun. The term "user-generated content" had yet to be coined. That hobby grew into Zagat Survey; 33 years later, we have over 375,000 surveyors and cover airlines, bars, dining, fast food, entertaining, golf, hotels, movies, music, resorts, shopping, spas, theater and tourist attractions in over 100 countries. Along the way, we evolved from being a print publisher to a digital content provider, e.g. **zagat.com** and Zagat mobile apps (for Android, iPad, iPhone, BlackBerry, Windows Phone 7 and Palm webOS). We also produce marketing tools for a wide range of blue-chip corporate clients. And you can find us on Google+ and just about any other social media network.

UNDERLYING PREMISES: Three simple ideas underlie our ratings and reviews. First, we believe that the collective opinions of large numbers of consumers are more accurate than those of any single person. (Consider that our surveyors bring some 583,000 annual transactions' worth of experience to this survey). Second, because there are many factors to be weighed when choosing a purveyor, we ask our surveyors to rate quality, display and service separately and then estimate the cost. Third, since people need reliable information in an easy-to-digest format, we strive to be concise and we offer our content on every platform – print, online and mobile. Our Top Ratings lists (pages 9–16) and indexes (starting on page 212) are also designed to help you quickly choose the best place for any occasion, and we've included an Online Sources section as well (Top Ratings, pages 272–273).

JOIN IN: To improve our guides, we solicit your comments – positive or negative; it's vital that we hear your opinions. Just contact us at **nina-tim@zagat.com.** We also invite you to join our surveys at **zagat.com.** Do so and you'll receive a choice of rewards in exchange.

New York, NY
May 23, 2012

Nina and Tim Zagat

How to Use This Guide

NYC is arguably the world's best city for food lovers, and its restaurants are only part of the reason. Equally exciting are its unmatched food shops, from old favorites like the Bronx's **Casa Della Mozzarella** (which nabs the Survey's top Quality rating) and **Zabar's** to hot newcomers like **Maison Ladurée** and **Ample Hills Creamery.** And if there's anything that NYers enjoy as much as good food, it's a good party, hence the city's abundance of caterers, florists and other experts. This guide brings together the best of all these resources, making it easy to find what you need whether you're cooking for one or throwing a bash for hundreds.

 IN THE KITCHEN: Home cooks can browse our top lists and indexes to find the right place to get ingredients of every kind – from freshly roasted coffee at **McNulty's** to handmade pastas at **Borgatti's Ravioli** – as well as kitchen equipment ranging from basic to professional-level. See our index of **Major Markets** (page 232) for one-stop shopping, our rundown of the city's **Greenmarket** locations (page 182) for farm-fresh fare and our **Green Glossary** to help you make sense of local/sustainable terminology (page 184). We also cover the city's newer markets – the **Brooklyn Flea, Fulton Stall, Hester Street Fair, New Amsterdam** – as well as the vendors who offer their wares there.

LET'S PARTY: For would-be hosts, we've included caterers and event planners who can do it all – whether you're looking for a tony affair from outfits like **Great Performances** and **Glorious Food** or a down-home spread from **Spoonbread Inc.** – as well as resources you'll need if you plan to DIY, such as florists (e.g. **Gramercy Flowers**), vintners (e.g. **Le Dû's Wines**) and party rental outfits that can supply everything from china and linens to tables and tents. Wedding cakes are covered too, as are prepared foods purveyors. Our **Party Sites** appendix (page 186) lists 357 of the best venues for entertaining, with options that can accommodate anything from an intimate dinner to a grand gala. It includes art galleries, mansions, lofts, formal gardens and more – not to mention the city's best bars, restaurants and hotels.

TASTEFUL TOURING: On page 13 we offer lists of must-visit places in some of the city's storied neighborhoods, e.g. Chinatown and Little Italy, where the mix ranges from the Italian dairy **Di Palo** and the Spanish import store **Despaña** to **Ten Ren Tea** and **Dragonland**; and the LES and East Village's blend of old (**Russ & Daughters, Streit's Matzo**) and newer (**Doughnut Plant, Il Laboratorio del Gelato**). These tours show that you really can go around the world on a MetroCard.

SURF'S UP: The few items that aren't available within the five boroughs can be conjured with the click of a mouse – these days just about anything can be ordered from just about anywhere and, in many cases, delivered the next day. Our **Online Resources** section (starting on page 272) covers 98 standouts ranging from fine artisan cheeses (**Cowgirl Creamery**) and premier-quality teas (**Upton Imports**) to far-flung confectioners (**Big Island Candies**) and growers of exotic legumes (**Rancho Gordo**).

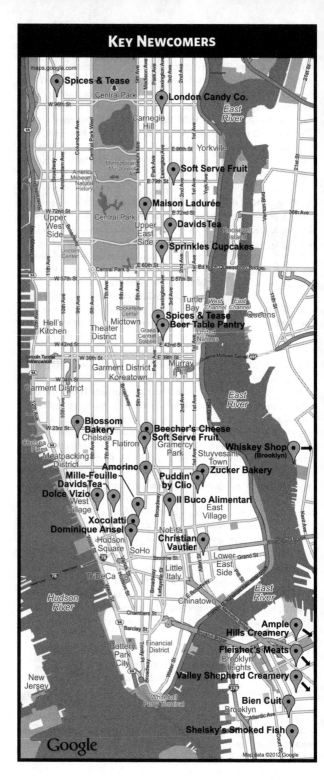

Spices & Tease
London Candy Co.
Soft Serve Fruit
Maison Ladurée
DavidsTea
Sprinkles Cupcakes
Spices & Tease
Beer Table Pantry
Blossom Bakery
Beecher's Cheese
Soft Serve Fruit
Whiskey Shop (Brooklyn)
Amorino
Mille-Feuille
Zucker Bakery
DavidsTea
Puddin' by Clio
Dolce Vizio
Xocolatti
Il Buco Alimentari
Dominique Ansel
Christian Vautier
Ample Hills Creamery
Fleisher's Meats
Valley Shepherd Creamery
Bien Cuit
Shelsky's Smoked Fish

Google

Vote at zagat.com

Key Newcomers

Our editors' picks among this year's arrivals. See full list on p. 212.

Amorino | *Ice Cream* | Village outpost of an Italian artisanal gelato chain

Ample Hills Creamery | *Ice Cream* | Locavore scoops in Prospect Heights

Beecher's | *Cheese/Dairy* | The Seattle fromage favorite comes to the Flatiron

Beer Table Pantry | *Beer* | On-the-go craft suds in Grand Central

Bien Cuit | *Baked Goods* | 'Well-done' bread and tarts for Cobble Hill

Blossom Bakery | *Baked Goods* | Vegan organic treats from the Blossom folks

Christian Vautier Le Concept | *Candy/Nuts* | Haute confections on the LES

DavidsTea | *Coffee/Tea* | Montreal tea merchant branches out to NYC

Dolce Vizio | *Baked Goods* | Tiramisu gets its own West Village shop

Dominique Ansel Bakery | *Baked Goods* | SoHo patisserie from a Daniel vet

Fleisher's Meats | *Meat/Poultry* | Lauded Kingston, NY, butcher hits Bklyn

Il Buco Alimentari | *Specialty Shop* | Artisan salumi and provisions in NoHo

London Candy Co. | *Candy/Nuts* | Sweets from Old Blighty on the UES

Maison Ladurée | *Baked Goods* | Paris' ballyhooed macarons fly to the UES

Mille-Feuille | *Baked Goods* | French patisserie facsimile in the Village

Puddin' by Clio | *Baked Goods* | East Villager upgrading the namesake dessert

Shelsky's | *Smoked Fish* | Old-style Jewish appetizing store for Boerum Hill

Soft Serve Fruit Co. | *Ice Cream* | Fresh fruit gets the soft-serve treatment

Spices & Tease | *Herbs/Spices* | Tea-and-spice market vendor sets up shop

Sprinkles | *Baked Goods* | Beverly Hills cupcakery comes to the UES

Valley Shepherd | *Cheese/Dairy* | Sheep cheeses from a NJ farm hit Bklyn

Whiskey Shop | *Wine/Liquor* | Every whiskey under the sun in Billyburg

Xocolatti | *Candy/Nuts* | SoHo haven for adventurous chocolate connoisseurs

Zucker Bakery | *Baked Goods* | Sticky buns and rugalach in the East Village

---

Coming Soon: The city's major markets are in expansion mode, with the venerable UESer **Agata & Valentina** set to open a Village store, **Whole Foods** readying a satellite on the East Side (and breaking ground on a site in Park Slope) and Brooklyn mini-chain **Union Market** preparing to cross the river with its first Manhattan outpost, in the East Village. Meanwhile, Williamsburg will get its first high-end grocery when the 15,000-sq.-ft. **Brooklyn Harvest Market** opens in the base of a luxury condo tower, sited beside the **Brooklyn Flea**'s waterfront digs. Billyburg cookware purveyor **Whisk** has a second, more ambitious Flatiron shop on the way, and is also opening a nearby vintner, **Flatiron Wine & Spirits. Dickson's Farmstand Meats** will branch out to TriBeCa with a roomy new retail store/restaurant, François Payard will add to his **FPB** fiefdom with a patisserie on Columbus Circle, his biggest yet, and **Lady M** has a Plaza Hotel offshoot in the works.

Ratings & Symbols

Zagat Top Spot	Name	Symbols	Category	Zagat Ratings			
				QUALITY	DISPLAY	SERVICE	COST

Area, Address & Contact
☒ **Tim & Nina's** ● *Seafood* ▽ 23 | 9 | 13 | I
Chelsea | 76 Ninth Ave. (bet. 15th & 16th Sts.) | 212-977-6000 | www.zagat.com

Review, surveyor comments in quotes
Fanatical fish fanciers find the fastest route to "fairly fared fin fare" is a foray to this "grungy grotto" in Chelsea, where the catch is "never more than a day old" and "the price is always net"; still, super-sensitive shoppers say the "surly staffers should be used as fishbait", especially because "they are often strung out"; P.S. check out the "daily East River specials" and Tim and Nina's catering service on the A train.

Ratings   **Quality, Display** & **Service** are rated on a 30-point scale.

0 – 9   poor to fair

10 – 15   fair to good

16 – 19   good to very good

20 – 25   very good to excellent

26 – 30   extraordinary to perfection

▽   low response | less reliable

Cost   Reflects our surveyors' average estimate of the price range, indicated as follows:

I   Inexpensive

M   Moderate

E   Expensive

VE   Very Expensive

Symbols
☒   highest ratings, popularity and importance
●   open until 8:30 PM or later
▣   mail order available via catalog, phone or web
⊘   no credit cards accepted

Top Quality

<u>29</u> Casa Della Mozz. | *Bx*
Borgatti's Ravioli | *Bx*
Lady M Cake
Korin Japanese
Le Dû's Wines
Di Palo Dairy
Simchick, L.
Russ & Daughters
Teuscher Chocolates
Murray's Cheese
Florence Prime Meat
Saxelby Cheese
Staubitz Market | *Bklyn*
Greenmarket | *multi*
La Maison Chocolat*
Sherry-Lehmann
Italian Wine
J.B. Prince
NYC Icy | *multi*
Sylvia Weinstock Cakes*

<u>28</u> Lobel's Meats
Ottomanelli & Sons | *multi*
Ample Hills | *Bklyn*

Harney & Sons
Ottomanelli's Meats | *Qns*
Maison Ladurée
Faicco's Pork | *multi*
Moore Bros. Wine
Terranova Bakery* | *Bx*
Salumeria Rosi Parmacotto
Dickson's Farmstand
Raffetto's
Pisacane
DavidsTea
S&S Cheesecake | *Bx*
Kee's Chocolates
Levain Bakery
Joe's Dairy
McNulty's
Jacques Torres | *multi*
L.A. Burdick
Burgundy Wine*
Orchard | *Bklyn*
Sahadi's | *Bklyn*
Marlow & Daughters | *Bklyn*
Blue Apron | *Bklyn*

BY CATEGORY

Major Markets are listed by the scores they received for the applicable department.

BAGELS/BIALYS

<u>26</u> Absolute Bagels
Kossar's Bialys
Ess-a-Bagel
Murray's Bagels
Bagelworks
<u>25</u> Hot Bagels/Bialys | *Bklyn*
H & H Midtown Bagels
David's Bagels

BREAD

<u>28</u> Terranova Bakery | *Bx*
Addeo Bakery | *Bx*
<u>27</u> Sullivan St. Bakery
Balthazar Bakery
Caputo Bakery | *Bklyn*
<u>26</u> Paneantico Bakery | *Bklyn*
Blue Ribbon Bakery
Eataly

CAKES

<u>29</u> Lady M Cake
Sylvia Weinstock Cakes

<u>28</u> S&S Cheesecake | *Bx*
<u>27</u> Ladybird Bakery | *Bklyn*
Villabate Pasticceria | *Bklyn*
Soutine
<u>26</u> Black Hound NY
Make My Cake

CANDY

<u>29</u> Teuscher Chocolates
La Maison Chocolat
<u>28</u> Kee's Chocolates
Jacques Torres | *multi*
L.A. Burdick
<u>27</u> Vosges Chocolat
<u>26</u> Neuhaus Chocolate
Leonidas

CATERERS/EVENTS

<u>26</u> Great Performances
Union Sq. Events
Abigail Kirsch | *multi*
Glorious Food
<u>25</u> Tastings by Payard

* Indicates a tie with property above; excludes place with low votes, unless otherwise indicated

23 Lassen & Hennigs | *Bklyn*
Arthur Ave. Caterers | *Bx*
Cer té

CAVIAR/SMOKED FISH
29 Russ & Daughters
28 Zabar's
Murray's Sturgeon
27 Petrossian
Sable's
Agata & Valentina
Barney Greengrass
26 Dean & DeLuca

CHEESE/DAIRY
29 Casa Della Mozz. | *Bx*
Di Palo Dairy
Murray's Cheese
Saxelby Cheese
28 Joe's Dairy
Dean & DeLuca
Zabar's
Alleva Dairy

COFFEE
28 McNulty's
27 Porto Rico Import | *multi*
Nespresso
D'Amico | *Bklyn*
26 Zabar's
25 Dean & DeLuca
Sensuous Bean
Fairway | *multi*

COOKIES
28 Levain Bakery
27 One Girl Cookies | *Bklyn*
Artopolis | *Qns*
26 Baked | *Bklyn*
Silver Moon Bakery
Two Little Red Hens
Patisserie Claude
25 City Bakery

COOKWARE/SUPPLIES
29 Korin Japanese
J.B. Prince
28 Zabar's
Cook's Companion | *Bklyn*
27 Williams-Sonoma
Sur La Table
26 Alessi
Broadway Panhandler

CUPCAKES
27 Ladybird Bakery | *Bklyn*
Sprinkles

26 Baked | *Bklyn*
Sugar Sweet
Two Little Red Hens
25 ChikaLicious
Blue Smoke Bake∇
Butter Lane | *multi*

DELIS/CHARCUTERIE
28 Salumeria Rosi
Marlow & Daughters | *Bklyn*
Schaller & Weber
27 Meat Hook∇ | *Bklyn*
Esposito & Sons Pork | *Bklyn*
26 Iavarone Bros. | *Qns*
Agata & Valentina
Salumeria Biellese

FLOWERS
27 Gramercy Park Flower | *multi*
Bloom
ZuZu's Petals | *Bklyn*
Zezé
26 Flowers of the World
Ariston
25 Dahlia
24 Windsor Florist∇

GIFT BASKETS
29 Russ & Daughters
Murray's Cheese
28 Jacques Torres | *multi*
L.A. Burdick
Orchard | *Bklyn*
25 Manhattan Fruitier
24 Fat Witch
23 Chelsea Mkt. Baskets

HEALTH/NATURAL
27 Whole Foods
26 Perelandra Natural | *Bklyn*
25 Fairway | *multi*
24 Bell Bates Natural
Back to the Land | *Bklyn*
23 Integral Yoga
A Matter of Health
Westerly Natural

HERBS/SPICES
29 Dean & DeLuca
27 Kalustyan's
Zabar's
25 Fairway | *multi*
Spices & Tease∇
23 Whole Foods
Foods of India
- La Boîte à Epice

ICE CREAM

28 Ample Hills | *Bklyn*
   Il Laboratorio/Gelato
27 Cones, Ice Cream
   Big Gay Ice Cream
   Fortunato Bros. | *Bklyn*
26 Van Leeuwen | *multi*
   Grom
   Eggers Ice Cream | *SI*

ICES/FROZEN YOGURT

29 NYC Icy | *multi*
26 Lemon Ice King | *Qns*
25 Dolly's Ices | *Bklyn*
   Ralph's Ices | *multi*
24 16 Handles | *multi*
22 Forty Carrots
   Red Mango | *multi*
   Popbar

MACARONS

28 Maison Ladurée
   Kee's Chocolates
27 Bouchon Bakery
26 Almondine Bakery
25 Financier Patisserie
24 Macaron Café

MAJOR MARKETS

27 Eataly
   Battery Place Market
   Zabar's
26 Citarella
   Dean & DeLuca
25 Agata & Valentina
   Whole Foods
   Grace's Market

MARKET VENDORS

29 Keith's Farm
   Flying Pigs Farm
28 Blue Moon Fish
   Beth's Farm
   DiPaola Turkeys
   Quattro's Game
27 3-Corner Farm
26 Martin's Pretzels

MEATS/POULTRY

29 Simchick, L.
   Florence Prime Meat
   Staubitz Market | *Bklyn*
28 Lobel's Meats
   Ottomanelli & Sons | *multi*
   Ottomanelli's Meats | *Qns*
   Faicco's Pork | *multi*
   Dickson's Farmstand

NEWCOMERS (RATED)

28 Ample Hills | *Bklyn*
   Maison Ladurée
   DavidsTea
27 Dominique Ansel
26 Sprinkles
25 Amorino
24 Shelsky's | *Bklyn*
   Zucker Bakery

NUTS/DRIED FRUITS

28 Sahadi's | *Bklyn*
27 Kalustyan's
26 Trader Joe's | *multi*
25 Economy Candy
24 Nut Box | *multi*
   Zabar's
   Fairway | *multi*
22 Aji Ichiban

OLIVES/PICKLES

28 Sahadi's | *Bklyn*
27 McClure's Pickles∇
   Pickle Guys | *multi*
   Teitel Brothers | *Bx*
26 Rick's Picks∇
   Titan Foods | *Qns*
   Eli's Manhattan
25 Pickles, Olives Etc.

PASTAS

29 Borgatti's Ravioli | *Bx*
28 Raffetto's
   Eataly
   Agata & Valentina
27 Piemonte Ravioli
   Pastosa Ravioli | *multi*
26 Durso's Pasta | *Qns*
   Citarella

PASTRIES

27 Bouchon Bakery
   Balthazar Bakery
   Villabate Pasticceria | *Bklyn*
   Dominique Ansel
   Artopolis | *Qns*
   Fortunato Bros. | *Bklyn*
26 Black Hound NY
   Almondine Bakery | *Bklyn*

PIES/TARTS

27 Soutine
26 La Bergamote
   Four & Twenty∇ | *Bklyn*
   Silver Moon Bakery
   Aunt Butchie's Desserts | *multi*
   Ceci-Cela

Steve's Key Lime Pies | *Bklyn*
25 | City Bakery

PREPARED FOODS

27 | Eataly
Lorenzo & Maria's
26 | William Poll
Dean & DeLuca
25 | Eli's Manhattan
Agata & Valentina
24 | Citarella
E.A.T.

PRODUCE

27 | Dean & DeLuca
26 | Eataly
Whole Foods
25 | Manhattan Fruit
Agata & Valentina
Eli's Manhattan
Garden of Eden | *multi*
Grace's Market

SEAFOOD

28 | Pisacane
Eataly
Citarella
27 | Lobster Place
Fish Tales | *Bklyn*
Red Hook Lobster* | *Bklyn*
26 | Dorian's Seafood
Agata & Valentina

SOUPS

27 | Zabar's
26 | Citarella
Dean & DeLuca

25 | Agata & Valentina
Whole Foods
Eli's Manhattan
Fairway | *multi*
24 | Eli's Vinegar

SPECIALTY SHOPS

28 | Sahadi's | *Bklyn*
Blue Apron | *Bklyn*
27 | Bklyn Larder | *Bklyn*
Despaña Foods | *multi*
Coluccio & Sons | *Bklyn*
Kalustyan's
Marlow & Sons | *Bklyn*
Teitel Brothers | *Bx*

TEA

28 | Harney & Sons
DavidsTea
McNulty's
27 | Porto Rico Import | *multi*
26 | Two for the Pot∇ | *Bklyn*
25 | Ten Ren Tea
Carry On Tea
24 | Empire Coffee/Tea

WINES/LIQUOR/BEER

29 | Le Dû's Wines
Sherry-Lehmann
Italian Wine
28 | Moore Bros. Wine
Burgundy Wine
Acker Merrall & Condit
27 | Bierkraft | *Bklyn*
Chambers St. Wines

BY ETHNIC FOCUS

AMERICAN

29 | Saxelby Cheese
27 | One Girl Cookies | *Bklyn*
Ladybird Bakery | *Bklyn*
26 | Ronnybrook Milk
Two Little Red Hens
25 | Eddie's Sweet | *Qns*

ASIAN

29 | Korin Japanese
Minamoto Kitchoan∇
25 | Ten Ren Tea
24 | Bangkok Grocery∇
21 | Tai Pan Bakery | *multi*
Kam Man*

CENTRAL EUROPEAN

28 | Schaller & Weber
25 | Duane Park
Stork's Pastry | *Qns*
24 | Andre's | *multi*
Glaser's Bake
23 | Hungarian Pastry

EASTERN EUROPEAN

27 | Petrossian
26 | Caviar Russe
East Village Meat
23 | Eagle Provisions | *Bklyn*
22 | M & I Int'l Foods | *Bklyn*

FRENCH

29 La Maison Chocolat
28 Maison Ladurée
   Jacques Torres | *multi*
   Burgundy Wine
27 Bouchon Bakery
   Balthazar Bakery

GREEK/SPANISH/MED.

27 O&CO.
   Despaña Foods | *multi*
   Artopolis | *Qns*
26 Titan Foods | *Qns*
   Mediterranean Foods | *Qns*
25 Poseidon

INDIAN/MIDEASTERN

28 Sahadi's | *Bklyn*
27 Kalustyan's
26 D'Vine Taste | *Bklyn*

   Damascus Bakery | *Bklyn*
23 Foods of India
   Spice Corner*

ITALIAN

29 Casa Della Mozz. | *Bx*
   Borgatti's Ravioli | *Bx*
   Di Palo Dairy
   Florence Prime Meat
   Italian Wine
28 Ottomanelli & Sons | *multi*

JEWISH (KOSHER‡)

29 Russ & Daughters
28 Murray's Sturgeon‡
27 Pickle Guys‡ | *multi*
   Kosher Bagel‡ | *Bklyn*
   Barney Greengrass
   Streit's Matzo‡

FOOD TOURS

NYC is a food shopper's paradise, from its flourishing Greenmarket system (see page 89) to the polyglot resources of its outer-boroughs. Here are some must-visit places in its most storied neighborhoods.

CHELSEA

29 Lucy's Whey∇
28 Dickson's Farmstand
   Jacques Torres
27 Doughnut Plant
26 BuonItalia
   Amy's Bread
   La Bergamote
   Salumeria Biellese

CHINATOWN/
LITTLE ITALY

29 Di Palo Dairy
27 Despaña Foods
26 Ceci-Cela
25 Ten Ren Tea
   Dragonland∇
24 Chinatown Ice Cream
23 Papabubble∇
21 Kam Man

EAST VILLAGE

29 NYC Icy
27 Porto Rico Import
   Big Gay Ice Cream
26 Barnyard Cheese∇
   Sigmund Pretzel∇
25 Momofuku Milk Bar
   Veniero's
23 Moishe's

FLATIRON/MURRAY HILL

29 J.B. Prince
28 Moore Bros. Wine
   L.A. Burdick
27 Beecher's
   Eataly
   Kalustyan's
25 City Bakery
   Todaro Brothers

GREENWICH VILLAGE/
WEST VILLAGE

29 Varsano's∇
   Murray's Cheese
28 Ottomanelli & Sons
   Raffetto's
   McNulty's
27 FPB∇
   Cones, Ice Cream
25 Amorino

LOWER EAST SIDE

29 Russ & Daughters
   Saxelby Cheese
28 Il Laboratorio/Gelato
27 Doughnut Plant
   Pickle Guys
   Sweet Life
   Streit's Matzo
26 Kossar's Bialys

MIDTOWN EAST

29 Tea & Honey▽
   Teuscher Chocolates
   Sherry-Lehmann
28 Neuchatel Chocolates▽
27 O&CO.
26 Neuhaus Chocolate
   Sprinkles
24 Japanese Culinary▽

MIDTOWN WEST

29 Minamoto Kitchoan▽
   La Maison Chocolat
27 Sullivan St. Bakery
   Petrossian
   Esposito Meat
   Chocolat Michel Cluizel▽
26 Grom
24 Macaron Café

SOHO/HUDSON SQ.

28 Harney & Sons
   Kee's Chocolates
   Joe's Dairy
   Jacques Torres
27 Balthazar Bakery
   Vosges Chocolat
26 Alessi
   Dean & DeLuca

UPPER EAST SIDE

29 Lady M Cake
   Teuscher Chocolates
   La Maison Chocolat
28 Maison Ladurée
   DavidsTea
26 Kusmi Tea▽
   Orwasher's Bakery

UPPER WEST SIDE

28 Salumeria Rosi
   Levain Bakery
   Jacques Torres
27 Bouchon Bakery
   Zabar's
   Barney Greengrass
26 Neuhaus Chocolate
25 Spices & Tease▽

BX: ARTHUR AVE.

29 Casa Della Mozz.
   Borgatti's Ravioli
   Vincent's Meat▽
28 Terranova Bakery
   Addeo Bakery
27 Calandra Cheese▽

Teitel Brothers
26 Madonia Bakery

BKLYN: BAY RIDGE/ BENSONHURST/ BOROUGH PARK

28 Faicco's Pork
27 Villabate Pasticceria
   Coluccio & Sons
   Lioni Mozzarella
26 Paneantico Bakery
   Royal Crown Pastry
22 Hinsch's

BKLYN: BKLYN HTS./ CARROLL GDNS./ COBBLE HILL

29 F. Monteleone Bakery▽
28 Sahadi's
27 One Girl Cookies
   Mazzola Bakery▽
   Stinky Bklyn
   Caputo Bakery
   D'Amico
26 Damascus Bakery

BKLYN: PARK SLOPE/ PROSPECT HEIGHTS/ GOWANUS

29 Fleisher's Meats▽
28 Ample Hills
   Blue Apron
27 Bklyn Larder
   Bierkraft
   Ladybird Bakery
26 Four & Twenty▽

BKLYN: GREENPOINT/ WILLIAMSBURG

28 Marlow & Daughters
27 Meat Hook▽
   Bedford Cheese
   Fortunato Bros.
   Marlow & Sons
26 Van Leeuwen
25 Brooklyn Kitchen
24 Peter Pan Donut▽

QNS: ASTORIA/ SUNNYSIDE/WOODSIDE

29 Cassinelli Food▽
28 Ottomanelli & Sons
27 Baruir's Coffee▽
   La Guli▽
   Butcher Block
   Artopolis
26 Titan Foods

Top Display

28 Maison Ladurée
Villabate Pasticceria | Bklyn
Lady M Cake
Brooklyn Farmacy | Bklyn
Moore Bros. Wine
La Maison Chocolat

27 Dylan's Candy Bar
Zezé
Sylvia Weinstock Cakes
Pomegranate | Bklyn
Manhattan Fruitier
Pour*
Teuscher Chocolates
Bottlerocket Wine
Williams-Sonoma
Nespresso

26 Gramercy Park Flower
Little Cupcake | multi
Vosges Chocolat
Eataly
Jacques Torres | multi
MarieBelle's Treats
Bloom

DavidsTea
Le Dû's Wines*
M&M's World
Bedford Cheese | Bklyn
One Girl Cookies | Bklyn
Italian Wine
Korin Japanese
Black Hound NY
Bklyn Larder | Bklyn
Murray's Cheese
Empire Cake
Artopolis | Qns
Lorenzo & Maria's
Sherry-Lehmann
Godiva | multi
Dickson's Farmstand

25 Petrossian
Harney & Sons
Sprinkles
Rice to Riches
Eleni's Cookies
Mona Lisa Pastry | Bklyn
Dean & DeLuca

Top Service

29 Moore Bros. Wine

28 Big Gay Ice Cream
Le Dû's Wines
Pour*

27 Biancardi Meats | Bx
Sylvia Weinstock Cakes
DavidsTea
Florence Prime Meat
Saxelby Cheese
Great Performances
Enoteca Di Palo

26 Bottlerocket Wine
Ottomanelli & Sons | multi
Dickson's Farmstand
Chambers St. Wines
Staubitz Market | Bklyn
Esposito Meat
Lobel's Meats
Italian Wine
Korin Japanese
East Village Wines
Harney & Sons

D'Vine Taste | Bklyn
Piemonte Ravioli

25 Borgatti's Ravioli | Bx
Simchick, L.
Di Palo Dairy
Brooklyn Farmacy | Bklyn
Butcher Block | Qns
Blue Apron | Bklyn
Bklyn Larder | Bklyn
Casa Della Mozz.* | Bx
McNulty's
Gramercy Park Flower
Ann Clair's Salumeria | Bx
Dorian's Seafood
Zezé
Heights Chateau | Bklyn
Maison Ladurée
Sherry-Lehmann
Big Nose Full Body | Bklyn
Blue Sky* | Bklyn
Lorenzo & Maria's*
Ottomanelli's Meats* | Qns

Best Buys

In order of Bang for the Buck rating.

CANDY/NUTS
1. Economy Candy
2. JoMart Chocolates▽ | *Bklyn*
3. Chocolate Room | *Bklyn*
4. Aji Ichiban
5. Mondel Chocolates
6. Nut Box | *multi*

CHEESE/DAIRY
1. Casa Della Mozz.
2. Di Palo Dairy
3. Alleva Dairy
4. Joe's Dairy
5. Lamarca
6. East Vill. Cheese

COFFEE/TEA
1. McNulty's
2. Porto Rico Import | *multi*
3. Empire Coffee
4. D'Amico | *Bklyn*
5. Ten Ren Tea
6. Oren's Daily Roast

COOKWARE
1. Cook's Companion | *Bklyn*
2. Brooklyn Kitchen | *Bklyn*
3. Broadway Panhandler
4. Macy's Cellar
5. Bowery Kitchen
6. Bari Rest. Equip.

HEALTH/NATURAL
1. Integral Yoga
2. Bell Bates Natural
3. Westerly Natural
4. Health Nuts | *multi*
5. A Matter of Health
6. Natural Frontier Mkt.

MAJOR GOURMET MKTS.
1. Trader Joe's | *multi*
2. Fairway | *multi*
3. Amish Mkt.
4. FreshDirect | *Qns*
5. Costco | *multi*
6. Westside Market

MEAT/POULTRY
1. Biancardi Meats | *Bx*
2. Faicco's Pork | *multi*
3. Calabria Pork | *Bx*
4. Esposito Meat
5. Bari Pork | *multi*
6. Florence Prime Meat

PREPARED FOODS
1. Iavarone Bros. | *Qns*
2. Cucina & Co.
3. Melange
4. Cucina Vivolo
5. Lamarca
6. D'Vine Taste | *Bklyn*

PRODUCE
1. Greenmarket | *multi*
2. Manhattan Fruit
3. Three Guys | *Bklyn*
4. #1 Farmers Mkt.
5. Annie's
6. Hong Kong Supermkt. | *multi*

SEAFOOD
1. Lobster Place
2. Randazzo's Seafood | *Bx*
3. Cosenza's Fish | *Bx*
4. Pescatore Seafood
5. Red Hook Lobster | *Bklyn*
6. Sea Breeze▽

SPECIALTY SHOPS
1. Sahadi's | *Bklyn*
2. Pickle Guys | *multi*
3. D'Vine Taste | *Bklyn*
4. Teitel Brothers | *Bx*
5. Mediterranean Foods | *Qns*
6. Titan Foods | *Qns*

WEDDING CAKES
1. Sal & Dom's | *Bx*
2. Cake Chef | *SI*
3. Villabate Pasticceria | *Bklyn*
4. Silver Moon Bakery
5. Rocco's Pastry
6. Glaser's Bake

WINES/LIQUOR/BEER
1. Moore Bros. Wine
2. Bottlerocket Wine
3. Pour
4. Big Nose Full Body | *Bklyn*
5. Astor Wines
6. Warehouse Wines

NYC SOURCES DIRECTORY

NYC Sources

Abigail Kirsch *Caterer*   26 | 25 | 24 | VE

Chelsea | Chelsea Piers | Pier 62 (entrance at Hudson River & 23rd St.) | 212-336-6060
Bronx | Botanical Garden | 200 Southern Blvd. (bet. Crotona Park & 175th St.) | 718-220-0300
Brooklyn Navy Yard | Stage 6 at Steiner Studios | 15 Washington Ave. (Flushing Ave.) | Brooklyn | 718-237-1919 ⌐⊄
Tarrytown | Tappan Hill Mansion | 81 Highland Ave. (bet. Benedict Ave. & Gunpowder Ln.), NY | 914-631-3030
www.abigailkirsch.com
By appointment only

The very "name equals quality and class", and Abigail Kirsch's by-word in "elegant" catering will "definitely deliver" "an exquisite job" that "takes all the guesswork out" of hosting an event either off-site or in the "beautiful surroundings" of her six tony venues; from "impeccably done" food and "exceptional presentation" to "superb service", clients both corporate and private can expect an affair "simply beyond reproach", though naturally the "spectacular" performance "doesn't come cheap."

⊠ Absolute Bagels ●⊄ *Bagels*   26 | 15 | 18 | I

W 100s | 2788 Broadway (bet. 107th & 108th Sts.) | 212-932-2052

A "first choice" in the Columbia area, this "no-frills" storefront gets "back to the basics" with "awesome" "hand-rolled" bagels that meld "just the right amount of chewiness" with a "crispy" outside; "efficient" staffers slather the rounds with "a large variety" of "yummy" spreads, and despite the "chaotic-at-times" "morning rush", "carb-lovers" are absolutely convinced the "taste and price" are "worth traveling" for.

Academy Floral Co. ⌐≡ *Flowers*   22 | 21 | 21 | M

W 100s | 2780 Broadway (107th St.) | 212-222-0771 | 800-231-7592 | www.academyfloral.com

Considered the "best and the brightest" among Columbia-area florists, this "family-run" neighborhood stalwart (dating from 1910) matches a "big-city selection" showcasing Dutch and South American blooms with "friendly", "personal" service; along with "interesting arrangements" in fishbowl-style vases, they put together gift baskets brimming with plants, fruit and candy, all at "reasonable" prices "for the quality."

⊠ Acker Merrall & Condit Co. ●⌐≡ *Wine/Liquor*   28 | 23 | 25 | E

W 70s | 160 W. 72nd St. (bet. B'way & Columbus Ave.) | 212-787-1700 | www.ackerwines.com

"New, aged or hard-to-find" – "whatever you're looking for in the world of fine wines", from "French classics", Barbarescos and Riojas to California Cabernets and Super Tuscans, you'll likely find it at this UWS "top" shop, a fixture since 1820; the staff offers "recommendations you can trust", and its online and live auction offerings and hosted dinners are "simply incomparable" – little wonder oenophiles consider it a "quantum leap ahead" of most in the genre.

Ackerson, T.B., Wine Merchants ● *Wine/Liquor*

∇ 25 | 24 | 26 | E

Ditmas Park | 1205 Cortelyou Rd. (Westminster Rd.) | Brooklyn | 718-826-6600

The "friendly, welcoming" and – "especially important for a wine store – very knowledgeable" staff "could make swill sound good" at this Ditmas Park "charmer", but luckily it stocks a "thumbs-up" selection focused on smaller-scale vineyards and featuring many organic and biodynamic labels; from the "witty" product descriptions and "shelves of glittering libations" to the reasonable prices and frequent tastings, it's an "inviting" "local" standby.

Acme Smoked Fish ⊅ *Caviar/Smoked Fish*

25 | 16 | 19 | M

Greenpoint | 30 Gem St. (15th St.) | Brooklyn | 718-383-8585 | www.acmesmokedfish.com

"Go to the source" say smoked-fish fanatics who find it more than "worth the schlep" to this family-owned wholesaler/smokehouse among Greenpoint's "warehouses and factories" for "steal deals" on a "top-quality selection" of "loxilicious" goods, including whitefish, sturgeon, sable, herring and chubs (they even "give samples"); however, know that its "no-frills utilitarian retail shop" opens to civilians on Fridays from 8 AM-1 PM only, and "be prepared to wait on line" at holiday time.

☑ Addeo Bakery ⊅ *Baked Goods*

28 | 20 | 23 | I

Bronx | 2352 Arthur Ave. (bet. Crescent Ave. & 186th St.) | 718-367-8316
Bronx | 2372 Hughes Ave. (186th St.) | 718-367-8316

"Nothing has changed" at these Bronx bakeries that remain as "authentic" and "friendly" as when your "great grandparents shopped here", turning out the same "wide variety" of "exceptionally good", "decent-priced" Italian breads as well as biscotti "like momma made"; "oh the aroma" – it's "worth" the "trek" to Hughes Avenue, where production takes place, though the goods are just as "fabulous" on Arthur Avenue; P.S. while you're there pick up some "fresh" "pre-made pizza dough", which is something of a regulars' "secret."

Agata & Valentina ● ▣ *Major Market*

25 | 23 | 22 | E

E 70s | 1505 First Ave. (79th St.) | 212-452-0690 | www.agatavalentina.com

"Don't go hungry" to this UES "high-end purveyor" of Italian-accented "gourmet" goods where devotees "dare you to leave with only what you came in for" once faced with the "outstanding" meats and seafood, "succulent" housemade pastas, "fresh and delicious" baked goods, "plentiful selection" of "first-rate" prepared foods and "exceptional" "spectrum of cheeses"; it "can get crazy" at "peak hours" when "bustle" and "tussle" fill the "narrow aisles", but "eager" staffers and "fair" (for the zip code) prices mean for most it "can't be beat" for "one-stop shopping"; P.S. a Village outpost at 64 University Place is expected this summer.

	QUALITY	DISPLAY	SERVICE	COST

Aji Ichiban *Candy/Nuts* | 22 | 21 | 17 | I |

Chinatown | 23 E. Broadway (bet. Catherine & Market Sts.) |
212-571-3755
Chinatown | 37 Mott St. (bet. Bayard & Pell Sts.) | 212-233-7650
www.ajiichiban.com.hk

It's "fun just to say 'Ichiban'", and even more so to peruse the
"amazing" Asian treats at these "cute" links of a Hong Kong chain
specializing in locally "unfamiliar", "attractively displayed" candy,
dried fruits and "savory" snacks; "get your dried salty plum fix" at
this "taster's paradise" where you can sample "anything you see",
but beware – the "wide selection of morsels" includes some that the
less-adventurous call "weird" ("Hershey's this is not").

Alessi ▣ *Cookware* | 26 | 24 | 19 | E |

E 60s | 30 E. 60th St. (bet. Madison & Park Aves.) | 212-317-9880
SoHo | 130 Greene St. (bet. Houston & Prince Sts.) | 212-941-7300
www.alessi.com

These "gorgeous" SoHo–East Midtown stores "excite all your
senses" with their "beautifully designed" "contemporary" Italian
cookware, kitchen accessories and tabletop items fashioned from
"polished" stainless steel, including espresso makers and other
"interesting coffee-related" equipment; "whimsical" yet functional
and "durable", these "clever", "museum-worthy" pieces make
"impressive gifts for all occasions"; P.S. contemplate your purchase
with a "fortifying espresso" and "delectable" bites at the
Greene Street "oasis."

Alice's Tea Cup, Chapter I ▣ *Coffee/Tea* | 22 | 22 | 20 | M |

W 70s | 102 W. 73rd St. (bet. Amsterdam & Columbus Aves.) |
212-799-3006

Alice's Tea Cup, Chapter II *Coffee/Tea*
E 60s | 156 E. 64th St. (bet. Lexington & 3rd Aves.) | 212-486-9200

Alice's Tea Cup, Chapter III *Coffee/Tea*
E 80s | 220 E. 81st St. (bet. 2nd & 3rd Aves.) | 212-734-4832

🆕 Wonderland *Coffee/Tea*
Union Sq | 18 W. 18th St. (bet. 5th & 6th Aves.) | 212-242-8818
www.alicesteacup.com

"Fantasy meets reality" via the "*Alice and Wonderland* theme" at this
"busy" UWS "fairyland" and its spin-offs, where "eclectic front-of-
the-store" shops vend an "extraordinary selection" of "loose teas in
bulk", along with Carroll-centric pots, mugs and paraphernalia; the
"storybook" decor also proves "too cute to pass up" for "mommies,
daughters" and "girlie" cliques who slip "down the rabbit hole" to sip
brew and nibble on "delectable scones", finger sandwiches
and "decadent desserts."

🅉 Alleva Dairy ▣ *Cheese/Dairy* | 28 | 20 | 23 | M |

Little Italy | 188 Grand St. (Mulberry St.) | 212-226-7990 |
800-425-5382 | www.allevadairy.com

They're "still doing it the old-fashioned way" at this "family-run"
Little Italy "icon", a circa-1892 "throwback" that remains a "superb"
source of "authentic Italian cheeses" ("fresh-made mozzarella",

ricotta and "some unusual imports") along with salami, prosciutto and assorted "grocery items from Italy"; the staff "aims to please" and prices are "fair" – "hope they never change."

Almondine Bakery ⊅ *Baked Goods*   26 | 21 | 21 | M

Dumbo | 85 Water St. (bet. Dock & Main Sts.) | Brooklyn | 718-797-5026

Park Slope | 442 Ninth St. (bet. 6th & 7th Aves.) | Brooklyn | 718-797-5026
www.almondinebakery.com

"Beautiful" French pastries, croissants "worth walking the bridge for" and some of the "best baguettes" in town keep sweet tooths and carbophiles coming back to baker extraordinaire Hervé Poussot's "delightful" Dumbo "jewel" and its "child-friendly" Park Slope offshoot, whose roomy cafe seating area encourages "hanging out"; "delicate macarons, delectable sandwiches" and a friendly "French-speaking staff" complete the "little-bit-of-Paris-in-NY" picture; P.S. "get there early for the almond croissants or you lose!"

Amanda Smith Caterers *Caterer/Events*   ▽ 27 | 23 | 27 | E

W 80s | 40 W. 86th St., Ste. 11A (Columbus Ave.) | 917-626-6055 | www.amandasmithcaterers.com
By appointment only

Boutique caterer Amanda Smith's client list includes some seriously swanky names (the Rothschilds, the Rockefeller Group), but regular folk planning a family festivity can also expect a specially designed menu that may incorporate Mediterranean, Pacific and Latin flavors, which reflect Smith's Mexican heritage and international travels; pretty presentation is a given, as is help organizing flowers, music, lighting and every aspect to make a do memorable, whether it's a wedding, gala, fancy fund-raiser or a simple picnic; P.S. there's also an outlet in Connecticut.

A Matter of Health ●▣ *Health*   23 | 15 | 19 | M

E 70s | 1478 First Ave. (77th St.) | 212-288-8280 | www.amatterofhealth.net

"They couldn't stock more" on the "crowded shelves" of this "local health and wellness" spot in the Yorkville vicinity, where an "amazing" "mishmash" of natural and organic items "to fit every need" is "packed" into a "tight" space tended by "helpful" staffers; it's "a bit of a maze" that can be "hard to get around", but when "convenience, price and selection" matter, neighbors say it's a "de facto go-to."

Ambassador
Wines & Spirits ●▣ *Wine/Liquor*   25 | 20 | 24 | E

E 50s | 1020 Second Ave. (54th St.) | 212-421-5078 | www.ambassadorwines.com

What an "amazing selection" of "unusual, upscale wines and spirits" – you may even find the label "you enjoyed in that restaurant last night" with the help of the "extremely knowledgeable" staff at this "inviting", family-owned Eastsider; there's a "special" walk-in refrigerator for "sake lovers", a "must-see" downstairs cellar room with an "exclusive feel", separate rooms for Burgundies, Bordeaux, dessert vintages, etc. – little wonder the neighborhood relies on it as an "excellent source."

American Beer Distributing *Beer* | 26 | 18 | 20 | M |

Cobble Hill | 256 Court St. (bet. Butler & Kane Sts.) | Brooklyn | 718-875-0226 | www.americanbeerbuzz.com

"They have everything" at this "no-frills" Cobble Hill brewmeister – even "obscure sodas", ciders, imported mineral waters, sports drinks and an "interesting selection" of glassware – but the real draw is the "phenomenal" 1,500-strong selection of bottled beers "spanning a breadth of styles and regions", from American micro-brews and Belgian, British and French ales to German doppelbocks; what really puts this longtimer over the top: "growler fill-ups" and delivery service in Brooklyn and Manhattan.

Amish Market ● *Major Market* | 22 | 20 | 19 | M |

E 40s | 240 E. 45th St. (bet. 2nd & 3rd Aves.) | 212-370-1761
Financial District | 53 Park Pl. (bet. Charles St. & W. B'way) | 212-608-3863
W 40s | 731 Ninth Ave. (bet. 49th & 50th Sts.) | 212-245-2360
www.amishfinefood.com

Don't expect much trace of the Pennsylvania Dutch, but these "go-to" markets are "fully stocked" with the "basics" plus "some higher-end items", including a "decent variety" of "fresh" fruits and vegetables, meat, fish, "tasty" baked goods, a few "more exotic cheeses", "better-than-average" prepared foods and random "surprises" (e.g. "thin-crust pizza" and "off-the-hook" olives); to skeptics the "uninspired" formula "falls flat", but locals appreciate an "easy" "last-minute" option, especially in the underserved area near Park Place.

NEW Amorino *Ice Cream* | 25 | 24 | 20 | M |

G Village | 60 University Pl. (bet. 10th & 11th Sts.) | 212-253-5599 | www.amorino.com

The first U.S. outpost of an Italy-based chain, this Village newcomer specializes in "delicious, creamy" all-natural Italian gelato presented "like artwork", with multiple flavors of your choice filling the "petals" of "flower-shaped cones"; "mouthwatering signage" dresses up already "cute" digs, and though it gets "super-busy with the younger set" at prime times and the "check-out process is a little awkward", everyone agrees its "super-premium" scoops are "so worth it"; P.S. "the best hot chocolate" is a cool-weather "treat."

NEW Ample Hills Creamery *Ice Cream* | 28 | 22 | 24 | M |

Prospect Heights | 623 Vanderbilt Ave. (St. Marks Ave.) | Brooklyn | 347-240-3926 | amplehills.com

Manhattanites "look for an excuse to trek to Brooklyn" so they can indulge in the "sublime" ice cream and sorbet made in-house from "locally sourced" dairy and eggs at this "kid-friendly" Prospect Heights parlor, where the scoops come in a "vast", ever-changing array of "unexpected" flavors (e.g. maple bacon, stout 'n' pretzels, "addictive" salted crack caramel); it's a "gem" of a "neighborhood hangout" where the "smiling" staff keeps things copacetic even in "warmer weather" when the lines can "stretch down the block."

	QUALITY	DISPLAY	SERVICE	COST

Amy's Bread ❶ *Baked Goods* — 26 | 22 | 21 | M

Chelsea | Chelsea Mkt. | 75 Ninth Ave. (bet. 15th & 16th Sts.) | 212-462-4338
W 40s | 672 Ninth Ave. (bet. 46th & 47th Sts.) | 212-977-2670
W Village | 250 Bleecker St. (Morton St.) | 212-675-7802
www.amysbread.com

Amy Scherber's "constantly buzzing" bakery trio remains a "carb-lovers' dream" thanks to its "wonderful artisan breads" – "iconic fennel, semolina and golden raisin" loaves, "addictive" black olive twists – that are "divine" as ever "after all these years"; its "sandwiches, pizzas and sweets" including "delicious" cakes are also voted "worth every calorie", and while seating is "limited", a bonus at the Chelsea Market branch is getting to watch the "bakers in action."

Andre's Hungarian 🖃🏵 *Baked Goods* — 24 | 18 | 19 | M

Forest Hills | 100-28 Queens Blvd. (67th Ave.) | Queens | 718-830-0266 | www.andresbakery.com

Andre's Cafe ❶ *Baked Goods*

E 80s | 1631 Second Ave. (bet. 84th & 85th Sts.) | 212-327-1105 | www.andrescafeny.com

"When you want a taste of the old world", head for this Forest Hills "treasure trove of Hungarian pastries" and "savory" specialties where the "moist chocolate babkas are unrivaled", the rugalach "sumptuous" and "oh, those strudels", "flaky and filled with fresh fruit" (or cabbage – "who knew?"); the bakery/cafe offshoot on the UES will also "take you back" to Budapest.

Angelica Flowers & Events *Flowers* — ∇ 24 | 23 | 22 | E

W Village | 436 Hudson St. (bet. Leroy & Morton Sts.) | 212-243-7302 | www.angelicaflowersandevents.com

Those who "can afford the best" are "always pleased" by this West Village florist, where designer Angelica Gomes gathers blossoms from around the world to create "gorgeous" arrangements, including signature single-color bouquets and dramatic sculptural displays; despite a star-studded client list that runs from celebs to Cartier and Condé Nast, service is so "good" that mere mortals who drop in feel "like the only customer in the store."

Ann Clair's Salumeria *Deli* — 25 | 22 | 25 | M

Bronx | 1130 Morris Park Ave. (bet. Tomlinson Ave. & Williamsbridge Rd.) | 718-409-1171 | www.annclairs.com

"Loyal" customers and "big-sandwich" buffs regard this Morris Park salumeria/caterer as a "fine example of a Bronx Italian deli" that has been treating patrons "like family" since 1972, dishing out "fresh" "high-quality" heros – up to six feet for parties – as well as red-sauce pasta faves, ultrafresh mozzarella and "terrific" housemade sausages; the moderate prices "are even better."

Annie's ❶ *Produce* — 20 | 18 | 19 | M

E 80s | 1330 Lexington Ave. (bet. 88th & 89th Sts.) | 212-427-8800

With its 24/7 accessibility and "good variety" of "fresh fruits and vegetables" (including organic choices), this Upper East Side market is deemed "fine for quick pickups" round the clock; but even with flowers and sundry groceries in the mix, the less-impressed shrug "ok" but "not worth a detour."

Anopoli Ice Cream Parlor ⌦ *Ice Cream* 24 | 21 | 22 | M

Bay Ridge | 6920 Third Ave. (bet. Bay Ridge & Ovington Aves.) | Brooklyn | 718-748-3863

A "classic diner with housemade ice cream – what more could you ask for?" gush groupies of this 115-year-old Bay Ridge "great throwback" to parlors of the past whose "old-time feel" is complete with original woodwork, a long soda-fountain counter and comfy green booths; it serves a full menu of Greek-American comfort fare, but those 16 nostalgic flavors scooped into banana splits and root beer floats or atop fresh pies and pound cake remain the "awesome" highlight here.

Anthi's ● *Prepared Food* - | - | - | M

W 80s | 614A Amsterdam Ave. (90th St.) | 212-787-1007

Greek gastronomic favorites – spanakopita, moussaka, pastitsio, ultrathick yogurt with nuts and other flavorings, plus sweets like baklava – are the attractions at this postage stamp–size Upper West Side prepared foods shop from Paul Likitsakos (whose family owned the Upper East Side's erstwhile Likitsakos); the on-site kitchen produces most of the dishes, but a select few are brought in from Astoria.

Appellation Wine & Spirits ●⌐ *Wine/Liquor* ▽ 26 | 21 | 26 | M

Chelsea | 156 10th Ave. (bet. 19th & 20th Sts.) | 212-741-9474 | www.appellationnyc.com

It's a "pleasure to shop" at this spacious, eco-oriented West Chelsea wine store where a customer "can ask anything and there's not a smirk in sight" thanks to "fantastic" staffers who ensure you'll "find just the right bottle"; the "well-selected and focused" array of organic, biodynamic, natural and "hard-to-find" wines are arranged by country and from light to full-bodied – an "interesting approach" – and there's a handy library of reference books to boot; P.S. it offers frequent tastings and classes.

AQ Kafé *Baked Goods* 23 | 21 | 19 | M

W 50s | 1800 Broadway (58th St.) | 212-541-6801 | www.aqkafe.com

Satisfy "Scandinavian cravings" at this "light, airy" Columbus Circle bakery/cafe where "novice and hard-core Swedes" alike deem the "plentiful herring and smorgasbord plates", sandwiches and other savories A-ok, but for most it's the "exemplary", "hard-to-come-by" Scandinavian breads – plus pastries from Balthazar – that really set it apart.

Ariston ⌐ *Flowers* 26 | 25 | 24 | E

Chelsea | 110 W. 17th St. (bet. 6th & 7th Aves.) | 212-929-4226 | 800-422-2747 | www.aristonflorist.com

E 40s | 425 Lexington Ave. (bet. 43rd & 44th Sts.) | 212-867-8880 | www.aristonfloralboutique.com

"Years of perfection" precede this family-owned Chelsea standout (with a newer East Side offshoot) as it transforms flora imported from around the globe into arrangements exhibiting a balance of "beautiful" and "tasteful"; "super-helpful" staffers are "well informed", and while it's "a bit pricey", the artistry is "lovely" and "they stand by their work."

Arthur Avenue Caterers *Caterer* | 23 | 18 | 21 | M |

Bronx | Arthur Avenue Retail Mkt. | 2344 Arthur Ave. (186th St.) | 718-295-5033 | www.arthuravenue.com

"Don't miss out" on the "real" deal at this catering service whose links to the Arthur Avenue Retail Market and the legendary Mike's Deli guarantee a bona fide taste of Italy "at your fingertips"; their homestyle spreads bring old-world flavor to a broad institutional and private clientele, courtesy of a team that aims to "make planning an event easy."

☑ Artisanal *Cheese/Dairy* | 27 | 23 | 22 | E |

Garment District | 483 10th Ave. (37th St.) | 212-239-1200 | 877-797-1200 | www.artisanalcheese.com 📧
By appointment only
Murray Hill | 2 Park Ave. (bet. 32nd & 33rd Sts.) | 212-532-4033 | www.artisanalbistro.com ◗

"Whatever your cheese fancy", "absolutely the place to be" is Terrance Brennan's "boisterous" (and "knock-you-over" aromatic) Murray Hill "mecca", where the "superior" retail display boasts an "extraordinary" international selection of some 250 "high-end" fromages "with prices to match", all meticulously housed in on-site caves and "sold at the peak of perfection"; the "overwhelming" choices "may be intimidating", but the "passionate" staff "can walk you through" with "great expertise" and ensure "you get what you pay for"; P.S. under separate ownership, the Garment District wholesale adjunct offers classes for fledgling fromagiers.

☑ Artopolis ◗📧 *Baked Goods* | 27 | 26 | 22 | M |

Astoria | Agora Plaza | 23-18 31st St. (bet. 23rd Ave. & 23rd Rd.) | Queens | 718-728-8484 | 800-553-2270 | www.artopolis.net

It's as if an "upscale" Athenian bakery "dropped from the sky and landed in Astoria" agree admirers agog over the "fantastic selection" of "artistic" cakes and "so-very-fresh" pastries, plus "French-style desserts", "superb" cookies and "savory items" at this "modern" standout; the "wonderful" breads and Greek specialties are deemed "truly worth a special trip" – just "secure those boxes" of *kourabiedes* and baklava for the "subway home", lest you finish them off before arriving.

Artuso Pastry *Baked Goods* | 24 | 21 | 22 | M |

Bronx | 670 E. 187th St. (Cambreleng Ave.) | 718-367-2515 | www.artusopastry.com

When you're seeking some of the "best cannoli on the continent" or other "old-time" Italian tastes, make tracks to this Arthur Avenue-area pasticceria, a family-run fixture since 1946 providing the likes of "seriously addictive" struffoli ("little honey balls that you get around Christmas"), "creamy-yet-light" tiramisu and a "vast variety" of other pastries; "go early in the day" and "fuhgeddaboudit on Sundays" if you're in a hurry – the lines can stretch "down the block."

Asia Market *Specialty Shop* ▽ 20 | 13 | 11 | I |

Chinatown | 71½ Mulberry St. (bet. Bayard & Canal Sts.) | 212-962-2020
What you can't find here "probably doesn't exist" say admirers of the "great variety" of culinary staples "from all over Asia" at this Chinatown grocer, where the supply of produce, herbs, dried goods, spices and teas features Thai, Indonesian, Malaysian and Filipino specialties; the quarters are "cramped" and the employees "stock the shelves and that's about it", but the "cheap" price tags help make it all "manageable."

Astor Bake Shop ● *Baked Goods* ▽ 23 | 22 | 20 | M |

Astoria | 12-23 Astoria Blvd. (14th St.) | Queens | 718-606-8439 | www.astor-bakeshop.com
It's "just what the neighborhood needed!" enthuse locals who're sweet on this "chill Astoria" bake shop/cafe, an "adorable oasis" helmed by "high-end" pastry chef George McKirdy (ex Veritas, Café Boulud); "delicious" European-American pastries, cakes and other confections are the focus here, though there's also a savory menu – "love it!"

Astor Wines & Spirits ●◨ *Wine/Liquor* 26 | 24 | 23 | M |

NoHo | 399 Lafayette St. (4th St.) | 212-674-7500 | www.astorwines.com
With "mammoth" (11,000-sq.-ft.) proportions and an "encyclopedic" selection spanning "any kind of wine, bubbly, spirit" or sake imaginable at "some of the best prices in the city", this NoHo behemoth remains a NYC "favorite"; "you could spend a day roaming" the "user-friendly layout" in search of that "hard-to-find bottle" – or "geek out" with the "well-versed" staffers who'll guide you to "real treasures" – at this "stellar cellar" that "has all your imbibing needs" covered, from "frequent tastings" and "free delivery" to a "varied calendar" of classes at the "educational" Astor Center upstairs.

Atlas Party Rentals *Party Rentals* 25 | 18 | 22 | E |

Mt. Vernon | 554 S. Columbus Ave. (Sandford Blvd.), NY | 212-929-8888 | 800-695-6565 | www.partyrenter.com
Lending a "friendly" shoulder to shindig-givers, this Mount Vernon-based rental outfit delivers "quality" goods – whether dishes and linens or tables, tents and dance floors – throughout the five boroughs and metro area (including Long Island, Westchester and parts of CT and NJ); incentives include "excellent customer service", 11th-hour availability and "better prices" than many of its Big Apple rivals.

Aunt Butchie's Desserts *Baked Goods* 26 | 19 | 22 | M |

Financial District | Whitehall Staten Island Ferry Terminal | 4 South St. (bet. Broad St. & B'way) | 212-742-2787
Dyker Heights | 6901 13th Ave. (Bay Ridge Ave.) | Brooklyn | 718-256-2933
Staten Island | 4864 Arthur Kill Rd. (bet. Bridge St. & Richmond Valley Rd.) | 718-227-0002
www.auntbutchies.com
From "beyond-amazing" NY cheesecake to chocolate-mousse and carrot gateaux, "all kinds of decadent choices" await at this Dyker

Heights bakery "heaven" with offshoots in the Staten Island Ferry Terminal and on SI's Arthur Kill Road; insiders advise "definitely try the sampler" when you're "entertaining" – it's a sure-to-"impress" "staple" at many a "family celebration" since "you get to taste" lots of house specialties "without buying multiple" cakes.

BabyCakes NYC ◐▤ *Baked Goods* | 24 | 22 | 22 | M |

LES | 248 Broome St. (bet. Ludlow & Orchard Sts.) | 212-677-5047 | www.babycakesnyc.com

"Heaven-sent for both vegans" and people with "food allergies and sensitivities", this "quaint little" LES "bakery experience" offers up "healthier" renditions of "birthday cakes", "cupcakes, cookies and treats" made without milk, soy, refined sugar and other trigger-point ingredients; if a few feel less than babied by "granddaddy prices", admirers retort "what's not to love?" – "gluten-free never tasted this good."

Back to the Land ◐ *Health* | 24 | 20 | 19 | M |

Park Slope | 142 Seventh Ave. (bet. Carroll St. & Garfield Pl.) | Brooklyn | 718-768-5654 | www.backtothelandnaturalfoods.com

"Lots of choice" means Park Slope's health conscious are "good to go" at this '70s-era "neighborhood resource", where the "surprisingly diverse" lineup runs to "better-than-average" natural and organic foods bolstered by supplements, "beauty aids and vitamins"; those low on green gripe it's an "expensive alternative" to the Food Coop, but backers counter "you can't beat the convenience."

Baconery ▤ *Baked Goods* | ▽ 25 | 24 | 24 | M |

Chelsea | 511 W. 33rd St. (bet. 10th & 11th Aves.) | 917-675-3385 | www.baconery.com

Lovers of "all things bacon" go hog wild at this new Chelsea bakery where the porcine-centric, salt-meets-sweet treats – fudgy bacon brownies, bacon marshmallows, bacon banana bread, peanut butter–bacon cookies – keep addicts "mesmerized by all the options"; there's a sample pack for the undecided, and even pig-shaped, you-know-what-flavor dog biscuits for pooches.

Bagel Bob's *Bagels* | 23 | 16 | 19 | I |

E 80s | 1638 York Ave. (bet. 86th & 87th Sts.) | 212-535-3838
G Village | 51 University Pl. (bet. 9th & 10th Sts.) | 212-533-2627 ⊄
www.bagelbobs.com

"Just what you'd expect" from a "local" "standby", this "NYU fixture" and its separately owned Yorkville counterpart are "reliable" for "tasty bagels" – "nothing more, nothing less"; besides being "one of the best food values" around ("don't miss" the half-off "discount" Mondays from 4 to 7 PM), they're "well-staffed" by "quick" counterfolk who ensure the line "moves really fast."

Bagel Hole ⊄ *Bagels* | 25 | 12 | 17 | I |

Park Slope | 400 Seventh Ave. (bet. 12th & 13th Sts.) | Brooklyn | 718-788-4014 | www.bagelhole.net

Fuhgeddabout those "overlarge monstrosities" because this Park Slope "hole-in-the-wall" is "one of the few places left" for a "fresh" "fix" of bagels "like they used to be": "normal-size", "shiny and dense" with a "rather crusty" crunch; the "old-fashioned quality" and "decent prices" really "hit the spot", but just don't think about dawdling because the space is "tiny" and the service wholly "no-nonsense."

Bagel Oasis ● Bagels   25 | 16 | 19 | I

Fresh Meadows | 183-12 Horace Harding Expwy. (L.I. Expwy.) | Queens | 718-359-9245 | 888-224-3561 | www.bageloasis.com

Only a short "hop off the LIE", this "oldie but goodie" in Fresh Meadows is a "welcome constant" of a half-century's standing where the housemade bagels "are the bomb" for fans of "fresh" "traditional" rounds turned out to "crispy" and "not-too-heavy" perfection "24 hours a day"; it's a "must" "stop-off" that never closes, and you don't really "need the excuse of going to the Hamptons to drop by."

Bagels & Co. Bagels   21 | 16 | 18 | M

E 70s | 1428 York Ave. (76th St.) | 212-717-0505 ✏
W 70s | 393 Amsterdam Ave. (79th St.) | 212-496-9400 ▭✏
Hillcrest | 188-02 Union Tpke. (Saul Weprin St.) | Queens | 718-217-7755
www.bagelsandco.com

"Observant folk" commend this cross-borough kosher trio for its "appetizing" lineup of "thick", almost "sandwich-size bagels" plus bialys and "Jewish-style dairy", all served up by "fast and friendly" staffers; the "consistent" quality and "convenient" "neighborhood" settings are "good in a pinch", as is the cost-effective catering service; P.S. closes two hours before sunset on Friday, and all day Saturday.

Bagels by the Park ✏ Bagels   23 | 18 | 21 | I

Carroll Gardens | 323 Smith St. (President St.) | Brooklyn | 718-246-1321 | www.bagelsbythepark.net

"Superior" bagels with "great toppings" along with "terrific wraps" and such at fair prices keep customers coming to this "convenient" Carroll Gardens mainstay, in spite of a "random ordering system" that can make for "rather slow" service; still, most "appreciate the Brooklyn-ness" of employees who evince a little "attitude" at times, and those who don't can "get it to go" and "eat in the park across the street" – "plus, they deliver."

Bagels on the Square ● Bagels   20 | 14 | 18 | I

W Village | 7 Carmine St. (bet. Bleecker St. & 6th Ave.) | 212-691-3041

If "big" is what "you care about", this 24/7 Village stop is a longtime source for ultra-"large", "doughy" bagels in a "wide variety of flavors" (e.g. oat bran, French toast) schmeared with a choice of 30-odd spreads by a "quick" crew; "traditionalists might find it disturbing", but it squares well when you're starved for "carbs" – "even at 2 AM."

Bagel Store Bagels   24 | 22 | 21 | I

Williamsburg | 349 Bedford Ave. (S. 4th St.) | Brooklyn | 718-218-7220 ▭
Williamsburg | 754 Metropolitan Ave. (bet. Graham Ave. & Humboldt St.) | Brooklyn | 718-782-5856
www.thebagelstoreonline.com

"Locals gather in line" at these "high-quality" Williamsburg joints boasting a "big selection" of "fresh and warm" "oversize" bagels in classic flavors as well as "gimmick" variations, matched with an endless variety of "exotic" cream cheeses ("sooo good"); insiders note the counter folk "get you in and out fast", and advise timing trips for "the fresh morning run."

Bagelworks, Inc. ◑ *Bagels*

| 26 | 16 | 20 | I |

E 60s | 1229 First Ave. (bet. 66th & 67th Sts.) | 212-744-6444

Despite its modest size, this "no-nonsense" nook works up an "excellent selection" of "wonderful" "classic" bagels hailed as "some of the best" on the UES; the goods are "fresh"-baked in the store and paired with "lots of spreads" at a "competitive price", and if the "very small" digs are often "crowded", to most it's well "worth the hassle for what you get in return."

Bake City Bagels *Bagels*

| ∇ 28 | 23 | 23 | M |

Gravesend | 357 Ave. X (bet. 1st & West Sts.) | Brooklyn | 718-339-0800

Generations of Gravesend bagel buffs have counted on this veteran supplier of "spectacular" old-fashioned rounds – "crisp outside, light and fluffy inside" – dressed up with classic toppings, though some prefer the newer-fangled flagel (the bagel's flattened, chewier, crustier cousin); sandwiches, wraps and coffee help make the place "great for breakfast" or lunch to go, or you can nosh in-house at a stand-up table.

☑ Baked ▣ *Baked Goods*

| 26 | 22 | 22 | M |

Red Hook | 359 Van Brunt St. (bet. Dikeman & Wolcott Sts.) | Brooklyn | 718-222-0345 | www.bakednyc.com

"Schlep to Red Hook?" – heck yeah, if you make this "charming, neighborhoody" bakery your "decadent" destination, with or without a "trip to Fairway"; "it's all about the chocolate chip cookies and brownies" here, not to mention the Brookster, an "illicit love child" of both, though the "sweet and salty caramel" "treats" and cupcakes are "also to-die-for" – dig in at the "comfortable" "large tables" where you can also "sit and read or chat."

Baked by Melissa ◑▣ *Baked Goods*

| 24 | 23 | 23 | M |

E 40s | 109 E. 42nd St. (bet. Lexington & Park Aves.) | 212-842-0220

Flatiron | 7 E. 14th St. (bet. 5th Ave. & University Pl.) | 212-842-0220

SoHo | 529 Broadway (Spring St.) | 212-842-0220 ⌿ www.bakedbymelissa.com

"Delicious" things come in small packages at Melissa Bushell's bakery trio devoted exclusively to "itty-bitty cupcakes" (about the diameter of a quarter) "so cute you could kiss them", in "exuberant" flavors and kaleidoscopic colors; 10 renditions – including red velvet, s'more and the signature multicolored 'tie-dye' – are always on hand, along with a rotating 'mini of the month' ("always a nice surprise"); P.S. they're "the perfect gift for friends or business associates" – and customers placing large orders can customize with a rainbow of flavors, icings, toppings and fillings.

Bakeri ⊞ Baked Goods
▽ 22 | 20 | 18 | M

Williamsburg | 150 Wythe Ave. (bet. 7th & 8th Sts.) | Brooklyn | 718-388-8037 | www.bakeribrooklyn.com

From the owners of Sweetwater, this "cute, tiny bakery/cafe" in Williamsburg specializes in breads, "devilish pastries and delights" and other German-Scandinavian baked goods, including a "delicious" orange brioche roll; although "service can be harried", regulars say the "very Brooklyn-French" decor is an ideal backdrop for "sitting in the front window seats with a good book for a while"; P.S. it also does wedding cakes.

Balady Foods ● Specialty Shop
- | - | - | I

Bay Ridge | 7128 Fifth Ave. (72nd St.) | Brooklyn | 718-567-2252

This well-stocked Middle Eastern grocery and butcher shop in Bay Ridge is a boon to neighborhood residents shopping for halal meats, cheeses, olives, pickles and baked goods, as well as a range of imported goods from spices, grains, nuts, dried fruits, candy and oils to housewares and hookahs; it's locally renowned for its annual Ramadan dinner, a feast that spills out on to the sidewalk.

☑ Balthazar Bakery Baked Goods
27 | 24 | 21 | E

SoHo | 80 Spring St. (bet. B'way & Crosby St.) | 212-965-1785 | www.balthazarny.com

"Even after all these years" this French bakery "addendum" to Balthazar remains a "scene" with "crowds spilling "out the door", all clamoring to "pay a pretty penny" for "absolutely top-drawer" "crusty and chewy baguettes" and other "exquisite" breads, "mouthwatering" pastries and "arguably the best croissants" around; it "smells like heaven" and is mightily "hard to resist" so "don't even try" – just "grab a tartine" and a "divine" hot chocolate and "pretend you're in Paris."

NEW B&B Empire Bagels
▽ 17 | 13 | 16 | M

Boerum Hill | 200 Clinton St. (bet. Atlantic Ave. & State St.) | Brooklyn | 718-858-6358 | www.bandbempire.com

This Boerum Hill start-up "prides itself on its Montreal-style bagels", which are hand-rolled and baked in a custom wood-fired brick oven to emerge sweeter, denser and more chewy than their classic U.S. counterparts; of course, "bagels are champion in Brooklyn", so local opinions unsurprisingly diverge, with some declaring the baked rounds "tasty", others rating them a solid "B", and the "underwhelmed" sticking to the soups, salads, sandwiches and such.

Bangkok Center Grocery ⊟ Specialty Shop
▽ 24 | 16 | 22 | I

Chinatown | 104 Mosco St. (bet. Mott & Mulberry Sts.) | 212-349-1979 | www.bangkokcentergrocery.com

"One of the only" options for "authentic Thai stuff" in town, this "compact" but "organized" Chinatown mart's wares include "all of the essentials for preparing" Siamese feasts, from imported sauces and fresh curry pastes to herbs and seasonings like fresh "kaffir lime leaves and Thai basil"; it's also a godsend "for newbies" since the "staff will cheerfully give you advice on just what you need."

	QUALITY	DISPLAY	SERVICE	COST

Barbarini Alimentari ❶ *Prepared Food* — ▽ 25 | 24 | 23 | E

Financial District | 225 Front St. (bet. Beekman St. & Peck Slip) |
212-227-8890 | www.barbarinimercato.com

Financial District denizens sigh "thank goodness" for this "hidden"
deli/cafe, a "neighborhood favorite" for "awesome" Italian prepared
foods like pastas and sandwiches, along with "fresh pastries" and
"top-notch" imported *alimenti* including cheeses, olive oils and "many
items that you can't find" elsewhere; the skylit eat-in area is "charming" too, and they have a catering service focused on office functions.

Bari Pork Store *Meat/Poultry* — 26 | 22 | 23 | M

Bensonhurst | 6319 18th Ave. (64th St.) | Brooklyn | 718-837-9773
Gravesend | 158 Ave. U (W. 7th St.) | Brooklyn | 718-372-6405 🖃
Staten Island | 1755 Richmond Rd. (bet. Dogan Hills & Seaver Aves.) |
718-667-7780

"Old-school Italian and proud of it", these separately owned
Brooklyn and Staten Island butcher shops/markets purvey "quality"
"fresh-cut" and cured meats along with a "diverse" selection of imported goods, antipasti and other "delicacies", but they're best
known for their "nothin'-like"-'em housemade sausages; other
strong suits are fresh-made mozzarella, pastas and *perfetto* prepared dishes (they also cater).

Bari Restaurant Equipment 🖃 *Cookware* — - | - | - | M

LES | 240 Bowery (bet. Houston & Prince Sts.) | 212-925-3845 |
www.bariequipment.com

"If you want restaurant-quality" cookware, small and large appliances, glassware and, yes, even kitchen sinks, "shop where the
pros" go – and save a bundle too – at this family-run LES outfit that's
been firing on all burners since 1949; the quarters may be a bit
cramped, but the rewards are many – from a myriad of specialty
utensils to "professional" house-brand pizza ovens and Turbo Air
freezers, you'll find it here.

☑ Barney Greengrass 🖃 *Caviar/Smoked Fish* — 27 | 18 | 18 | E

W 80s | 541 Amsterdam Ave. (bet. 86th & 87th Sts.) |
212-724-4707 | www.barneygreengrass.com

For "classic" smoked fish in its "many forms", "step back in time" to
this circa-1908 "treasure", a still-family-run "old-school" UWS "appetizing emporium" that "can't be beat" for "excellent-quality"
goods including the "silkiest, fattiest lox around" (plus the "gold
standard of Nova") served by "crusty" staffers; sure, it's "costly"
and "a little dingy", but legions of "nostalgic" admirers declare "may
it never change!"; P.S. "long lines for brunch" in the adjoining eatery
can be trying, but they're "worth the wait – and the salt."

Barnyard Cheese Shop 🖃 *Cheese/Dairy* — ▽ 26 | 23 | 22 | E

E Village | 149 Ave. C (bet. 9th & 10th Sts.) | 212-674-2276 |
www.barnyardcheese.com

It's "like going to a friend's" at this East Village "community cheese
shop", where "extremely personable" types oversee an artisanal selection starring locally sourced varieties augmented by Swiss and

Bavarian imports, plus charcuterie and other gourmet nibbles; loyalists "love their sandwiches" as well, and if tabs run "a little high for the neighborhood", it won't cost you the farm.

Baruir's Coffee ⊜ *Coffee/Tea* ▽ 27 | 15 | 19 | M

Sunnyside | 40-07 Queens Blvd. (bet. 40th & 41st St.) | Queens | 718-784-0842 | www.baruirscoffee.com

What's said to be a "thousand-year-old" copper roaster has been churning out "excellent" coffee beans at this small, family-run Sunnyside storefront since 1966; most patrons get their "dependable" cuppa to go since much of the space is devoted to Balkan dried goods (nuts, fruit, spices, herbs and tea), and the lone table in the back is usually taken by old-world grandpa types; P.S. its iced coffee never gets watery thanks to housemade pure-coffee ice cubes.

Battery Place Market *Major Market* 27 | 25 | 26 | M

NEW **Financial District** | Goldman Sachs Bldg. | 240 Murray St. (bet. North End Ave. & West St.) | 212-323-6965

Financial District | 77 Battery Pl. (3rd Pl.) | 212-786-0077 ◐
www.batteryplacemarkets.com

With locations in the base of a Battery Park 'green' luxury condo and in the Goldman Sachs Building, this "much-needed" "upscale" Financial District grocer stocks the "finest-caliber" cheeses, prepared foods, bakery items, charcuterie and more, with focus on goods from "small producers and local artisans"; in a zone that's short on food markets, it's particularly appreciated for its grass-fed meat counter and "organic vegetables and fruit", though the pricing on some items is "definitely for the Wall Street banker" budget.

Bayard Street Meat Market *Meat/Poultry* 21 | 15 | 13 | M

Chinatown | 57 Bayard St. (Elizabeth St.) | 212-619-6206

Little Italy | 79 Elizabeth St. (bet. Grand & Hester Sts.) | 212-925-5766 ◐

The range of "fresh" and marinated beef, pork, poultry, game and "specialty" animal parts (think pig's ears, duck's feet) on offer at these Chinatown–Little Italy meat marts is so "fantastic", "if you can't find it here, it may not exist"; "bargain prices" make it "worthwhile" to battle the "crowds", especially at the "block-long", "jampacked" Elizabeth Street branch, where those willing to "walk single file" also find a fish counter and a small sit-down section to nosh on Chinese bakery goods, wontons, sushi and such.

Bay Ridge Bakery *Baked Goods* 25 | 22 | 23 | M

Bay Ridge | 7805 Fifth Ave. (78th St.) | Brooklyn | 718-238-0014 | www.bayridgebakery.com

"Fresh, fresh, fresh" fawn fans who fall head over heels for the "fine selection of cakes and pies" and other "yum" treats at this "family-run" Bay Ridge bakery, which "specializes in Greek pastries"; it also excels at special-occasion gateaux, from towering traditional wedding cakes to imaginative custom birthday creations, and there's a "friendly", "helpful" staff on hand for advice.

	QUALITY	DISPLAY	SERVICE	COST

Beacon Wines & Spirits ◐ ▣ *Wine/Liquor*   23 | 20 | 19 | M

W 70s | 2120 Broadway (74th St.) | 212-877-0028 | www.beaconwine.com
How "convenient" – you can "pick up a bottle or two to accompany
what you've just bagged at Fairway" at this "welcoming" UWS
"bright spot" offering an "extensive selection" of wines (including
some 2,000 white and sparkling vintages in the chiller at all times),
plus high-end bourbons, scotches, cognacs and rums; a few grouse
that the "prices are not the best in the neighborhood", but staffers
who are "mindful" of whatever "budget you express" can point you
to the "unusually good" array of affordable options.

❷ Bedford Cheese Shop ◐ ▣ *Cheese/Dairy*   27 | 26 | 24 | E

Williamsburg | 229 Bedford Ave. (N. 4th St.) | Brooklyn |
718-599-7588 | 888-484-3243 | www.bedfordcheeseshop.com
"One of the seven wonders of Williamsburg", this "adorable little"
corner nook is a "cheese lover's paradise" flaunting over 150 "extraordinary" fromages "well chosen" "from around the world" by a
"very helpful" staff that's "quick to offer samples and suggestions";
it's "equally good" for upmarket, locavore-oriented groceries
("jams, condiments, meats") and bread from the area's best bakeries, and while it'll "make a bit of a dent in your wallet", the "outstanding" quality keeps it ever "popular"; P.S. true turophiles can
join their cheese-of-the-month club.

NEW Beecher's Handmade   27 | 23 | 24 | M
Cheese Counter ▣ *Cheese/Dairy*

Flatiron | 900 Broadway (bet. 19th & 20th Sts.) | 212-466-3340 |
877-907-1644 | www.beechershandmadecheese.com
Proving that "gourmet American cheese" is not an oxymoron, this
"upscale", tri-level Flatiron "outpost of the Seattle favorite" offers an
"unbeatable selection" of "fabulous" domestic "artisanal" fromages,
including those "you can see them making" in-house before they
travel to a downstairs aging cave; they can be on the "pricey" side,
but to most it's "oh-so-worth-it" when you factor in the "courteous",
"helpful" staff and additive-free accompaniments – not to mention
the "decadent" dishes from the adjacent cafe, packaged to go.

Bee Desserts ▣ *Baked Goods*   ▽ 24 | 16 | 19 | M

W Village | 94 Greenwich Ave. (bet. Jane & W. 12th Sts.) |
212-366-6110 | www.beedesserts.com
"Adorable all-natural honey cakes" in a variety of flavors (try the
chocolate-covered version) are "simply heaven" and the "main attraction" at this Brazilian-influenced West Village cafe, which also
offers a lunch and dinner menu; each little cake is wrapped in foil,
and "the boxed variety sets make excellent hostess gifts" – "go and
see what the buzz is all about."

Beekman Liquors ◐ ▣ *Wine/Liquor*   24 | 20 | 23 | M

E 40s | 500 Lexington Ave. (bet. 47th & 48th Sts.) | 212-759-5857 |
www.beekmanliquors.com
"Everything" the "wine enthusiast" "needs and more" can be found
at this compact contender near Grand Central that stores its "huge"

stash of "domestic and imported vintages", including "rare" varietals (with an emphasis on California and French selections), vertically; an extensive array of liquors and a "long tradition" of "knowledgeable, friendly" service "make the experience even better than its good prices would alone."

🆕 Beer Table Pantry *Beer* ▽ 26 | 20 | 22 | M

E 40s | Grand Central Terminal | main concourse, Graybar Passage (42nd St. & Lexington Ave.) | 212-922-0008 | www.btpantry.com

You can "stock up on craft beer on your way on or off a train" at this tiny Grand Central offshoot of Park Slope's Beer Table, where shelves of "choice" bottled beers plus 64-ounce growlers – filled from a rotating on-tap selection – tempt many a commuter; the "limited" offerings include a few products from local producers, including beef jerky, jam, pickles and baked goods from ScratchBread.

Belfiore Meats *Meat/Poultry* ▽ 25 | 18 | 24 | M

Staten Island | 2500 Victory Blvd. (Willowbrook Rd.) | 718-983-0440 | www.belfiorecatering.com

"Excellent fresh meats" head the list of offerings at this "old-fashioned" SI Italian butcher/"salumeria"/specialty shop, which is also appreciated for its prepared foods and imports from the motherland, all at "moderate prices"; "good service" extends to catering if you don't care to cook, or need a business lunch whipped up in a hurry.

Bell Bates
Natural Food Market ⬛ *Health* 24 | 16 | 18 | M

TriBeCa | 97 Reade St. (bet. Church St. & W. B'way) | 212-267-4300 | www.bellbates.com

It's "one-stop shopping" for the crunchy crowd at this "huge" TriBeCa natural-food bellwether, known for stocking an "excellent selection" of goods in bulk that includes "hard-to-find dried herbs and spices", coffee, tea, dried fruits and nuts and just about "everything you could want"; it's also a wholesome haven for lunch thanks to its prepared foods and salad and juice bars.

Belle Fleur ⬛ *Flowers* ▽ 28 | 28 | 28 | VE

Flatiron | 134 Fifth Ave., 4th fl. (bet. 18th & 19th Sts.) | 212-254-8703 | www.bellefleurny.com

Count on "something truly spectacular" from this Flatiron "florist extraordinaire", a mother-and-daughter-run studio that's "absolutely wonderful to work with" and "consistently" creates "beautiful modern arrangements" for all occasions with "never a dud"; the "top-tier" results are predictably "pricey", but "savvy" types who cite the optimal "cost-to-quality ratio" consider it "worth every penny" to please a "very special" someone.

Ben & Jerry's *Ice Cream* 24 | 17 | 18 | M

Garment District | Macy's | 151 W. 34th St., 4th fl. (bet. 6th & 7th Aves.) | 212-594-0018 🌙

W 40s | Rockefeller Ctr. | 30 Rockefeller Plaza, concourse level (bet. 49th & 50th Sts.) | 212-218-7843

(continued)
Ben & Jerry's
W 100s | 2722 Broadway (104th St.) | 212-866-6237 ◗
www.benandjerrys.com
"Rich ice cream" in "funky flavors" with "clever pun" names
("Cherry Garcia is the bomb!") is the deal at this philanthropic chain
that "does the trick when you need something cold and sweet" on
"summer evenings"; if snobs sniff "stay in Vermont", convinced that
it's best left to "slack-jawed tourists", most melt when they see the
"familiar" sign, insisting it's a "reliable" "place to indulge."

Ben's Best ◗▣ *Deli*
25	16	19	M

Rego Park | 96-40 Queens Blvd. (63rd Dr.) | Queens |
718-897-1700 | www.bensbest.com
"Now we're talking" rejoice deli devotees at this Rego Park "neighborhood tradition" (since 1945) that's still "the real deal" for "quintessential Jewish" staples including "rich, delicious" pastrami,
corned beef and other "top-notch" noshes; the interior is "appropri-
ately schlocky", but never mind, because the "great quality" is
"worth the trip", and its stellar "name and reputation" extends to
"rib-sticking" platters for private and business catering.

Ben's Kosher Deli ◗▣ *Deli*
22	17	18	M

Garment District | 209 W. 38th St. (7th Ave.) | 212-398-2367
Bayside | Bay Terrace | 211-37 26th Ave. (Bell Blvd.) | Queens |
718-229-2367
800-344-2367 | www.bensdeli.net
"When you have a hankering" for a "classic kosher" "fix", these
"solid" Garment District–Bayside delis uphold the "traditional" "experience" with a "big selection" of "old-style" faves including "excellent pastrami", house-cured corned beef and knishes; purists say
"it's not your grandma's best", but it "more than satisfies" most, and
the delivery and catering services can supply "everything one
needs" for "holiday dinner" or hosting "the in-laws."

Bergen Bagels ◗⊅ *Bagels*
23	15	17	I

Boerum Hill | 473 Bergen St. (Flatbush Ave.) | Brooklyn | 718-789-7600
Fort Greene | 486 Myrtle Ave. (Hall St.) | Brooklyn | 718-789-9300
www.bergenbagel.com
"Some of the best bagels in the neighborhood" draw a "constant
stream of customers" to this Boerum Hill "joint" (with a Fort Greene
follow-up), where an evolving array of cream cheeses in some
"amazing" flavors complements the "fresh-out-of-the-oven" holes;
"the space itself is tight", but "quick service" keeps the "busy weekend" traffic flowing.

Berried Treasures ⊅ *Produce*
▽ 29	25	26	E

Location varies | 646-391-3162
"Legendary" strawberries are the signature offering of "sweetheart"
Greenmarket veteran Franca Tantillo, a farmer and ex-nutritionist
who "grows a great selection" of "delicious" produce "with great
care" at her Catskills farm; besides several sorts of berries, her trea-

sures include fingerling and other potatoes, tomatoes, herbs and various beans – everything at this stall is deemed "to die for."

Berry Fresh Farm ● *Specialty Shop* ▽ 25 | 21 | 18 | M
Astoria | 43-26 Ditmars Blvd. (bet. 47th & 48th Sts.) | Queens | 718-204-1662

A "huge variety of fruits and vegetables" lures locals into the narrow aisles of this big, "wonderful" Astoria grocery store, which also offers "fresh fish" on ice, a "great" butcher counter and deli with prepared foods manned by "super-friendly guys" and a selection of imported Italian products; "affordable" prices and "tons of parking" seal the deal.

Berrywild ● *Ice Cream* 21 | 18 | 18 | M
E 60s | 818 Lexington Ave. (63rd St.) | 212-838-3911
Murray Hill | 427 Third Ave. (30th St.) | 212-686-5848
www.berrywildyogurt.com

When that craving for a dish of "berry delicious" "guilt-free frozen yogurt" with "fresh" or dried fruit hits, head to these "bright", "clean" shops – and there are also smoothies and crêpes at the Murray Hill branch; those less wild for its frozen product yawn it's yet another "Pinkberry clone" and "typical of the new chains popping up", i.e. "add toppings", and it starts to get "berry expensive."

Best Cellars ● *Wine/Liquor* 22 | 24 | 23 | M
W 80s | 2246 Broadway (bet. 80th & 81st Sts.) | 212-362-8730 | www.bestcellars.com

A "go-to for that last-minute bottle", this "handy" Upper Westsider manned by an "energetic" staff is also the "perfect Wine for Dummies shop" for those who aren't necessarily oeno-"savvy"; the "beautiful displays" and "really good category system" allow you to walk in with "just a flavor profile in mind and come out with an inexpensive" choice, plus the "interesting tastings" also "expand your horizons", especially if you're an "experimenter."

Best Yet Market ● *Specialty Shop* 23 | 20 | 22 | I
Harlem | 2187 Frederick Douglass Blvd. (118th St.) | 212-377-2300
Astoria | 19-30 37th St. (bet. 19th & 20th Aves.) | Queens | 718-721-7500
www.bestyetmarket.com

The "name says it all" according to backers of these "up-and-coming" Astoria and Harlem "neighborhood markets", "welcome" links in a statewide chain where the "amazing selection", "reasonable" cost and "helpful" service come as a "pleasant surprise"; known for "fresh" fruits and veggies and dynamite meat counters, they also "can have some great deals" storewide – "just don't tell too many people."

❷ Beth's Farm Kitchen ▣ *Specialty Shop* 28 | 25 | 26 | M
Location varies | 800-331-5267 | www.bethsfarmkitchen.com

There's "excellent flavor in every jar" of small-batch preserves produced by the Hudson Valley's Beth Linskey, who graces the Greenmarket with "fabulous jams, jellies and chutneys" galore, including "all the basics" plus "gourmet" specialties like a strawberry-rhubarb jam blend ("one of life's little pleasures"), "peppered chutneys" and "delicious pickled vegetables" made from "local produce"; the "delightful" stand staffers are free with "helpful" advice, and the "gift boxes make great presents" for epicures on your list.

Betty Bakery *Baked Goods*   ▽ 26 | 23 | 23 | E

Boerum Hill | 448 Atlantic Ave. (bet. Bond & Nevins Sts.) | Brooklyn | 718-246-2402 | www.bettybakery.com

"Beautifully decorated" special-event "creations" for nuptials, birthdays and really "all occasions" crafted by wedding-cake pros Cheryl Kleinman and Bijoux Doux's Ellen Baumwoll are just the jumping-off point at this colorful, retro-inspired Boerum Hill bakery kitted out with a 1920s-era green stove; sweet tooths also turn to it for everyday "fresh, real and amazing" strawberry shortcake, "cute cookies and petit fours" and "really wonderful" cakes (coconut, red velvet), all of them "outstanding."

Between the Bread *Caterer*   23 | 19 | 19 | M

W 50s | 145 W. 55th St. (bet. 6th & 7th Aves.) | 212-581-1189 | www.betweenthebread.com

Long an off-site caterer to the corporate world, this Midtown prepared foods store sustains meetings and functions with its "fresh" and "yummy" New American spreads, from "picnic"-style lunches and "gourmet-quality sandwiches" to full dinner menus and holiday buffets; past clients include NASDAQ, Chanel and Michael Kors, and event planning services are available for a little extra dough.

☒ Biancardi Meats *Meat/Poultry*   28 | 25 | 27 | M

Bronx | 2350 Arthur Ave. (bet. Crescent Ave. & 187th St.) | 718-733-4058

"What an incredible place" rave carnivores of this family-owned Arthur Avenue "meat heaven", where the "high-quality" beef, lamb, pork, poultry and "outstanding" sausages are offered alongside harder-to-find viands like rabbit, pheasant, tripe and sweetbreads; in business since 1932, it's an Italian-style "throwback" to the days of meat "trimmed to order" by butchers with "excellent skills" – factor in "good prices", and no wonder you'll see "license plates from several states" parked outside.

NEW Bien Cuit *Baked Goods*   ▽ 23 | 22 | 18 | E

Cobble Hill | 120 Smith St. (bet. Dean & Pacific Sts.) | Brooklyn | 718-852-0200 | www.biencuit.com

"High-end" artisan bread comes to Cobble Hill via this French bakery from an alum of Philadelphia's Le Bec-Fin, whose "amazing" crusty loaves (the moniker means 'well done') are offered alongside "gorgeous, delicious" sweet and savory tarts and other pastries, plus "wonderful sandwiches"; its simple, brick-walled storefront features an open kitchen at its center and a few tables up front for on-site munching, and though there are a few complaints about service miscues, many a local "wakes up on Saturday mornings dreaming about this place."

QUALITY DISPLAY SERVICE COST

Bierkraft ●◻ *Beer* 27 | 21 | 24 | M

Park Slope | 191 Fifth Ave. (bet. Berkeley Pl. & Union St.) | Brooklyn | 718-230-7600 | www.bierkraft.com

"Wow, that's a lot of beer" – the "unbeatable" 1,000-plus selection at this "Park Slope gem" encompasses "fabulous" craft brews "from all over the world", plus the "frothy" favorites on tap lead sudsophiles to say "growlers are the way to go" ("who doesn't like refills?"); prices are on the "expensive" side, but with pluses like "hearty sandwiches" to "keep the drinkers nice and full" and a "really dedicated" staff, to most it's "worth" the "extra dough."

Big Apple Florist ◻ *Flowers* ▽ 27 | 23 | 28 | E

E 40s | 228 E. 45th St. (bet. 2nd & 3rd Aves.) | 212-687-3434 | 800-554-0001 | www.bigappleflorist.com

"Superb quality and design" and "dependable service" are the calling cards of this "pricey" Grand Central florist that turns out "fresh and lovely" flower arrangements and bouquets designed in-house to suit corporate events, weddings and more; there are also potted plants and gift baskets (which can be ordered online), not to mention convenient same-day Manhattan delivery.

NEW Big Gay Ice Cream Shop *Ice Cream* 27 | 23 | 28 | I

E Village | 125 E. Seventh St. (bet. Ave. A & 1st Ave.) | 212-533-9333 | www.biggayicecream.com

Known for its out-and-proud mobile unit ("keep on truckin'") dispensing "gourmet soft-serve ice cream" extraordinaire, this roving favorite put down roots post-Survey with an already-mobbed East Village storefront, where its conventional flavors (vanilla and chocolate) get accessorized with "exquisite toppings" from wasabi-pea-dust to cayenne pepper; the combos come with "equally appealing" "gay"-insider names (the Bea Arthur, Salty Pimp), and service is "super-friendly", making for one "special cone indeed" – "this is why we live in NY."

Big Nose Full Body ● *Wine/Liquor* 24 | 24 | 25 | M

Park Slope | 382 Seventh Ave. (bet. 11th & 12th Sts.) | Brooklyn | 718-369-4030 | www.bignosefullbody.com

"Cheerful", "super-helpful" staffers who "really know their stuff" guide you to "the bottle you're looking for" at this "small", "boutique-y" Park Slope wine store offering some 350 "not-your-everyday" labels, including organic and small-vineyard bottlings; a healthy "selection of inexpensive" choices and "great tastings on Saturdays" are other pluses.

Billy's Bakery ●◻ *Baked Goods* 24 | 22 | 20 | M

Chelsea | 184 Ninth Ave. (bet. 21st & 22nd Sts.) | 212-647-9956
NoLita | 268 Elizabeth St. (Houston St.) | 212-219-9956
TriBeCa | 75 Franklin St. (bet. B'way & Church St.) | 212-647-9958
www.billysbakerynyc.com

Billy is out of the picture but his partners bake on at this "kitschy" Chelsea cupcake place made to feel like "grandma's kitchen" – that is if "grandma had attractive gay men icing" the treats at the counter – along with its offshoots in TriBeCa and NoLita; the "smell alone is hypnotic" and the slices of banana-red-velvet and chocolate gateaux "utterly sinful", but it's the "moist", "addictive" cupcakes that lure "lines out the door" on weekends; P.S. local delivery orders can now be placed via the website.

Birdbath *Baked Goods* | 23 | 21 | 21 | M |

E Village | 223 First Ave. (bet. 13th & 14th Sts.) | 646-722-6565 ●⊟
NEW **E Village** | 35 Third Ave. (bet. 9th & 10th Sts.) | 212-201-1902
LES | New Museum | 235 Bowery (Prince St.) | 646-442-8140
SoHo | 160 Prince St. (bet. Thompson St. & W. B'way) | 212-612-3066
TriBeCa | 200 Church St. (Thomas St.) | 212-309-7555
www.buildagreenbakery.com

You'll "want to eat everything in sight", from the "shockingly" "delicious cookies" and pastries to the "memorable" muffins and "savory treats" at City Bakery owner Maury Rubin's blossoming bunch of eco-conscious bakeries, which includes a branch "charmingly housed" in SoHo's "old Vesuvio" space; the "inventive" "temptations" are made with "good-for-you" organic and local ingredients and everything in its sustainably outfitted environs is greenminded – little wonder bicyclists get discounts.

Bis.Co.Latte ☒ *Baked Goods* ▽ | 24 | 21 | 22 | M |

W 40s | 667 10th Ave. (47th St.) | 212-581-3900 | www.biscolatte.com
"So many flavors, not enough money" to sample them all quip visitors to this "biscotti-lovers' heaven" in Hell's Kitchen offering some 70 rotating "scrumptious choices" from fig and date to New Orleans praline, all best enjoyed with a latte brewed from Illy coffee; linger "as long as you like" while munching your "lovely" "hard cookies" or spoon up hearty soups and other savories, served by staffers who "make you feel like part of the family."

Bisous, Ciao *Baked Goods* ▽ | 25 | 25 | 25 | E |

LES | 101 Stanton St. (Ludlow St.) | 212-260-3463 | www.bisousciao.com
Exquisite, "bite-of-heaven" French-style macarons are the *specialité* of this dainty Lower East Side boutique, which began as a mail-order business; arranged in rows in glass cases, the colorful treats come in "amazing" flavors both classic (chocolate, pistachio) and seasonal (fall cranberry, spring violet) and are packaged in "tasteful" sleek black boxes; P.S. custom orders can be placed for bridal showers and other events.

❷ Bklyn Larder ● *Specialty Shop* | 27 | 26 | 25 | E |

Park Slope | 228 Flatbush Ave. (Bergen St.) | Brooklyn |
718-783-1250 | www.bklynlarder.com
Hailed as a "terrific addition to the Park Slope foodie scene", this gourmet pantry (co-owned by Francine Stephens of the famed across-the-street pizzeria Franny's) is "jam-packed" with "extraordinary" "artisanal foodwares" including "better-than-sex" cheeses (from an on-site cave), "seriously good" house-cured meats, chocolates, oils and condiments, plus "first-rate" prepared foods and sandwiches "as tasty as they look"; the "ridiculous prices" draw

some fire, but the "enthusiastic" staff's "generous with the samples" and for "amazing finds" you "won't see elsewhere" it's "so worth it."

☑ Black Hound New York ◑ ▣ *Baked Goods*
26 | 26 | 23 | E

E Village | 170 Second Ave. (bet. 10th & 11th Sts.) | 212-979-9505 | 800-344-4417 | www.blackhoundny.com

"Just taking a deep breath" at this "tiny" East Villager "can give a chocoholic a rush" agree "serious" sweet tooths who find the "indulgent", "expensive" jam-filled cookies, tarts, truffles and "really special" cakes – including "cute" mini-sizes – more than "worth the splurge"; a few sourpusses say the treats "under-deliver on flavor", but the tail-wagging majority insists the inventory here is "as pleasing to the taste buds as it is to the eye."

☑ Bloom *Flowers*
27 | 26 | 23 | VE

E 50s | 541 Lexington Ave. (50th St.) | 212-832-8094 ▣
NEW Financial District | 255 Murray St. (West St.) | 646-429-6269
www.bloomflowers.com

"Wow!" is the response to the "magnificent" floral work from this Midtown emporium (with a new Battery Park City offshot), where "artists" assemble "awesome" "dense arrangements" in a store that also serves as a showroom for stylish furniture and home accessories; yes, the blooms are "frightfully expensive" here, but they "last a long time" and, "when price is no object", are guaranteed "to impress the object of your desires"; P.S. other services include interior design and event-planning.

Bloomingdale's Cookware ◑ ▣ *Cookware*
25 | 24 | 18 | E

E 50s | Bloomingdale's | 1000 Third Ave. (bet. 59th & 60th Sts.) | 212-705-2237 | 800-472-0788 | www.bloomingdales.com

Truly a "one-stop" bonanza for "all your cooking needs", the famed East Side department store's kitchen section is stocked with a "well-edited" yet "comprehensive" array of "high-quality" cookware, bakeware and gadgets that are equally "high-cost" – though if you wait for "super-sale days" then you can "buy what you have always craved", and "bring it back if you're not satisfied" (just a few of "Bloomies' perks"); however, shoppers are of two minds regarding the service: "excellent" vs. "just try to find a salesperson that knows something about the products."

NEW Blossom Bakery *Baked Goods*
▽ 26 | 23 | 23 | M

Chelsea | 174 Ninth Ave. (bet. 20th & 21st Sts.) | 212-242-3339 | www.blossomnyc.com

The brownies, cookies, cakes, quiches, croissants and other "delicious", "super-high-quality" baked treats are all organic and vegan at Chelsea's new specialty bakeshop, an offshoot of the vegetarian cafes of the same name; spiced hot chocolate is another lure within its diminutive, cheery brick-walled digs, so even if you're an omnivore, "if you love sweets, you won't be disappointed"; P.S. Blossom du Jour, serving savory vegan fare, is next door.

	QUALITY	DISPLAY	SERVICE	COST

❷ Blue Apron Foods *Specialty Shop* | 28 | 24 | 25 | E |

Park Slope | 814 Union St. (7th Ave.) | Brooklyn | 718-230-3180 |
www.blue-apron-foods.com

A "little slice of luscious in Park Slope", this "small but wonderful" gourmet shop is "chock-full" of "all things delicious", notably a bounty of "lovely cheeses" and charcuterie and a "carefully selected" mix of "high-quality" goods from premium pastas to Jacques Torres chocolates and fresh bread from top bakeries; the "friendly" "pro" staff offers "great guidance" too, so while this nook is "expensive" and "a little overcrowded", it's a major "benefit" for the neighborhood considered well "worth visiting – and often."

Blue Marble Ice Cream ● *Ice Cream* | 26 | 21 | 22 | M |

Cobble Hill | 196 Court St. (bet. Congress & Warren Sts.) | Brooklyn |
718-858-0408
Prospect Heights | 186 Underhill Ave. (St. Johns Pl.) | Brooklyn |
718-399-6926
www.bluemarbleicecream.com

"Creamy, custardlike", "full-flavored", "ridonkulously good" ice cream is the thing at this eco-friendly Brooklyn duo whose seasonally rotating selection is made from farm-fresh dairy and served by "lovely" staffers; the Cobble Hill nook simply serves scoops, but the roomier Prospect Heights branch also offers baked goods, pours La Colombe coffee and In Pursuit of Tea and has a play space for young 'uns.

❷ Blue Moon Fish ⌦ *Seafood* | 28 | 21 | 24 | M |

Location varies | no phone | www.bluemoonfish.com

Showcasing seafood so "truly fresh" "guests will think you caught dinner yourself", this North Fork fish merchant is a Greenmarket fixture for "amazing" "local, seasonal catch" (filleted, whole and some smoked) courtesy of "cheerful" folk who'll give "knowledgeable" advice on "even the most mysterious" offerings; moonstruck fans of the "sky-high" "quality and value" say it's "so worth suffering" lines that "stretch forever", but those who surface early get "the best selection."

Blue Ribbon Bakery Market *Specialty Shop* | 26 | 22 | 23 | E |

W Village | 14 Bedford St. (bet. Downing & Houston Sts.) |
212-647-0408 | www.blueribbonrestaurants.com

The Bromberg Brothers' West Village nook allows enthusiasts of the "oh-so-good" bread baked in a 150-year-old oven at nearby sibling Blue Ribbon Bakery the chance to take a loaf home, albeit at "not-cheap" prices; it specializes in "delectable" open-faced 'toast' sandwiches, and the sorts of things that make an "amazing picnic" – chances are you also "won't be able to leave without buying" some "grainy mustard, homemade hot sauce, carefully sourced" Mexican honey or soy sauce.

Blue Sky Bakery ⌦ *Baked Goods* | 27 | 23 | 25 | M |

Park Slope | 53 Fifth Ave. (bet. Bergen St. & St. Marks Ave.) |
Brooklyn | 718-783-4123

Park Slopers find "heaven in a homemade muffin" at this bakery on the Fifth Avenue strip, where the "excellent" signature items come fresh-made "in the most interesting flavors" (pumpkin-banana-walnut, zucchini-chocolate-strawberry), along with croissants, cupcakes and other delectables; the staff offers "service with a smile", so nab a marble-topped table in the "cozy cafe" or dither at the counter and "wave at the baker while you decide which scrummy to indulge in", but beware – they close around lunchtime.

Blue Smoke
Bake Shop *Baked Goods*
∇ 25 | 20 | 22 | M

NEW **Financial District** | 255 Vesey St. (bet. North End Ave. & West St.) | 212-889-2363
Murray Hill | 116 E. 27th St. (bet. Lexington & Park Aves.) | 212-447-6058 ●⬛
www.bluesmoke.com

It has the "Danny Boy [Meyer] touch" declare dessert mavens sweet on this bakery counter inside the Murray Hill smokehouse – and now inside its Battery Park City sibling as well – specializing in Southern-style baking "at its best" with treats like Bourbon-pecan pie, red-velvet cake and Boston-cream cupcakes; it's a solid "resource for parties, and just plain indulging", with "decent" prices and "friendly" service to ice the cake.

Bomboloni ● *Baked Goods*
22 | 22 | 21 | M

W 60s | 187 Columbus Ave. (bet. 68th & 69th Sts.) | 212-877-3080 | www.bomboloni.com

"Addicting" namesake "donut-like creations" with "fun", seasonal jam, cream and fruit fillings (strawberry, chestnut, peanut-butter cup) are the "to-die-for" specialty of this Upper Westsider from chef David Ruggerio; however, the "tastes of Italy" here also extend to "high-quality" gelato in some 20 flavors, with waffle-style pizzelle cookies as the crowning touch.

Bond Street
Chocolate *Candy/Nuts*
∇ 27 | 26 | 23 | E

E Village | 63 E. Fourth St. (bet. Bowery & 2nd Ave.) | 212-677-5103 | www.bondstchocolate.com

It's a "delightful surprise in the East Village" gush sweet tooths who stumble upon Lynda Stern's tiny, brick-walled sweets shop producing "wonderful", quirky chocolates, from edible gold leaf–dusted statues of Jesus, Moses and the Virgin of Guadalupe and tins of metallic silver skulls to dark bonbons with boozy fillings like bourbon or elderflower liquor; works of art all, it's no wonder they're showcased in a lovely antique jewelry case.

Bonsignour ● *Prepared Food*
∇ 27 | 23 | 23 | M

W Village | 35 Jane St. (8th Ave.) | 212-229-9700

Casual and cordial, this petite West Villager is "perfect" on the run given its smart selection of fresh-made muffins and other baked goods, plus prepared foods including sandwiches, soups and salads, desserts and such dinner entrees as lasagna, lamb stew or inventive daily specials; the area natives see it as an upmarket version of a "neighborhood take-out joint."

	QUALITY	DISPLAY	SERVICE	COST

◪ Borgatti's Ravioli & Egg Noodles ⊟ *Pasta*

29	20	25	I

Bronx | 632 E. 187th St. (bet. Belmont & Hughes Aves.) | 718-367-3799 | www.borgattis.com

"Step back to the old days" at this "no-frills" Bronx "shrine" proffering "sublime" "creamy pillows" of ravioli "like nonna used to make", as well as "fresh, delicate" "outstanding" pastas ranging from "light whole wheat" to squid ink; it's all "made and sold with a smile" by a "lovely" family that operates its business "with pride" – "no wonder it's been around for generations" ("please never stop!"); P.S. expect a "line out the door" around holidays.

Botta di Vino ◑ *Wine/Liquor*

▽ 24	25	24	M

Red Hook | 357 Van Brunt St. (bet. Dikeman & Wolcott Sts.) | Brooklyn | 347-689-3664 | www.bottadivino.net

Among the "coolest wine shops" going, this "wonderful" Red Hook vintner specializes in Italian varietals, carrying some 400 labels assembled by an owner with "superior knowledge" who'll help guide your choice; it stands out with a rustic iron-and-wood setting that includes a glass-paneled section in the floor allowing views into the cellar, which houses seasonally featured wines from other countries, and where weekly tastings are held by candlelight.

◪ Bottlerocket Wine & Spirit ▭ *Wine/Liquor*

25	27	26	M

Flatiron | 5 W. 19th St. (bet. 5th & 6th Aves.) | 212-929-2323 | www.bottlerocketwine.com

Perfect for those who "get overwhelmed" in traditional wine stores and "just plain fun" for the "savvy", this Flatiron shop's "brilliant setup" amounts to "smart" "kiosk" displays presenting its "well-curated" 365 labels sorted by theme or category ("value", "gift ideas", "region", etc.), with a "fact sheet" explaining each bottle; it's "really easy", but "if you can't navigate it", a staff willing to "bend over backwards" is "at your service."

◪ Bouchon Bakery *Baked Goods*

27	24	22	E

NEW **W 40s** | Rockefeller Ctr. | 1 Rockefeller Plaza (bet. 48th & 49th Sts.) | 212-782-3890

W 60s | Shops at Columbus Circle | 10 Columbus Circle (bet. 58th & 60th Sts.) | 212-823-9366 ◑ www.bouchonbakery.com

When you want to "embrace your inner cookie monster", head to Thomas Keller's bakery/take-out counter "just down the corridor" from his "casual" same-name cafe offering "dramatic" views of Columbus Circle; the "delicate macarons" may be the "best" "outside of Paris", while the other "French-style treats" – "delicious" breads, "decadent", "beautiful" pastries, sandwiches and soups – are *"fantastique"*; "be prepared" for "long lines", minimal seating and "Time Warner Center prices" – "although compared to Per Se" upstairs, it's a "steal!"; P.S. the Rockefeller Center offshoot opened post-Survey.

Bowery & Vine ● ▣ *Wine/Liquor* ▽ 22 | 22 | 21 | M

LES | 269 Bowery St. (bet. Houston & Stanton Sts.) | 212-941-7943 | www.boweryandvine.com

Now "conveniently located next to Whole Foods", this "trendy" LES wine store's "large inventory" runs from "amazing bargains to memorable vintages" (the latter stored in a temperature-controlled room) along with a solid "selection of sparkling wines" and spirits, including some "quirky options"; "eager-to-help" staffers are ready to offer "respectful advice" or "help you pick out something special", and online ordering allows at-home browsing.

Bowery Kitchen Supplies ▣ *Cookware* 23 | 14 | 15 | M

Chelsea | Chelsea Mkt. | 75 Ninth Ave. (bet. 15th & 16th Sts.) | 212-376-4982 | www.shopbowery.com

Whether you're a "serious cook" or just "envision yourself as one", you'll discover "everything you could ever need for your kitchen, in one shiny spot" at this moderately priced Chelsea Market "wonderland for foodies"; shop for "tons of gadgets", cookware, cutlery, "hard-to-find tools and supplies", appliances, even "professional" worktables for the "ultimate chef" – just be prepared to "wade through a lot" of "haphazardly displayed" items on your "treasure hunt" for that "pan of your dreams."

Bread Alone ▣ *Baked Goods* 25 | 21 | 22 | M

Location varies | 845-657-3328 or 800-769-3328 | www.breadalone.com

"Rich, toasty flavors" are the hallmark of the "wholesome, dense" "artisanal-style" bread sold by this Ulster County outfit's three organic bakeries in the Catskills and at Greenmarket locations around the city; the "fabulous granola", "breakfast pastries", muffins, scones, croissants, "rolls and cookies" also have a solid "fan base" – clearly they're "all made with plenty of TLC"; P.S. insiders say "whole, fresh loaves are preferable to the pre-packed."

Broadway Panhandler ▣ *Cookware* 26 | 22 | 20 | M

G Village | 65 E. Eighth St. (bet. B'way & University Pl.) | 212-966-3434 | 866-266-5927 | www.broadwaypanhandler.com

A "browser's paradise" for "anyone who likes to cook or entertain", this Village "oldie but goodie" is a "favorite" of "gourmet" chefs, "amateurs" and "armchair foodies" alike for its "stocked-floor-to-ceiling" selection of "weird, technical" tools and equipment, "fantabulous cookware" and "all the kitchen accoutrements you'd ever want or need" offered at "fair prices"; yes, it's a "little difficult to navigate", but luckily the "oh-so-knowledgeable" staff "always steers you in the right direction."

Brooklyn Beer & Soda *Beer* ▽ 25 | 18 | 22 | M

Prospect-Lefferts Gardens | 507 Flatbush Ave. (Lefferts Ave.) | Brooklyn | 718-622-8800 | www.bkbeerandsoda.com

There's an "almost endless variety of brews" at this supermarket-size, warehouse-style Prospect-Lefferts suds seller spotlighting rare, craft and small-batch beers along with the usual Buds; "great" service helps make visits here good "fun", and "not-expensive" prices don't hurt either; P.S. get drafts to go via its 64-ounce growlers filled from the 16 rotating taps of local microbrews.

Brooklyn Brew Shop ⌨ *Beer* ∇ 26 | 22 | 26 | M

Location varies | Brooklyn | no phone |
www.brooklynbrewshop.com

Brew-it-yourself suds is the idea behind this artisanal beer biz that hawks one-gallon home-fermenting kits (choose from starter mixes like Chestnut Brown Ale, Everyday IPA and Coffee & Donut Stout) and related equipment (get yer bottle-capper here) to help novices create their own cold one; there's no brick-and-mortar location, just Greenmarket and flea-market locales, in addition to online ordering.

Brooklyn Cupcake ⌨ *Baked Goods* 27 | 24 | 23 | M

Williamsburg | 335 Union Ave. (bet. Grand & Maujer Sts.) |
Brooklyn | 347-762-2253 | www.brooklyncupcake.com

"Why don't these cupcakes get more press?" wonder devotees of this Williamsburg bakery where "both the cake and the frosting are outstanding"; "unique" flavors like guava con queso and more traditional offerings like red velvet are "a slice of heaven" considered well "worth every pound you'll gain", so the only downside is "how hard it is to decide" which one you want.

Brooklyn Fare ● *Major Market* ∇ 26 | 23 | 24 | M

Downtown Bklyn | 200 Schermerhorn St. (Hoyt St.) | Brooklyn |
718-243-0050 | www.brooklynfare.com

"Surprisingly high quality" comes to Downtown Brooklyn via this gourmet grocery and cafe, "the place to go" for top-flight produce, seafood, meat and game along with pastas and other "well-selected" specialty goods (not to mention its serious beer section); since it's also a "fine local source for innovate and fresh prepared foods" from its full kitchen – whether "delish" sandwiches, short ribs, lasagna or more "unusual items" – "indulgent" types are "truly temped" to "buy every day's meals here."

Brooklyn Farmacy *Ice Cream* 25 | 28 | 25 | M

Carroll Gardens | 513 Henry St. (Sackett St.) | Brooklyn |
718-522-6260 | www.brooklynfarmacy.blogspot.com

Its "throwback"-to-1920s-soda-shops feel is so "authentic", you may "start twisting your imaginary handlebar 'stache" while waiting for your "stellar egg cream" at this Carroll Gardens "retro" fountain set in a "beautiful old" 1920s pharmacy; its "wonderful" Adirondack Creamery ice cream and sundaes topped with "made-from-scratch" syrups spark "wonderful reminiscences" of "childhood" – and endear it to "families" in an area "full of hipsters, trendsetters" and "speakeasies."

Brooklyn Flea *Specialty Items* 22 | 19 | 21 | M

Fort Greene | Williamsburg Savings Bank Bldg. | 1 Hanson Pl.
(Flatbush Ave.) | Brooklyn | 718-935-1052
Fort Greene | Bishop Loughlin Memorial High School | 176 Lafayette Ave.
(bet. Clermont & Vanderbilt Aves.) | Brooklyn | 718-935-1052

(continued)

(continued)
Brooklyn Flea
Williamsburg | East River Waterfront (bet. 6th & 7th Sts.) | Brooklyn | 718-928-6603
www.brooklynflea.com

If you're "itching for" an "adventure", these Brooklyn "bohemian bazaars" are a "wildly popular weekend destination" that host "fabulous" food vendors among their myriad booths, bringing together a "mouthwatering" medley from the likes of Asia Dog, Choncho's Tacos, Rick's Picks, Porchetta, the Red Hook Lobster Pound and many more; it's "a lot of fun" to "spend the day" "browsing and noshing", though the "overwhelming" crowds and "crazy" "lines can be rough."

Brooklyn Ice Cream Factory ◐⇚ *Ice Cream*   25 | 17 | 19 | M
Dumbo | Fulton Ferry Landing Pier | 1 Water St. (Old Fulton St.) | Brooklyn | 718-246-3963
Greenpoint | 97 Commercial St. (Manhattan Ave.) | Brooklyn | 718-349-2506
www.brooklynicecreamfactory.com

The "super-long lines" can be "endless" at this scoop of "Cape Cod in Dumbo" (with a Greenpoint follow-up) on a "hot day" – especially "now that the world has discovered Brooklyn" – "but stay" because the "fresh, fresh, fresh", "out-of-this-world", "true old-fashioned" ice cream is so "worth it"; "you can't beat the quality" or the "view of the skyline" from the "scenic" Fulton Ferry pier, plus the flavors are "divine" – this may be "NY's best factory."

Brooklyn Kitchen ▤ *Cookware*   25 | 21 | 22 | M
Williamsburg | 100 Frost St. (bet. Manhattan & Meeker Aves.) | Brooklyn | 718-389-2982 | www.thebrooklynkitchen.com

"Brew your own beer, ferment your own kombucha, stuff your own sausages" or shop for "really cool" vintage and top-notch "kitchen supplies" at this "DIY" cookware "mecca" in Williamsburg; another prime reason for "urban homesteaders" to "flock": it now stocks "very fine" butchered beef, lamb, pork and poultry from its affiliate, the Meat Hook.

Brooklyn Liquors ◐ *Wine/Liquor*   24 | 19 | 22 | I
Sunset Park | Costco | 976 Third Ave. (bet. 37th & 38th Sts.) | Brooklyn | 718-499-2257 | www.brooklynliquors.com

Although it's "not affiliated with Costco" next door, this Sunset Park vendor is "similarly value-priced", offering "quaffable" wines and spirits that "don't cost much", especially if you buy "in volume"; the selection is "somewhat limited", but there are "excellent choices" to be found, as well as "unbeatable specials", plus the "friendly", "knowledgeable" staff is "willing to help novices" and experts alike.

Brooklyn Oenology *Wine/Liquor*   - | - | - | M
Greenpoint | 209 Wythe Ave. (bet. 3rd & 4th Sts.) | Brooklyn | 718-599-1259 | www.brooklynoenology.com

This "wonderful" winery HQ housed in a converted Greenpoint warehouse offers "great" French and Bordeaux varietals made under contract with a host vineyard on Long Island's North Fork (even the labels on the bottles have been designed by neighborhood artists); it also vends other NY State wines, and operates a tasting room where you can meet the "nice" vintners and taste their wares – "makes buying local" even more "pleasant."

Brooklyn Wine Exchange ⌨ *Wine/Liquor*   25 | 23 | 23 | M

Cobble Hill | 138 Court St. (bet. Atlantic & Pacific Sts.) | Brooklyn | 718-855-9463 | www.brooklynwineexchange.com

"Another winner from the people who brought us Smith & Vine", this "nice-looking newcomer" in Cobble Hill is already "a hangout for wine-lovers" who appreciate its "amazing selection" of "unusual" finds (including sustainable, biodynamic and organic varieties), and its favorable "price-to-quality ratio"; "frequent tastings" and "great classes" held at least once a week in an on-premises classroom plus a "helpful" staff bolster its standing as a "real neighborhood spot."

Brouwerij Lane ●⊄ *Beer*   ∇ 28 | 23 | 28 | M

Greenpoint | 78 Greenpoint Ave. (Franklin St.) | Brooklyn | 347-529-6133 | www.brouwerijlane.com

Offering "beers from everywhere", this "lesser-known" Greenpoint "gem" owned by brew broker Ed Raven carries some 170 "fantastic" imported and domestic labels with a focus on small, American craft brewers; 64-ounce growlers filled from one of the 19 taps dispensing a rotating selection of drafts (including house specialties Jever, Gaffel and Gosser) can "elevate a night of hanging with your buds", and if you need help deciding, the "great guys" on staff "sure know what they're talking about."

Bruno Bakery ●⌨ *Baked Goods*   24 | 24 | 21 | M

G Village | 506 La Guardia Pl. (bet. Bleecker & Houston Sts.) | 212-982-5854

Pasticceria Bruno ● *Baked Goods*

Staten Island | 1650 Hylan Blvd. (Alter Ave.) | 718-987-5859
Staten Island | 676 Forest Ave. (bet. Bement & Burgher Aves.) | 718-448-0993
www.pasticceriabruno.com

"Your head spins in a million directions" as you take in the "beautiful pastries, cakes and homemade gelato" at this "real-deal" "authentic Italian" bakery in Greenwich Village (with two SI branches); "sit and enjoy your espresso" with a "classic" "delicious" "treat" from "pastry chefs extraordinaire Biagio" and Salvatore Settepani and indulge in the "people-watching opportunities" too – "what a fabulous way to end an evening."

Bruno Ravioli ● *Pasta*   21 | 18 | 20 | M

Gramercy | 282 First Ave. (bet. 16th & 17th Sts.) | 212-254-2156 | www.brunoravioli.com

"Such abundance, such variety, so tasty!" – it's a "neighborhood savior" say supporters of this Gramercy offshoot of a Hackensack-based centurion, where "interesting ravioli", "delicious tortellini" and other fresh pastas, sauces, breads and housemade mozzarella

QUALITY DISPLAY SERVICE COST

Visit zagat.com   47 and prepared foods provide all you need for "a quick meal"; a few find the offerings "nothing to write home to mama about", but most are glad to have it as a "basic" "neighborhood option."

BuonItalia 🖃 *Specialty Shop*   26 | 20 | 18 | M

Chelsea | Chelsea Mkt. | 75 Ninth Ave. (bet. 15th & 16th Sts.) | 212-633-9090 | www.buonitalia.com

"Italophiles flock" to this Chelsea Market staple, an "excellent" resource for "authentic provisions of all kinds", most notably "artisanal pastas", "to-die-for" truffles, the "finest" cured meats, 50-plus cheeses and lots of "hard-to-find" "imported indulgences" direct from The Boot; the "service is a bit aloof", but for "stocking up on" delicacies you "don't see anywhere else", it's "heaven"; P.S. prepared foods are sold at the deli counter and cafe.

☑ Burgundy Wine Company 🖃 *Wine/Liquor*   28 | 23 | 24 | E

Chelsea | 143 W. 26th St. (bet. 6th & 7th Aves.) | 212-691-9092 | 888-898-8448 | www.burgundywinecompany.com

As the name suggests, this "cool niche for Pinot lovers" in Chelsea specializes in fine wines from, yes, the Bourgogne region in France, as well as Rhônes and Oregonians, all carefully chosen and, *naturellement,* on the "pricey" side (although there's a "good selection" for under $20 too); bottles are displayed with short descriptions for the cognoscenti, or you can get one of the "friendly" "wine geeks" on staff to give you a hand, while daily tastings and live jazz on Wednesdays are other enticements.

Butcher Block *Specialty Shop*   27 | 23 | 25 | M

Sunnyside | 43-46 41st St. (Queens Blvd.) | Queens | 718-784-1078

This "fantastic" Sunnyside "find" is on the small side for an all-in-one grocery, but as a source for Irish and British goods it's possibly the largest in the five boroughs; area expats stock up on a "reasonably priced", "practical selection" of canned and dried goods, condiments, tea, sweets, beverages and personal-care items from familiar British Isles brands (there's even a wall of crisps), as well as produce, while "helpful and informed" "real old-school butchers" offer choice cuts and huge, hot to-go meals.

Buttercup Bake Shop *Baked Goods*   22 | 21 | 20 | M

E 50s | 973 Second Ave. (bet. 51st & 52nd Sts.) | 212-350-4144 ●
LIC | 41-21 28th St. (41st Ave.) | Queens | 212-350-4144
www.buttercupbakeshop.com

"Oh, how I love thee" – "if only I could live in a red-velvet cupcake" daydream devotees of these "cozy" East Side–LIC twins reminiscent of "small-town bake shops"; "sweet tooths" would "walk a mile for a spoonful" of their "beyond-addictive" frosting, and suggest "try the amazing banana pudding" too, and though a few find the goods "overly" sugary and "on the dry side", the majority retorts "what more could you want, other than a glass of milk?"

	QUALITY	DISPLAY	SERVICE	COST

Butterfield Market 🖃 *Specialty Shop*   25 | 23 | 21 | E

E 70s | 1114 Lexington Ave. (bet. 77th & 78th Sts.) | 212-288-7800 |
www.butterfieldmarket.com

NEW **Baked by Butterfield** *Baked Goods*

E 70s | 1102 Lexington Ave. (77th St.) | 212-988-0196 |
www.bakedbybutterfield.com

"Year after year", this circa-1915 food market and caterer "keeps up
its high standards", supplying the UES with a tasteful array highlighting "excellent" produce, "fresh sandwiches", "delicious prepared
foods" and shelves stocked with "exquisite" "specialty items"; add
"courteous and quick" service and it's "right up there with the best" for
an "easy dinner at home", "but bring your wallet" – "you pay for" the
"zip code"; P.S. the offshoot a few doors down opened post-Survey,
specializing in cake-style donuts that are baked, not fried.

Butter Lane   25 | 21 | 22 | M

Cupcakes *Baked Goods*

E Village | 123 E. Seventh St. (bet. Ave. A & 1st Ave.) |
212-677-2880 ◑

Park Slope | 240 Seventh Ave. (bet. 4th & 5th Sts.) | Brooklyn |
718-369-0466
www.butterlane.com

Its "French buttercream will change your world – at least on a bad
day" say sweet tooths enamored with this "adorable" East Village
bakery (with a Park Slope offshoot that opened post-Survey), where
you can "pick your own" cupcake flavor and icing – "who could ask
for anything more?"; it has "serious locavore" cred (the "totally
moist" "little treasures" here are made from organic and locally
sourced ingredients), plus you can learn to make your own at a baking class – "so much fun!"

Caffé RomaPastry ◑🖬 *Baked Goods*   22 | 19 | 18 | M

Little Italy | 385 Broome St. (Mulberry St.) | 212-226-8413

"Delectable is the word" longtime customers use to describe the
"terrific" cannoli, tiramisu, ricotta cheesecake and other "classic
Italian pastries", plus housemade gelato, that have been turned out
by this "venerable" bakery since 1891; the "quaint" setting's "nothing fancy" and it gets "crazy busy" on weekends, but sipping a cappuccino or a "well-made espresso" at one of the "old-style tables" is
"a true Little Italy experience."

Cake Chef   ∇ 28 | 23 | 22 | M

Bakery 🖬 *Baked Goods*

Staten Island | 957 Jewett Ave. (Victory Blvd.) | 718-448-1290 |
www.cake-chef.com

"Heavenly brownie bites", the "very best cookies" and "delicious"
cakes, pies and tarts are among the "tasty treats" supplied by this
"old-fashioned" Staten Island bakery, where even the gluten-free
crowd can order custom-made delicacies; just remember that the
goodies are baked in small batches, so place an order or "get there
early", especially "on weekends."

	QUALITY	DISPLAY	SERVICE	COST

Cake Man Raven
Confectionery ◑ *Baked Goods*

QUALITY 24 | DISPLAY 16 | SERVICE 17 | COST M

Fort Greene | 708A Fulton St. (bet. Oxford St. & Portland Ave.) | Brooklyn | 718-694-2253 | www.cakemanraven.com
It's "worth the trip to Fort Greene" to find "divine" red velvet cake baked by the "quirky" eponymous Southern owner of this shop according to "wowed" partisans who cite "delicious", "fluffy" carrot and pineapple-coconut cakes as runners-up to the "memorable" house "favorite"; aficionados endure "ridiculously long lines" and service just this side of "nonexistent" to purchase up to four "big" "hunks" (whole cakes must be ordered in advance) – "nothing tops" it.

ⓩ Calabria Pork Store ▣ *Meat/Poultry*

27 | 23 | 23 | M

Bronx | 2338 Arthur Ave. (bet. 183rd & 187th Sts.) | 718-367-5145
A "throwback to the old days", this "sublime" Arthur Avenue Italian deli is famed for the countless "heavenly" cured sausages hanging from its ceiling ("you'll go nuts with the choices"), while the fresh pork-y products from the butcher counter are "as good as it gets"; housemade mozzarella plus plenty of imported delights at "great value" ensure "many regular customers" – about "the only thing missing is the sawdust."

Calandra Cheese Co. ▣ *Cheese/Dairy*

∇ 27 | 19 | 25 | M

Bronx | 2314 Arthur Ave. (bet. Crescent Ave. & 187th St.) | 718-365-7572
Dating from the 1930s, this unassuming Arthur Avenue shop "is truly an artisan" when it comes to crafting the "very freshest" Italian cheeses, and its housemade specialties – the "most delicate" ricotta and "delicious" mozzarella in either the standard or the enriched scamorza and caciocavallo varieties – "can't be beat"; with an imported selection also on hand, far-flung formaggio fanciers only "wish this store were closer."

California
Wine Merchants ◑▣ *Wine/Liquor*

∇ 24 | 23 | 24 | M

Financial District | 15 Bridge St. (bet. Broad & Whitehall Sts.) | 212-785-7285 | www.cawinemerchants.com
With a spotlight on small producers from across the Golden State, 95% of this FiDi vintner's wines are "well-chosen" California labels running from "everyday drinkers to cellar gems", offered at a "good range of prices"; the "modern, spacious" digs are manned by "knowledgeable" owners who are "hyped about wine and eager to share", and better still, that West Coast vibe ensures they're "not pushy."

Calvisius Caviar ◑ *Caviar/Smoked Fish*

∇ 29 | 25 | 25 | VE

E 50s | Four Seasons Hotel | 58 E. 58th St. (bet. Madison & Park Aves.) | 212-207-8222 | www.calvisiuscaviar.com
This chichi caviar boutique and lounge in the lobby of the Four Seasons Hotel in Midtown puts a sustainable spin on all things eggscellent, offering the likes of farm-raised, imported-from-Italy osetra and white sturgeon available in tins or, for those who eat in, served atop warm potato purée with sips of Dom Perignon; tabs are in the ka-ching realm, but then "is there such a thing as cheap caviar?"

	QUALITY	DISPLAY	SERVICE	COST

Cannelle Patisserie *Baked Goods*   ▽ 29 | 22 | 19 | M

Jackson Heights | 75-59 31st Ave. (78th St.) | Queens |
718-565-6200 | www.cannellepatisserie.com

Pastry chefs who honed their skills at the Waldorf-Astoria are behind this "fantastic" bakery/cafe whose "highly unlikely" location in a Jackson Heights strip mall has habitués exalting "finally" – Queens has a "top"-quality patisserie; its "light, flaky croissants", "fabulous" gateaux Breton, éclairs, tarts *et tout comme ça* "rival the best of France", and while there are often "lines" out the door, devotees declare the goods "worth the wait" – especially given "amazing-value" prices that are "simply the icing on the cake."

⌷ Caputo Bakery ⊅ *Baked Goods*   27 | 20 | 21 | I

Carroll Gardens | 329 Court St. (bet. Sackett & Union Sts.) |
Brooklyn | 718-875-6871

"Crispy, warm loaves fly off the shelves" at this Carroll Gardens "institution" that for more than a century has been baking "heavenly" Italian breads (seeded or plain), ciabatta, olive and semolinas, plus a prosciutto-packed lard version that aficionados deem downright "remarkable" ("forget the cardiologist"); low prices and a counter crew that includes "entertaining older ladies" complete the "true Brooklyn-Italian experience."

Carnegie Deli ●▤⊅ *Deli*   23 | 17 | 16 | E

W 50s | 854 Seventh Ave. (55th St.) | 212-757-2245 |
800-334-5606 | www.carnegiedeli.com

A "fresser's dream" and "must-visit" for "every tourist", this "been-around-forever" (since 1937) Midtown deli is touted as "the gold standard for corned beef" and "pastrami champ" by boosters who don't mind the "bustle" and "gruff, seasoned" staff; crowds can be "a hassle" and "your wallet will be a lot lighter when you leave", but it's "still a destination" whether "once in a lifetime or once a month."

Carolina Country Store *Specialty Shop*   - | - | - | I

Brownsville | 2001 Atlantic Ave. (Saratoga Ave.) | Brooklyn |
718-498-8033

Dixie expats pining for Southern comfort take to this rustic larder on a remote (to say the least) stretch in Brownsville, where the cornucopia extends to country ham, smoked sausage, hoop cheese, backwoods BBQ sauces, cane syrup and other sundries, down to old-fashioned cookies and candy; the tabs are affordable, and the homespun setting rightly recalls the Tar Heel State.

Carrot Top Pastries ▤ *Baked Goods*   23 | 17 | 20 | M

Inwood | 5025 Broadway (214th St.) | 212-569-1532
Washington Heights | 3931 Broadway (bet. 164th & 165th Sts.) |
212-927-4800 ●
www.carrottoppastries.com

Upper Manhattanites declare "you'd be hard-pressed to find better carrot cake" than the "amazing" creations baked at this "high-quality" Washington Heights–Inwood duo, which also offers cheesecake, flan, muffins, "oversized rugalach" that "rock" and lots more;

it's all baked at the 165th Street location, but both branches boast pleasingly affordable prices that keep 'em "coming back for more."

Carry On
Tea & Sympathy ❶ 🗉 *Coffee/Tea*

25 | 20 | 21 | M

W Village | 110 Greenwich Ave. (bet. 12th & 13th Sts.) | 212-989-9735 | www.teaandsympathynewyork.com

Pop in "for everything British" at this next-door annex to the West Village's Tea & Sympathy, a carry-out shop that's "small" but "stocked so well" with "wonderful, eclectic U.K. products", from a "lovely tea" selection to "quaint" pots, condiments, biscuits, boiled sweets and scads of other "English goodies"; "cute" decor that's "worthy of a Monty Python sketch" and "cheeky, fun" employees well endowed with "wit" have the homesick saying it's "just like Blighty"; P.S. it also caters, with deliveries made via an authentic London cab.

☒ Casa Della Mozzarella 🗉 *Cheese/Dairy*

29 | 25 | 25 | M

Bronx | 604 E. 187th St. (Arthur Ave.) | 718-364-3867

"Mozzarella doesn't get any better" than at this circa-1922 Arthur Avenue mecca, esteemed as "the definitive source" for "the freshest", "creamiest" "homemade" mozz "this side of the Atlantic" (it's rated No. 1 for Quality in NYC); with the house's own olive oil, imported cheeses and "ridiculously good" salumi from the "accommodating" "counter guys" to round out the "sensory overload" of "old-world Italian delights", this is the "real deal."

Cassinelli Food Products ⌀ *Pasta*

▽ 29 | 19 | 25 | I

Astoria | 31-12 23rd Ave. (31st St.) | Queens | 718-274-4881

Consider "throwing out your pasta machine" – after all, "how can you beat" this Astoria stalwart's made-on-premises "phenomenal, fresh" fettuccine, linguine, tortellini, ravioli and more unusual varieties like perciatelli (a long tubular shape), all offered up "with a smile"?; partisans praise the carborrific goods' "unbelievable" flavor and texture, and those who live a stone's throw away just feel "lucky to have these guys in the neighborhood."

Cathcart & Reddy ❶ *Baked Goods*
(fka DessertTruck Works)

25 | 20 | 23 | I

LES | 6 Clinton St. (bet. Houston & Stanton Sts.) | 212-228-0701 | www.desserttruck.com

Its bakers once dispensed their "amazing" desserts from a refurbished former postal truck, but they have come to a stop at this "surprisingly cozy", recently renamed LES pastry shop/cafe; now the "yum" "fun" continues with macarons, molten-chocolate cake and the like, plus a chocolate bread pudding so "unbelievable" it beat Bobby Flay on *Throwdown*.

Catskill Bagel Co. *Bagels*

▽ 22 | 18 | 20 | I

Ditmas Park | 1416 Cortelyou Rd. (bet. Marlborough & Rugby Rds.) | Brooklyn | 718 282-5014

Ditmas Park's "go-to bagel spot", this "terrific" Cortelyou Road shop is a source of "terrific" housemade rounds in an area short on high-quality carbs; its extensive, affordable chalkboard menu also features a serious "variety of wraps, sandwiches, spreads" and such.

Caviar Russe ◐☰ *Caviar* | 26 | 23 | 23 | VE |

E 50s | 538 Madison Ave., 2nd fl. (bet. 54th & 55th Sts.) | 212-980-5908 | 800-692-2842 | www.caviarrusse.com

Those with a taste for "top-end" caviar swim to this "impressive" Midtown Russian restaurant/boutique and indulge in an extravagant array of domestic and imported eggs, plus mother-of-pearl accessories to go with, as well as smoked fish, gourmet goodies like foie gras and truffles and deluxe gift samplers delivered in insulated bags; prices are predictably "high", but "red-carpet service" from "knowledgeable" staffers make the dent in your wallet easier to accept.

Ceci-Cela *Baked Goods* | 26 | 21 | 20 | M |

Little Italy | 55 Spring St. (bet. Lafayette & Mulberry Sts.) | 212-274-9179 | www.cecicelanyc.com

"Sinfully delicious napoleons", "to-die-for" éclairs, tarts, madeleines, "flakey, buttery croissants" and other "sweets and savories" looking like "works of art" add up to "a taste of Paris" at this Little Italy patisserie; a "pipsqueak of a place" it may be, but it's "the real thing", from the "good, strong coffee" served in the "quaint little sitting area" to the "dash" of "sassy" service "to spice it up" a bit; P.S. it also specializes in wedding cakes.

Ceriello Fine Foods ☰ *Specialty Shop* | 24 | 19 | 21 | E |

E 40s | Grand Central Mkt. | Lexington Ave. (43rd St.) | 212-972-4266 ◐
Douglaston | 4435 Douglaston Pkwy. (Northern Blvd.) | Queens | 718-428-2494
877-613-6637 | www.ceriellofinefoods.com

"Gorgeous prime meats" presented in a "terrific display" make this Grand Central Market stall "very convenient for picking up" the likes of fresh sausage, dry-aged porterhouse or stuffed pork roast "on the way to the train"; while the "reliable" quality's "worth every penny", the Queens HQ is a cheaper source of the same, along with "homemade mozzarella" and "old-world Italian" imports.

Cer té *Caterer/Events* | 23 | 18 | 18 | M |

W 50s | 20 W. 55th St. (bet. 5th & 6th Aves.) | 212-397-2020 | www.certenyc.com

The Midtown "gem" Cer té Cafe is also a "best-kept secret" for catering, providing a globally inflected lineup of "creative and generally tasty" fare à la "gourmet sandwiches", salads and hot dishes to corporate clients in the vicinity; they also service full-scale events, including past affairs at venues such as the Whitney and Carnegie Hall.

☑ Chambers Street Wines ◐☰ *Wine/Liquor* | 27 | 24 | 26 | E |

TriBeCa | 148 Chambers St. (bet. Greenwich St. & W. B'way) | 212-227-1434 | www.chambersstwines.com

Perfect when you "need an impress-the-boss bottle", this "excellent" wine shop "buried" on a TriBeCa "backstreet" carries an "unusually good selection of Loire and biodynamic wines" among its "interesting" stock of small-producer and "hard-to-find" vintages; "decent" (if not cheap) prices lure "experienced wine-buyers", who can be found "ogling the aged stuff", but whether you're "a geek" or a "novice", the "passionate" staff will "happily guide you."

Charbonnel et Walker ▣ Candy/Nuts ∇ 23 | 26 | 22 | E

E 40s | Saks Fifth Ave. | 611 Fifth Ave., 8th fl. (bet. 49th & 50th Sts.) | 212-588-0546 | www.charbonnel.co.uk

Never mind the "outrageous prices" – the decadently "delicious" treats at this Saks Fifth Avenue outpost of the venerable London confectioner, the royal manufacturer to Her Majesty the Queen, are worth every pound; sit at the counter below the elegant chandelier and indulge in rich brownies, puddings and drinking chocolate, or bring a bit of Britain home with prettily packaged champagne truffles, cocoa-dusted almonds and the signature silky plain chocolates.

Cheese of the World Cheese/Dairy 26 | 21 | 21 | M

Forest Hills | 71-48 Austin St. (Queens Blvd.) | Queens | 718-263-1933 | www.cheeseoftheworldforesthills.com

They've been "doing it right" "for ages" at this Forest Hills "mom-and-pop" cheesemonger, "iconic" in the area for its "amazing selection" of some 400 "hard-to-find" fromages "from around the globe", hewn from huge wheels at "incredibly good prices" by a "knowledgeable staff"; figure in charcuterie and "accoutrements like jam" and crackers, and the worldly-wise agree it's "sure to please."

Chelsea Market Baskets ▣ Specialty Shop 23 | 23 | 21 | M

Chelsea | Chelsea Mkt. | 75 Ninth Ave. (bet. 15th & 16th Sts.) | 212-727-1484 | 888-727-7887 | www.chelseamarketbaskets.com

Assemble an "eclectic" gift basket "for any person's passions" at this Chelsea Market "catch-all store", which custom-fills totes and hampers with a "super assortment" of "things you don't find everywhere", whether English preserves, candy, cookies, coffee, toys, "New York–centric" items or "you name it"; the goods are "cleverly displayed", and the "outstanding staff" "will accommodate" your choices so you only "pay as much as you can afford."

Chelsea Wine Vault ▣ Wine/Liquor 24 | 24 | 23 | M

Chelsea | Chelsea Mkt. | 75 Ninth Ave. (bet. 15th & 16th Sts.) | 212-462-4244 | www.chelseawinevault.com

The "wondrously eclectic", "well-displayed" wines at this Chelsea Market vintner include "uncommon" labels from around the globe on offer at "every price" point; frequent seminars held in its cellar-esque digs and "tastings that lead you down new paths" add to the "educational" aspect, as does the "cheerful", "insanely helpful" staff there to "giddily" guide you whether you want a "$7 bottle or a $2,000 one."

Cheryl Kleinman Cakes Baked Goods ∇ 28 | 26 | 27 | E

Boerum Hill | 448 Atlantic Ave. (bet. Bond & Nevins Sts.) | Brooklyn | 718-237-2271

By appointment only

"Perfect, unforgettable" wedding and special-occasion cakes are "thoughtfully rendered" by this high-end Boerum Hill "class act" whose "beautiful design and color sense" matches the "delicious"-ness quotient whether for a tiered traditional model or something creatively modern; those looking for an everyday treat find cupcakes, cookies and pastries at Betty Bakery, the retail outlet.

ChikaLicious ● *Baked Goods* | 25 | 22 | 23 | M |

E Village | 204 E. 10th St. (bet. 1st & 2nd Aves.) | 212-475-0929 | www.dessertclubchikalicious.com

Sweet tooths "can't rave enough" about this "cute little" East Village "boutique" outlet of the well-known dessert bar across the street, where "the art" of treats is expressed in "cookies to kill for" and "cheesecake to die for", not to mention "incredible éclairs" and other "sublime" pastries to take out or eat at the stand-up counter; there's "always a line", but that's the price of "bliss."

Chinatown | 24 | 16 | 19 | I |
Ice Cream Factory ●⊞ *Ice Cream*

Chinatown | 65 Bayard St. (bet. Elizabeth & Mott Sts.) | 212-608-4170 | www.chinatownicecreamfactory.com

"Adventurous flavors" "galore" "reflect the neighborhood" at this Chinatown ice cream "institution", where you can get "good old-fashioned vanilla" but it's the likes of "delish" red bean, lychee and green tea that "steal the show"; although it's too "tiny" for seating, it's the "perfect" place "if you crave" scoops "after a C-town feeding."

Choco Bolo *Baked Goods* | ▽ 21 | 20 | 20 | E |
(fka Best Chocolate Cake in the World)

E 80s | 1046 Madison Ave. (bet. 79th & 80th Sts.) | 212-535-2253 ●▤
NoLita | 55A Spring St. (bet. Lafayette & Mulberry Sts.) | 212-343-2253 ●▤
NEW **W 70s** | 2058 Broadway (71st St.) | 212-799-2253
Dumbo | 68 Jay St. (Water St.) | Brooklyn | 718-246-2253 ▤
www.chocobolo.com

These links of a Lisbon-founded mini-chain specialize in two "excellent" iterations of Valrhona flourless cake – dark or milk chocolate – both filled with delicate layers of gooey ganache, meringue and mousse; beyond the "tasty" signature gateaux, there's coffee and scoops from Il Laboratorio del Gelato.

Chocolate Bar ●▤ *Candy/Nuts* | 25 | 23 | 23 | E |

W Village | 19 Eighth Ave. (bet. Jane & 12th Sts.) | 212-366-1541 | www.chocolatebarnyc.com

The "sinful", "spicy hot chocolate definitely warms the soul" and "makes you feel like a kid again" say those "over the moon" about this West Villager's "decadent" sweets; "if you need a gift that looks as good as it tastes", load up on the namesake specialty, crafted from Belgian chocolate and packaged in decorative boxes and wrappers, or go for the lollipops – now these are "delicacies" "for grown-ups."

The Chocolate Room ●▤ *Candy/Nuts* | 25 | 23 | 22 | M |

Cobble Hill | 269 Court St. (bet. Butler & Douglass Sts.) | Brooklyn | 718-246-2600

(continued)

(continued)

The Chocolate Room

Park Slope | 86 Fifth Ave. (bet. St. Marks Pl. & Warren St.) |
Brooklyn | 718-783-2900
www.thechocolateroombrooklyn.com

"There's no better way to end an evening" than at this "chocoholic's paradise", a "wonderful" candy shop/cafe twosome in Park Slope and Cobble Hill (where you can "watch them making" desserts "through the window"); try the chocolates from famed confectioner Fritz Knipschildt or indulge in the "supremely delicious" baked creations like "blackout cake that lights up the night" or brownie sundaes – and "for a special treat", pair them with "wines and spirits."

Chocolat Michel Cluizel   Candy/Nuts   ▽ 27 | 25 | 23 | VE

W 40s | 584 Fifth Ave. (bet. 47th & 48th Sts.) | 646-415-9126 |
www.chocolatmichelcluizel.com

"When you need a high-quality chocolate fix", "break open the piggy bank" and head for this swish Midtown mecca boasting bonbons, salted caramel bars, pastries and other "luxury" sweets you just "can't say no to" (including kosher varieties), all imported from France; yes, these "elegantly decadent" delectables come at a price, but to the *enchanté* they're oh-so-"worth it!"

Choice Greene   *Prepared Food*   ▽ 27 | 23 | 19 | M

Fort Greene | 214 Greene Ave. (bet. Cambridge Pl. & Grand Ave.) |
Brooklyn | 718-230-1243 | www.choicebrooklyn.com

Choice Market ●   *Prepared Food*

Clinton Hill | 318 Lafayette Ave. (Grand Ave.) | Brooklyn | 718-230-5234

This "gourmet" duo enjoys a "trendy" rep, with the Clinton Hill cafe vending "delightful" baked goods and prepared foods that can attract "long lines" while the Fort Greene grocer stocks a full range of choice specialty items; it's further evidence that "Brooklyn has become the new Manhattan", so expect prices "similar to those in the city."

Choux Factory   *Baked Goods*   23 | 17 | 21 | I

E 40s | 865 First Ave. (bet. 48th & 49th Sts.) | 212-223-0730
E 80s | 1685 First Ave. (bet. 87th & 88th Sts.) | 212-289-2023 ●

If you want "delicate, light" cream puffs like a "melting cloud of yum in your mouth", these East Side branches of a Japanese chain are a "choux-in"; "wonderful" staffers dispense the "addictive", "made-fresh daily", piped-to-order puffs in a "variety of flavors", and there's the "bonus" of "strong, smooth" Kona coffee to sip as you savor.

Christian Vautier   - | - | - | E
Le Concept   *Candy/Nuts*

LES | 254 Broome St. (Orchard St.) | 212-473-3200 |
www.cvleconcept.com

The eponymous Parisian chocolatier has teamed up with a NYC pastry chef to open this new LES confectioner, where the made-fresh-daily truffles, bars, pastries, macarons and more are decidedly French, though some of the flavorings travel the globe a bit (e.g. bonbons filled with Sichuan pepper ganache); its petite, brick-walled space

QUALITY DISPLAY SERVICE COST

with a bright-pink awning houses a small seating area where the treats can be enjoyed on-premises along with Dallis Brothers coffee.

Christos Steak House ● *Meat/Poultry* | 25 | 22 | 24 | VE |

Astoria | 41-08 23rd Ave. (bet. 41st & 42nd Sts.) | Queens | 718-726-5195 | www.christossteakhouse.com

Doing double duty, this "Greek-style steakhouse" in Astoria has an on-premises butcher shop offering poultry, game and prime meats, including "beautiful" "thick steaks" and other cuts "nicely marbled and aged to perfection"; Hellenic-accented sausages and charcuterie round out the offerings, but keep in mind that the "Manhattan quality" is matched with "very expensive" prices.

Chung Fat Supermarket ● *Specialty Shop* | ▽ 22 | 13 | 10 | I |

Flushing | 41-82 Main St. (bet. Maple & Sanford Aves.) | Queens | 718-886-9368 | www.cfsupermarket.com

"You can get everything here" say those in the know about this Flushing behemoth, a sprawling Asian market that has plenty of "locals' appeal" thanks to its bonanza of meats, seafood, "exotic fruits" and vegetables, and countless packaged, canned and frozen staples from the Far East; what's more, the "low prices" are a lifesaver when your funds thin out.

Ciao Bella Gelato *Ice Cream* | 26 | 19 | 19 | M |

E 40s | Grand Central Terminal | dining concourse (42nd St. & Vanderbilt Ave.) | 212-867-5311 ●
E 90s | 27 E. 92nd St. (bet. 5th & Madison Aves.) | 212-831-5555
NoLita | 285 Mott St. (bet. Houston & Prince Sts.) | 212-431-3591 ●
800-435-2863 | www.ciaobellagelato.com

Those looking for a "little taste of Italy" via the "pure deliciousness" of "creamy", "delectable gelato" or a "supreme sorbet" seek scoops at this "hit-the-spot" chain; the "fabulous flavors" on offer "may not be as newfangled as some", but to ice cream freaks they're still "plenty delicious" – and hard to beat "on a sultry NYC day."

Cipriani Le Specialità ▭ *Baked Goods* | 26 | 23 | 21 | VE |

E 40s | 110 E. 42nd St. (bet. Lexington & Park Aves.) | 212-557-5088 | www.cipriani.com

The Cipriani clan's offspring opposite Grand Central includes a cafe dispensing sandwiches and other "great lunch fare", while the bakery/prepared foods annex boasts high-end Italian baked goods like breadsticks, "divine rosetta rolls" and pastries, as well as "delicious" pastas and such to "take home and devour"; olive oils, vinegars, sauces and other house-imported specialty products are also on offer.

Citarella ●▭ *Major Market* | 26 | 24 | 22 | E |

E 70s | 1313 Third Ave. (75th St.) | 212-874-0383
G Village | 424 Sixth Ave. (9th St.) | 212-874-0383
W 70s | 2135 Broadway (75th St.) | 212-874-0383
www.citarella.com

"The best of everything under one roof" entices the faithful to this "top-quality" "gourmet purveyor", well known as "one of the most reliable" and "customer-oriented" sources for "fabulous", "swimmingly fresh" seafood and "exceptional" "prime meats" trimmed with the "friendly" humor of "a hometown butcher"; it's also a "treasure hunt" of "excellent produce", "superb prepared foods", "delicious" deli items, a "curated selection of cheeses" and "outta sight" breads and baked goods – despite the "commensurate" "hefty cost", seekers of "first-class" rations find it "hard to do better."

City Bakery *Baked Goods*   25 | 22 | 19 | E

Flatiron | 3 W. 18th St. (bet. 5th & 6th Aves.) | 212-366-1414 | www.thecitybakery.com

"You often see Maury Rubin hanging out" at his Flatiron bakery/cafeteria where the "swoon"-inducing goodies run from "world-famous pretzel croissants" to "picture-perfect tarts", "fantastic" pastries and cookies (including "surprisingly good" vegan varieties), and that "decadent hot chocolate"; on the savory side, there's a "genius salad bar" and "superior" prepared foods made of Greenmarket produce, and though it's all "a bit spendy" and a "zoo" with "confused" service at peak times, devotees "wouldn't mind getting locked in for the night" all the same; P.S. it also does a big catering business.

Cleaver Co. *Caterer/Events*   ∇ 27 | 19 | 26 | E

Chelsea | Chelsea Mkt. | 75 Ninth Ave. (bet. 15th & 16th Sts.) | 212-741-9174 | www.cleaverco.com
By appointment only

For cuisine so "flavorful" it makes any occasion "unique", Mary Cleaver's "fab" Chelsea Market caterer hews to organic, "local and sustainable" ingredients (many from the Greenmarket) to produce "fresh and delicious" global fare "displayed with an awareness" that "allows the food to shine"; the "extraordinary service" extends to all-inclusive event planning for private parties, weddings and corporate functions, and her handiwork can be sampled at a tiny next-door restaurant, the Green Table.

Clinton St.   26 | 20 | 21 | M
Baking Company ●⏦ *Baked Goods*

LES | 4 Clinton St. (bet. Houston & Stanton Sts.) | 646-602-6263 | www.clintonstreetbaking.com

"If you have a sweet tooth", this "too-popular" little bakery/cafe is the Lower East Side "authority", dispensing "the best cookies" and other "wonderful baked goods" including "delicious" biscuits, muffins and scones; just know that on weekends you'll have to fight your way through "lines down the block", because the eatery's famously "divine" pancakes and waffles "live up to the hype"; P.S. it also does custom birthday cakes.

Cocoa Bar ● *Candy/Nuts*   21 | 18 | 15 | M

LES | 21 Clinton St. (bet. Houston & Stanton Sts.) | 212-677-7417
Park Slope | 228 Seventh Ave. (bet. 3rd & 4th Sts.) | Brooklyn | 718-499-4080
www.cocoabarnyc.com

Boasting "both day and night personalities", this LES–Park Slope java/vino bar duo is a favored local choice for "something sweet" – notably "to-die-for" Belgian bonbons and "wonderful desserts" – paired with coffee or a "late glass of wine"; its attractive chocolate boxes and assortments are perfect when you need a last-minute gift, but in truth it's most appreciated as a "nice place to hang out", where they "let people lounge for hours" – it'll surely be "popular forever."

Colette's Cakes *Baked Goods* ▽ 27 | 27 | 25 | VE

W Village | 681 Washington St. (bet. Charles & W. 10th Sts.) | 212-366-6530 | www.colettescakes.com
By appointment only

Like "spectacular" "works of art", the sculptural, "imaginative" (and sometimes humorous) special-occasion cakes created by painter-turned-West-Village-baker Colette Peters are as "delicious" as they are "beautiful" to behold, as her long list of celeb clients suggests; naturally such creations come "at a price", but the "splurge" is "worth it" – "you're paying for quality."

Colson Patisserie *Baked Goods* ▽ 24 | 22 | 19 | M

Park Slope | 374 Ninth St. (6th Ave.) | Brooklyn | 718-965-6400 | www.colsonpastries.com

A "wee gem", this "busy" French-Belgian Park Slope patisserie is the "real deal", featuring "fantastic" pastries and croissants, pain au chocolat, brioche, "noteworthy financiers" and all the *classiques*, along with "delectable" sandwiches and coffee; the "pleasant" staff and "child-friendly" vibe cement its status as a neighborhood standby.

☑ Coluccio & Sons *Specialty Shop* 27 | 21 | 22 | M

Borough Park | 1214 60th St. (bet. 12th & 13th Aves.) | Brooklyn | 718-436-6700 | www.dcoluccioandsons.com

"Here's the real deal" promise partisans of this family-run specialty grocer in "unfancy" Borough Park boasting an "extensive" array of "authentic Italian" goods "to make your mouth water", most of them imported "from all parts of the motherland"; it's an "excellent source" of "wonderful" cheeses, 80 varieties of pasta, olives, condiments, oils and other "favorites" "at the best prices" – no wonder "those in the know swear by this place."

Columbus Circle Wines & Spirits ◑▣ *Wine/Liquor* 25 | 21 | 22 | M

W 50s | 1802 Broadway (bet. CPS & 58th St.) | 212-247-0764 | www.columbuscirclewines.com

"High-end and boutique wines" plus some more "reasonably priced" bottles are all "clearly laid out" at this Columbus Circle wine shop; "spot-on" help from the "friendly" personnel and an enomatic tasting system that allows customers to sip several samples completes the solid "neighborhood experience."

Commodities Natural Market ◑ *Health* ▽ 25 | 16 | 16 | M

E Village | 165 First Ave. (bet. 10th & 11th Sts.) | 212-260-2600 | www.commoditiesnaturalmarket.com

"It may look small", but this East Village health food fixture is "stocked to the ceiling" with "everything you need" in the way of natural noshables, from a "staggering" selection of organic produce to packaged items "not found elsewhere"; the lines are "slow-moving" and the "narrow aisles" are often "packed with young" bohos, but "character" renders it a welcome "alternative to the big chains."

☑ Cones, Ice Cream Artisans ● ⊟ *Ice Cream*

27 | 21 | 22 | M

W Village | 272 Bleecker St. (bet. Morton St. & 7th Ave.) | 212-414-1795
Maybe "corn flavor" ice cream "sounds crazy" but, like all of the 30-plus "outrageous", "creamy", "intense" options at this "delightful" West Village cone-u-copia owned by a couple of Argentinean brothers, it's "shockingly tasty"; the "super-premium" cream here is made daily with "fresh ingredients", so though it strikes some as "a bit pricey", most "would make a detour" from anywhere for scoops so "fabulous."

The Cookie Jar ☷ *Baked Goods*

∇ 27 | 25 | 24 | M

Staten Island | 1226 Forest Ave. (bet. Jewett Ave. & Llewellyn Pl.) | 718-448-3500 | www.cakechefcookiejar.com
The "sister to Cake Chef", this "pretty little" Staten Island bakery turns out "yummy" fresh-made cookies that are "the next best thing to your mother's" – and in "a variety like no other" (about 100 per day); customers murmuring "decisions, decisions . . ." just "take some of each", or better yet fill one of the dozens of "neat cookie jars" on sale here.

☑ A Cook's Companion ☷ *Cookware*

28 | 24 | 24 | M

Brooklyn Heights | 197 Atlantic Ave. (bet. Clinton & Court Sts.) | Brooklyn | 718-852-6901 | www.acookscompanion.com
"Chockablock with the best of everything a home cook needs", this Brooklyn Heights "resource" is a "favorite" for everything from "gadgets and aprons" to "electronics like waffle irons and slow cookers" from "all the best brands", as well as more "unusual items like a spaetzle maker"; "dedicated" staffers are "unobtrusive but always available for assistance" – a bonus since sometimes those "treasures" are really "stashed away" in its "small"-ish space.

Cork & Bottle ● *Wine/Liquor*

23 | 19 | 21 | M

E 60s | 1158 First Ave. (bet. 63rd & 64th Sts.) | 212-838-5300
A "well-curated" selection makes this veteran (since 1933) East Side vino vendor a "handy local" fallback where "helpful" sales-folk assist all who browse the 1,000-plus wines and spirits on offer, with an emphasis on Californian, Australian and Spanish regions; Manhattan delivery and reasonable tabs are other endearments.

Corner Café & Bakery *Baked Goods*

23 | 21 | 18 | M

E 90s | 1246 Madison Ave. (bet. 89th & 90th Sts.) | 212-860-4340 ●
E 90s | 1645 Third Ave. (92nd St.) | 212-860-8060 ●
E 90s | 1659 Third Ave. (93rd St.) | 212-860-8060
www.cornercafe-bakery.com
These UES bakeries "fill the street with mouthwatering smells" from the "scrumptious" "treats" made within – muffins, cakes, the "best red-velvet cupcakes", rugalach – augmented with "thoughtful" prepared foods at the 1645 Third Avenue location (which also has a

QUALITY | DISPLAY | SERVICE | COST

"comfortable" full-service cafe); service can be "indifferent" at times, but the "good value" compensates; P.S. it also caters.

Corrado Bread & Pastry *Baked Goods*   22 | 20 | 19 | M

E 70s | 1390 Third Ave. (79th St.) | 212-288-2300
E 70s | 960 Lexington Ave. (70th St.) | 212-774-1904
E 90s | 1361 Lexington Ave. (bet. 90th & 91st Sts.) | 212-348-8943
W Village | 35 Christopher St. (Waverly Pl.) | 212-242-3534
www.corradobread.com

Aggregators extraordinaire, these shops assemble an "enticing" variety of goods from the tri-state region's finest bakeries, including "interesting breads", "fantastic muffins", "gorgeous pastries" and cakes; there's also "fresh sandwiches" and other lunch fare, so even though a few mutter about "helter-skelter service", the "convenience" keeps 'em "pretty darn crowded" all the same.

Cosenza's Fish Market *Seafood*   25 | 22 | 23 | M

Bronx | 2354 Arthur Ave. (186th St.) | 718-364-8510

"It don't get much better" for "briny mollusks" than the just-shucked clams and oysters at this Arthur Avenue staple, a venerable purveyor of "the freshest fish" where fin fans can net the likes of *vongole* and *scungilli*; family-owned friendliness means "the boys will always have a suggestion", and you can even enjoy some bivalves on the spot thanks to the raw bar set up out on the sidewalk.

Costco Wholesale ●◑▣ *Major Market*   23 | 15 | 14 | I

Harlem | East River Plaza | 517 E. 117th St. (Pleasant Ave.) |
212-896-5873 | 800-774-2678
Sunset Park | 976 Third Ave. (bet. 37th & 38th Sts.) | Brooklyn |
718-965-7603
Astoria | 32-50 Vernon Blvd. (bet. B'way & 33rd Rd.) | Queens |
718-267-3680
Staten Island | 2975 Richmond Ave. (Independence Ave.) | 718-982-9000
www.costco.com

"Clear your refrigerator and pantry" before "stocking up" at this "no-frills" warehouse chain, where cost-conscious cohorts willing to "schlep bulk" flock for "great buys" on "industrial sizes" of "staples" like "passable" "mass-produced baked goods", "daunting" "chunks of cheese", "humongous" cuts of meat (perfect "for freezing"), "giant packs" of produce and "really cheap" cooking supplies; it's "a bit overwhelming" and "service leaves much to be desired", but "let's face it" – if you're "on a budget" or "have a family of 12", it's "a steal."

Court Pastry Shop ⊘ *Baked Goods*   26 | 19 | 22 | I

Cobble Hill | 298 Court St. (bet. Degraw & Douglass Sts.) |
Brooklyn | 718-875-4820

Almost "a picture of time standing still", this Cobble Hill Sicilian bakery "has been around forever" (actually since 1948) "and deservedly so", considering its "wow"-inducing "handmade" sweets all "done right", including cookies and "excellent biscotti", "outstanding cannoli", sfogliatelle and the like; although it can be "hard" to choose among the "not-to-be-missed" options, in summertime "the house-made ices are a cooling treat" while you make up your mind.

QUALITY | DISPLAY | SERVICE | COST

Court Street Grocers *Major Market* ▽ 29 | 28 | 27 | E

Carroll Gardens | 485 Court St. (Nelson St.) | Brooklyn |
718-722-7229 | www.courtstreetgrocers.com

An "expertly curated" selection of "high-end" grocery items, "amazing sandwiches" and prepared foods plus a high-quality roster of meats and cheeses have made this Carroll Gardens shop a "great addition to the neighborhood" according to admirers who also praise the "very friendly workers"; all of that and a "great, casual" atmosphere have led at least one regular to dub its narrow, meticulously appointed space "my favorite local."

Cousin John's 22 | 19 | 19 | M
Cafe & Bakery ◑ *Baked Goods*

Park Slope | 70 Seventh Ave. (bet. Berkeley & Lincoln Pls.) |
Brooklyn | 718-622-7333 | www.cousinjohnsbakery.com

"One of the originals in gentrified Park Slope", this bakery "mainstay" is known for "really good croissants", cookies, "wonderful pastries" and "the best strawberry shortcake"; a few shrug "mediocre", but locals eating breakfast or lunch in the "cozy cafe" or watching the bakers in the open kitchen declare it's "great having John as a cousin."

Crespella *Baked Goods* - | - | - | M

Park Slope | 321 Seventh Ave. (9th St.) | Brooklyn | 718-788-2980 |
www.crespellabk.com

The namesake Italian spin on the crêpe comes to Park Slope via this dessert nook right by the subway on Seventh Avenue, done up in a maroon palette with Italian sayings on the wall; the choices include sweet fillings (Nutella, strawberry, tiramisu) or savory (mortadella, ricotta, prosciutto) to eat at the counter with or without an espresso.

Crumbs Bake Shop 🗐 *Baked Goods* 22 | 22 | 21 | M

E 50s | 501 Madison Ave. (bet. 52nd & 53rd Sts.) | 212-750-0515 |
877-278-6270

E 70s | 1371 Third Ave. (bet. 78th & 79th Sts.) | 212-794-9800 |
877-278-6270◑

Financial District | 87 Beaver St. (bet. Hanover & Pearl Sts.) |
212-480-7500 | 877-278-6270

G Village | 124 University Pl. (bet. 13th & 14th Sts.) |
212-206-8011 | 877-278-6270◑

G Village | 37 E. Eighth St. (University Pl.) | 212-673-1500 |
877-278-6270◑

Murray Hill | 254 Park Ave. S. (21st St.) | 212-995-1400

W 40s | 43 W. 42nd St. (bet. 5th & 6th Aves.) | 212-221-1500 |
877-278-6270◑

W 70s | 350 Amsterdam Ave. (bet. 76th & 77th Sts.) |
212-712-9800 | 877-278-6270◑

🆕 **W 100s** | 2814 Broadway (109th St.) | 212-865-4500
🆕 **Elmhurst** | Queens Center Mall | 90-15 Queens Blvd. (90th St.) |
Queens | 718-271-8800
www.crumbs.com

Additional locations throughout the NY area

The "colossal cupcakes" this "popular", proliferating chain is known for come "elaborately decorated" and in "tons" of "crazy flavors" like cookie dough, red velvet and caramel chew; such "sugar bombs" will likely "derail any diet", but they're a "knee-buckling experience" that "can make the most stressed-out NYer smile" – including the observant, as all of the "indulgences" here, including cookies, scones and brownies, are kosher.

☑ Crush Wine & Spirits ◐☐ *Wine/Liquor* | 27 | 25 | 25 | E |

E 50s | 153 E. 57th St. (bet. Lexington & 3rd Aves.) | 212-980-9463 | www.crushwineco.com

A "lovely, well-stocked shop" with a "modern feel", this "upscale" Midtown wine merchant focusing on small producers is "right up there" for oenophiles, while novices can count on "great recommendations" from a staff that "knows all there is to know"; the 2,500 labels include "high-end" and "rare" vintages stored in a temperature-controlled room called the Cube, but there's also a solid showing of everyday bottles, and it's all offered at "competitive prices."

Cucina & Co. *Prepared Food* | 22 | 21 | 18 | M |

E 40s | MetLife Bldg. | 200 Park Ave. (45th St.) | 212-682-2700 ◐
Garment District | Macy's Cellar | 151 W. 34th St. (bet. 6th & 7th Aves.) | 212-868-2388 ◐
W 40s | Rockefeller Ctr. | 30 Rockefeller Plaza, concourse level (bet. 49th & 50th Sts.) | 212-332-7630
www.patinagroup.com

Commuters and the lunchtime legions can grab something "fresh and tasty" at these "convenient" pit stops in Macy's, Rock Center and the MetLife Building, which "efficiently" ply "a broad selection" of Med-style prepared foods, mainly sandwiches, salads and pastas; maybe "they don't have the 'wow' factor", but "reliability" keeps them "busy" at peak hours and makes them a "value" office-catering staple.

Cucina Vivolo *Prepared Food* | 22 | 20 | 18 | M |

E 50s | 222 E. 58th St. (bet. 2nd & 3rd Aves.) | 212-308-0222
E 70s | 138 E. 74th St. (bet. Lexington & Park Aves.) | 212-717-4700 ◐
www.vivolonyc.com

Upper Eastsiders who "don't feel like cooking" can "pick up a wonderful meal" at this offshoot of the nearby Italian eatery Vivolo where the pastas, salads, panini and desserts taste like they "whipped it up for you in your own" *cucina*; whether takeout or delivery suits your mood, it's handy for "a quick lunch or dinner."

Cupcake Cafe *Baked Goods* | 24 | 21 | 19 | M |

W 40s | 545 Ninth Ave. (bet. 40th & 41st Sts.) | 212-268-9975 | www.cupcakecafe.com

"Famous" for the "beautiful-to-behold" "buttercream flowers" that crown its cupcakes, this Hell's Kitchen bakery's creations amount to "edible art", whether for "special occasions" or just a "fun" "pick-me-up"; muffins and custom cakes are other standouts among the "treasure trove" of options, though a few who find the signature product "photo worthy but not super-delicious" say donuts are "the real gems" here; P.S. it also offers cake-decorating classes.

Cupcake Kings *Baked Goods* ▽ 24 | 24 | 22 | M

Sheepshead Bay | 1613 Voorhies Ave. (Sheepshead Bay Rd.) | Brooklyn | 718-513-4747 | www.cupcakekingsny.com

"Yummy" is the verdict on the cupcakes at this "tucked-away" Sheepshead Bay bakery known for "specialty flavors" like Ferrero Rocher, Key lime pie and piña colada, with muffins, macarons, croissants, cookies and custom cakes completing the princely array; all come dispensed by a "friendly, helpful" staff in candy-pink digs that are rentable for little kids' parties, while coffee and herbal tea help keep the big kids "returning."

Dahlia *Flowers* 25 | 22 | 21 | M

E 40s | Grand Central Terminal | 42nd St. ramp (Vanderbilt Ave.) | 212-697-5090
E 40s | Grand Central Terminal | dining concourse (42nd St. & Vanderbilt Ave.) | 212-697-5090
E 40s | Grand Central Terminal | main concourse, Biltmore Passage (42nd St. & Vanderbilt Ave.) | 212-697-5090
W 40s | Rockefeller Ctr. | 30 Rockefeller Plaza, concourse level (bet. 49th & 50th Sts.) | 212-247-2288
www.dahlia-nyc.com

For the Midtown commuter set "catching that train" at Grand Central or scurrying through Rock Center, these blossom stops are "especially" handy peddlers of "pretty and fresh" bouquets that last way "longer than flowers bought at the corner deli"; between the high "value" and "polite", "eager-to-please" service, they're sure "to make a workday happier."

Damascus Bread & 26 | 18 | 22 | I
Pastry Shop ▤ *Baked Goods*

Brooklyn Heights | 195 Atlantic Ave. (bet. Clinton & Court Sts.) | Brooklyn | 718-625-7070 | www.damascusbakery.com

Known for the "best pita to be found" and other "authentic" Middle Eastern flatbreads, this circa-1930 Brooklyn Heights Syrian bakery also turns out "luscious" savory and sweet pastries – spinach pies, baklava and other "sticky delights" – so "delicious" you can "gain 10 pounds just looking in the window"; "charming owners" preside over the old-style, "no-frills" setting, where dips, spreads, "wonderful feta cheese, nuts" and similar "specialties" are other reasons it's "worth the trip."

Ⓩ D'Amico ▤ *Coffee/Tea* 27 | 16 | 22 | I

Carroll Gardens | 309 Court St. (bet. Degraw & Sackett Sts.) | Brooklyn | 718-875-5403 | 888-814-7979 | www.damicofoods.com

Still the neighborhood "standard to judge by", this circa-1948 Carroll Gardens "coffee lovers' oasis" perfumes the block with the "delicious aroma" of its "black gold" as a wide assortment of the "best beans" are "freshly roasted" daily and sold from sacks lining the floor; with a sandwich board and "fine" Italian groceries as well, it's a "homey" emporium that's a favorite local trip "back in time."

	QUALITY	DISPLAY	SERVICE	COST

Daniel's Bagels ◑ *Bagels* | 24 | 15 | 17 | I |

Murray Hill | 569 Third Ave. (bet. 37th & 38th Sts.) | 212-972-9733 | danielsbagelsnyc.com

"Proper-size", "less-doughy" bagels topped with "quality" cream cheeses prove as "irresistible" as the "fair prices" to the Murray Hill 'hoodies who frequent this "solid" local stalwart; given the scarcity of nearby rivals, it's convenient and "appetizing" enough to be "worth the long lines" and occasional "attitude" from the "flustered" staff.

David Burke at Bloomingdale's ◑ *Caterer/Events* | 21 | 19 | 17 | E |

E 50s | Bloomingdale's | 150 E. 59th St. (bet. Lexington & 3rd Aves.) | 212-705-3800 | www.burkeinthebox.com

Besides being a "break from a shopping spree" "at Bloomie's", this "creative" New American cafe from big-name chef David Burke is "a treat" for in-store or off-site catering, enlivening events with a cleverly "tasteful" range of its signature hors d'oeuvres and other "excellent" eats; but though it's a "well-run" operation, a hard-to-please few feel it's "not special enough."

David's Bagels ⊄ *Bagels* | 25 | 16 | 19 | I |

Gramercy | 331 First Ave. (bet. 19th & 20th Sts.) | 212-780-2308 | www.davidsbagelsnyc.com

For "flavor and freshness", fans swear this Gramercy nook's "great big" puffy bagels are "some of the best" around, with a dozen "delish" varieties that make it a solid "competitor" to the better known hole hawkers; even if the space "could use some dressing up", its standing in the neighborhood ensures "business is brisk on weekends."

NEW DavidsTea *Coffee/Tea* | 28 | 26 | 27 | M |

E 60s | 1124 Third Ave. (66th St.) | 212-717-1116 🖃
W Village | 275 Bleecker St. (bet. Jones & Morton Sts.) | 212-414-8599 ◑
www.davidstea.com

Bringing a spot of "tea culture" to Manhattan, this Montreal-based loose-leaf company arrived with "flying colors" to launch UES and Village outposts; "gracious" staffers who "really know the merchandise" are "more than happy to help" customers navigate the "well-organized", "amazing assortment" of brews and tisanes, and they "know how to prepare" a cuppa properly too, so why not "save your Lipton pennies" and "splurge."

Dean & DeLuca 🖃 *Major Market* | 26 | 25 | 21 | VE |

E 80s | 1150 Madison Ave. (85th St.) | 212-717-0800
SoHo | 560 Broadway (Prince St.) | 212-226-6800
800-221-7714 | www.deandeluca.com
Additional locations throughout the NY area

"Everything's a wow" at this dean of "fancy schmancy" gourmet grocers, an "inspiring" gastronomic showplace that goes "above and beyond" with the "gorgeously displayed" likes of "excellent" produce, "superior" prepared foods, "heavenly" baked goods "poised for a photo shoot", "luscious", "less-common" cheeses, an "encyclopedic" lineup of "hard-to-find" specialty items, "wonderful" spices, coffee and teas, "pristine seafood" and a "super selection" of "high-quality" cookware; it "caters to the rich and shameless" with notoriously "over-the-top" pricing, but even for "window shopping" this is "foodie" "nirvana."

Delillo Pastry Shop 🖃 *Baked Goods*

25 | 21 | 22 | M

Bronx | 610 E. 187th St. (bet. Arthur & Hughes Aves.) | 718-367-8198 | www.delillopastryshop.com

An "Arthur Avenue treasure" since 1925, this "traditional Italian pasticceria" moved into bigger down-the-block digs not long ago (which may outdate the above Display score), but it can still be counted on for handmade "sfogliatelle that sing", "the best cannoli", biscotti, sesame-seed cookies and all "the best recipes from the century-before-last"; far-flung devotees declare it's "worth trekking to the Bronx" for such "quality."

Deluxe Food Market ● *Specialty Shop*

▽ 23 | 16 | 14 | I

Chinatown | 79 Elizabeth St. (bet. Grand & Hester Sts.) | 212-925-5766

"In addition to regular Asian groceries", the "terrific assortment" at this "funky" "one-stop" destination in C-town includes a "wide range" of "interesting" meats, fish and "prepared and marinated foods" that are "always fresh due to turnover"; "half supermarket and half dining hall", it's a "great bargain" but often gets "mind-blowingly crowded", so "watch out."

De Robertis
Pasticceria & Caffe ●🖃 *Baked Goods*

23 | 21 | 22 | I

E Village | 176 First Ave. (bet. 10th & 11th Sts.) | 212-674-7137 | www.derobertiscaffe.com

This "delightful" "time capsule" conjuring "old NY" is a "no-glitz", "real-deal" Italian bakery, now in the hands of fourth-generation De Robertises, turning out "delicious" pignoli cookies, biscotti, pastries and other "traditional" sweets; a "glass" of "the best cappuccino" or an ice in the "quaint", "original" back room "is a must" for nostalgists who "hope it never changes."

☑ Despaña Foods 🖃 *Specialty Shop*

27 | 23 | 23 | E

Little Italy | 408 Broome St. (bet. Cleveland Pl. & Lafayette St.) | 212-219-5050 | www.despananyc.com
Jackson Heights | 86-17 Northern Blvd. (bet. 86th & 87th Sts.) | Queens | 718-779-4971 | www.despanabrandfoods.com 888-779-8617

"*Que bueno!*" cheer champions of these "top-notch importers" of "the best of Spain" in Jackson Heights and Little Italy, where "helpful" staffers oversee an "enticing" trove of "hard-to-find" "delicacies", notably "luxurious" Serrano and Ibérico ham, housemade chorizo and a "terrific" array of cheeses; given the "awesome" lineup of "wonderful olive oils", rice and grains, cooking implements and grocery "basics" "from the home country", it's something "really special"; P.S. the Manhattan store's back counter turns out "incredibly tasty" sandwiches and tapas too.

QUALITY | DISPLAY | SERVICE | COST

Despaña Vinos Y Mas 🖃 *Wine/Liquor* ▽ 28 | 24 | 24 | E

Little Italy | 410 Broome St. (bet. Cleveland Pl. & Lafayette St.) | 212-219-1550 | www.despanafinewines.com

When "you need a cava that isn't Freixenet" or seek that vintage "you once had in San Sebastián", try this "wonderful" wine store spun off from the Spanish specialty-foods standout Despaña, and sited next door to its Little Italy flagship; it's a "tiny" source for some 400 regional wines and sherries from Spain (50 or so under $25) – many of which otherwise "can't be found outside the mother country" – with helpful tasting notes and a staff ready to guide novices; P.S. there are free wine-and-food pairings the fourth Tuesday of every month.

🗹 Dickson's 28 | 26 | 26 | E
Farmstand Meats 🖃 *Meat/Poultry*

Chelsea | Chelsea Mkt. | 75 Ninth Ave. (bet. 15th & 16th Sts.) | 212-242-2630 | www.dicksonsfarmstand.com

"Foodies and locavores" applaud the "real butchery" at Jacob Dickson's sleek Chelsea Market meat mart, where the "incredible display" of "outstanding" humanely raised beef, lamb, pork, goat and poultry from regional farms strikes most as "well worth" the "high prices"; housemade sausages are another specialty, and at lunchtime there are "delicious", "freshly made" sandwiches of pulled pork, pastrami and such, and it even offers butchering classes; P.S. a TriBeCa offshoot is in the works that will include a full-service restaurant.

🗹 Di Palo Fine Foods 🖃 *Cheese/Dairy* 29 | 24 | 25 | M

Little Italy | 200 Grand St. (bet. Mott & Mulberry Sts.) | 212-226-1033 | www.dipaloselects.com

"Absolutely the best" for "fabulous" Italian formaggio, this "old-world" Little Italy "classic" with "several generations" of family-owned history behind it is "cherished" as an "unsurpassed" showcase for housemade ricotta and mozzarella ("a religious experience"), "delectable" parmigiano, pecorino and other imports, as well as "superior" Boot-style "goodies" from pasta to prosciutto; the "warm" staff "will take care of you" "when it's your turn", and even the weekend "mob scene" is "well worth the detour" when only "the real thing" will do.

🗹 DiPaola 28 | 14 | 22 | M
Turkey Farm 🖙 *Meat/Poultry*

Location varies | 609-587-9311 | www.dipaolaturkeyfarm.com

Admirers of the "excellent natural turkey products" purveyed by this "reliable" Hamilton, New Jersey–based Greenmarket regular "give thanks" all year long for whole "tasty, lean", farm-raised birds that are "so good, you don't mind eating leftovers for a week"; "fresh breasts", "deboned thighs", the "very best" Italian-style sausages (spicy or sweet, with plenty of samples on hand) and "delicious" ground meat for burgers, "risotto, chili or other recipes" are also "worth every penny."

	QUALITY	DISPLAY	SERVICE	COST

Dishes *Prepared Food*   24 | 22 | 18 | M

E 40s | 6 E. 45th St. (bet. 5th & Madison Aves.) | 212-687-5511
E 40s | Grand Central Terminal | dining concourse (42nd St. & Vanderbilt Ave.) | 212-808-5511 ◗
E 50s | 399 Park Ave. (bet. 53rd & 54th Sts.) | 212-421-5511

Dishes at Home ◗ *Prepared Food*

E 40s | Grand Central Mkt. | Lexington Ave. (43rd St.) | 212-370-5511
www.dishestogo.com

"A step up" for "takeaway", this "quality" chainlet lays out an "awe-some" variety of "surprisingly" "flavorful" and "creative" soups, sal-ads and other "addictive" dishes for the "chaotic" noontime crowds near Grand Central; "ridiculous" lines prove they're "doing some-thing right", though penny-pinchers advise "watch those prices."

NEW Dolce Vizio *Baked Goods*   ▽ 25 | 25 | 24 | M

W Village | 131 Christopher St. (Hudson St.) | 646-669-7432 | www.dolceviziotiramisu.com

It's all tiramisu, all the time, at this contemporary-yet-"cozy" new Italian bakery in the West Village devoted entirely to "*delizioso*" riffs on the classic ladyfingers-and-mascarpone cake, including mango and Nutella renditions as well as build-your-own options (column A: soaking liquid, Column B: toppings); take the luscious layers to go or eat in – Italian espresso and "friendly" staffers add to the "warm" vibe.

Dolly's Ices ◗⇄ *Ice Cream*   25 | 12 | 20 | I

Mill Basin | 5800 Ave. U (58th St.) | Brooklyn | 347-582-1075

"Real" housemade Italian ices and ice cream in a "seemingly endless" range of "yum" flavors have made this Mill Basin "tiny shack" a "neighborhood staple" despite its "out-of-the-way" lo-cation near King's Plaza mall; maybe it's "not much to look at" and service comes with occasional attitude, but that "adds to the charm" attest addicts who "suffer from withdrawal" when the place closes for winter.

NEW Dominique Ansel Bakery *Baked Goods*   27 | 25 | 25 | E

SoHo | 189 Spring St. (Thompson St.) | 212-219-2773 | www.dominiqueansel.com

Pastry chef and Daniel alum Dominique Ansel has created a "glori-ous piece of heaven" with his new SoHo patisserie, where the canelés, "citrusy madeleines", pies, tarts, cookies, "must-try" kouign amann and other "amazing" French treats are as "lovely to look at" as they are "delicious"; factor in sandwiches and savories served by an "incredibly nice staff" in a roomy, 50-seat, all-white shop, plus the "surprise treat" of a glass-enclosed conservatory in back, and although the "underwhelmed" complain it's "overpriced", most consider it "worth every penny" for such "quality."

Donna Bell's Bake Shop *Baked Goods*   ▽ 24 | 24 | 25 | M

W 40s | 301 W. 49th St. (bet. 8th & 9th Aves.) | 212-219-2773 | www.donnabellsbakeshop.com

There's "always a sweet aroma in the air" at this "cute", homey Hell's Kitchen bakery, thanks to the "high-quality" Southern-accented lineup that includes red velvet and coconut cakes, "to-die-for" brownies and lemon bars and "delicious muffins"; "extremely nice and attentive" hospitality is one more reason it's considered a "much needed addition" to the neighborhood.

Donut Pub ● *Baked Goods*

| 22 | 15 | 19 | I |

Chelsea | 203 W. 14th St. (7th Ave.) | 212-929-0126 | www.donutpub.com

On the hole, there's "nothing fancy" about this "old-school" (circa 1964) donut dive in Chelsea, but it "can't be beat" for "really good versions" of all the "standards" (no newfangled "chai tea" flavors here), alongside pastries, bagels, sandwiches and cups of joe, all sold "cheap" to a "waiting line" that "moves fast"; the "nondescript" counter-and-stool setup won't win any prizes, but the 24/7 schedule makes it just the spot when you're cruising for a "late-night" cruller.

Dorian's
Seafood Market ▣ *Seafood*

| 26 | 22 | 25 | E |

E 80s | 1580 York Ave. (83rd St.) | 212-535-2256 | www.doriansseafood.com

Appreciated as an "old-style fishmonger", this "small" Yorkville outfit purveys "terrific" "fresh seafood" as well as smoked fish and "delicious" prepared foods like poached salmon, chowders and more; the "superb service" includes on-the-spot oyster shucking and free delivery, and though it can "cost you a fin and a leg", "the best quality" means "you get what you pay for."

Dough ⊘ *Baked Goods*

| ∇ 26 | 22 | 21 | M |

Bed-Stuy | 305 Franklin Ave. (Lafayette Ave.) | Brooklyn | 347-533-7544

This "friendly" Bed-Stuy standout from the Choice Market folks specializes in airy, delicate, "delicious" yeast donuts with a "rainbow" of "creative" glazes like dulce de leche with almonds or bright-pink hibiscus, as well as filled versions plumped with the likes of chai cream, Nutella or spiced plum; new batches come out often as the day goes on, as do the pots of French-press coffee to go with – no wonder "long lines form daily" at prime times.

Doughnut Plant *Baked Goods*

| 27 | 17 | 20 | M |

Chelsea | 220 W. 23rd St. (bet. 7th & 8th Aves.) | 212-675-9100
LES | 379 Grand St. (bet. Essex & Norfolk Sts.) | 212-505-3700 ⊘
www.doughnutplant.com

A "pioneer" when it comes to "decadent", "drool-worthy donuts", this recently renovated Lower East Side factory and its newer, roomier offshoot inside the Chelsea Hotel supply "sublime" examples, "fried, baked, glazed and stuffed" in 35 seasonally rotating "marvelous", "wild flavors" like chestnut, tres leches, blackout and PB&J, all made with "fresh, natural ingredients"; it's "kinda pricey" and you should "be prepared for long lines", but "you'll forget about" all that "from bite one."

Dragonland Bakery 🍞 Baked Goods ▽ 25 | 20 | 21 | I

Chinatown | 125 Walker St. (Baxter St.) | 212-219-2012

"Racks and racks" of Chinese-style buns "stuffed with everything from custard to sweetened red beans to wieners" are the main attraction at this Chinatown bakery, though an assortment of cakes and crustless, premade sandwiches also entice peckish passersby; the atmosphere is strictly "average on-the-go", but the "ready and friendly staff" and "super-cheap" prices make that easy to overlook.

Dry Dock Wine & Spirits ● Wine/Liquor ▽ 28 | 27 | 28 | M

Red Hook | 424 Van Brunt St. (Van Dyke St.) | Brooklyn | 718-852-3625 | www.drydockny.com

Moored in Red Hook, this boutique liquor store "fills a void" with its "excellent", Italian-leaning lineup of some 500 "smartly chosen" wines ("biodynamic" offerings included) and "deep bench" of small-batch bourbons and single-malt scotches; given the "fair prices", "thoughtful suggestions" from a "friendly" staff, tastings on weekends and free neighborhood delivery of cases, "thrilled" locals marvel "what more could you ask?"

Duane Park Patisserie ▣ Baked Goods 25 | 18 | 18 | E

TriBeCa | 179 Duane St. (bet. Greenwich & Hudson Sts.) | 212-274-8447 | 877-274-8447 | www.duaneparkpatisserie.com

"TriBeCa's favorite neighborhood patisserie" is this "quiet" veteran specializing in "excellent" Austrian, French and German treats like "petits fours to die for", "gorgeous", "artistic" special-occasion cakes, "beautifully decorated" cookies, lemon curd tarts and other "quality" goodies baked "with heart"; "service is iffy", especially when it's busy in the usually "relaxing" cafe, but there's a "little park across the street" to retreat to once you've nabbed your sweet; P.S. it also offers online ordering.

Durso's Pasta & Ravioli Co. ▣ Pasta 26 | 21 | 24 | M

Flushing | 189-01 Crocheron Ave. (Utopia Pkwy.) | Queens | 718-358-1311 | www.dursos.com

"Good luck getting out" of this "lovely, family-owned" "local gem" in Flushing "without a big bag of goodies", notably "fresh, delicious light pastas" that'll "melt in your mouth", plus "incredible sauces", sausages and cheeses or a "spectacular selection" of Italian prepared dishes "better than your momma made"; it's all dished up by a staff of "professionals" who are "animated" and "helpful" – "we've never been disappointed."

☒ D'Vine Taste ●▣ Specialty Shop 26 | 20 | 26 | M

Park Slope | 150 Seventh Ave. (bet. Carroll St. & Garfield Pl.) | Brooklyn | 718-369-9548 | www.dvine-taste.com

"For that ingredient you can't find anywhere", this Park Slope Middle Eastern mart plies a "terrific array" of "excellent cheeses" and specialty grocery "treats" like spreads, dried fruits and a "great selection of spices", all at "reasonable prices"; with counters also vending an "amazing selection of prepared and baked goods" and a staff of

QUALITY DISPLAY SERVICE COST

"the world's nicest people", the "lucky folks" in the neighborhood "can't praise this shop enough."

Ⓩ Dylan's Candy Bar ◑▣ *Candy/Nuts* | 23 | 27 | 19 | E |

E 60s | 1011 Third Ave. (60th St.) | 646-735-0078 | 866-939-5267 | www.dylanscandybar.com

This "real-life Candyland" on the East Side is a "delight for the senses" declared "worth a special trip" given its 5,000-strong selection of "unusual and classic" candies, many "sold in bulk", spread over three "heavenly" floors; it "takes you back to your childhood" – in fact, "nostalgia is all around you" in the form of Charleston Chews, Mallo Cups, etc. – but just know it all "comes with a hefty price tag"; P.S. there's an ice cream/coffee bar "to boot."

Eagle Provisions *Meat/Poultry* | 23 | 18 | 21 | M |

Greenwood Heights | 628 Fifth Ave. (18th St.) | Brooklyn | 718-499-0026

Located just south of Park Slope in Greenwood Heights but "spiritually based in Krakow", this old-school "neighborhood grocery" specializes in "hard-to-find Eastern European" comestibles and "fine cured meats", including house-smoked kielbasa; its "little-of-everything" selection includes an "extensive" array of oils, vinegars and similar provisions at "fair" prices, but most "amazing" of all may be its 2,000-label lineup of imported and microbrew beers.

Eastern District *Specialty Shop* | - | - | - | M |

Greenpoint | 1053 Manhattan Ave. (bet. 123rd & 124th Sts.) | Brooklyn | 718-349-1432 | www.easterndistrictny.com

Artisanal cheeses and craft beers of the local-regional variety – particularly products of Brooklyn origin – are championed by this Greenpoint grocer, which also deals in cured meats, made-to-order sandwiches (vegetarian and not), cupcakes, jarred goods, party platters and cheeseboards; another locals' lure: refillable growlers and a rotating selection of draft suds to put in 'em.

East Side Bagel ◑ *Bagels* | 21 | 18 | 21 | M |

E 70s | 1496 First Ave. (78th St.) | 212-794-1403

When you need a "basic" UES "fix", this steady stalwart "has all the essentials" for "breakfast or any time" with its "surprisingly" serviceable selection of puffed-up bagels, spreads and standard salads and sandwiches; also favored for its house-baked black-and-white cookies, it can be "very convenient" even if the overall verdict is "average"; P.S. it also caters.

**East Village
Cheese Store** ⊟ *Cheese/Dairy* | 23 | 17 | 19 | I |

E Village | 40 Third Ave. (bet. 9th & 10th Sts.) | 212-477-2601

"It's hard to control yourself" when confronted with the "bargains galore" at this East Village cheesemonger, a "no-frills" "treasure trove" where an "amazing variety" of fromage retails at prices "not to be believed" (like those "unbeatable" $2.99 daily specials); cold cuts, spreads and "assorted snacks" are also available, and while the occasional pick may be "past its prime", "the careful shopper" can count on "big savings"; P.S. "no credit cards."

East Village Meat Market *Meat/Poultry*   26 | 20 | 22 | M

E Village | 139 Second Ave. (bet. 9th St. & St. Marks Pl.) | 212-228-5590

"The last of the great Ukrainian butchers" in the East Village, this "friendly", "old-fashioned" market "entices" with "prime" viands, "wonderful smoked meats" (including "the best kielbasa in the world"), plus "good-quality" poultry and "delicious fresh-baked turkey"; imported Eastern European comestibles and "reasonable prices" are other lures for devoted customers, many of whom "have been shopping here since the '70s."

East Village Wines *Wine/Liquor*   26 | 21 | 26 | M

E Village | 138 First Ave. (St. Marks Pl.) | 212-677-7070 | www.eastvillagewines.com

"Friendly" merchants "who know their market well" and offer plenty of "affordable" bottles earn this "little" East Village wine-and-spirits shop kudos from local clients ("love these guys"); among its 400-odd labels, small-production vintages and Iberian bottles are the focus, and a modest number of organic picks are stocked as well.

E.A.T. ◐ 🗺 *Prepared Food*   24 | 22 | 18 | VE

E 80s | 1064 Madison Ave. (bet. 80th & 81st Sts.) | 212-772-0022 | www.elizabar.com

"Doing it right" since 1973, Eli Zabar's UES cafe and prepared foods emporium still "measures up" with an "impressive" slate of "greatest hits" like "terrific" breads and "bakery treats" as well as "interesting sandwiches", salads and "high-end deli" fare; it's known for its "laughably expensive" prices and "attitude to boot", but nonetheless it remains "very popular with locals" and "often so crowded."

🆉 Eataly ◐ 🗺 *Major Market*   27 | 26 | 22 | E

Flatiron | 200 Fifth Ave. (bet. 23rd & 24th Sts.) | 212-229-2560 | www.eataly.com

"Mamma mia!" – the Batali-Bastianich team's "Disneyworld" of "all things Italian", a "vast" outpost of a Turin chain, is voted NYC's No. 1 Major Market thanks to its "dazzling" array of stations dispensing "artisanal bread" and 400 cheeses from Italy plus housemade mozz, "heavenly" fresh or dry pastas, "top-notch" prepared foods (eat in or take out), countless "imported gourmet" goods, "incredible" meats and seafood and "fantastic" produce; there's also cookware, coffee bars, a gelateria and next-door wine shop, as well as a cooking school overseen by Lidia Bastianich, so despite "not-cheap" pricing, it's been drawing "madhouse" crowds from day one.

Economy Candy 🗺 *Candy/Nuts*   25 | 20 | 20 | I

LES | 108 Rivington St. (bet. Essex & Ludlow Sts.) | 212-254-1531 | www.economycandy.com

"Amazing" "candy nostalgia" is the "blockbuster" attraction at this circa-1937 Lower East Side "wonderland" that's "packed floor-to-ceiling" with "retro and international" "sugary treats", including innumerable "old-school brands you never knew were still in production", plus "fresh nuts, dried fruit and halvah" too; "bargain prices" are yet another reason it's the "perfect" place to show the "kids and grandkids" what a "classic" is all about.

Eddie's Sweet Shop ●⊄ *Ice Cream* | 25 | 22 | 22 | I |

Forest Hills | 105-29 Metropolitan Ave. (72nd Rd.) | Queens | 718-520-8514

"Everything screams authenticity" at this century-old Forest Hills "landmark" that's as "well loved" as ever for its "exceptional" homemade ice cream, "fudge sundaes to die for" and malteds that are a "must"; "antique refrigerators, tile floors and marble counters" add to the sense that you've taken a "time machine to a gentler age", but it's the "creamy" frozen treats that truly "merit the visit."

Edible Arrangements   *Caterer* | 22 | 24 | 21 | E |

E Village | 100 St. Marks Pl. (bet. Ave. A & 1st Ave.) | 212-982-7200
Garment District | 62 W. 38th St. (bet. 5th & 6th Aves.) | 212-221-8300
Harlem | 2035 Fifth Ave. (bet. 125th & 126th Sts.) | 212-831-6041
NEW W 50s | 1756 Broadway (56th St.) | 646-490-4000
Bronx | 2021 Williamsbridge Rd. (bet. Lydig & Neill Aves.) | 718-823-4646 ☰
Flatbush | 402 Ave. M (4th st.) | Brooklyn | 718-645-0100
Sheepshead Bay | 1736 Sheepshead Bay Rd. (bet. Shore Pkwy. & Voorhies Ave.) | Brooklyn | 718-535-7909 ☰
Williamsburg | 601 Lorimer St. (bet. Conselyea St. & Skillman Ave.) | Brooklyn | 718-389-0700
Astoria | 30-47 Steinway St. (bet. 30th & 31st Aves.) | Queens | 718-943-6775
Flushing | 154-08 Northern Blvd. (154th St.) | Queens | 718-463-7848
877-363-7848 | www.ediblearrangements.com
Additional locations throughout the NY area

"In lieu of flowers", this "innovative" global chain is out "to please the eye and the palate" with "pretty" displays of fruit ("chocolate-dipped is the best") cut and arranged to resemble flora and "delivered fresh" and "ready to eat"; spoilers say it's a "corny" "novelty" that's "expensive for what it is", but they're outvoted by those who appreciate a "unique gift" for a "centerpiece" or "to cheer someone up" – just "don't let it sit too long."

Eggers Ice Cream Parlor ●⊄ *Ice Cream* | 26 | 21 | 23 | I |

Staten Island | 1194 Forest Ave. (bet. Llewellyn Pl. & Mundy Ave.) | 718-981-2110
Staten Island | 7437 Amboy Rd. (Yetman Ave.) | 718-605-9335
"Ice cream–aholics" can "feel like a kid again" at these separately owned SI parlors dispensing "the best" frozen scoops with that genuine "homemade taste", along with a range of "old-fashioned" candy; both proffer ice-cream cakes and pies, but the Forest Avenue original also offers housemade chocolates, while the Amboy Road offshoot, set in a vintage drugstore, is the scene of many a birthday party.

Egidio Pastry Shop 🖃 *Baked Goods* | 25 | 23 | 23 | M |

Bronx | 622 E. 187th St. (Hughes Ave.) | 718-295-6077

"Holy cannoli" – it's a century old, and this Bronx pasticceria is still known for "excellent Italian pastries", cakes, biscotti and cookies, including what may be the "best" pignoli variety "on the continent"; but despite the "delicious" baked goods, in summer insiders insist "you're here for the ices" in a staggering array of "traditional" flavors; P.S. it also does wedding cakes and gingerbread houses at Christmastime.

Eileen's Special Cheesecake ●🖃 *Baked Goods* | 25 | 18 | 21 | M |

NoLita | 17 Cleveland Pl. (Kenmare St.) | 212-966-5585 | 800-521-2253 | www.eileenscheesecake.com

A "must for any cheesecake-lover", this "exceptional" NoLita bakery has "been around forever" (well, since 1976) turning out "light", "fluffy" versions in varieties from Key lime to dulce de leche – good thing the individual-size ones allow you to sample different flavors "without feeling too guilty"; though it does a big web-order business, locals claim it as one of their own "hidden gems" that happily "isn't priced for tourists."

Eleni's Cookies 🖃 *Baked Goods* | 22 | 25 | 22 | E |

Chelsea | Chelsea Mkt. | 75 Ninth Ave. (bet. 15th & 16th Sts.) | 212-255-7990 | 888-435-3647

E 90s | 1266 Madison Ave. (bet. 90th & 91st Sts.) | 212-831-3170 www.elenis.com

There's a "cookie for every occasion" ("Oscars parties, elections, football games, etc.") at this Chelsea Market bakery and its UES sib boasting a "staggering variety" of "creative" customizable designs that fans enthuse are "so pretty you don't want to eat them"; sourpusses counter the goods are "better to look at than eat" and sport "ridiculous prices", but even critics concede these "smart, adorable" edible "artworks" make a "statement"; P.S. there are also cupcakes and flavored popcorn, and all items are kosher and nut-free.

Eli's Bread *Baked Goods* | 26 | 21 | 19 | E |

E 40s | Grand Central Mkt. | Lexington Ave. (43rd St.) | 212-831-4800 | www.elizabar.com

"Bread for all occasions" tempts carbophiles at Eli Zabar's stall in Grand Central Market ("finally, a location that's easy to get to") stocking his famously "delish" hearth-baked loaves, rolls, bagels and crisps; maybe "just looking at all their goodies will put on the pounds", but acolytes claim eating 'em warm "verges on a religious experience" – even if for some it's an act of faith to pay prices "high to the point of ridiculousness."

Eli's Manhattan ●🖃 *Major Market* | 25 | 24 | 21 | VE |

E 80s | 1411 Third Ave. (80th St.) | 212-717-8100 | www.elizabar.com

Procure "everything you might want and then some" at Eli Zabar's "upmarket" market, which indulges Upper Eastsiders with a cornucopia of "quality" gourmet goods taking in "fabulous breads" and other bakery "delights", droves of "delicious" cheeses, an "excellent" stock of specialty items, "inspired" prepared foods (notably the myriad "tasty" "homemade soups"), "wonderful" meats", "dependable" fish and an "abundant display" of "lovely produce"; "superb" "quality is assured" throughout, though "sticker shock" can be "an issue" for those who feel it's "really too expensive for everyday."

Eli's Vinegar Factory ● ☰ *Major Market*   24 | 22 | 18 | VE

E 90s | 431 E. 91st St. (bet. 1st & York Aves.) | 212-987-0885 | www.elizabar.com

Though "a little out of the way" on the East Side's periphery, Eli Zabar's gourmet market–cum-cafe flagship rewards the schlep with an "extensive" choice of "first-rate" comestibles, from pristine "fresh" produce and "dependably" "excellent" house-baked breads to "wonderful" specialty groceries, "prime meats" and seafood, a "great variety" of "interesting cheeses" and "gorgeous sandwiches" and prepared foods; some are sour on the "sky-high prices" ("totally outrageous"), but for followers the overall appeal is "oftentimes worth it."

Elm Health *Health*   ∇ 24 | 17 | 17 | M

Chelsea | 56 Seventh Ave. (14th St.) | 212-255-6300 | www.elmhealth.net

A "vast array" of organic, fresh and frozen "foods and fancies" lines the shelves of this Chelsea grocery, along with herbs and spices, nuts, grains, granola mixes and such by the pound, plus gluten-free products and heaps of other "health-related items" that are "hard to find elsewhere"; capping it off are juices, smoothies, "lunches to go", "monthly offers" so you can "stock up", a full pharmacy and help from a "knowledgeable" staff.

Emack & Bolio's ● *Ice Cream*   25 | 16 | 18 | M

E 80s | 1564 First Ave. (bet. 81st & 82nd Sts.) | 212-734-0105
SoHo | 73 W. Houston St. (W. B'way) | 212-533-5610
W 70s | 389 Amsterdam Ave. (bet. 78th & 79th Sts.) | 212-362-2747 ⌽
www.emackandbolios.com

"Thank you, Boston, for sharing" gush groupies of the "dangerous", "well-made" ice cream dished up in "dozens" of "fantastic, creative flavors" by these "hopping" outposts of the Beantown mini-chain; though the less-enthused wonder "what's the fuss?", most are willing to overlook sometimes-"snarky" service and "costly" prices because those "terrific" "creamy" scoops taste "sooo good."

Empire Cake ☰ *Baked Goods*   26 | 26 | 25 | M

Chelsea | 112 Eighth Ave. (bet. 15th & 16th Sts.) | 212-242-5858 | www.empirecake.com

An offshoot of an upscale outfit in Scarsdale, this "cute" Chelsea baker uses high-quality ingredients to prepare "creative and delicious" baked goods with a retro-snack twist, meaing it's the "perfect destination for those who always wondered what a Twinkie would taste like if it weren't made by a team of scientists"; there's also a "divine" lineup of more classic desserts, like Southern red velvet and organic carrot cakes.

Empire Coffee & Tea Co. 🖃 *Coffee/Tea* | 24 | 18 | 22 | I |

W 40s | 568 Ninth Ave. (bet. 41st & 42nd Sts.) | 212-268-1220 | 800-262-5908 | www.empirecoffeetea.com

A "mom-and-pop" shop "wedged" in "behind the Port Authority", this circa-1908 Hell's Kitchen survivor continues to carry an "awesome selection" of "top-quality" teas and "roasted-to-perfection" coffees ("including some unusual varieties"), all priced for "value"; the "helpful staff" also doles out cookies and candy, and patrons can "comfortably" browse a "wide-ranging" hoard of "accessories" like grinders, brewers and kettles.

Empire Market *Meat/Poultry* | ▽ 23 | 21 | 23 | M |

College Point | 14-26 College Point Blvd. (bet. 14th Ave. & 14th Rd.) | Queens | 718-359-0209 | www.empire-market.com

Beloved as an "old staple of the community", this family-owned College Point shop purveys a plethora of organic, nitrate-free meats, including hams, wursts, franks and such made in their own smokehouse ("one of the few left in NYC"), as well as fresh meats, poultry and an array of chicken and turkey sausages; it's been in business since the 1850s, with the fourth generation now at the helm, and these folks truly "take pride in their products."

☑ Enoteca Di Palo *Wine/Liquor* | 27 | 25 | 27 | M |

Little Italy | 200 Grand St. (bet. Mott & Mulberry Sts.) | 212-680-0545

"Unusual" vintages turn up at this all-Italian vino vendor annex to Little Italy's Di Palo Fine Foods, where 250-odd labels representing every region of The Boot yield "some very interesting" varietals "from small producers" at the "right price point"; "to help you choose", the staffers provide "knowledgeable" "assistance" and host regular tastings in the handsome, wood-beamed space – *salute!*

☑ Esposito & Sons Pork Store 🖂 *Meat/Poultry* | 27 | 19 | 24 | M |

Carroll Gardens | 357 Court St. (bet. President & Union Sts.) | Brooklyn | 718-875-6863

It's "quality all the way" at this "real-deal", "old-school", third-generation Carroll Gardens Italian butcher that's been plying "excellent" pork in its many forms since 1922, most notably via a selection of "standout" house-cured sausages (salami, pepperoni and sopressata "you can't stop eating"); it's also a "standby" for imported provisions, aged cheeses and fresh mozzarella, as well as sandwiches and prepared foods like lasagna, eggplant parm and "delicious" arancini.

☑ Esposito Meat Market *Meat/Poultry* | 27 | 20 | 26 | M |

Garment District | 500 Ninth Ave. (38th St.) | 212-279-3298 | www.espositomeatmarket.com

"A true old-time butcher shop", this Garment District stalwart is "famous for its pork" but also offers "optimum-quality" veal, lamb and poultry, plus "hard to find" game meats like buffalo, rabbit and venison – "not to mention" some of the "best sausages in town"; a family-owned biz that's "been around forever", it's known more for "wonderful service and value" than "fancy-dancy" displays.

Ess-a-Bagel ◐▣ Bagels

| 26 | 16 | 18 | I |

E 50s | 831 Third Ave. (bet. 50th & 51st Sts.) | 212-980-1010
Gramercy | 359 First Ave. (21st St.) | 212-260-2252
www.ess-a-bagel.com

"Bagels the size of hubcaps" will "hold you all day" at this ess-ential East Side duo, where "superior", "incredibly fresh" rounds that earn "props" for "perfect texture" ("crisp on the outside, soft and chewy on the inside") are topped with a "mind-boggling" choice of spreads; the "salty" "counter guys" exhibit "plenty of NY 'tude", but there's "nothing ersatz" here and "major lines on the weekends" only confirm a "hands-down winner" – "'nuff said."

Faicco's Pork Store Meat/Poultry

| 28 | 23 | 25 | M |

W Village | 260 Bleecker St. (bet. 6th & 7th Aves.) | 212-243-1974
Bay Ridge | 6511 11th Ave. (bet. 65th & 66th Sts.) | Brooklyn | 718-236-0119

"If you're not Italian, you will be as soon as you walk through the door" of these "old-world" butchers/salumerias, "go-to destinations" for "terrific" housemade sausages (fresh, dried and cured) and "expertly cut" pork and meats "of all varieties", plus "excellent" cheeses, oils, vinegars, housemade sauces, "ready-made specialties" and more; "fair prices" and "counter guys" who're "all smiles" ensure these "institutions" remain "perfect local" standbys; P.S. the circa-1940 Village branch is the original, while the Bay Ridge offshoot is bigger.

Fairway Major Market

| 25 | 19 | 18 | M |

E 80s | 240 E. 86th St. (bet. 2nd & 3rd Aves.) | 212-595-1888
Harlem | 2328 12th Ave. (bet. 132nd & 133rd Sts.) | 212-234-3883 ◐
W 70s | 2127 Broadway (74th St.) | 212-595-1888 ◐
Red Hook | 480-500 Van Brunt St. (Reed St.) | Brooklyn | 718-694-6868 ◐
Douglaston | 242-02 61st Ave. (Douglaston Pkwy.) | Queens | 718-432-2100 ◐
www.fairwaymarket.com

"If it exists, you can find it" at this UWS gourmet "mainstay" and its "warehouse-size" offshoots, where shoppers are "spoiled" by the "phenomenal selection", "reliable quality" and "fair prices" on produce that's "perfection" "piled high", a "super" assortment of "enticing" cheeses, "delicious prepared foods", a "profusion" of natural items, a "world market" of "tempting" specialty goods, "outstanding" seafood and "the freshest" "prime meat"; it takes "sterner stuff" to cope with the "chaotic" "throngs", but loyalists "never tire" of this all-purpose "paradise."

Family Health Foods Health

| ▽ 22 | 14 | 18 | M |

Staten Island | 1789 Victory Blvd. (Manor Rd.) | 718-442-0357
Staten Island | 4888 Arthur Kill Rd. (Richmond Valley Rd.) | 718-967-9674
www.familyhealthfoods.com

In business for more than 35 years, these "friendly" health food stores supply Staten Islanders with organic produce, nuts and dried fruits, vitamins, herbs, natural remedies and items for the wheat-, dairy- and gluten-sensitive set; a "consistently good" deli counter at the Victory Boulevard branch offers sandwiches, salads, hot foods and made-on-the-premises baked goods.

Family Store *Specialty Shop*   ▽ 24 | 23 | 26 | M

Bay Ridge | 6905 Third Ave. (bet. Ovington Ave. & 69th St.) | Brooklyn | 718-748-0207 | www.familystorecooks.com

"You name it", they "know how to make" it at this "good-value" Bay Ridge "favorite", a Med–Middle Eastern "gem" that "caters to anyone's palate" with a wealth of dry goods and a wide-ranging roster of like-"home-cooked (but yummier)" prepared foods; boasting daily specials from sandwiches to entrees to "spectacular" cheesecake, it has "everything your dinner table needs and then some", delivered by staffers who live up to the name – they're so "super nice", you "feel like part of the family."

Fat Witch Bakery ☐ *Baked Goods*   24 | 21 | 21 | M

Chelsea | Chelsea Mkt. | 75 Ninth Ave. (bet. 15th & 16th Sts.) | 212-807-1335 | 888-419-4824 | www.fatwitch.com

"Super-rich" brownies "par excellence" in "addictive" flavors (caramel, oatmeal-walnut, cappuccino) work magic on Chelsea Marketgoers who warn "good luck eating just one" – though those fearful of becoming "a little plump around the broomstick" go for the "mini-sizes"; the deal gets sweeter "during the witching hour" (weekdays after 5 PM) when all unwrapped morsels are half-price; P.S. its gift packaging "rocks."

Fay Da Bakery *Baked Goods*   20 | 18 | 15 | I

Chinatown | 191 Center St. (Hester St.) | 212-966-8934 ⊟

Chinatown | 83 Mott St. (Canal St.) | 212-791-3884 ⊟

Garment District | 257 W. 34th St. (8th Ave.) | 212-868-8881 ◗⊟

Elmhurst | 86-12 Justice Ave. (B'way) | Queens | 718-205-5835 ⊟

Flushing | 136-18 39th Ave. (College Point Blvd.) | Queens | 718-321-1759 ◗⊟

Flushing | 37-11 Main St. (bet. 37th & 38th Aves.) | Queens | 718-888-9890 ⊟

NEW **Flushing** | Skyview Mall | 40-24 College Point Blvd. (Roosevelt Ave.) | Queens | 718-461-1888

Flushing | 41-60 Main St. (Sanford Ave.) | Queens | 718-886-4568 ⊟

Flushing | 46-15 Kissena Blvd. (Juniper Ave.) | Queens | 718-353-0730 ⊟

Forest Hills | 107-50 Queens Blvd. (Continental Ave.) | Queens | 718-268-8882 ◗⊟

www.fayda.com

"Grab a tray and a pair of tongs and you're set" at this Chinese bakery chain where customers choose from a "yummy" array of baked and steamed buns (both savory and sweet), cookies, "gorgeous" cakes and pastries, and wash 'em down with "delicious" bubble tea; it's on the "crowded" and "chaotic" side, with sometimes "brash" service, but "more-than-reasonable" prices make all that easy to overlook.

	QUALITY	DISPLAY	SERVICE	COST

Fellan Florist *Flowers* ∇ 24 | 22 | 23 | E

E 60s | 1243 Second Ave. (65th St.) | 212-421-3567 |
800-335-5267 | www.fellan.com

"For years" a bastion of "high quality", this venerable bloom biz's "beautiful displays" of globally sourced flowers still make the grade with well-heeled Upper Eastsiders who declare "no one is better"; be it bouquets or gift baskets, their mastery is sure to draw "thank you's and compliments" provided you can afford the rather "steep price."

Ferrara Bakery & Cafe ◐ ▤ *Baked Goods* 22 | 23 | 18 | M

Little Italy | 195 Grand St. (bet. Mott & Mulberry Sts.) |
212-226-6150 | 800-533-6910 | www.ferraracafe.com

"Old-school Italian pastry heaven" is what fans call this Little Italy "institution" that has lured generations with pasticceria staples like "ethereal" lobster tails and sfogliatelle, "delicious" cannoli and rainbow cookies, torrone, gelato, espresso and sodas that give a glimpse of "the way things used to be"; however, vocal critics citing "tourist" "overcrowding", "slow", "attitudinous" service and "commercial quality" say "it's not what it used to be" – but then again "it has its reputation for a reason."

Fifth Avenue Chocolatiere ▤ *Candy/Nuts* ∇ 25 | 22 | 22 | E

E 40s | 693 Third Ave. (bet. 43rd & 44th Sts.) | 212-935-5454 |
www.5thavenuechocolatiere.com

Sweet tooths find "something chocolatey for every occasion" at this "quality" East Side confectioner that's been making some of the "smoothest, richest" all-kosher treats from Belgian chocolate since 1973; there are "amazing truffles" in "sublime" flavors like raspberry, tiramisu and coconut, as well as "interesting" novelty shapes like owls, squirrels, sailboats, airplanes and even Cadillacs, fashioned from one of its 10,000 molds.

Filling Station *Specialty Shop* 25 | 24 | 23 | M

Chelsea | Chelsea Mkt. | 75 Ninth Ave. (bet. 15th & 16th Sts.) |
212-989-3868 | www.thefillingstationnyc.com

Epicures fuel up at this Chelsea Market "great concept" whose oleaginous inventory features "excellent olive oils" – some 15 imported and domestic varieties – which customers purchase in bottles that they can bring "back to refill" at a 10% discount; other renewable offerings include "special" vinegars, sea salts (both flavored and not) and unrefined sugars, not to mention growlers of craft beer chosen from a "rotating selection."

Financier Patisserie *Baked Goods* 25 | 24 | 20 | M

NEW **E 40s** | 245 Park Ave. (47th St.) | 212-687-9000
E 40s | Grand Central Terminal | main concourse, 42nd St. Passage
(42nd St. & Vanderbilt Ave.) | 212-973-1010 ◐
E 50s | 983 First Ave. (54th St.) | 212-419-0100
E 50s | 989 Third Ave. (59th St.) | 212-486-2919
Financial District | Winter Garden | 3-4 World Financial Ctr. (Vesey &
West Sts.) | 212-786-3220

(continued)

(continued)

Financier Patisserie

Financial District | 35 Cedar St. (bet. Pearl & William Sts.) | 212-952-3838 ●
Financial District | 62 Stone St. (bet. Mill Ln. & William St.) | 212-344-5600 ●
NEW **Financial District** | 90 Nassau St. (Fulton St.) | 212-748-6000
Flatiron | 688 Sixth Ave. (22nd St.) | 212-367-8900
NoHo | 740 Broadway (Astor Pl.) | 212-228-2787
W 40s | 1211 Sixth Ave. (48th St.) | 212-381-4418
www.financierpastries.com

These proliferating "taste-of-Paris" patisseries proffer "gorgeous" French sweets that "live up to their appearance", including "to-die-for" éclairs, tarts, "the best macarons" and "delicate" croissants, plus sandwiches and salads for the lunch crowd; "clean and bright-looking" digs make up for any service miscues, while the "delicious" "tiny" financiers given "free with coffee" further sweeten the deal.

First Avenue
Wines & Spirits ● *Wine/Liquor*

22 | 18 | 22 | M

Gramercy | 383 First Ave. (bet. 22nd & 23rd Sts.) | 212-673-3600

"Pick up the basics" or something more unusual at this Gramercy "neighborhood" wine shop, a "spacious" "standby" that "beats many" with a selection embracing California boutique labels as well as far-flung imports, some stashed in a "vintage room in back"; "prices are more than good" and the "salespeople know what they're talking about", though a few followers fret it's "not what it used to be."

Fischer Bros. & Leslie 🖃🗷 *Meat/Poultry*

24 | 16 | 21 | E

W 70s | 230 W. 72nd St. (bet. B'way & West End Ave.) | 212-787-1715 | www.fischerbros.com

The "broad range" of "super-fresh" glatt kosher meat and poultry has drawn Upper Westsiders to this "old-world but up-to-date" butcher shop/deli since 1949, as have its "gourmet sausages" and prepared foods like gefilte fish and "the best" barbecue chicken, overseen by a "helpful" staff; it doesn't take credit cards, so bring plenty of cash to settle the "expensive" bill.

🔁 Fish Tales 🖃 *Seafood*

27 | 24 | 24 | E

Cobble Hill | 191A Court St. (bet. Bergen & Wyckoff Sts.) | Brooklyn | 718-246-1346 | www.fishtalesonline.com

Expect "fish so fresh you want to slap them" at this "classy" little Cobble Hill market, an "excellent" purveyor of "treasures from the sea" where "the best catch of the day" is lovingly laid out on ice and a slew of premade fin fare is "cooked to a tee"; "it's not cheap", but the "personal service" is "always a pleasure" and hey, "quality costs."

NEW Fleisher's
Grassfed & Organic Meats *Meat/Poultry*

∇ 29 | 24 | 28 | E

Park Slope | 192 Fifth Ave. (Sackett St.) | Brooklyn | 718-398-6666 | www.fleishers.com

"What a thrill to have it here" enthuse Park Slope fans of this off-shoot of the renowned Upstater practicing the utmost in "modern butchery" with its nose-to-tail treatment of "humanely raised", pastured, all-natural animals from small, local, sustainable farms, resulting in some of the "best-tasting" beef, pork, lamb and poultry going, not to mention "great sausages" in 15 varieties, bacon, cold cuts, dairy, pot pies and – proving nothing is wasted – tallow soap; "sure, it costs more", but given the "wonderful" quality and "excellent", "no-attitude" service, most declare "hang the expense."

29	18	27	M

Z Florence
Prime Meat Market 🖃 *Meat/Poultry*
W Village | 5 Jones St. (bet. Bleecker & 4th Sts.) | 212-242-6531
A "NYC treasure" since 1936, this tiny West Village butcher shop is beloved for its "finest"-quality meats aged in-house and "cut to your exact specifications" by "friendly" countermen who show "superb attention" to their craft; the "charm" is enhanced by the "screen door", "sawdust on the floor" and "house cat", not to mention the "reasonable" prices (as a particular "bargain" the "Newport steak is a classic"); P.S. it also vends sausages, game and organic poultry, but whatever your order, consider calling ahead to "save time."

▽ 26	24	22	E

Flowers by Reuven *Flowers*
Fort Greene | Brooklyn Navy Yard | 63 Flushing Ave., Bldg. 5, Ste. 601 (bet. Adelphi St. & Canton Ave.) | Brooklyn | 718-403-0369 | www.flowersbyreuven.net
By appointment only
"Beautiful", "unique" flower arrangements are the perennial stock in trade of this Fort Greene–based blossom vet (since 1973, though it recently relocated from Manhattan); its fresh designs are built with Holland-import buds and geared toward weddings, bar and bat mitzvahs, soap-opera sets and corporate clients, and it also offers event-design services; P.S. delivery in Manhattan only.

26	24	24	VE

Flowers of the World 🖃 *Flowers*
Financial District | 110 Maiden Ln. (bet. Pearl & Water Sts.) | 212-425-2234
W 50s | 150 W. 55th St. (bet. 6th & 7th Aves.) | 212-582-1850
800-582-0428 | www.flowersoftheworld.com
"Popular for window-shopping" owing to their "spectacular" storefront displays, this longtime Financial District florist and its greener Midtown branch fashion "exquisite", "uniquely arranged" bouquets to "delight any recipient" while providing "excellent service" from skilled studio hands; though they're undeniably "costly", deeppocketed partisans confide "you get what you pay for."

29	21	24	E

Z Flying Pigs Farm 🖃 *Meat/Poultry*
Location varies | 518-854-3844 | www.flyingpigsfarm.com
"The best heritage pork out there" keeps customers flying to this Upstate farm's Greenmarket stall proffering all parts of the pig, notably bacon, sausage, hot dogs and "the best smoked ham this side of heaven", plus, for poultry people, there's chicken as well as eggs "too good to waste on baking"; none of it comes cheap, but factor in "amazing" quality, "very nice" service and the satisfaction of supporting "local" farmers, and to most it's a "win-win-win!"

QUALITY | DISPLAY | SERVICE | COST

F. Monteleone
Bakery & Cafe 📋 *Baked Goods*   ▽ 29 | 26 | 23 | M

Carroll Gardens | 355 Court St. (bet. President & Union Sts.) | Brooklyn | 718-852-5600

"Excellent" breads, cakes, pastries, the "best cannolis" and house-made gelato have made this Italian bakery a beloved Carroll Gardens institution, but it's the "wide variety" of traditional cookies that really stands out here; it also sells loaves from the famed Cammareri Bros. (now wholesale-only), and it's all overseen by a "first-rate" staff.

Foods of India *Herbs/Spices*   23 | 17 | 17 | I

Murray Hill | 121 Lexington Ave. (bet. 28th & 29th Sts.) | 212-683-4419

"They have everything" to flavor a subcontinental spread at this Murray Hill spice shop, a long-standing "go-to for all things Indian" that "hasn't changed in years" according to fans of its broad array of "fresh", "exotic" seasonings; best of all, it'll put the kick in your curry at prices that are "often less" than the competition's.

Foragers City Grocer ● *Major Market*   ▽ 26 | 23 | 18 | E

NEW **Chelsea** | Gem Hotel | 300 W. 22nd St. (8th Ave.) | 212-243-8888
Dumbo | 56 Adams St. (Front St.) | Brooklyn | 718-801-8400
www.foragerscitygrocer.com

Sized like a bodega but stocked like a fancy-foods emporium, this "favorite" Dumbo grocery is strong on organic, regionally sourced and "unusual" items, including cheeses (more than 100 kinds), grass-fed meat, sustainable seafood, vegetables harvested from a Columbia County farm, NYC-made goods and an array of tempting prepared foods; it was joined post-Survey by a roomier Chelsea sib whose additional perks include an on-site cafe and an adjacent wine store.

Foremost RAM Caterers *Caterer*   ▽ 23 | 21 | 20 | VE

Moonachie | 65 Anderson Ave. (Romeo St.), NJ | 201-664-2465 | www.foremostcaterers.com

Most maintain this "top-of-the-line kosher caterer" is "the very best" of its kind, with a "friendly" team devising "creative" glatt menus of "excellent", globe-trotting fare to provision off-premises occasions; whether for private get-togethers or at the "event level" – e.g. galas at sites like the Plaza Hotel, Ellis Island and the Museum of Natural History – they "deliver what they promise."

🗹 Formaggio Essex 📋 *Cheese/Dairy*   27 | 21 | 25 | E

LES | Essex Street Mkt. | 120 Essex St. (bet. Delancey & Rivington Sts.) | 212-982-8200 | www.formaggioessex.com

In an Essex Street Market berth not much bigger than a "shoebox", this offshoot of a beloved Cambridge, MA, gourmet store squeezes in an "amazing selection" of the "highest-quality" imported European cheeses and "excellent" housemade charcuterie, plus high-end olive oils, pastas, beans, grains and baked goods; it's "not cheap", but "passionate", "personable" staffers who "share their expertise" – "no matter how busy" they are – compensate; P.S. it also does a big web-order business.

	QUALITY	DISPLAY	SERVICE	COST

Z Fortunato Bros. ◐ 🍽 ⌺ *Baked Goods* — 27 | 23 | 21 | M

Williamsburg | 289 Manhattan Ave. (Devoe St.) | Brooklyn |
718-387-2281

"One of the great Italian pastry shops from the old school", this
Williamsburg "institution" has been around since "way before the
neighborhood got trendy", maintaining its reputation with
"better-than-mama's" cannoli, sfogliatelle, lobster tails, cookies
and marzipan treats almost "too gorgeous to eat"; the "unpretentious" vibe makes it a "nice place to sit with a cup of coffee", but just
keep in mind the "step-back-in-time" milieu is complete with
a "cash-only" policy.

Forty Carrots *Ice Cream* — 22 | 17 | 17 | M

E 50s | Bloomingdale's | 1000 Third Ave., 7th fl. (bet. 59th & 60th Sts.) |
212-705-3085 | www.bloomingdales.com

It's "the frozen yogurt that started it all, and it's still the ultimate"
dish devotees of Bloomie's "popular" seventh-floor oasis, where
special-formula fro-yo made its NYC debut in the 1970s and has
been dispensed in "generous helpings" ever since; the cafe also offers "fresh-tasting" salads, sandwiches and such, but "hungry"
hordes "taking a break from shopping" say the "decadent" icy stuff
is the "main attraction."

Four & Twenty — ▽ 26 | 19 | 24 | M
Blackbirds ⌺ *Baked Goods*

Gowanus | 439 Third Ave. (8th St.) | Brooklyn | 718-499 2917 |
www.birdsblack.com

Doing a "formidable job" with fruit pies and other "amazing"
buttery-crusted creations, this "charming" shop "off the beaten
path" in Gowanus offers a "daily changing" array of pies like "what
grandma made but with a twist" – apple-cheddar, honeyed fig,
salted caramel – crafted by hand in an open kitchen and sold by the
slice ("call in advance" to order 'em whole); with its "homey" space
sporting "rustic wood" tables, "sweet" service and Irving Farm coffee, it's perfect for on-site snacking.

FPB 🍽 *Baked Goods* — ▽ 27 | 25 | 21 | E

NEW **Financial District** | 210 Murray St. (bet. North End Ave. &
West St.) | 212-566-8300

G Village | 116 W. Houston St. (bet. Sullivan & Thompson Sts.) |
212-995-0888
www.fpbnyc.com

François Chocolate Bar *Baked Goods*

W 50s | Plaza Hotel | 1 W. 58th St., lower level (5th Ave.) |
212-986-9241 | www.fcchocolatebar.com

"Thank God he is back" sigh fans of François Payard and his
Downtown patisseries providing "too-good-to-be-true" treats like
macarons, tarts and "to-die-for" croissants that have devotees declaring "I'm back in Paris!"; there's also a small outlet inside the
Plaza Hotel's lower-level arcade, where out-of-towners and others
"refuel for more shopping", and a 1,100-sq.-ft. venue is in the works
at 3 Columbus Circle.

	QUALITY	DISPLAY	SERVICE	COST

FreshDirect ● *Major Market* | 23 | 15 | 22 | M |

LIC | 23-30 Borden Ave. (23rd Ave.) | Queens | 866-283-7374 | www.freshdirect.com

"Shopping's a breeze" thanks to this LIC-based online grocery service, "a busy NYer's lifesaver" with an "easy-to-navigate site" proffering "loads" of "moderately priced" gourmet products for "convenient" "on-time delivery"; given "extensive" offerings running to "wonderful" "parbaked breads", "delicious" top-grade cheeses, a "nice selection" of deli fare, "quality" prepared foods (some created by "name chefs"), "fresh and reliable fish", "fantastic" meat and "seasonal produce" that's "better than the fruit market down the street", repeat customers wonder "how did we survive without them?"

Fulton Stall Market *Produce* ▽ 25 | 22 | 21 | M |

Financial District | South Street Seaport | South St. (bet. Beekman & Fulton Sts.) | no phone | www.fultonstallmarket.com

Occupying the open-air stalls vacated by the old Fulton Fish Market, this "small but fun" seasonal bazaar's dozen or so vendors include "local" farmers hawking "some very good produce" conveyed fresh from upstate; there's also "much to choose from" in the way of baked goods, dairy products, prepared snacks and regional wines – it's well worth a "walk-through."

Garden of Eden | 23 | 22 | 18 | E |
Gourmet Market ●▣ *Major Market*

Chelsea | 162 W. 23rd St. (bet. 6th & 7th Aves.) | 212-675-6300
Union Sq | 7 E. 14th St. (bet. 5th Ave. & University Pl.) | 212-255-4200
W 100s | 2780 Broadway (107th St.) | 212-222-7300
Brooklyn Heights | 180 Montague St. (bet. Clinton & Court Sts.) | Brooklyn | 718-222-1515
www.edengourmet.com

"When you need a break from the megastores", these "quite compact" gourmet marts are a "terrific alternative" with "enticing displays" of "high-quality" edibles including "yummy" baked goods, cheeses "from the commonplace to the exotic", "tasty" deli fare, "shelves filled with" "one-of-a-kind specialty items", "excellent" meats and "impeccable produce" that's "the next best thing to the farmer's market"; fans of "fast, efficient" provisioning are always "glad there's one in the neighborhood."

Garnet Wines & Liquors ●▣ *Wine/Liquor* 26 | 18 | 21 | M |

E 60s | 929 Lexington Ave. (bet. 68th & 69th Sts.) | 212-772-3211 | www.garnetwine.com

A "real jewel" in the eyes of UES oenophiles, this longtime "wine bargain champ" still delivers "the best value" around – "hands down" – on a "wide variety" of "top-notch" global labels (notably Italian and French producers), along with "excellent" liquors and champagnes; the style's a bit "rough and ready" and some suggest the admittedly "sharp" staff's attitude "could be improved", but "in terms of pricing and quality" you "can't beat" it.

	QUALITY	DISPLAY	SERVICE	COST

Gary Null's
Uptown Whole Foods ◐ *Health*

20 | 14 | 15 | E

W 80s | 2421 Broadway (89th St.) | 212-874-4000

No relation to the well-known natural superstores, this Upper West Side health food "favorite" packs "loads of interesting" items from supplements to "organic veggies" into "the littlest" space; diet-conscious sorts say the selection's "very tempting", but holdouts warn of "high prices", "crowded aisles" that "can be quite confusing" and staffers who sometimes "act like they're doing you a favor."

Glaser's Bake Shop ⊘ *Baked Goods*

24 | 19 | 24 | I

E 80s | 1670 First Ave. (bet. 87th & 88th Sts.) | 212-289-2562 | www.glasersbakeshop.com

A family-run "fixture in Yorkville forever" (well, since 1902), this "anciently wonderful" German bakery boasts "original wooden display cases" bulging with goods that "look and taste like grandma made them", including "amazing" black-and-white cookies, brownies, Danishes and "to-die-for" cakes (and they do wedding and other special-occasion versions); "welcoming", "accommodating" service and "very fair" prices ice the cake – "if you feel nostalgia for the old days, this is the place to come."

Glorious Food *Caterer*

26 | 24 | 24 | VE

E 70s | 504 E. 74th St. (bet. East River & York Ave.) | 212-628-2320 | www.gloriousfood.com
By appointment only

"When you want the best", this "exceptional" UES caterer of four decades' standing is "always a winner" for "the whole shebang", including, yes, glorious cuisine ("anything from homestyle to cutting-edge") in lavish presentations and first-class service; whether for a small soiree or a full-scale blowout, clients can "rely on" a "perfectly executed" spread – even if you "need to take out a mortgage" to settle the bill, "it'll be worth it."

Godiva Chocolatier *Candy/Nuts*

23 | 26 | 23 | E

E 40s | MetLife Bldg. | 200 Park Ave. (44th St.) | 212-697-9150 ◐ ⊑
E 50s | 560 Lexington Ave. (bet. 50th & 51st Sts.) | 212-980-9810 ⊑
NEW E 50s | 650 Fifth Ave. (bet. 51st & 52nd Sts.) | 212-664-1258
E 60s | 793 Madison Ave. (67th St.) | 212-249-9444 ⊑
Financial District | 21 Fulton St. (South St.) | 212-571-6965 ⊑
Financial District | 33 Maiden Ln. (Nassau St.) | 212-809-8990 ⊑
W 40s | 1460 Broadway (bet. 41st & 42nd Sts.) | 212-840-6758 ⊑
W 50s | Shops at Columbus Circle | 10 Columbus Circle (bet. 58th & 60th Sts.) | 212-823-9462 ◐ ⊑
W 50s | 745 Seventh Ave. (50th St.) | 212-921-2193
Elmhurst | Queens Center Mall | 90-15 Queens Blvd. (90th St.) | Queens | 718-271-3603
800-946-3482 | www.godiva.com
Additional locations throughout the NY area

The "luscious display" of "beautifully wrapped" chocolates "never fails to elevate your mood" declare devotees who "love" this "consistent" chain's "diverse and imaginative" goods, including milk and dark "divine" truffles and "themed creations" – plus, the rewards club "entitles you" to a "free" monthly treat; however, those unimpressed with the "quality-price" ratio retort "in this day of chocolatiers", we'd "rather spend our calories elsewhere."

Good & Plenty To Go   *Prepared Food*   ∇ 21 | 19 | 20 | M

W 40s | 410 W. 43rd St. (bet. 9th & 10th Aves.) | 212-268-4385 | www.goodandplentytogo.com

"A neighborhood staple" for the Theater District's lunchtime throngs, this "tiny" comfort kitchen in the Manhattan Plaza center turns out "very homey" prepared foods aplenty, with a revolving lineup of "quality sandwiches", "outstandingly good" soups and specialties like bourbon-baked ham and walnut cookies; it's "nothing fancy", and that suits longtime loyalists fine; P.S. it also does a big catering business.

Good Beer Store ● *Beer*   ∇ 27 | 24 | 26 | M

E Village | 422 E. Ninth St. (bet. Ave. A & 1st Ave.) | 212-677-4836 | www.goodbeernyc.com

It's brewski bliss at this East Village beer bazaar whose nearly 600 labels (80% American craft brews; 20% Belgian, German and British) can make for an occasionally "overwhelming" shopping experience (hint: just "ask the staff to point you in the right direction"); there's also a dozen taps flowing with an ever-changing lineup that customers can buy by the refillable growler or sample at an in-store cafe serving charcuterie to go with pints and tasting flights – the smitten swear this place should be redubbed "Great Beer."

Gorzynski Ornery Farm ⊟ *Produce*   ∇ 26 | 24 | 25 | M

Location varies | 845-252-7570

"It's always a pleasure to see what he's brought down" declare "enchanted" admirers of grower John Gorzynski, a Greenmarket regular "for lo these many years" and "the real deal" for produce trucked from "his farm up north"; the "great variety" includes "fresh and delicious" root vegetables and fruit of "much higher" quality than the norm, and the curious can count on "friendly and helpful" tips "on how to prepare the exotic greens" and such.

Gotham   24 | 19 | 22 | M
Wines & Liquors ●◗▤ *Wine/Liquor*

W 90s | 2517 Broadway (94th St.) | 212-932-0990 | www.gothamwines.com

Upper Westsiders shop the "bargains" at this "unpretentious" wine outlet, a stalwart that still "beats many in the nabe" with "solid deals" on a "wide selection" that's "nothing too exotic" but "encompasses many tastes"; it's "reliable" "if you know what you're doing", and observant oenophiles can draw on a "wonderful kosher" section running to 300 bottles.

Gourmet Garage ●◗▤ *Major Market*   20 | 18 | 16 | E

E 60s | 301 E. 64th St. (bet. 1st & 2nd Aves.) | 212-535-6271
E 90s | 1245 Park Ave. (96th St.) | 212-348-5850
SoHo | 453 Broome St. (Mercer St.) | 212-941-5850

(continued)

Gourmet Garage

W 60s | 155 W. 66th St. (bet. Amsterdam Ave. & B'way) |
212-595-5850
W Village | 117 Seventh Ave. (bet. Christopher & W. 10th Sts.) |
212-699-5980
www.gourmetgarage.com

Parked in "its own niche", this "upscale grocer" chainlet is a
"shopping-friendly" supplier of "dependable" gourmet products including "assorted varieties" of baked goods, "wide" cheese choices,
"consistently good" prepared foods and deli items, "appetizing"
produce and "very acceptable" coffee; the "relaxed" style "serves a
purpose", though detractors drive at prices "on the high side" for
what they consider "ordinary quality" and "so-so" selection.

Grab Specialty Foods ◐ *Specialty Shop* 26 | 19 | 22 | E

Park Slope | 438 Seventh Ave. (bet. 14th & 15th Sts.) | Brooklyn |
718-369-7595 | www.grabspecialtyfoods.com

Though "a relatively small" outfit, this specialty shop grabs South
Slopers' attention with "top-quality offerings" like "fantastic" artisanal cheeses, charcuterie, baked goods, Nunu and Mast Brothers
chocolates, gourmet groceries and even a "very good beer selection" from local brewers (decanted into growlers); it's all-around accessible "for the right occasion", though some protest "steep
prices" given the "other on-par options in the immediate area";
P.S. gift-givers can check out its kitchen and picnic accessories and
made-to-order baskets.

Grace's Marketplace ◐▭ *Major Market* 25 | 23 | 20 | VE

E 70s | 1237 Third Ave. (71st St.) | 212-737-0600 |
www.gracesmarketplace.com

This enduring Upper East Side gourmet market stays in the neighborhood's good graces with "friendly" service and inventory that's
"lovely to behold and taste", extending to "glorious" baked goods,
an abundance of "the best cheeses", prepared foods "tasty" enough
"to pass off as your own", "quality meats and poultry" from "helpful
butchers", "always-fresh" produce and various "difficult-to-find"
specialty items; granted, it's "crowded" and "expensive", but loyalists insist it's a "pleasure spending too much money" here.

Gracious Home ▭ *Cookware* 26 | 21 | 21 | E

E 70s | 1220 Third Ave. (70th St.) | 212-517-6300
W 60s | 1992 Broadway (67th St.) | 212-231-7800 ◐
800-338-7809 | www.gracioushome.com

An "indispensable" "one-stop wonder" for "apartment-dwellers",
this UES-UWS duo's kitchen departments stock "quality appliances" (and "replacement parts"), "splendid" cookware, utensils,
cutlery, gadgets and "anything else you can imagine" to "make a
meal or throw a party"; true, "you can probably get it cheaper elsewhere", the shelves "can be cluttered" and the "old-school NY service" is "variable", but all agree it's "super-convenient" to have the
"best selection" all "under one roof."

	QUALITY	DISPLAY	SERVICE	COST

☑ Gramercy Park
Flower Shop ▭ *Flowers*   27 | 26 | 25 | E

Chelsea | Chelsea Mkt. | 75 Ninth Ave. (bet. 15th & 16th Sts.) |
212-475-4989 | 888-747-4424
Gramercy | 236 Third Ave. (bet. 19th & 20th Sts.) | 212-475-4989
Dumbo | 28 Adams St. (Water St.) | Brooklyn | 212-475-4989
www.gramercyflowers.com

Purveying petals in Gramercy for over a century, this urbane florist
and its Chelsea and Dumbo offshoots boast a "courteous staff" of
designers who "completely understand what you want" as they
fashion "fresh, gorgeous" blooms into "beautiful arrangements"; for
"a magnificent gift or treat for yourself", it "never fails to deliver."

Grandaisy Bakery   *Baked Goods*   25 | 19 | 21 | M

SoHo | 73 Sullivan St. (bet. Broome & Spring Sts.) | 212-334-9435
TriBeCa | 250 W. Broadway (Beach St.) | 212-334-9435
W 70s | 176 W. 72nd St. (Amsterdam Ave.) | 646-274-1607
www.grandaisybakery.com

"Fantastic artisanal" breads are the showstoppers at this bakery
threesome where the yeasty lineup ranges from the "addictive" focaccia to one of the "best Pullman loaves in NY", and there are also
"delightful nibbles" like the "terrific" olive rolls, "sublime" thin-crust
pizzas and seasonal panettone; its storefronts are on the "small and
simple" side, but never mind – they "always smell great."

Grande Harvest Wines ● *Wine/Liquor*   22 | 21 | 19 | E

E 40s | Grand Central Terminal | main concourse, Graybar Passage
(42nd St. & Vanderbilt Ave.) | 212-682-5855 | www.ghwines.com

"Convenient" when you're "rushing to make the train", this Grand
Central vino depot caters to the Metro North–bound with a variety
that's "not as big" as some but still "passable" for Californian and
French vintages from small producers, as well as organic and kosher
selections and single-malt scotches; it's run by "knowledgeable"
types, and even if "you'll pay a buck or two more", the location's
ideal "on the go."

Grand Wine & Liquor ●◑▭ *Wine/Liquor*   22 | 17 | 19 | M

Astoria | 30-05 31st St. (30th Ave.) | Queens | 718-728-2520 |
www.grandwl.com

Like a "League of Nations of wine", this Astoria vet's vintages span
a "fantastic selection" "from all over the world", "especially from
Greece" and "typically underrepresented" areas of Eastern Europe,
not to mention Asia and South America; "friendly" staffers oversee
the sizable space, and the "affordable" prices are as worthy of a trip
as the "interesting" inventory.

☑ Great Performances   *Caterer*   26 | 24 | 27 | E

Hudson Square | 304 Hudson St. (Spring St.) | 212-727-2424 |
www.greatperformances.com
By appointment only

After decades in the biz this "excellent" Hudson Square caterer/
event planner still puts on a "fabulous" show, earning a standing

ovation for its "imaginative and well-presented" menus – often starring local and sustainable ingredients – and "charming and courteous" staff; it's "among the best" for weddings, socials and corporate dos mounted at "BAM and many other venues" (e.g. Jazz at Lincoln Center, the Plaza, Sotheby's); P.S. in season, it employs produce sourced from Katchkie, its own upstate organic farm.

GreatWall Supermarket ● *Specialty Shop* | 19 | 14 | 12 | I |

Dumbo | 6722 Fort Hamilton Pkwy. (67th St.) | Brooklyn | 718-680-2889
Elmhurst | 77-00 Queens Blvd. (bet. 77th & 78th Sts.) | Queens | 718-205-0181
Flushing | 137-45/61 Northern Blvd. (bet. Leavitt St. & Linden Pl.) | Queens | 718-353-9828
Flushing | 144-50 Northern Blvd. (bet. 147th St. & Parsons Blvd.) | Queens | 718-321-8019
www.gw-supermarket.com

"They have everything" for Chinese cooking at these "huge" outposts of an Asian supermarket chain, "solid" suppliers of "real-deal" rations like "very fresh veggies and fruits", meats and seafood (some "you've never seen before") that are also wall-to-wall with "hard-to-find Far East" groceries; sure, they're "crowded" and it "helps to have a translator", but given such "great prices", supporters shrug "that's part of the fun."

The Greene Grape ●▣ *Wine/Liquor* | 22 | 19 | 23 | M |

Fort Greene | 765 Fulton St. (bet. S. Oxford St. & Portland Ave.) | Brooklyn | 718-797-9463 | www.greenegrape.com

"Pick up a bottle" on "the trip home" at this Fort Greene wine merchant that's a "local favorite" for its "limited" but "excellent" stock centered on small, family-run vintners, as well as a "small choice of premium spirits"; it hosts tastings of "rarely seen" varietals and gets points for its "really reasonable price range" as well.

Greene Grape Provisions ●▣ *Specialty Shop* | ▽ 27 | 21 | 25 | E |

Fort Greene | 753 Fulton St. (S. Portland Ave.) | Brooklyn | 718-233-2700 | www.greenegrape.com

Bringing "more choice" to Fort Greene with its "variety of excellent foods", this gourmet market "matchbox" (sib of the nearby Greene Grape wine shop) stocks an often-organic mix with highlights like "fresh meat" and fish, local produce, "nice cheeses" and even microbrews; "it's going to cost you", but the staff is "warm and knowledgeable" and "you always know the quality's superb."

Greenmarket *Produce* | 29 | 24 | 23 | M |

Union Sq | Union Sq. | B'way & 17th St. | 212-788-7476 | www.grownnyc.org | Mon./Wed./Fri./Sat., Year-round
For a full list of Greenmarket locations, see page TK

"The farm comes to the city" via this "beloved" network of markets throughout the five boroughs (the Union Square "mecca" is the largest), where regional growers and producers vend "gorgeous", just-picked produce and "the freshest" meats, cheese, seafood, "homemade" baked goods, flowers and "fabulous" finds "you didn't know existed"; they're "a must-visit for foodies", chefs from "many of the top restaurants" and local-sustainable enthusiasts who concur quality "doesn't get better" – especially if you "get there early."

Greenwich Produce ● *Produce*   ▽ 28 | 26 | 21 | M

E 40s | Grand Central Mkt. | Lexington Ave. (43rd St.) | 212-490-4444

"When cruising the Grand Central Market", this produce vendor with stalls set up at either end is handy for an "excellent selection" of "beautiful" fruit and vegetables, offered alongside other "quality merchandise" like nuts and fresh-cut flowers (some of them edible); the pickings "can be pricey", but it's still a "great stop on the way home to Connecticut."

Grom ● *Ice Cream*   26 | 22 | 20 | E

W 50s | 1796 Broadway (bet. Columbus Circle & 58th St.) | 212-974-3444
W 70s | 2165 Broadway (bet. 76th & 77th Sts.) | 212-362-1837
W Village | 233 Bleecker St. (Carmine St.) | 212-206-1738
www.grom.it

"Gelato *magnifico*", "sublime" sorbets and "wow"-worthy granitas in "exquisite", "delicate" flavors are the draw at these West Side outposts of an Italian chain where the "authentic" frozen product is made in-house using "the very best" (mostly imported) ingredients; "long lines" and "stratospheric" prices don't faze fans, who say even "chintzy portions" hardly matter given that the "creamy", "super-smooth" "dee-lish" treats "taste like 1,000 calories per lick."

Güllüoglu 🗐 *Baked Goods*   23 | 19 | 18 | M

E 50s | 982 Second Ave. (52nd St.) | 212-813-0500 ●
Brighton Bch | 231 Brighton Beach Ave. (Brighton First Pl.) | Brooklyn | 347-577-6150 ●
NEW Astoria | 30-92 31st St. (31st Ave.) | Queens | 718-406-9100
www.gulluoglubaklava.com

Everything is "authentic and delicious" – particularly the many iterations of the "best baklava away from the Bosporus" – at these "real-deal" outposts of a 130-year-old Turkish dessert company; although the "sticky", honey-soaked specialties are the "highlight of the place", there's also Turkish coffee, salads and savory pastries – and if the service is a little "loopy", it's still way "cheaper than a trip to Istanbul"; P.S. Astoria is takeout-only.

Gustiamo 🗐 *Specialty Shop*   - | - | - | E

Bronx | 1715 W. Farms Rd. (Sheridan Expwy.) | 718-860-2949 | www.gustiamo.com

"Love their stuff" gush *amici* of this Bronx-based importer of Italian goods, where pricey but "wonderful artisanal foods" (many "not available anywhere else") – including top-quality pastas, oils, vinegars and jarred items – are carefully chosen from small suppliers and shipped exclusively from The Boot; while the store's situated well off the beaten path, it's popular with online shoppers who can procure its regional delicacies and gift baskets through the website.

	QUALITY	DISPLAY	SERVICE	COST

H & H Midtown Bagels East ◐▣ *Bagels*

| 25 | 17 | 19 | M |

E 80s | 1551 Second Ave. (bet. 80th & 81st Sts.) | 212-734-7441 | www.hhmidtownbagels.com

"Fresh", "fluffy", "hot", "oversized" bagels and "everything that goes with 'em" make this UES shop (no relation to the erstwhile, similarly monikered Westsider) a "mob scene" on weekends – but insiders say "don't be put off by the long lines" because they "move quickly"; other pluses include "great catering", "ship-anywhere" delivery and "around-the-clock" hours, which are just the thing for a "late-night drunken bagel run."

Harlem Vintage ◐▣ *Wine/Liquor*

| ▽ 27 | 26 | 27 | M |

Harlem | 2235 Frederick Douglass Blvd. (bet. 120th & 121st Sts.) | 212-866-9463 | www.harlemvintage.com

"Bravo!" cheer locals who "no longer have to travel" for "quality wine and spirits" thanks to this "excellent" Harlem "boutique" shop, whose "well-chosen stock" includes smaller and lesser-known vintners (e.g. it goes "out of the way to highlight female winemakers"); the "first-rate" staff is likably "down-to-earth", and Thursday, Friday and Saturday tastings provide a chance to "try new things."

Harney & Sons ▣ *Coffee/Tea*

| 28 | 25 | 26 | M |

SoHo | 433 Broome St. (bet. B'way & Crosby St.) | 212-933-4853 | 888-427-6398 | www.harney.com

It's always tea time at this "beautiful" SoHo outpost of a Millerton, NY, shop that has gained a wide following for its "marvelous", "reasonably priced" teas, which can be sampled at a tasting bar, and there's also a "nice little cafe in back" for enjoying a cuppa with scones and other treats; its "bazillion varieties" (well, 250) – black, white, green, oolong, herbal, fruit, decaf, kosher – are packaged in trademark tins and displayed on wooden shelves, along with pots and assorted accoutrements, and overseen by a "friendly", "über-knowledgeable" staff.

Hawthorne Valley Farm *Produce*

| ▽ 28 | 25 | 25 | M |

Location varies | 518-672-7500, ext. 2 | www.hawthornevalleyfarm.org

"One to look for", this Greenmarket booth "abounds" with organic and biodynamic foods straight from a Columbia County farm, including the freshest veggies, grass-fed beef and pork, "excellent yogurt" and dairy products, and baked goods that prove "healthy and delicious don't have to be mutually exclusive"; eco-conscious eaters can also unearth granola, herbs and eight varieties of sauerkraut.

Health & Harmony ◐▣ *Health*

| - | - | - | M |

W Village | 470 Hudson St. (bet. Barrow & Grove Sts.) | 212-691-3036

Green-leaning West Villagers sing the praises of this health-food hideaway as a "great neighborhood resource" where the "wonderful selection" of "organic supplies" includes produce and cheeses, plus sugarless baked goods, "gluten-free" items, vitamins and a full range of natural groceries; the staff knows what's what, and an in-store dietitian's on hand with wholesome pointers if you call ahead.

Health Nuts *Health*   22 | 17 | 18 | M

E 40s | 835 Second Ave. (bet. 44th & 45th Sts.) | 212-490-2979 ◐ ⌑
E 60s | 1208 Second Ave. (bet. 63rd & 64th Sts.) | 212-593-0116 ◐ ⌑
W 90s | 2611 Broadway (bet. 98th & 99th Sts.) | 212-678-0054 ◐ ⌑
Bayside | Bay Terrace | 211-35 26th Ave. (Bell Blvd.) | Queens |
718-225-8164

"Get that special something for your crazy diet" at this long-running chain, which satisfies "your health-food needs" via "small" outlets "jammed" with "quality brands" of staples plus "vegetarian prepared foods" and a handful of organic produce and dairy items; critics contend it's "feeling its age in the Whole Foods era", but most are still "glad it's nearby."

❷ Heights Chateau ◐ ⌑ *Wine/Liquor*   25 | 24 | 25 | M

Brooklyn Heights | 123 Atlantic Ave. (bet. Clinton & Henry Sts.) |
Brooklyn | 718-330-0963 | www.heightschateau.com

"Trust them" to "really know their wine" at this Brooklyn Heights mainstay, where a "comprehensive" lineup of worldwide labels "in all price ranges" ("bottles from small vineyards" included) is "well curated" by "experts" whose recommendations are "always spot-on"; bourbons and single-malt scotches also make a strong showing, and "frequent tastings" and "liberal discounts" on cases help explain why there's "no better" option in the area.

Heights Prime Meats *Meat/Poultry*   ∇ 27 | 24 | 25 | E

Brooklyn Heights | 59 Clark St. (bet. Henry & Hicks Sts.) | Brooklyn |
718-237-0133

The "goods are grand" at this "friendly and small" "old-fashioned butcher" and deli in Brooklyn Heights, which sells fresh and aged prime meats (including grass-fed beef), organic poultry and a variety of nitrate-free sausages, as well as pasta sauces; while the prices are "unfortunately suited to millionaire-row incomes", regulars say the "good quality" makes it the "best butcher shop in the Heights."

‖NEW‖ Heritage Meat Shop ⌑ *Meat/Poultry*   ∇ 27 | 21 | 25 | M

LES | Essex Street Mkt. | 120 Essex St. (bet. Delancey & Rivington Sts.) |
212-539-1111 | www.heritagemeatshop.com

When you need to know the pedigree of your pork chop, this new Essex Street Market outpost of the online artisanal butcher Heritage Foods USA fills the bill; its "lovely" counter staff shepherds conscientious carnivores as they select cuts from heirloom animals humanely raised on independent farms, including beef, pork, goat, poultry and more, plus bacon and "holy cow"–good salumi; no wonder meat-lovers declare it a "great place to buy" and "worth every penny" of the unsurprisingly higher-than-supermarket prices.

Hershey's Times Square ◐ *Candy/Nuts*   21 | 25 | 18 | M

W 40s | 1593 Broadway (48th St.) | 212-581-9100 | www.hersheys.com

If you can't get "to Pennsylvania to the HQ", "pay homage to your chocolate gods" at this neon-signed "mecca" smack dab in Times Square, "one of the most foot-traveled sites on the globe"; "unless they're on a Jacques Torres fast", many "NYers" may pass it by, citing a "gimmicky" setting and "supermarket" quality, but "tourists" smitten by the "intoxicating" smells, "nostalgia" factor and "limited edition" products you "can't find elsewhere" find it "loads of fun."

Hester Street Fair *Specialty Items*   21 | 20 | 20 | M

LES | Hester & Essex Sts. | no phone | www.hesterstreetfair.com

"Walk, shop and chow down" at this seasonal LES weekend "street fair", where the 50-plus stalls include "friendly vendors" of "so much yummy food", from cookies, brownies and pretzels to Luke's Lobster rolls; it's on the "smaller" side (think a "mellow cousin to the Brooklyn Flea"), but if you "go hungry" there's more than "enough to keep yourself occupied" here.

Hinsch's *Ice Cream*   22 | 21 | 22 | I

Bay Ridge | 8518 Fifth Ave. (bet. 85th & 86th Sts.) | Brooklyn | 718-748-2854

"Old Bay Ridge lives" on at this "cute", circa-1924 "classic" soda fountain serving 16 flavors of "fabulous" ice cream, "shakes, malts, egg creams" and "great" chocolates", all "housemade" "from scratch"; the "Formica-and-stainless steel" setting adds to the sense that you've taken "a step back in time", while "NY-style" servers "full of character" and affordable prices make the experience "really fun."

H Mart ● *Specialty Shop*   22 | 15 | 14 | I
(fka Han Ah Reum Market)

Garment District | 25 W. 32nd St. (bet. 5th & 6th Aves.) | 212-695-3283
Flushing | 141-40 Northern Blvd. (Bowne St.) | Queens | 718-358-0700
Flushing | 156-40 Northern Blvd. (Roosevelt Ave.) | Queens | 718-888-0005
Flushing | 29-02 Union St. (29th Ave.) | Queens | 718-445-5656
www.hmart.com

Loaded with "authentic" goods "not carried in everyday" markets, this Korean "superstore" foursome in the Garment District and Flushing comprises a "one-stop" "resource" for "exploring" "fabulous fresh fish, meats, veggies and fruit" plus a plethora of "Asian staples" and "hard-to-find ingredients"; sure, conditions can be "hectic", but it's got "character" and "you can't beat the value."

Holey Cream *Ice Cream*   ▽ 21 | 19 | 20 | M

W 50s | 796 Ninth Ave. (53rd St.) | 212-247-8400 | www.holeycream.com

Holey "decadence" – this Hell's Kitchen dessert-debauchee's delight is hailed for "introducing the donut–ice cream sandwich" to NYC – choose a hot, "sublime", made-on-site sinker, an ice cream flavor, topping and icing, then "pray that a heart attack doesn't follow"; the heavenly "sugar overload" also includes cupcakes, cookies, sundaes and more, "oh my."

Hong Kong Supermarket *Specialty Shop*   19 | 13 | 12 | I

Chinatown | 68 Elizabeth St. (Hester St.) | 212-966-4943
Elmhurst | 82-02 45th Ave. (B'way) | Queens | 718-651-3838 ●
(continued)

QUALITY | DISPLAY | SERVICE | COST

(continued)

Hong Kong Supermarket

Flushing | 37-11 Main St. (bet. 37th & 38th Aves.) | Queens | 718-539-6868 ●

"If it's anything Asian, they've got it" at this California-based mega-mart chain, "the be-all and end-all" for "a plethora" of Far Eastern provisions from "fresh" seafood, meats and produce to "basic" groceries to "hard-to-find" "exotica"; its branches are a "real learning experience" complete with "tight aisles" and "madhouse" crowds, but "at these prices" you "can't go wrong."

Hot Bagels & Bialys ● *Bagels*

| 25 | 17 | 21 | I |

Midwood | 1615 Kings Hwy. (E. 17th St.) | Brooklyn | 718-627-9868
Bagels "chewy and dense with a perfect crust" (the "nearest thing to heaven") plus "can't-be-beat" bialys earn this unpretentious storefront a reputation as the carbophile's "Shangri-La of Midwood"; its ever-steamy windows hint at the fact that its traditionally made goods, available in the usual range of flavors, are made fresh throughout the day – and sold into the wee hours.

Hot Bialys & Bagels *Bagels*

| 23 | 15 | 18 | I |

Forest Hills | 116-63 Queens Blvd. (78th Ave.) | Queens | 718-544-0900
Known for producing some of the "best bagels in Queens" – plus namesake bialys (many a NYer's "basic necessity") – since the early 1980s, this Forest Hills "joint" retains the "same wonderfully blah decor" as ever; a few longtimers, citing a change in ownership, fear this "once-great" place is slipping to merely "above-average", but to most it remains a "reliable" "classic", and a serious "value" to boot.

House of Spices ▣ *Herbs/Spices*

| ▽ 26 | 18 | 19 | M |

Flushing | 127-40 Willets Point Blvd. (Northern Blvd.) | Queens | 718-507-4600 | www.hosindia.com

An "interesting concept" for an out-of-the-way Flushing warehouse, this well-established Indian importer is home to a "tremendous array of spices for all" your South Asian culinary needs; it's also a bountiful cache of beans, nuts, oils, pickles, pastes, chutneys, sweets and frozen meals, typically sold wholesale but also retailed for nice prices to those willing to venture out.

Hudson Valley Foie Gras ▣ *Meat/Poultry*

| ▽ 29 | 22 | 24 | E |

Location varies | 845-292-2500 | www.hudsonvalleyfoiegras.com
While fattened duck liver is its specialty, this Sullivan County farm's Greenmarket stall is also a "great source for whole duck", as well as a "top-notch" selection of products, including duck prosciutto and duck leg confit, that come from fowl raised cage-free on 200 acres of land; customers can also order everything but the quack through the farm's online store.

Hungarian Pastry Shop ●⊄ *Baked Goods*

| 23 | 18 | 19 | I |

W 100s | 1030 Amsterdam Ave. (111th St.) | 212-866-4230
"For generations", Columbia students have been coming to this Hungarian bakery/cafe in Morningside Heights to "read Hegel while

munching on hamentaschen", as well as "out-of-this-world" chocolate mousse cake, "lovely strudels" and butter cookies and tortes like "grandma used to make" – all chased by "bottomless cups of coffee"; even if you're not there to study, it's a "nice, quiet place to hang out."

Iavarone Bros. 🗐 Prepared Food 26 | 22 | 24 | M
Maspeth | 6900 Grand Ave. (69th St.) | Queens | 718-639-3623 | www.ibfoods.com

"You never have to cook again" given the "numerous choices" of "real Italian" prepared foods at this "old-style", third-generation fixture in Maspeth, where the "mouthwatering" housemade specialties are sure to "fool your family"; they're also "reliable" for cheeses, pastas, a "marvelous" deli counter and "premium" meats (notably the store-made sausage) from "top-notch" butchers, and while they're "not cheap", for most the "quality" and "excellent service" are "well worth the extra bucks"; P.S. it also does a big web-order business.

Ice Cream House Ice Cream 24 | 19 | 22 | M
NEW **Borough Park** | 3624 15th Ave. (37th St.) | Brooklyn | 718-972-0222
Flatbush | 1725 Ave. M (E. 18th St.) | Brooklyn | 718-972-0222
NEW **Williamsburg** | 873 Bedford Ave. (Myrtle Ave.) | Brooklyn | 718-972-0222
www.theicecreamhouse.com

"Yum" – Brooklynites scream for "fresh", "not-very-expensive" kosher and vegan ice cream at these cross-borough triplets vending scoops and soft-serve in a "great variety" of flavors both "classic and modern", plus other frozen-dessert fundamentals like fro-yo, sorbet and ice cream cakes; the unpretentious, brightly hued setups "sport similar layouts", and all close for Shabbat.

Ideal Cheese 🗐 Cheese/Dairy 27 | 21 | 23 | E
E 50s | 942 First Ave. (52nd St.) | 212-688-7579 | 800-382-0109 | www.idealcheese.com

An "incredible assortment" of "luscious" cheeses "from around the world" plus an "excellent array" of "go-withs" (e.g. "meats, pâtés, crackers" and even beer) help this Sutton Place shop "live up to its name", while "first-cabin" service from "knowledgeable" folk push it over the top; they'll even "pack goodies to take away for the weekend", so "you'll leave every time with a smile" – or at least saying 'cheese.'

NEW Il Buco Alimentari Specialty Shop ▽ 25 | 24 | 23 | E
NoHo | 53 Great Jones St. (bet. Bowery & Lafayette St.) | 212-837-2622 | www.ilbuco.com

"Outstanding" house-cured salumi is the star at this Italian market inside Il Buco's "charming" new wine bar/eatery, which also dispenses artisanal cheeses, housemade pastas, breads and gelato, not to mention "some of the best sandwiches" around, plus dry goods like sea salt, olive oils and vinegars; it's all overseen by a "helpful, knowledgeable" counter crew, and for those who want to *mangia* on the spot, there's an adjacent cafe area that's a combination coffee bar/*vineria*.

	QUALITY	DISPLAY	SERVICE	COST

Il Cantuccio 🔲 *Baked Goods* ▽ 26 | 22 | 24 | M

W Village | 91 Christopher St. (bet. Bleecker St. & 7th Ave.) |
212-647-8787 | www.ilcantuccionyc.com

It's the "best addition to the West Village in years" enthuse early-goers to this outpost of a bakery in Prato, Italy, whose specialty is "soft, chewy, excellent" *cantucci*, a more tender version of biscotti; there's also traditional Tuscan salt-free bread (perfect for pairing with some good salami), focaccia and pizza, all baked on-site and served by "real Italian" staffers whose "friendliness" makes this a pleasant "spot to linger" – as does the back patio on warm days.

☑ Il Laboratorio del Gelato ◑🔲 *Ice Cream* 28 | 18 | 21 | M

LES | 188 Ludlow St. (Houston St.) | 212-343-9922 |
www.laboratoriodelgelato.com

"Serious craft" goes into the "out-of-this-world" "artisanal" gelato at this LES parlor, once again voted No. 1 for Ice Cream in this Survey, whose "silky-smooth" scoops come in an "inventive" array of "lush", "complex" flavors that cognoscenti "can't ever get enough" of; it's slightly pricey and you may have to "stand in line", but "who cares" – "this is art"; P.S. it's equipped with an espresso bar and seating for 20.

In Pursuit of Tea 🔲 *Coffee/Tea* ▽ 28 | 23 | 27 | E

SoHo | 33 Crosby St. (bet. Broome & Grand Sts.) | 646-964-5223 |
866-878-3832 | www.inpursuitoftea.com

"Exceptional-quality teas", many sourced from small producers in remote areas around the globe, are the specialty of this importer with a teacup-size SoHo storefront; its "wonderful", "informative" staffers "clearly love" the house inventory and "are happy to talk about" all of the loose-leaf varieties on hand (the full inventory is available online), which, given the "top quality", can be on the "expensive" side; P.S. it also vends tea pots and accessories.

Insomnia Cookies ◑🔲 *Baked Goods* 22 | 17 | 20 | I

NEW **E 80s** | 1579 Second Ave. (82nd St.) | 212-628-7771
G Village | 50 W. Eighth St. (6th Ave.) | 212-228-2373 |
877-632-6543
NEW **Murray Hill** | 482 Third Ave. (33rd St.) | 212-725-0600
W 70s | 405 Amsterdam Ave. (bet. 79th & 80th Sts.) | 212-595-3800
www.insomniacookies.com

"As the name implies, these are the ideal midnight snack" say devotees of the "big", "amazing", "melt-in-your-mouth" cookies and brownies dispensed by the NYC branches of an East Coast chain; the "addictive" wares are "great for students" and anyone else with "late-night sugar cravings" – since it's open till 3 AM daily, you can always "get a fix", and best of all, "they deliver."

Integral Yoga Natural Foods ◑🔲 *Health* 23 | 18 | 22 | M

W Village | 229 W. 13th St. (bet. 7th & 8th Aves.) | 212-243-2642 |
www.integralyoganaturalfoods.com

"Jam-packed with natural goodies", this West Village health-fooder "attracts a loyal crowd" seeking "everything vegetarian", including a "terrific selection" of organic produce, vegan baked goods, pre-

	QUALITY	DISPLAY	SERVICE	COST

pared foods, vitamins and "cosmetic products"; the merchandise is "moderately priced" ("especially bulk items" like grains, beans, nuts and spices), and the "civilized" vibe makes it a "very Zen" spot to "stop in after yoga" at the studio next door.

International Grocery 🖃 *Specialty Shop*

| 24 | 17 | 19 | I |

(fka Ninth Avenue International Grocery)

W 40s | 543 Ninth Ave. (bet. 40th & 41st Sts.) | 212-279-1000 | www.internationalgrocerynyc.com

A "treasure trove" for "innovative cooks", this "ancient" (since 1967) Mediterranean souk in Hell's Kitchen flaunts a "wide choice" of "exotic ingredients" – notably "beautiful vats of spices" – at "very reasonable" per-pound prices; those who "keep navigating" beyond the "bulk items" will encounter "interesting stuff" encompassing cheeses, olives and "fresh" Greek specialties like the "heavenly" homemade taramosalata.

In Vino Veritas ● *Wine/Liquor*

| ▽ 22 | 21 | 23 | M |

E 70s | 1375 First Ave. (74th St.) | 212-288-0100

A veritable landmark on the Upper East Side, this circa-1933 wine store stocks an impressive lineup spotlighting Italian imports in "pretty" digs that preserve antique touches like a stained-glass frontage, Murano lamps and cast-iron filigree dating from the 1800s; it stays true to the "neighborhood" regulars with affordable pricing and "friendly and knowledgeable" advice from a staff that's always "happy to talk about wine."

🅉 Italian Wine Merchants 🖃 *Wine/Liquor*

| 29 | 26 | 26 | E |

Union Sq | 108 E. 16th St. (bet. Irving Pl. & Union Sq. E.) | 212-473-2323 | www.italianwinemerchants.com

"Like a museum for wine", this Union Square "boutique" deals mostly in "fine Italian" vintages, showcasing an "amazing selection" from "all regions" (rare finds included) displayed "art-gallery" style and curated by a "most informed" staff that's ready with "wonderful service and recommendations"; insiders say "you'd better cash in a CD" first – but to most it's worth the "splurge" since if it's "on their shelves, you know it has to be good"; P.S. it holds tastings on Saturdays.

🅉 Jacques Torres Chocolate 🖃 *Candy/Nuts*

| 28 | 26 | 23 | E |

Chelsea | Chelsea Mkt. | 75 Ninth Ave. (bet. 15th & 16th Sts.) | 212-229-2441
Hudson Square | 350 Hudson St. (King St.) | 212-414-2462
W 40s | Rockefeller Ctr. | 30 Rockefeller Plaza, concourse level (bet. 49th & 50th Sts.) | 212-664-1804
W 70s | 285 Amsterdam Ave. (bet. 73rd & 74th Sts.) | 212-787-3256
Dumbo | 66 Water St. (bet. Dock & Main Sts.) | Brooklyn | 718-875-9772

🅉 Jacques Torres Ice Cream *Ice Cream*

Dumbo | 62 Water St. (bet. Dock & Main Sts.) | Brooklyn | 718-875-9772 www.mrchocolate.com

"Willy Wonka has nothing" on "chocolate wizard" Jacques Torres and his burgeoning mini-empire, where the "mind-boggling variety" of "vaunted" confections runs from "glorious" truffles and other "grown-up" bonbons to "chocolate-covered cornflakes" and "warm, melty" cookies; "snazzy presentation" is a given, while the "high prices" are deemed "oh, so worth it", especially when you can "watch the candy get made" at some branches, and even the kiosk at Chelsea Market serves the "incomparable" hot chocolate deemed so "heavenly" it's "sinful"; P.S. the location next to the Dumbo original specializes in "OMG" ice cream.

Japanese Culinary Center 🗏 *Cookware*

▽ 24 | 25 | 25 | E

E 40s | 711 Third Ave. (bet. 44th & 45th Sts.) | 212-661-3333 | www.japaneseculinarycenter.com

The Far East comes to East Midtown at this retail arm of New York Mutual Trading, truly a "must-see for those serious about Japanese cooking"; the ever-"expanding" selection ranges from "high-quality" cast-iron pots, knives and modern ceramics to soba noodle–making machines and specialty items like the Sushi Robot, as well as imported comestibles, more than 130 kinds of sake and 40 types of shochu; P.S. complete your education with tasting seminars and cooking classes.

Japan Premium Beef, Inc. *Meat*

▽ 29 | 25 | 26 | VE

NoHo | 57 Great Jones St. (Bowery) | 212-260-2333

In-the-know carnivores question whether "there is a better cut of beef in the city" than those exemplars found at this sleek NoHo Japanese butcher, which specializes in domestically bred, Kobe-style Wagyu beef; whether it's sold as rib-eyes, the "best strip steaks ever" or cuts trimmed on request for Japanese BBQ, the luxurious, intensely marbled meat comes at a premium – "but man, is it worth it."

Java Joe *Coffee/Tea*

- | - | - | M

Park Slope | 414 Eighth St. (bet. 4th & 5th Sts.) | Brooklyn | 718-369-6026 | www.javajoebrooklyn.com

"Good to have them in the neighborhood" declare Park Slopers of this "special place" that has been luring java-jonesing locals to its tiny storefront for 20 years with a fragrant inventory of more than 65 "high-quality" coffee varieties roasted to order in small batches; its "fun, quirky" and "warm" staff also vends a line of high-quality teas, plus all the necessary brew paraphernalia, such as French presses and kettles.

Jay & Lloyd's Kosher Deli ❶ *Deli*

22 | 16 | 20 | M

Sheepshead Bay | 2718 Ave. U (bet. 27th & 28th Sts.) | Brooklyn | 718-891-5298 | www.jayandlloydskosherdeli.com

"Quaint" and "authentic", this "old-fashioned Jewish deli" in Sheepshead Bay maintains a rep as a "solid" supplier of "fresh", "delicious" pastrami, corned beef ("mmmm"), chopped liver and all "the staples", dished over the counter with a "personal, homey touch"; those short on shekels find it "a bit pricey", but nonetheless it's "worth a visit" if you're in the "neighborhood."

🗹 J.B. Prince 🖃 Cookware
29 21 20 E

Murray Hill | 36 E. 31st St., 11th fl. (bet. Madison & Park Aves.) |
212-683-3553 | www.jbprince.com

"Hidden on the 11th floor of a nondescript building in Murray Hill" is this "real pro" "insider's place" where a "who's who of chefs" – along with "serious and affluent" home cooks – buy their "top-of-the-line" equipment at accordingly "high prices"; you can "stock up on anything from a sous-vide machine to madeleine pans" and fine knives, including lots of "hard-to-find" items, and the impressive inventory is overseen by a staff that's "helpful even if you're not Danny Meyer."

Jerome Florists Flowers
▽ 24 19 20 E

E 90s | 1379 Madison Ave. (96th St.) | 212-289-1677 |
800-848-4316 | www.jeromeflorists.com

This upscale UES petal-peddling veteran (since 1929) supplies "beautiful", elegant floral arrangements comprising high-end fresh-from-Holland blooms, scoring points for "personal service"; flower fanciers say it's worth the "trip Uptown" to make a purchase, but on-line ordering and "very good" delivery are handy too.

🗹 Joe's Dairy 🖗 Cheese/Dairy
28 15 24 I

SoHo | 156 Sullivan St. (bet. Houston & Prince Sts.) |
212-677-8780

It's formaggio "heaven" at this circa-1925 SoHo "throwback" of an Italian "specialty cheese store" that dispatches "wonderful", "made-daily" mozzarella ("fresh and smoked") that'll have you swearing the city's "zoned for cows"; there's also a solid "selection of sausages, sopressata" and so on, with ridiculously "reasonable" prices sealing the deal – but remember to "go early" because the "mozz" sometimes "runs out."

JoMart Chocolates 🖃 Candy/Nuts
▽ 28 24 23 M

Marine Park | 2917 Ave. R (bet. Nostrand Ave. & 29th St.) |
Brooklyn | 718-375-1277 | www.jomartchocolates.com

A "terrific experience for palate, eye and nose", this Marine Park "jewel" dating to 1946 is rated "worth a trip from anywhere" and is always filled with "happy faces"; the "fabulous displays" of "excellent" "handmade chocolates" stir memories aplenty – fans fondly "remember the Easter bunnies" and "solid" milk "turkeys" made from molds – and thankfully, the "wonderful" staff "still does a great job at all that holiday stuff", including custom orders.

Jordan's Lobster Dock Seafood
24 15 20 M

Sheepshead Bay | 1 Harkness Ave. (Knapp St.) | Brooklyn |
718-934-6300 | www.jordanslobsterdock.com

Docked near "the mouth of Sheepshead Bay", this family-owned "institution" lets you "pick your own" from a cache of the "freshest" "live lobsters", either for steaming on-site or to fetch "home for cooking"; "sure, it's a little low-rent", but "excellent quality" at a "very reasonable cost" gives crustacean connoisseurs plenty of claws to "absolutely love the place."

Joyce Bakeshop *Baked Goods*   ▽ 25 | 22 | 21 | M

Prospect Heights | 646 Vanderbilt Ave. (bet. Park & Prospect Pls.) | Brooklyn | 718-623-7470 | www.joycebakeshop.com

"Yummy" baked goods have made this Prospect Heights bakery and cafe a "neighborhood favorite" that's so popular the "tables are always taken" by locals lured in by the well-crafted treats and coffee from Brooklyn roaster Gorilla; thanks to the glass-walled kitchen, you can watch the cupcakes, cookies and seasonal pies and tarts as they come out of the ovens, and there are sandwiches and soups as well.

Jubilat Provisions ⊅ *Meat/Poultry*   - | - | - | I

Greenwood Heights | 608 Fifth Ave. (17th St.) | Brooklyn | 718-768-9676

"Whatever you buy will be delicious" according to boosters of this Polish butcher south of Park Slope in Greenwood Heights, which tempts carnivores with the promise of "wonderful" house-smoked kielbasas that hang from the ceiling, as well as a host of other pork products including ham, bacon and "juicy, tasty" sausages; non-pork offerings like sauerkraut and pickled herring are also packed into this storefront, whose diminutive "size belies its powerful food."

Junior's ❶⌐ *Baked Goods*   21 | 18 | 18 | M

E 40s | Grand Central Terminal | dining concourse (42nd St. & Vanderbilt Ave.) | 212-983-5257
E 40s | Grand Central Terminal | main concourse, Biltmore Passage (42nd St. & Vanderbilt Ave.) | 212-692-9800
W 40s | Shubert Alley | 1515 Broadway (45th St.) | 212-302-2000
Downtown Bklyn | 386 Flatbush Ave. Ext. (Dekalb Ave.) | Brooklyn | 718-852-5257
800-958-6467 | www.juniorscheesecake.com

It's still "all about the cheesecake" at this circa-1950 Downtown Brooklyn "institution" – with outposts in Grand Central and the Theater District – where the faithful flock for those "heavenly", "creamy", "wonderfully fresh" cakes that have made it "world famous"; the rest of the menu is "essentially diner fare", so consider springing just for a "giant" slice of the house specialty, since it "could feed a whole family" anyway.

☑ Kalustyan's ⌐ *Specialty Shop*   27 | 20 | 19 | M

Murray Hill | 123 Lexington Ave. (bet. 28th & 29th Sts.) | 212-685-3451 | 800-352-3451 | www.kalustyans.com

Dubbed "the mother lode of spices" for its "endless variety" of "superb" Indian and Mideastern seasonings, this "amazing" Murray Hill "bazaar" is also a "staggering" grocery "cornucopia" where "chefs looking for inspiration" can browse a "brilliant selection" of items both "common and exotic" – "wonderful dried fruit", nuts, rice, beans, frozen foods, "teas galore", fresh flatbreads, cookware or "you name it" – all at "pretty reasonable prices"; add a "hidden" "cafe upstairs" serving "delish" prepared specialties, and there's "always a lot to discover."

	QUALITY	DISPLAY	SERVICE	COST

Kam Man ◐▣ *Specialty Shop* — 21 | 15 | 11 | I

Chinatown | 200 Canal St. (bet. Mott & Mulberry Sts.) |
212-571-0330 | www.newkamman.com

"No matter what you need for an Asian kitchen, they've got it" at
this Chinatown vet, still a "best bet" for "authentic" Eastern eats
(dried goods, frozen items, sweets, teas and prepared specialties
like BBQ duck) along with the equipment to cook them with and
"dishes to serve them in" from the housewares section downstairs;
it takes "patience to hunt" around and there's "very little service",
but the "great buys" make for many happy kampers all the same;
P.S. the upper level deals in beauty supplies.

K & D Wines & Spirits ◐▣ *Wine/Liquor* — 26 | 21 | 24 | M

E 90s | 1366 Madison Ave. (bet. 95th & 96th Sts.) | 212-289-1818 |
www.kdwine.com

Long a "go-to" for Carnegie Hill oenophiles, this "neighborhood grog
shop" features some 4,000 "fairly priced" wines "from around the
globe", ranging from "regular stock" to "high-quality, unusual" vintages; "particularly good" guidance from "knowledgeable salespeople", tastings Thursday–Saturday and "prompt", no-minimum
delivery offered "free of charge" in Manhattan further explain
its "staying power."

Katagiri ▣ *Specialty Shop* — 23 | 17 | 17 | M

E 50s | 224 E. 59th St. (bet. 2nd & 3rd Aves.) | 212-755-3566 |
www.katagiri.com

"Handy" for "all things Japanese", this diminutive Upper East Side
mart is a long-standing (since 1907) purveyor of "high-quality"
goods, from "fresh fish" and produce to "authentic" ingredients like
"soba noodles, aji-mirin, natto or fresh shiso leaves"; sushi and
bento boxes are also available, and although prices strike some as "a
little expensive", for "last-minute" "essentials" it's "your best bet"
in these parts.

Katz's Delicatessen ◐▣ *Deli* — 25 | 16 | 17 | M

LES | 205 E. Houston St. (Ludlow St.) | 212-254-2246 |
800-446-8364 | www.katzdeli.com

Founded in 1888, this "legendary" LES "retro experience" is the
"prototypical" "no-frills" deli, which "sets the bar" with "bench-
mark" hand-sliced pastrami and corned beef that "bring tears of
joy" to those with "cravings" for "traditional Jewish" fare; true,
it's also "chaotic", "touristy" and "anything but cheap", but if you
"don't go expecting white-glove treatment" the "prime quality" and
"character" are "worthy of its fame"; P.S. it's now open round-the-
clock on weekends.

⊠ Kee's Chocolates *Candy/Nuts* — 28 | 21 | 22 | E

SoHo | 80 Thompson St. (bet. Broome & Spring Sts.) | 212-334-3284
W 40s | HSBC Bldg. | 452 Fifth Ave. (40th St.) | 212-525-6099
www.keeschocolates.com

"Chocolate goddess" Kee Ling Tong offers "the most gastronomi-
cally forward" bonbons of "any chocolatier in the city" according to

acolytes of her tiny SoHo storefront and Midtown kiosk, where the "dreamlike" handcrafted confections' "smooth texture" and "exotic" flavors – from "addictive" crème brûlée and passion fruit to "particularly sinful" Asian-accented "black sesame" – "satisfy even the most discriminating palates"; just "get there early" as the "best ones are gone by midday" – "that's how fresh they are, and how popular."

🅱 Keith's Farm 🌱 *Produce*　　29 | 24 | 23 | M
Location varies | 845-856-4955
"Hands down the best garlic available anywhere" is the highlight "you don't want to miss" at this Greenmarket go-to for "fresh, organic, delish" produce, the stand of Orange County, NY, farmer/author Keith Stewart, "one of the pioneers and heroes of the local food movement"; regulars relish the likes of "lovely potatoes, tomatoes and greens" as well as the "solid information and friendly advice" that accompany everything on offer.

🅱 Korin Japanese　　29 | 26 | 26 | E
Trading Corp. 🖃 *Cookware*
TriBeCa | 57 Warren St. (bet. Church St. & W. B'way) | 212-587-7021 | 800-626-2172 | www.korin.com
Shopping this cutting-edge Japanese "authority" in TriBeCa is "like visiting a fine art gallery" given its "superb" collection of traditionally handcrafted knives, to which aficionados say "nothing else" in town "comes close"; maybe the "amazing" blade "of your dreams" is so "expensive" you'll be tempted to "display it in a frame", but the other wares, like "sets of sushi molds", sashimi tools, cast iron and ceramic pots and sake accessories, are a "steal", and it's all presided over by a "wonderful" staff.

Koryodang *Baked Goods*　　▽ 22 | 21 | 17 | M
Garment District | 31 W. 32nd St. (bet. B'way & 5th Ave.) | 212-967-9661 ●
Flushing | 156-19 Northern Blvd. (157th St.) | Queens | 718-762-0104
Flushing | 39-02 Union St. (39th Ave.) | Queens | 718-762-6557
www.koryodang.com
"Korean pastries and breads" are the calling cards of these outposts of a Seoul-based bakery chain whose specialties include green-tea cakes, rice donuts, bean-paste buns and shaved ice; that it pours coffee and bubble tea makes it a good place to "just hang out with friends" during the day, though when "it's jumping at night", service can be a bit "brusque" ("have your $$$ ready").

Kosher BagelHole *Bagels*　　27 | 21 | 23 | I
Flatbush | 1423 Ave. J (15th St.) | Brooklyn | 718-258-4150
Flatbush | 1431 Coney Island Ave. (bet. Aves. J & K) | Brooklyn | 718-377-9700
www.kosherbagelhole.com
With two locations in Flatbush, this old-school bagelry's "delicious" rolled holes cause loyalists to reach for hyperbole ("sublime"), embracing "attitude behind the counter" as the proper accompaniment

QUALITY DISPLAY SERVICE COST

to a "brilliantly boiled and baked bagel"; there's also the usual array of spreads and toppings, plus soups, wraps and salads, and it also does "great" kosher catering.

❷ Kossar's Bialys ⌨✏ *Bagels* | 26 | 13 | 17 | I |

LES | 367 Grand St. (bet. Essex & Norfolk Sts.) | 212-473-4810 | 877-424-2597 | www.kossarsbialys.com

It doesn't get "better", "fresher" or "more authentic" for bagels, bulkas and bialys than at this circa-1935 Lower East Side "landmark", a "bare-bones" storefront turning out "superb" "old-country" carbs "baked daily" (they're "hot! hot! hot!") the way "bubbie's bubbie used to make"; here "nothing changes" and you "can't beat the prices", so "get down" to Grand Street and sample the "real thing" – but just "don't go on Saturdays because they're closed."

Kusmi Tea *Coffee/Tea* | ▽ 26 | 24 | 24 | E |

E 60s | 1037 Third Ave. (bet. 61st & 62nd Sts.) | 212-355-5580 | www.us.kusmitea.com

A "gem" on the East Side, this "inviting Parisian import" specializes in "absolutely delicious" teas of the "highest quality" packaged in "beautiful" colorful tins and presented in a sleekly "gorgeous" space; 140-plus years of "integrity" goes into the "large selection of flavored and herbal" blends (detox, "Russian-style" Prince Vladimir, etc.), while "friendly" staffers who "know their tea" ensure it's a prime "place for a gift" – but "oh, those prices!"

La Bagel Delight *Bagels* | 22 | 18 | 21 | I |

Brooklyn Heights | 90 Court St. (bet. Livingston & Schermerhorn Sts.) | Brooklyn | 718-522-0520

Dumbo | 104 Front St. (Adams St.) | Brooklyn | 718-625-2235

Fort Greene | 73 Lafayette Ave. (Elliot Pl.) | Brooklyn | 718-246-3744 ⌨

Park Slope | 284 Seventh Ave. (bet. 6th & 7th Sts.) | Brooklyn | 718-768-6107

www.labageldelight.com

"Big, fluffy" bagels and "everything that goes with them" is the deal at this Brooklyn bunch, where the "friendly and efficient" service will have you "out the door in no time", "schmear" and "coffee" in hand; the "real community vibe" means you get to "kibbutz at the same time" – still, what's with the "silly name"?; P.S. the Park Slope branch also boasts a salad bar and hot prepared dishes.

La Bergamote *Baked Goods* | 26 | 25 | 19 | E |

Chelsea | 177 Ninth Ave. (20th St.) | 212-627-9010

W 50s | 515 W. 52nd St. (bet. 10th & 11th Aves.) | 212-586-2429 ◗

www.labergamotenyc.com

Find the "true French cafe experience" at this Chelsea patisserie whose "gorgeous and delicious pastries" are showcased in "pretty" quarters in Chelsea and at a "lovely" West Hell's Kitchen offshoot; regulars praise the likes of "jewellike tarts" and "irresistible" *souris au chocolat* (chocolate mice) as well as some of the "best croissants in NYC", even if it's all offered up with a bit of "attitude."

	QUALITY	DISPLAY	SERVICE	COST

La Boîte à Epice 🖃 *Herbs/Spices* | - | - | - | E |

W 50s | 724 11th Ave. (bet. 51st & 52nd Sts.) | 212-247-4407 | www.laboiteny.com

From a chef who has worked for big names like Daniel Boulud, this Hell's Kitchen sliver specializes in unusual spice blends inspired by the owner's travels, including some 40 mixtures, such as Mishmash (crystallized honey, saffron, lemon), Ararat (Urfa biber, smoked paprika, fenugreek) and Pierre Poivre (a mix of eight peppers); also on offer are biscuits – actually sweet and savory cookies – that change seasonally and are developed in collaboration with an artist whose work adorns the packages; P.S. open Wednesday to Friday, 3–7 PM.

🗹 L.A. Burdick Handmade Chocolates ◑🖃 *Candy/Nuts* | 28 | 24 | 23 | E |

Flatiron | 5 E. 20th St. (bet. B'way & 5th Ave.) | 212-796-0143 | www.burdickchocolate.com

This "welcome addition" to the Flatiron is a "charming" cafe/sweets shop from the New Hampshire–based confectioner known for its "exquisitely crafted and flavored" artisanal chocolates, ranging from animal shapes (those trademark "tiny mice" are "conversation pieces") to "all sorts of truffles", bonbons, bars and dipped fruit; there are also "terrific pastries in a vaguely Viennese" style, perfect for nibbling on-site with some hot chocolate so "heavenly", the "Swiss Miss would hang up her apron if she tried it."

NEW La Cremeria *Ice Cream* | ▽ 22 | 20 | 20 | M |

Little Italy | 178 Mulberry St. (bet. Broome & Kenmare Sts.) | 212-226-6758 | www.la-cremeria.com

Although Little Italy doesn't lack for gelato, this import from the old country (there's also a branch in Capri) claims to use imported ingredients like Piedmontese hazelnuts, Sicilian pistachios and Valrhona chocolate in its gelati, sorbetti and granitas; be warned that the hours are also authentically Italian – the shop is closed during the winter season.

🗹 Ladybird Bakery *Baked Goods* | 27 | 24 | 23 | E |

Park Slope | 1112 Eighth Ave. (bet. 11th & 12th Sts.) | Brooklyn | 718-499-8108 | www.ladybirdbakery.com

A longtime "Park Slope treasure" (it was the original location of Two Little Red Hens), this "teeny", "friendly" storefront is beloved by the neighborhood for its "top-quality baked goods" – "addictive" scones and cookies, "fantastically good" fruit tarts and cupcakes – that "taste just like granny's"; it specializes in "truly delicious" birthday and wedding cakes, and while there are a few grumbles about "Manhattan prices", most don't mind much considering that the decorations are "so freakin' beautiful."

🗹 Lady M Cake Boutique 🖃 *Baked Goods* | 29 | 28 | 23 | VE |

E 70s | 41 E. 78th St. (bet. Madison & Park Aves.) | 212-452-2222 | www.ladymconfections.com

This "refined" UES boutique is famed for its "exquisite" signature mille crêpes gateau (comprising numerous layers of custard and

	QUALITY	DISPLAY	SERVICE	COST

pastry) and other "light, delicious, dainty" cakes displayed like gems in a "jewel box"; it fairly "drips with elegance" – you may "feel like you have to be dressed-up" just to enter – and prices are accordingly "expensive", but "ladylike" devotees declare it "well worth the splurge"; P.S. a new Plaza Hotel outlet is in the works.

La Guli ⏺☰ *Baked Goods* ▽ 27 | 22 | 20 | M

Astoria | 29-15 Ditmars Blvd. (bet. 29th & 31st Sts.) | Queens | 718-728-5612 | www.laguli.com

Astorians have been coming to this family-run Italian bakery "for years" (since 1937) for both "traditional" sweets ("delicious" cannoli, "great" marzipan, Sicilian pignoli tarts, gelato) and seasonal delights like Christmas gingerbread houses, Easter grain pie and summertime ices; the decor, like the treats, is "old-time", with the original terrazzo floors and wooden cabinetry still intact to remind customers that they're "patronizing" an "institution."

☑ La Maison du Chocolat ☰ *Candy/Nuts* 29 | 28 | 24 | VE

E 70s | 1018 Madison Ave. (bet. 78th & 79th Sts.) | 212-744-7117
Financial District | 63 Wall St. (bet. Hanover & Pearl Sts.) | 212-952-1123
W 40s | Rockefeller Ctr. | 30 Rockefeller Plaza (49th St., bet. 5th & 6th Aves.) | 212-265-9404
www.lamaisonduchocolat.com

It's "the next best thing" to being in Paris sigh the smitten who "swoon over" the "spectacular variety" of "divine", "luxurious" French chocolates in *très* "unique" flavors at this "upscale" Madison Avenue boutique/cafe and its Rock Center and Financial District branches; prices are in the "investment-banker" range, but the "delectable" goods in "beautiful", haut packaging and "insanely smooth" hot chocolate are deemed "well worth it" – it's the "best way to self-medicate after a bad day."

La Maison du Macaron *Baked Goods* ▽ 28 | 25 | 22 | E

Chelsea | 132 W. 23rd St. (bet. 6th & 7th Aves.) | 212-243-2757 | www.nymacaron.com

A "true macaron mecca", this Chelsea patisserie has earned favorable comparisons to "Laudurée in Paris" for its "amazing" meringue cookie sandwiches, whose wide variety of flavors includes caramel, pistachio and chocolate; savory treats like a "super" croque monsieur and "fantastic" ham-and-cheese croissant round out the offerings, and if they're served with *un peu* of "traditional French crankiness", at least "your mouth will be in heaven."

Lamarca ⏺⇹ *Prepared Foods* 26 | 19 | 23 | M

Gramercy | 161 E. 22nd St. (3rd Ave.) | 212-673-7920

"Dependably tasty" pastas and other from-scratch prepared foods (just "pick a sauce" and "choose a container size" to go) endear this "small" shop to busy Gramercy locals, including Baruch and SVA students who particularly appreciate its "good prices"; another house specialty is cheese, offered in some 40 varieties, all properly aged thanks to an in-house cave, and there are also cured meats and baked goods; P.S. no credit cards and no weekend hours.

	QUALITY	DISPLAY	SERVICE	COST

Lamazou 🖃 Cheese/Dairy — 26 | 19 | 24 | M

Murray Hill | 370 Third Ave. (bet. 26th & 27th Sts.) | 212-532-2009 | www.lamazoucheese.com

"Treat yourself" at this "tiny" but "impressive" Murray Hill European cheese and prepared-foods shop that garners praise for its "spectacular variety" of fromage and draws "lunchtime lines" for its "excellent" sandwiches made with "fresh, authentic ingredients"; "charming" service and low prices have locals "loving this place."

Landmark Wine & Sake ● Wine/Liquor — ▽ 24 | 23 | 26 | M

Chelsea | 167 W. 23rd St. (bet. 6th & 7th Aves.) | 212-242-2323

"If you're a beginner at sake", the "best place to start" may be this Chelsea emporium boasting a 300-strong selection, plus some 200 sojus; it also works "for your everyday wine needs" with a "reasonably priced" global inventory marked by eclectic labels from France, Italy and California (notably Pinot Noirs), all displayed in an attractive, tasting bar–equipped space and overseen by "very helpful" staffers.

La Newyorkina Ice Cream — - | - | - | M

Location varies | no phone | www.lanewyorkina.com

For a "treat that doesn't feel overly indulgent" on "a hot day", pastry chef Fany Gerson fashions frozen Mexican *paletas* (i.e. "hip ice-pops") from seasonal, local ingredients in distinctive flavors like coconut, avocado, hibiscus, tamarind and her signature "mango dusted with chile powder"; in warmer months they're on offer at local markets including the Hester Street Fair, and in winter you can find them at the East Village's Big Gay Ice Cream Shop.

L'Arte del Gelato Ice Cream — 25 | 21 | 21 | M

Chelsea | Chelsea Mkt. | 75 Ninth Ave. (bet. 15th & 16th Sts.) | 212-366-0570

W Village | 75 Seventh Ave. S. (Barrow St.) | 212-924-0803 ●🖃 www.lartedelgelato.com

When "in need of a major indulgence", you "can't go wrong" with this West Village–Chelsea Market twosome's "silky", "sinfully rich", "seriously top-of-the-line" gelato, made fresh daily in a revolving "range of flavors" (traditional and "unusual") and dispensed by a staff that's "very willing" to supply samples; come summer, "look for their mobile cart" in Lincoln Center Plaza.

Las Palomas Productos Mexicanos 🖃 Specialty Shop — - | - | - | I

W 100s | 219 W. 100th St. (B'way) | 212-729-3469

At first glance it looks like an ordinary bodega, but at this tiny, packed-to-the-rafters Upper Westsider, every item is either imported from Mexico or made locally in the traditional way; the offerings span fresh tortillas (yellow and blue corn, flour), cheeses, sausage, dried beans, spices – including, of course, chiles, from fresh poblanos, jalapeños and serranos to a myriad dried ones – plus lots more "things you don't find at other places" like fresh epazote, not to mention south of the border–made Coca-Cola, prized for containing cane sugar rather than corn syrup.

Lassen & Hennigs ● *Caterer*

25 | 21 | 21 | M

Brooklyn Heights | 114 Montague St. (bet. Henry & Hicks Sts.) | Brooklyn | 718-875-6272 | www.lassencatering.com

A "core resource" that's "been around forever" in Brooklyn Heights, this "classic" deli has also built a "reliable" off-site catering business focused on private get-togethers and office lunches; with a "helpful" staff and "nicely presented" spreads starring "high-quality" prepared foods and baked goods, it's somewhat "predictable" but it "always delivers."

❷ Le Dû's Wines ⌨ *Wine/Liquor*

29 | 26 | 28 | E

W Village | 600 Washington St. (bet. Leroy & Morton Sts.) | 212-924-6999 | www.leduwines.com

"When you can't find it anywhere else", this "excellent West Village" vintner run by "charming" "top sommelier" Jean-Luc Le Dû (formerly of top-tier restaurant Daniel) lovingly displays a "carefully chosen stock" of "world-class wines" highlighting "hard-to-get or obscure" vintages "from all regions", plus spirits and sake; "informative" staffers are "happy to guide" greenhorns and conduct weekly tastings, but as this is "not just the same old" selection, don't be surprised if prices are "on the high side."

Led Zeppole ●⇪ *Baked Goods*

∇ 22 | 17 | 20 | I

E Village | 328 E. 14th St. (bet. 1st & 2nd Aves.) | 212-228-2807 | www.ledzeppolenyc.com

A "whole lotta love goes into every bite" at this down-the-block spin-off of the East Village favorite Artichoke Basille's Pizza, where sugar-dusted-dough groupies can gorge on "kick-ass zeppoles", cannoli, funnel cakes and cream puffs prepared "fresh" by "friendly" counterfolk; there's also housemade Italian ice (expect flavors like mango and PB&J), but the digs barely bigger than a fried Oreo mean "you have to stand or take it to go."

Le Marais ●⌨ *Meat/Poultry*

23 | 19 | 20 | VE

W 40s | 150 W. 46th St. (bet. 6th & 7th Aves.) | 212-869-0900 | www.lemarais.net

"Fabulous" glatt kosher meats are for sale at this butcher shop, which shares its name and premises with a Theater District brasserie; regulars laud the "quality" of the steaks, poultry, game and homemade beef jerky, noting "you wouldn't know it was kosher unless you got a heads-up"; while skeptics say the offerings are "priced to a captive market", admirers counter they're "worth the money."

❷ Lemon Ice King of Corona ●⇪ *Ice Cream*

26 | 14 | 18 | I

Corona | Corona Park | 52-02 108th St. (52nd Ave.) | Queens | 718-699-5133 | www.thelemonicekingofcorona.com

Hailed as the "perfect summer treat" since 1944, this "landmark" stand near Corona Park vends "incomparable" housemade Italian ices in its trademark lemon variety as well as an "incredible" array of "classic" and "far-out" flavors; loyal subjects savoring "the real stuff" insist it's "worth the excursion" and "long lines" – "don't settle for less."

	QUALITY	DISPLAY	SERVICE	COST

Lenny's Bagels ⊘ *Bagels* — 21 | 15 | 17 | I

W 90s | 2601 Broadway (bet. 98th & 99th Sts.) | 212-222-0410
"Reliable" "chewy-but-not-too-chewy" bagels – including "several unusual flavors" like "My 2 Sons" (sunflower and poppy seeds) – as well as your usual "deli-type foods" are dispensed at this Upper West Side standby that's "not H & H" but is "decent" and "reasonable" pricewise; there are "a few tables if you want to eat in" but the "dumpy" decor may make you think twice.

Leonard's Market ▣ *Seafood* — 26 | 21 | 25 | E

E 70s | 1437 Second Ave. (bet. 74th & 75th Sts.) | 212-744-2600 | www.leonardsnyc.com
Family-operated for three generations, this circa-1910 Yorkville outfit remains a steadfast source of "off-the-boat fresh" seafood and prime cut-to-order meats (with sidelines in smoked fish and game birds), proffered with "expert advice on how to prepare" any purchase; steep pricing can be a sticking point, but the neighborhood regulars know you "can't get better quality" or service.

Leonidas ▣ *Candy/Nuts* — 26 | 24 | 23 | E

E 50s | 485 Madison Ave. (bet. 51st & 52nd Sts.) | 212-980-2608
Financial District | 120 Broadway (Thames St.) | 212-766-6100
Financial District | 3 Hanover Sq. (bet. Pearl & William Sts.) | 212-422-9600
Financial District | 74 Trinity Pl. (bet. Rector & Thames Sts.) | 212-233-1111
800-900-2462 | www.leonidas-chocolate.com
"Such a rich, tasty, luscious indulgence" – these links of the Brussels-based chain are a "favorite guilty pleasure" for "Belgian-chocolate aficionados" who "go often to satisfy" "cravings"; the "exquisite" bonbons come "beautifully wrapped" in Ballotin boxes ("excellent gifts") and, though they're "priced for people with deep pockets", big spenders say they're "reasonable" "compared to other fancy" shops; P.S. the "tiny espresso bars" Downtown (sharing space with Manon Cafe) "give out free pieces" with your java.

Leo's Bagels *Bagels* — 24 | 20 | 18 | M

Financial District | 3 Hanover Sq. (bet. Pearl & William Sts.) | 212-785-4700 | www.leosbagels.com
Finally "you can get" a "wow-inducing" "NY bagel" in the Financial District, thanks to the "very lucky" appearance of this "reasonable" lunch and breakfast spot (opened by a co-founder of Murray's) where the carbs are rolled by hand, baked on the premises and available in "broker's dozens"; that there's "no competition nearby" might explain why service sometimes slips.

Le Pain Quotidien *Baked Goods* — 23 | 22 | 18 | M

E 40s | 937 Second Ave. (bet. 49th & 50th Sts.) | 646-240-4670
E 60s | 833 Lexington Ave. (bet. 63rd & 64th Sts.) | 212-755-5810
E 70s | 252 E. 77th St. (bet. 2nd & 3rd Aves.) | 212-249-8600
NoHo | 65 Bleecker St. (bet. B'way & Lafayette St.) | 646-797-4922
SoHo | 100 Grand St. (Mercer St.) | 212-625-9009

(continued)

Le Pain Quotidien

W 60s | 60 W. 65th St. (bet. B'way & CPW) | 212-721-4001
W 70s | 50 W. 72nd St. (bet. Columbus Ave. & CPW) | 212-712-9700
W 80s | 494 Amsterdam Ave. (84th St.) | 212-877-1200
W 90s | 2463 Broadway (91st St.) | 212-769-8879
W Village | 801 Broadway (11th St.) | 212-677-5277
www.lepainquotidien.us
Additional locations throughout the NY area

"Giving chains a good name", this Belgian bakery/cafe outfit and its "ubiquitous" branches offer "quality" "organic fare" that's a "dependable" and "easy option" for your "daily bread" given its "outstanding" "old-world-style" loaves and "wonderful pastries", not to mention "freshly made soups, sandwiches and salads"; the "high standards" and "homey" "European feel" are a "crowd-pleaser" even with service that occasionally "needs more *allez*."

Les Halles Market ● *Meat/Poultry*

| 23 | 21 | 20 | E |

Murray Hill | 411 Park Ave. S. (bet. 28th & 29th Sts.) | 212-679-4111 | www.leshalles.net

"Prime quality" is the hallmark of this "super" butcher adjoining the longtime Murray Hill brasserie, where expertly cut "French-style meats" lead a lineup that also includes sausage ("the merguez is exceptional") and seasonal specials like wild game; to confirm that the goods are worth their "costly" price tag, carnivores can "sit down and enjoy" a preview at the restaurant.

🛿 Levain Bakery ▣ *Baked Goods*

| 28 | 18 | 23 | M |

Harlem | 2167 Frederick Douglass Blvd. (117th St.) | 646-455-0952
W 70s | 167 W. 74th St. (bet. Amsterdam & Columbus Aves.) | 212-874-6080
www.levainbakery.com

This "minuscule" UWS bakery (with a slightly roomier Harlem offshoot) "reigns supreme" with its "heavenly", "moist, rich", "gargantuan" chocolate chip cookies ("more like a meal than a snack") that devotees claim "make life worth living" and repay "every penny and pound"; insiders also "don't pass up" the "fabulous" breads, "buttery" scones and brioche – and to sweeten the deal, each day's unsold goods are donated to charity.

LIC Market *Specialty Shop*

| ▽ 25 | 25 | 24 | M |

LIC | 21-52 44th Dr. (23rd St.) | Queens | 718-361-0013 | www.licmarket.com

Long Island City denizens rely on this "little gem" of a market as an "oasis" offering a select, natural-leaning stash of "awesome gourmet" groceries plus jars of housemade specialties like fig jam, olive tapenade and pickled baby carrots; there's also a "homey" eatery in back, where the same "quality" comestibles show up on the menu.

Liddabit Sweets ▣ *Candy/Nuts*

| ▽ 25 | 21 | 24 | M |

Location varies | no phone | www.liddabitsweets.com

Signature beer-and-pretzel caramels are among the "cool" confections handmade in small batches by a duo of young, artisan candymakers who use as many organic and local ingredients as possible; visitors to their stall at the Brooklyn Flea most weekends (and the New Amsterdam market in season) also find "excellent" brittles, lollipops, jellies and honeycomb among the "delicious treats"; P.S. its goods are available at numerous gourmet retail outlets, and can be ordered online.

Liebman's ● Deli — 24 | 20 | 20 | M

Bronx | 552 W. 235th St. (Johnson Ave.) | 718-548-4534 | www.liebmansdeli.com

If you're "wondering where all the old-school Jewish delis have gone, look no further" than this Bronx bastion, a "local" fixture since the 1950s where the kosher "delights" are "an embarrassment of riches"; with the "finest cold cuts" (notably "wonderful pastrami"), knishes and other classics prepared to "perfection", it's "worth a trip to Riverdale even if you can't afford to live there"; P.S. it now serves wine and beer, and also caters.

LifeThyme Natural Market ●◑▣ Health — 22 | 16 | 18 | M

G Village | 410 Sixth Ave. (bet. 8th & 9th Sts.) | 212-420-9099 | www.lifethymemarket.com

Expect far "more than vitamins and protein shakes" at this Greenwich Village "crunchy" haven, where the "excellent range" of "natural and organic" goods encompasses everything from the "usual" groceries and produce to "alternative" eats like raw foods, "creative" prepared dishes and "vegan cakes and brownies" from a "healthy bakery"; though the layout's somewhat "narrow and crowded", prices are "fair" and "you can get help if you ask."

Li-Lac Chocolates ▣ Candy/Nuts — 26 | 24 | 23 | E

E 40s | Grand Central Mkt. | Lexington Ave. (43rd St.) | 212-370-4866 | 866-898-2462●
W Village | 40 Eighth Ave. (Jane St.) | 212-924-2280 | 866-898-2462
Sunset Park | 213 50th St. (2nd Ave.) | Brooklyn | 718-567-9500
www.li-lacchocolates.com

A "veteran" "all-American" confectioner, this West Village "institution" is under new ownership but still producing "the best fudge", "unbeatable buttercrunch", "delicious caramels" and "marvelous handmade chocolates" in a multitude of "artistic" shapes "almost too good to eat"; a few still "miss the atmospheric Christopher Street store", but most focus on the treats' own "old-time" appeal, whether to satisfy a "craving" or as a "great hostess gift"; P.S. the Grand Central outpost is just the ticket for an "impulse" purchase, and there's a retail shop at the Sunset Park factory too.

Lily O'Brien's ●◑▣ Candy/Nuts — 22 | 22 | 19 | M

W 40s | 36 W. 40th St. (bet. 5th & 6th Aves.) | 212-575-0631 | www.lilyscafenyc.com

Appreciated as a "wonderful little gem" in "touristy Bryant Park", this Midtown chocolatier offers "fantastic" imported Irish sweets handmade in the Emerald Isle (think sticky toffee truffles, honeycomb crisp and hazelnut torte), along with prettily wrapped collections and gift baskets; there's "a limited selection" but you get "a free piece" to sample in its "cute", cocoa-hued cafe, where you can sip "the finest hot chocolate" and nibble on croissants, cakes, cookies and "awesome macarons" baked on the premises; P.S. it now serves sandwiches and soups.

Lindt Chocolate Shop *Candy/Nuts*

| 25 | 24 | 22 | M |

E 50s | Rolex Bldg. | 665 Fifth Ave. (53rd St.) | 212-754-5191
W 50s | 692 Fifth Ave. (54th St.) | 212-582-3047
www.lindtusa.com

Links of the Swiss chain with a "worldwide reputation" for "quality", these Midtown boutiques offer "heavenly" bonbons that are like "the Goldilocks of chocolates – not too sweet, not too bitter, just right"; perennial favorites such as "dreamy" Lindor truffles star among a "vast assortment" of goodies that remain a "draw" despite "competition from the independents", and they "make very nice gifts" to boot, so you can "spread the joy."

✷ Lioni Fresh Mozzarella *Cheese/Dairy*

| 27 | 18 | 19 | M |

Bensonhurst | 7803 15th Ave. (bet. 78th & 79th Sts.) | Brooklyn | 718-232-1411 | www.lioniheroes.com

This mom-and-pop deli in Bensonhurst will have you "hooked" on "super-fresh" mozzarella that's "soft", "delicious" and "dripping with cream", not to mention the smoked and dried varieties and ricotta; the massive sandwich menu has more than 125 "super-size" heros that are named for Italian celebrities, taste "terrific" and can "feed a family of four" – factor in "decent" prices, and "what more could you ask for?"

Little Brown Chocolate
Bakery & Coffee ☻ *Baked Goods*

| 21 | 18 | 19 | M |

E 80s | 1269 Lexington Ave. (bet. 85th & 86th Sts.) | 212-828-2233 | www.ourlittlebrown.com

The 'chocolate and coffee love affair' is the motto of this UES "neighborhood hangout" from Oded Brenner, founder of Max Brenner chocolate, which is appreciated for its organic Kobricks java, Nutella lattes and, of course, "delicious hot chocolate", plus housemade pastries and chocolates; a dissatisfied few claim it all "looks better than it is", but the fact that the small quarters are "always packed" speaks for itself.

Little Cupcake Bake Shop *Baked Goods*

| 23 | 26 | 22 | M |

NoLita | 30 Prince St. (Mott St.) | 212-941-9100 ☻
Bay Ridge | 9102 Third Ave. (91st St.) | Brooklyn | 718-680-4465
www.littlecupcakebakeshop.com

A "little slice" of "sugar heaven" in Bay Ridge, this "niche bakery" is guaranteed to make your "mouth water" with its enticing variety of "wonderful cupcakes", baked in-house along with puddings, pies and layer cakes; lodged in a "cute" cafe space, it's "pretty expensive" for the area, but unsurprisingly it still "attracts the crowds"; P.S. the NoLita branch opened post-Survey.

| | QUALITY | DISPLAY | SERVICE | COST |

Little Pie Company ⌐ *Baked Goods* | 24 | 20 | 20 | M |

W 40s | 424 W. 43rd St. (bet. 9th & 10th Aves.) | 212-736-4780 | www.littlepiecompany.com

"Worth the stop again and again", this Theater District bakery is famed for its "superlative" fresh-baked pies, an "addictive" fusion of "top-quality" fillings and "crust that melts in your mouth" – particularly the "must-have" sour cream–apple-walnut variety; a "staple for Thanksgiving" ("order early") "or any occasion", all agree it "deserves its status as a dessert destination."

Lloyd's Carrot Cake *Baked Goods* | ▽ 29 | 15 | 24 | M |

NEW **E 90s** | 1553 Lexington Ave. (99th St.) | 212-831-9156
Bronx | 6087 Broadway (246th St.) | 718-548-9020
www.lloydscarrotcake.com

"Wow, what a carrot cake!" enthuse admirers in the know who maintain that the eponymous, made-from-scratch specialty at this tiny, family-run Bronx baker (with a new East 90s offshoot) is "by far the best in the city"; it's a frill-free operation and the small selection of other cakes and pies is "not as good", but when an "excellent" dessert can double as a vegetable, "what's better?"

Ⓩ Lobel's Prime Meats ⌐ *Meat/Poultry* | 28 | 24 | 26 | VE |

E 80s | 1096 Madison Ave. (bet. 82nd & 83rd Sts.) | 212-737-1373 | 800-556-2357 | www.lobels.com

Now in its fifth generation of family ownership, this "first-class" UES "institution" is still renowned for the "unquestionable quality" of its "sublime meats", from "awesome Wagyu", lamb and filet mignon to hot dogs and specialty items; each "unforgettable" cut is "custom" trimmed with genuine "graciousness" by "expert" butchers, and while it's notorious for charging "a king's ransom", don't hesitate to "rob a bank" – "you'll agree it's worth every penny"; P.S. the online ordering and shipping service "works like a Swiss clock."

Ⓩ Lobster Place ⌐ *Seafood* | 27 | 24 | 24 | M |

Chelsea | Chelsea Mkt. | 75 Ninth Ave. (bet. 15th & 16th Sts.) | 212-255-5672 | www.lobsterplace.com

"One step away from buying your fish off the boat", this Chelsea Market staple provides an "overflowing bounty" of "amazingly fresh" seafood, whether it's the eponymous "excellent" lobsters or "just about anything else from the ocean"; finatics also applaud the "personal" service, "fair" prices and "abundant selection of sushi" and prepared foods – "what more do you want?"

Locanda Verde *Baked Goods* | 26 | 24 | 19 | E |

TriBeCa | Greenwich Hotel | 377 Greenwich St. (Moore St.) | 212-925-3797 | www.locandaverdenyc.com

Nestled inside the Greenwich Hotel's "vibrant" Italian eatery, this TriBeCa bakery counter showcases "second-to-none" desserts courtesy of pastry chef Karen DeMasco, who oversees a "lovely" display devoted to the "fantastic" likes of olive oil coffee cake, polenta muffins, strawberry scones and lemon tarts; since attracting notice in sweet-tooth circles, it's quickly become a "must-go."

	QUALITY	DISPLAY	SERVICE	COST

L'Olivier ⌨ *Flowers* | ▽ 27 | 29 | 22 | VE |

Chelsea | 213 W. 14th St. (7th Ave.) | 212-255-2828
E 70s | 19 E. 76th St. (bet. 5th & Madison Aves.) | 212-774-7676
800-255-2828 | www.lolivier.com

Everything's coming up roses at Olivier Giugni's eponymous floral design ateliers in Chelsea and on the UES, where a simple bouquet can double as decorative art and a typical table centerpiece contains flora from across the globe; it's the perfect place, in other words, to find an arrangement for "somebody very difficult to satisfy", and though the cost is also demanding, "beauty is sometimes worth the price."

NEW London Candy Co. ⌨ *Candy* | ▽ 25 | 23 | 25 | M |

E 90s | 1442 Lexington Ave. (94th St.) | 212-427-2129 |
www.thelondoncandycompany.com

For sweets that are simply smashing, English expats and local sugar fiends head to this "cheerful" new UES British candy emporium proffering hard-to-find dainties imported from Old Blighty, a "quite tempting array" of "old favorites" (Cadbury chocolates, Nestlé Lion Bars, Maynard Wine Gums) and contemporary items (treats from London-based Hope and Greenwood) that taste like a "bite of" U.K. "heaven"; the premises are plastered with Union Jacks and feature a cafe that sells Stumptown coffee and, of course, "incomparable teas."

☑ Lorenzo & Maria's Kitchen *Prepared Food* | 27 | 26 | 25 | VE |

E 80s | 1418 Third Ave. (bet. 80th & 81st Sts.) | 212-794-1080

"They pull you in" with "enticing" displays at this classy Yorkville kitchen, celebrated since 1978 for "superb takeout" and catering centered on "delicious" "homemade" prepared foods (including meat, fish and "charming little chicken pot pies"), plus cookies, cakes and tarts; the "wonderful" cooking commands premium prices, but "if you're feeling flush" this is "one of the best."

Los Paisanos *Meat/Poultry* | ▽ 26 | 19 | 27 | M |

Cobble Hill | 162 Smith St. (bet. Bergen & Wyckoff Sts.) | Brooklyn |
718-855-2641 | www.lospaisanosmeatmarket.com

A Smith Street "tradition" dating to 1965, this "small" but "fabulous" butcher and Italian deli packs "a lot to choose from" in the way of "meat specialties" like dry-aged beef, pork and chicken (all organic) supplemented by sausage, cold cuts and exotic rarities (ostrich, anyone?); add a "great array" of pastas, cheeses and olive oils proffered "without attitude or high prices", and paisanos promise it's "worth the trip from any other neighborhood."

Lucy's Whey ⌨ *Cheese/Dairy* | ▽ 29 | 26 | 29 | E |

Chelsea | Chelsea Mkt. | 75 Ninth Ave. (bet. 15th & 16th Sts.) |
212-463-9500 | www.lucyswhey.com

"Cheesemongers who care" offer a "personal shopping experience" at this "welcome addition to Chelsea Market", an offshoot of the East Hampton fromage shop that specializes in "top-quality" American farmstead cheeses "you won't find elsewhere" (no won-

QUALITY | DISPLAY | SERVICE | COST

der it's "pricey"); if you "don't know what you want" they'll "happily cut you slivers" to try, and if you seek a party platter "they can take care of that too."

Lung Moon Bakery ✏ *Baked Goods*　▽ 20 | 14 | 15 | I
Chinatown | 83 Mulberry St. (bet. Bayard & Canal Sts.) | 212-349-4945
Long a "go-to" for "traditional Chinese pastries", this durable Chinatown bakery ranks with "the best" for its specialty moon cakes, available year-round but "a must during moon festival time"; loyalists lured into its orbit by "consistent quality" and "good prices" claim it's also "worth a try" for pork and chicken buns, bean cakes, custard tarts and seasonal treats.

Macaron Café 🖃 *Baked Goods*　24 | 19 | 17 | E
E 50s | 625 Madison Ave. (59th St.) | 212-486-2470
Garment District | 161 W. 36th St. (bet. B'way & 7th Ave.) | 212-564-3525
www.macaroncafe.com
"Delicious" macarons "so authentic they'll transport you to Paris with one bite" are the raison d'être of this Garment District Gallic nook and its East Side sib, "tiny" showcases for a "colorful display" of their signature cookie in 20 froufrou flavors; there are also sandwiches, salads and Mariage Frères teas, and if it's all "a bit pricey", it sure beats paying "the airfare" to France; P.S. an East 40s store is in the works at 750 Third Avenue.

Macy's Cellar ◗🖃 *Cookware*　23 | 21 | 16 | M
Garment District | 151 W. 34th St. (bet. 6th & 7th Aves.) | 212-695-4400, ext. 1468 | 800-456-2297 | www.macys.com
A cook's "heaven below" the famed Midtown department store, this basement kitchenware section is so "extensive" you'll find "stuff you never knew existed but gotta have" extol loyalists who scoop up cookware, cutlery, appliances and gadgets from "larger, well-known brands"; when it's "running promotions" you can "pick up a real steal" – but just "be prepared to find" it "without much help from the scarce staff."

Madonia Bakery ✏ *Baked Goods*　26 | 21 | 21 | I
Bronx | 2348 Arthur Ave. (187th St.) | 718-295-5573
"Buy extra" because "you'll eat some on the way home" urge aficionados of this "family-owned" Arthur Avenue bakery, an "old-world" Italian holdout where the "fabulous" "specialty breads" (especially the "divine" olive and prosciutto loaves) emerge from the ovens "crusty but light as a feather"; "cannoli filled on the spot" and "amazing" cookies also account for its "must-stop" status in the neighborhood.

Magnolia Bakery ◗🖃 *Baked Goods*　21 | 21 | 18 | M
E 40s | Grand Central Terminal | dining concourse (42nd St. & Vanderbilt Ave.) | 212-682-3588
NEW **E 50s** | Bloomingdale's | 1000 Third Ave., 1st fl. (bet. 59th & 60th Sts.) | 212-265-5320
W 40s | 1240 Sixth Ave. (49th St.) | 212-767-1123

(continued)

Magnolia Bakery
W 60s | 200 Columbus Ave. (69th St.) | 212-724-8101
W Village | 401 Bleecker St. (11th St.) | 212-462-2572
www.magnoliabakery.com

"Gimme sugar!" cry "the faithful" at this wildly "popular" West Village "destination" (with Midtown and UWS spin-offs), a "cute", "old-fashioned" bakery that "still rules" with "luscious" cupcakes "like June Cleaver used to bake" topped with "oh-so-buttery" pastel frosting sweet enough to "make your teeth ring", plus other "goodies" like "out-of-this-world" banana pudding; you'll have to contend with "mile-long" lines of "tourists" to experience the Bleecker Street original's "charm", but the other locations "don't have the crazy crowds."

☑ NEW Maison Ladurée *Baked Goods*   28 | 28 | 25 | VE
E 70s | 864 Madison Ave. (bet. 70th & 71st Sts.) | 646-558-3157 | www.laduree.fr

"Do you wear these little jewels or eat them?" muse admirers of what may be "the most treasured macarons on the planet", displayed like bijoux, at this UES outpost of the famed Parisian "luxury" confectioner, whose *magnifique* array of "crisp, airy", flown-in-from-France meringue sandwich cookies come in a "colorful" array of "decadent flavors"; devotees who brave "ever-present, lengthy lines" and "very expensive" prices declare the "superb" quality and "coddling" service "well worth" it – it's "the next best thing to a trip to Paris"; P.S. one of those "beautiful boxes" makes the "perfect gift."

Maison Prive *Caterer/Events*   - | - | - | E
Location varies | 914-843-5068 | www.maison-prive.com
By appointment only

Trained in the kitchens of Thomas Keller, Daniel Boulud and other top-drawer chefs, husband-and-wife team Jennifer and James Vellano have channeled their culinary expertise into this boutique catering enterprise, which is based in New Rochelle but does events in NYC, the Hamptons, Westchester and Lower Connecticut; generally eschewing set menus, they tailor dishes to their high-end clients, building them around seasonal, sustainable ingredients.

Make My Cake *Baked Goods*   26 | 22 | 21 | M
Harlem | 121 St. Nicholas Ave. (116th St.) | 212-932-0833
Harlem | 2380 Adam Clayton Powell Jr. Blvd. (139th St.) | 212-234-2344
www.makemycake.com

"Definitely one of Harlem's best bakeries", this Southern specialist makes its name with "homestyle" desserts like sweet potato cheesecake, "truly amazing" red velvet renditions, butter-cream and German chocolate cakes, cupcakes and other "tasty treats"; it's "not cheap", but given the "outstanding quality" and hospitality from a staff of "great folks", it's a "worthwhile stop" for birthdays, weddings and catering.

	QUALITY	DISPLAY	SERVICE	COST

Malaysia Beef Jerky ⌨️🏮 *Meat/Poultry* ▽ | 25 | 15 | 21 | I

Chinatown | 95A Elizabeth St. (bet. Grand & Hester Sts.) |
212-965-0796 | www.malaysiabeefjerky.com

"One of Chinatown's best-kept secrets", this simple storefront is devoted exclusively to "mouthwatering jerky" prepared Singapore-Malaysian style, with chunks of beef, pork and chicken coated in regular or spicy sauce, grilled to tenderness "right before your eyes" and purveyed as whole or thin-sliced tidbits; clued-in meat eaters who deem it a "must-try" gloat "this is the real stuff."

M & I International Foods 🌑 *Specialty Shop* | 22 | 20 | 10 | I

Brighton Bch | 249 Brighton Beach Ave. (bet. Brighton 1st &
Brighton 2nd Sts.) | Brooklyn | 718-615-1011

"Like a trip to Eastern Europe", this Slavic supermarket in Brighton Beach is a double-decker "mecca" "straight out of central casting" where the "vast selection" includes meat and sausage, "excellent smoked fish" and caviar, "unbelievable breads" and pastries, cheeses, imported groceries and "freshly prepared foods" like chicken Kiev and beef stroganoff; the more authentic items "can be a little rough" "on American palates" and service is "brusque" ("it helps if you speak Russian"), but "good buys" abound – and it's "always an adventure."

M&M's World 🌓⌨️ *Candy* | 21 | 26 | 17 | M

W 40s | 1600 Broadway (48th St.) | 212-295-3850 |
www.mymms.com

Three floors of "everything M&M" make this 25,000-sq.-ft. Times Square emporium a "kid's dream" and a "happy place" for anyone wanting "a fix" of those "glorious round candies" (including some "varieties you can't get elsewhere"), on one wall displayed more than a million strong in a "dizzying variety" of colors; there are also toys, "magnets, mugs, bags" and "every piece of branded kitsch you could want", and while naturally it's "mobbed with tourists" and prices are higher than at the "drugstore or supermarket" – "man is it fun!"

Mangia *Prepared Food* | 23 | 22 | 18 | M

E 40s | 16 E. 48th St. (bet. 5th & Madison Aves.) | 212-754-7600
Flatiron | 22 W. 23rd St. (bet. 5th & 6th Aves.) |
212-647-0200 🌑
Garment District | 45 W. 39th St. (bet. 5th & 6th Aves.) |
212-921-9100
W 50s | 50 W. 57th St. (bet. 5th & 6th Aves.) | 212-582-5882
www.mangiatogo.com

Desk-setters declare this "convenient" threesome "top-notch" for lunch "in a hurry" thanks to an all-but-"overwhelming" selection of "beautifully displayed" prepared foods comprising "well-crafted sandwiches" and panini, "gourmet salad bars", pizzas, hot or cold specialty items and the "temptation" of "lovely" baked goods; they're a "costly" option, but "better quality and choice" "packs 'em in" – and they're also known for "efficient" office catering; P.S. the Garment District branch offers organic fare.

	QUALITY	DISPLAY	SERVICE	COST

Manhattan Fruit Exchange ●◑⊞ *Produce* — 25 | 22 | 17 | I

Chelsea | Chelsea Mkt. | 75 Ninth Ave. (bet. 15th & 16th Sts.) | 212-989-2444

"If it grows in the earth, they'll have it" at this Chelsea Market "cornerstone", a "premier" purveyor of an "awesome" variety of "beautiful" fruits and veggies that's well stocked with "exotics" you'd have "trouble finding elsewhere", not to mention "assorted cheeses", candy, nuts and other "goodies"; that "they only accept cash" is a "downside", but nonetheless it's "hard to shop anywhere else" given the "dirt-cheap" prices.

☑ Manhattan Fruitier ▣ *Specialty Shop* — 25 | 27 | 24 | VE

Murray Hill | 105 E. 29th St. (bet. Lexington & Park Aves.) | 212-686-0404 | www.mfruit.com

"One to go to" when you aim to "make an impression", this Murray Hill maestro specializes in "first-class" gift baskets laden with "beautiful" presentations of exotic fruit, filled out with a gourmet array of chocolates, caviar, artisanal cheeses, dried fruits and nuts; with "excellent" options in all sizes and "great service" (including online ordering and delivery), it's "just perfect" for that "very special" someone – though naturally going for a "top choice" means paying "top dollar."

Marché Madison ● *Prepared Food* — 21 | 20 | 19 | VE

E 70s | 931 Madison Ave. (74th St.) | 212-794-3360 | www.marchemadisonvin.com

"If you're in the neighborhood", this "cute little" Upper East Side stalwart plies "good to high-quality" provisions spanning produce, deli dishes and the immediate area's "most extensive selection of prepared foods" like rotisserie chicken; then again, critics caution "because of the location" it's "frightfully expensive" for "nothing out of the ordinary."

Margot Pâtisserie *Baked Goods* — 23 | 18 | 19 | M

W 70s | 2109 Broadway (74th St.) | 212-721-0076

"Tasty French-style pastries" that are "some of the best" on the UWS are the thing at this "small", "very European" bakeshop, a "hidden treasure" known to locals as a "reliable" supplier of croissants, pain au chocolat, fruit tarts, cakes and baguette sandwiches at "reasonable prices"; it's also an "old-fashioned" haven where would-be boulevardiers can "relax and have a good café au lait."

MarieBelle's Fine Treats & Chocolates ▣ *Candy/Nuts* — 26 | 26 | 23 | E

SoHo | 484 Broome St. (bet. W. B'way & Wooster St.) | 212-431-1768 | www.mariebelle.com

"Chocolate as art" sums up the ornate, "ladylike" confections at Maribel Lieberman's "delightful" SoHo shop, where the "delicious" morsels come "exquisitely presented" and are "worth every sou" of the "king's ransom" they cost; as for the "cute cafe" in back, aficionados say it's "like being in Paris" to sit there and sip "fabulous" "rich Aztec" hot chocolate.

	QUALITY	DISPLAY	SERVICE	COST

Market *Specialty Shop* ▽ 24 | 23 | 25 | M

Ditmas Park | 1211 Cortelyou Rd. (Westminster Rd.) | Brooklyn | 718-284-4446 | www.mimishummus.com

Yes, it's "tiny", but "don't underestimate" this "welcome addition" to Ditmas Park, an adjunct to the neighboring eatery Mimi's Hummus that "enriches the neighborhood" with "overflowing" shelves of "selective" gourmet goods; it concentrates on Middle Eastern specialties, but also stocks "artisanal cheeses", "delicious" jams, coffee and tea, bread from Sullivan Street Bakery, small-brewery beer and more, with a "smiling staff" that takes care to "rotate inventory" so there's "always something new."

⊠ Marlow & Daughters *Meat/Poultry* 28 | 24 | 25 | E

Williamsburg | 95 Broadway (Berry St.) | Brooklyn | 718-388-5700 | www.marlowanddaughters.com

"Better than fantastic" is the word from meat mavens who "couldn't get along without" this Williamsburg butcher (from the team behind Diner and Marlow & Sons), where the sausage is made in-house and the beef, pork and poultry is sourced from local and sustainable suppliers "they vet" so carnivores can "enjoy eating with a clear conscience"; it also carries a few grocery items like local cheeses and produce, and while "it's on the expensive side", boosters advise "save up" – the quality's "just about the best."

⊠ Marlow & Sons ● *Specialty Shop* 27 | 23 | 21 | E

Williamsburg | 81 Broadway (Berry St.) | Brooklyn | 718-384-1441 | www.marlowandsons.com

"Part market, part restaurant", this next-door annex to Williamsburg's Diner is a general store spliced with an "informal" wine-and-oyster bar/eatery; at the front market epicureans can choose from a "delicious" assortment of organic dairy, pastries and chocolates, and though prices run steep, the "welcoming feel" and staffers who "really care" help make it "satisfying in all ways."

Martha's Country Bakery ● *Baked Goods* 22 | 24 | 21 | M

Astoria | 3621 Ditmars Blvd. (bet. 36th & 37th Sts.) | Queens | 718-545-9737
Bayside | 41-06 Bell Blvd. (41st Ave.) | Queens | 718-225-5200
Forest Hills | 70-28 Austin St. (70th Rd.) | Queens | 718-544-0088
www.marthascountrybakery.com

Queens natives are "so glad" these "cheery" bakeries are giving local competitors a "run for their money" with its "wonderful" housemade selection of "indulgent" cakes, cupcakes, pies and other old-fashioned "sweets"; they're "popular" spots with "value" rates, so no surprise the "cozy" cafe areas "get busy" with folks who "can't wait to dig in."

Martin Bros. ▽ 24 | 21 | 24 | M
Wines & Spirits ●▣ *Wine/Liquor*

W 100s | 2781 Broadway (107th St.) | 212-222-8218 | www.martinbrotherswine.com

Given "so many choices per square foot", this stalwart UWS vintner is a "fabulous" wellspring for spirits featuring 2,500 international wines both mainstream and "unusual" (Burgundy and Bordeaux are strong suits) and upwards of 150 single-malt whiskeys; extra incentives include regular tastings and "amazingly" "helpful and amusing" staffers who "know their stuff."

Martine's Chocolates 🖃 Candy/Nuts

| 25 | 23 | 23 | E |

E 50s | Bloomingdale's | 1000 Third Ave., 6th fl. (bet. 59th & 60th Sts.) | 212-705-2347 ◗
E 80s | 400 E. 82nd St. (bet. 1st & York Aves.) | 212-744-6289
www.martineschocolates.com

"Gifts to the neighborhood", these East Side chocolatiers concoct "fresh", handmade "luxe" treats in view on the premises, both in the "irresistible" Bloomie's original, where shoppers gladly "schlep to the sixth floor", as well as its "keyhole" of an outpost; high prices are a hallmark, as is the "vast selection" of "exotic shapes" (the newest molds are dogs and frogs), but it's the "brilliant quality" that has the smitten asking "may I sleep here?"

Martin's Pretzels 🖃 Baked Goods

| 26 | 17 | 22 | I |

Location varies | 315-628-4927 | www.martinspretzels.com
For "top quality" "without equivocation", this longtime Greenmarket vendor "lives up to the hype" with its "always fresh" hand-rolled hard pretzels, "excellent" "crunchy" twists available in salty or plain, traditional or whole-wheat versions; addicts who "crave them regularly" sigh "thank goodness they're always there."

Mast Brothers Chocolate 🖃 Candy/Nuts

∇ | 25 | 20 | 20 | E |

Williamsburg | 105 N. Third St. (bet. Berry St. & Wythe Ave.) | Brooklyn | 718-388-2625 | www.mastbrothers.com
"The smell is intoxicating" at this Williamsburg factory, where a pair of "expert" siblings makes "superb" artisanal chocolate from scratch, roasting and grinding cacao beans imported from small farms and crafting "amazing" bars ("wrapped in beautiful paper") and bonbons, plus now a back bakery turns out cakes and cookies too; a few skeptics call the goods "ordinary and overpriced", but most who visit its vintage warehouse–style space or pick up bars at gourmet markets around town aver they're simply "awesome."

Mauzone Caterer

| 21 | 14 | 18 | M |

Flushing | 72-30 Main St. (bet. 72nd & 73rd Aves.) | Queens | 718-261-7723
This long-established Flushing purveyor of kosher prepared dishes "like mama makes" provides the likes of "crispy" fried chicken, kugel, soups and sides for off-site catering; sure, it could be "more innovative", but when your wedding, party or event's "gotta" satisfy "that requirement and seal", the quality's "consistently" "very good."

Max & Mina's Homemade Inc. ◗⊄ Ice Cream

∇ | 25 | 23 | 27 | M |

Flushing | 71-26 Main St. (bet. 71st Rd. & 72nd Ave.) | Queens | 718-793-8629 | www.maxandminasicecream.com
One to "put on your bucket list", this Queens-based "standard-bearer" for kosher ice cream creates "crazy-delicious" concoctions

in the "wildest flavors", e.g. lox, horseradish, Cajun and red wine, but churns out the "typical ones" too; the brainchild of a biochemist, its scoops are "highly addictive", and if you "make a run" to the Flushing store-cum-lab, the "really nice" staff "will cheerfully give samples"; P.S. closes early on Friday and all day Saturday.

Max Brenner, Chocolate by the Bald Man ❶ ⌨ *Candy/Nuts*

| 22 | 24 | 18 | E |

G Village | 841 Broadway (bet. 13th & 14th Sts.) | 646-467-8803 | www.maxbrenner.com

The "only thing missing is Willie Wonka" at this "buzzy" Village "paradise for chocolate lovers", a link in the Israeli-founded "novelty" chain dedicated to the "magical cocoa bean" in many "fun" "forms and permutations" (the "chocolate pizza is a must"); it's "overrun by tourists", "service takes an age" and "it'll cost you" too, but those seeking a "satisfying" "sugar overload" say it's "worth the craziness."

Mazzola Bakery ⊘ *Baked Goods*

| ∇ 27 | 24 | 22 | M |

Carroll Gardens | 192 Union St. (Henry St.) | Brooklyn | 718-643-1719

Carroll Gardens locals have "only the best to say about" this "classic" "neighborhood institution", a circa-1927 Italian bakery that's mazzively adored for an "excellent" lineup of "classic" breads and rolls ("no better in the city") led by its prosciutto-packed lard loaves; partisans also plug the "fabulous coffee" and "mouthwatering croissants", muffins and pastries.

McCabes Wines & Spirits ❶ *Wine/Liquor*

| 22 | 19 | 21 | M |

E 70s | 1347 Third Ave. (77th St.) | 212-737-0790 | www.mccabeswine.com

Vintages "for every taste and pocketbook" qualify this "old-fashioned" shop as an UES "oenophile's local choice", where the "small" space is "crammed" with French, German and boutique California wines, along with 300 kosher labels, single-malt scotches and small-batch bourbons out of a "whiskey-lover's dream"; cited for "last-minute convenience" and a "friendly" staff to clue in "the uninitiated", it's typically "bustling."

McClure's Pickles ⌨ *Specialty Shop*

| ∇ 27 | 21 | 23 | M |

Location varies | 917-673-8795 | www.mcclurespickles.com

"These brothers know their pickles" rave devoted jarheads at this Greenmarket and Brooklyn Flea "favorite", whose "juicy, well-seasoned" specimens are made "fresh" from local produce and offered in two "amazingly good" types: "real" garlic dills and a spicy variety "with a nice kick"; tickled fans also tout the brine-based Bloody Mary mix ("I'm obsessed") and relish.

⦿ McNulty's Tea & Coffee Co. ❶⌨ *Coffee/Tea*

| 28 | 23 | 25 | M |

W Village | 109 Christopher St. (bet. Bleecker & Hudson Sts.) | 212-242-5351 | 800-356-5200 | www.mcnultys.com

"They've been here forever" (well, since 1895), and this West Village "gem" remains a "nirvana for real coffee-lovers" given its

QUALITY | DISPLAY | SERVICE | COST

"terrific inventory" of "high-quality" brews bolstered by "apothecary jars" filled with "more teas than you can shake a stick at"; "pro" staffers will "steer you" to the perfect blend at a "decent price", and the "wonderful aromas" suffusing the "vintage" digs are "an intoxicating experience" – "some things never change, thank God!"

The Meadow 🔲 *Specialty Shop* ▽ 29 | 28 | 26 | E

W Village | 523 Hudson St. (bet. Charles & 10th Sts.) | 212-645-4633 | 888-388-4633 | www.atthemeadow.com

An outpost of a Portland, OR, shop owned by Mark Bitterman, author of *Salted: A Manifesto on the World's Most Essential Mineral,* not surprisingly this "beautiful", minuscule West Villager specializes in the aforementioned seasoning, offering a "most impressive" selection of some 100 artisan varieties hailing from more than 25 countries; the rest of the eclectic goods overseen by a "helpful" staff includes high-end chocolate bars, specialty cocktail bitters (from Angostura and Peychaud's to an organic line by Urban Moonshine), syrups and even fresh flowers; P.S. it also offers classes and workshops.

The Meat Hook *Meat/Poultry* ▽ 27 | 23 | 26 | M

Williamsburg | 100 Frost St. (bet. Leonard St. & Manhattan Ave.) | Brooklyn | 718-349-5033 | www.the-meathook.com

"Noticeably tastier" meat is the métier of this "funky" Williamsburg butcher that shares space with the Brooklyn Kitchen and is renowned for its "knowledgeable" staff whose on-site butchering of "awesome" stock from small "local" producers yields "excellent" housemade sausages and charcuterie, as well as grass-fed beef, lamb and pork; it's "not a huge selection", but cuts "of the highest class" and "fair prices" hook "hordes" of carnivores who consider it "heaven on earth."

Mediterranean Foods ◑🔲 *Specialty Shop* 26 | 20 | 22 | M

Astoria | Agora Plaza | 23-18 31st St. (bet. 23rd Ave. & 23rd Rd.) | Queens | 718-721-0221
Astoria | 30-12 34th St. (30th Ave.) | Queens | 718-728-6166
www.mediterraneanfoodsny.com

"This is where to shop" for "high-quality" Greek specialties agree hungry Hellenists at this Astoria duo, home to a "wide variety" of imported victuals including "fabulous" "fresh fetas" and other cheeses, olives "picked by those who know", oils, yogurts and packaged foods; with cordial service and "low, low prices", it's a "must-visit" for your next "ethnic-inspired" spread.

Melange ◑ *Prepared Food* 23 | 15 | 19 | M

E 60s | 1188 First Ave. (bet. 64th & 65th Sts.) | 212-249-3743
E 60s | 1277 First Ave. (bet. 68th & 69th Sts.) | 212-535-7773
www.melangefinefood.com

Bringing the "Middle East to the Upper East", this duo is "packed" with an affordable mélange of Levantine and Med prepared foods, including "incredible" falafel, hummus and "wonderful baklava"; they're also "convenient" for dried fruits and nuts, and they have a "great cheese selection", with user-friendly "suggestions" from the staff on the side.

Michael-Towne Wines & Spirits ● *Wine/Liquor*

▽ 27 24 23 M

Brooklyn Heights | 73 Clark St. (Henry St.) | Brooklyn | 718-875-3667

A "neighborhood staple for sure", this "outstanding" Brooklyn Heights liquor mart lets the locals go to town browsing an "admirable", globe-trotting wine selection and a "huge range" of spirits with strengths in bourbons, single malts and sakes; the "excellent choices" are overseen by a "competent" team, and though views vary on the cost ("fair" vs. "expensive"), "discounts" on cases and Thursday–Saturday tastings are extra fillips.

Migliorelli Farm ✑ *Produce*

25 21 20 M

Location varies | 845-757-3276 | www.migliorelli.com

For "selection and quality", this Greenmarket veteran "stands out" as "one of the best" purveyors of "wonderful" seasonal produce "picked fresh" in the Hudson Valley by third-generation farmers "who really care"; it's "reliable" for a "wide variety" ("greens are the best bets") at a "decent price", and dedicated vegheads are grateful the goods "keep coming" through the fall and winter.

Milk & Cookies Bakery ●▤ *Baked Goods*

25 20 20 M

W Village | 19 Commerce St. (bet. Bedford St. & 7th Ave.) | 212-243-1640 | www.milkandcookiesbakery.com

"Give yourself a little treat" at this "charming" West Village "gem", which custom-bakes "wonderful" "fresh" cookies to order once you name your preference of dough flavor and mix-ins; premade cookies, bars and brownies are on hand to sweeten the deal, and everything's a "divine" match for "delicious ice cream sandwiches", shakes and sundaes via Il Laboratorio del Gelato and Ronnybrook Farms Dairy milk ("how can you go wrong?").

Mill Basin Kosher Deli ▤ *Deli*

24 19 20 M

Mill Basin | 5823 Ave. T (59th St.) | Brooklyn | 718-241-4910 | www.millbasindeli.com

Still furnishing the Jewish soul food of "childhood memories", this "real kosher deli" in Mill Basin is an enduring "delight" that appeals to "lots of neighborhood people" with "fabulous" standards like pastrami, corned beef and chopped liver; the circa-1972 surroundings are strictly "old-world style", but "lovely" "original art" by Erté and Lichtenstein displayed throughout sure "classes it up a bit"; P.S. it has a new in-house catering facility that seats 75.

NEW Mille-Feuille ▤ *Baked Goods*

▽ 25 18 23 M

G Village | 552 La Guardia Pl. (bet. Bleecker & 3rd Sts.) | 212-533-4698 | www.millefeuille-nyc.com

"You'll think you've just landed in Paris" attest admirers of this "tiny", "very French" Greenwich Village patisserie from a classically trained French pastry chef, a newly minted source for "outstanding" croissants and brioche, "fine macarons" in many flavors and, *naturellement,* the namesake many-layered cake; "good prices" further sweeten the deal.

	QUALITY	DISPLAY	SERVICE	COST

Minamoto Kitchoan ⊟ *Candy/Nuts* ▽ 29 | 29 | 26 | E

W 40s | Swiss Center Bldg. | 608 Fifth Ave. (49th St.) | 212-489-3747 | www.kitchoan.com

"Delicate", "divine Japanese sweets" are oh-so-"beautifully displayed" at this "peaceful" Midtown "oasis" offering a taste of Tokyo via "traditional" wagashi – the "artistic" confections served at tea; given that these "unique" treats come "elegantly" wrapped "with the utmost precision" by "über-polite" staffers, they make "exceptional" if "expensive" gifts, but remember: "this is not your American candy, loaded with sugar", so it "may not suit all Western tastes."

Miss Mamie's Spoonbread Too ◐ *Caterer* 20 | 15 | 17 | M

Harlem | 366 W. 110th St. (bet. Columbus & Manhattan Aves.) | 212-865-0700

Miss Maude's Spoonbread Too ◐ *Caterer*

Harlem | 547 Lenox Ave. (bet. 137th & 138th Sts.) | 212-690-3100 www.spoonbreadinc.com

As "down-home" as they come "north of the Mason Dixon line", Norma Jean Darden's "authentic Harlem outpost of Southern home cooking" is a "standby" caterer that furnishes "tasty eats" with "all the trimmings", whether "the best fried chicken", catfish and greens or innovative choices with international twists; run by a "nice-as-can-be" crew, it provisions events both off-site and in the "charming" eateries Miss Mamie's and Miss Maude's for big names like Russell Simmons, Bill Gates and Jazz at Lincoln Center.

Mister Wright ◐⊟ *Wine/Liquor* 25 | 23 | 24 | M

E 80s | 1593 Third Ave. (bet. 89th & 90th Sts.) | 212-722-4564 | www.misterwrightfinewines.com

"He's my kind of guy" enthuse admirers of this "well-run" Yorkville stalwart, a "wonderland of wine" whose "amazing selection" of vintages from around the world is bolstered by a "large inventory of better liquors"; with a "bright", "spacious" floor plan and an "extremely knowledgeable" staff to assist in finding "the perfect bottle in any price range", it's an "all-around" resource that "does it right."

Mitchel London Foods *Prepared Food* 25 | 22 | 21 | E

E 60s | 22A E. 65th St. (bet. 5th & Madison Aves.) | 212-737-2850 | www.mitchellondonfoods.com

A go-to for "well-prepared, if expensive" prepared foods like flank steak, tuna salad and mini-chicken pot pies, this little Upper East Side shop is also a source for "to-die-for" cupcakes and holiday pies (the crust alone is "worth every calorie"); cynics claim it's all "stuff you can really make yourself", but to devotees the convenience and "wow taste" is well "worth the dollars"; P.S. they're also a "pleasure to deal with" for office catering.

Moishe's ⊟⊐ *Baked Goods* 23 | 16 | 19 | I

E Village | 115 Second Ave. (bet. 6th & 7th Sts.) | 212-505-8555 A "blast from the past" that "hasn't changed since forever", this East Village Jewish bakery is a '60s-vintage "mainstay" for "truly authentic kosher" goods that "your grandmother will love" and "so will you"; for anyone coveting "awesome" babka and rugalach, "wonderful" challah, hamantaschen, mandelbrot and traditional breads, it's "like a sweet old friend"; P.S. closed Friday and Saturday.

Momofuku Milk Bar ●⊟ *Baked Goods*   25 | 19 | 19 | M

E Village | 251 E. 13th St. (bet. 2nd & 3rd Aves.) | 212-777-7773
W 50s | Chambers Hotel | 15 W. 56th St. (bet. 5th & 6th Aves.) | 212-777-7773
NEW W 80s | 561 Columbus Ave. (87th St.) | 212-777-7773
NEW Carroll Gdns | 360 Smith St. (Second Pl.) | 347-660-6658
Williamsburg | 382 Metropolitan Ave. (Havemeyer St.) | Brooklyn | 212-777-7773
www.momofuku.com

"Creative, cool and scrumptious" sums up David Chang's "nontypical" East Village bakery and its offshoots, where pastry chef Christina Tosi's "imagination" yields "fantastic" pork buns and "delightful" desserts including "sublime" cookies, "truly addicting" crack pie and soft-serve ice cream in "out-of-the-box" flavors; it's on the "expensive" side, and while you can "stand while you swoon" at "crowded" communal tables at the original location, the rest are takeout-only – "but you won't be sorry"; P.S. it also does wedding cakes.

⊠ Mona Lisa Pastry Shop ●⊟ *Baked Goods*   24 | 25 | 22 | M

Bensonhurst | 1476 86th St. (bet. Bay 8th St. & 15th Ave.) | Brooklyn | 718-837-9053 | www.monalisabakery.com

"Worth the trip" for the "best of old-style Italian desserts", this big, long-running Bensonhurst bakery's masterpieces include "delicious pastries" ("try a cannoli"), breads, cheesecake, layer cookies and gelato, accompanied by panini and pizzas; an "outdoor cafe" where idlers "can sit with an espresso and watch the world go by" completes the picture.

Mondel Chocolates ⊟ *Candy/Nuts*   24 | 19 | 22 | M

W 100s | 2913 Broadway (114th St.) | 212-864-2111 | www.mondelchocolates.com

A "wonderful neighborhood institution", this family-owned Morningside Heights "old-fashioned candy shop" has been dispensing a "nice array of confections", including "first-rate", "housemade chocolates" since the 1940s; although a few grumps gripe it's "a bit dated" and a tad "expensive", generations of Columbia students and other sweet-toothed supporters say the "high quality" is why "people come from all over the city" to partake.

Montague St. Bagels ● *Bagels*   ▽ 23 | 16 | 20 | M

Brooklyn Heights | 108 Montague St. (bet. Henry & Hicks Sts.) | Brooklyn | 718-237-2512 | www.montaguebagels.com

"Big, fluffy" baked-on-site hand-rolled bagels "keep lines long" at this "cramped, popular" hole-in-the-wall, which bagel buffs boast is "the best in Brooklyn Heights", especially given its unconventional flavors, e.g. French toast; an extensive lineup of spreads, sandwiches, wraps and muffins adds to the appeal, as does 24-hour service.

	QUALITY	DISPLAY	SERVICE	COST

☑ Moore Brothers Wine Co. ◐▣ *Wine*   28 | 28 | 29 | M

Flatiron | 33 E. 20th St. (bet. B'way & Park Ave. S.) | 212-375-1575 |
866-986-6673 | www.moorebrothers.com

They "exhibit the highest degree of care" at this "one-of-a-kind"
Flatiron vintner from Philly-area connoisseurs Greg and David Moore,
which is once again voted No. 1 for Service in NYC thanks to the efforts of its "most knowledgeable" expert staff; the "terrific handpicked" wines from European "artisanal producers" are "shipped
properly in refrigerated trucks" and displayed at the "correct tem-
perature" in a "pristine", two-story space, and the fact that they're
offered at "excellent value" gives those "not blessed with trust funds"
moore reason to "love it all"; P.S. insiders tout its "tasting events."

Morrell & Co. ▣ *Wine/Liquor*   26 | 24 | 23 | E

W 40s | Rockefeller Ctr. | 1 Rockefeller Plaza (bet. 5th & 6th Aves.) |
212-688-9370 | 800-969-4637 | www.morrellwine.com

This handsome hideaway across from the Rockefeller Center rink
"truly distinguishes itself" with an "amazing", 5,000-strong lineup
of "fine wines", plus top-shelf liquors, made "accessible" by
"classy", "amiable and informative" staffers; yes, the price tag is
"top dollar", but "if you're willing to spend" you'll "always find something to satisfy"; P.S. along with "noteworthy" tastings and classes,
it offers wedding registration, consignment and online futures sales.

Mother Mousse *Baked Goods*   25 | 21 | 22 | E

Staten Island | 2175 Hylan Blvd. (bet. Lincoln & Midland Aves.) |
718-987-4242
Staten Island | 3767 Victory Blvd. (Travis Ave.) | 718-983-8366
www.mothermousse.com

When you're "in the mood for mousse", these "small", slightly "expensive" but "fabulous" SI bakeries whip up their "decadent" namesake from "fresh ingredients" in several flavors to produce
"delightful cakes" "for birthdays", weddings and "special occasions"; they're staffed by a "pleasant-to-deal-with" crew and also
"do up really elegant gift baskets" filled with cookies and more.

Mother's Bake Shop ◐⊘ *Baked Goods*   ∇ 20 | 16 | 19 | I

Bronx | 548 W. 235th St. (Johnson Ave.) | 718-796-5676 |
www.mothersbakeshop.com

For "real Jewish" baked goods "like mom and grandma made", this
Riverdale kosher vet turns out "well-made staples" such as babka,
"light-as-a-feather" rugalach, black-and-white cookies, cakes, old-
world breads and sandwiches; it's both "reliable" and "reasonably
priced", though noodges shrug it's "ok for a local bakery" but "nothing special"; P.S. closes early on Friday and all day Saturday.

Mount Carmel
Wine & Spirits ◐▣ *Wine/Liquor*   ∇ 24 | 21 | 22 | M

Bronx | 609 E. 187th St. (bet. Arthur & Hughes Aves.) | 718-367-7833 |
www.mountcarmelwines.com

"Wonderful purchases are in store" at this Bronx bastion "near Arthur
Avenue", which mounts about the "largest assortment of Italian wines

and liqueurs" around, with vintages from all regions ("look for that rare bottle") and a "wall" of 190 grappas that's a "definite must" for aficionados; prices are "not obscene", and with "genuinely helpful" staffers on hand even nonlocals "look forward to" the visit.

Movable Feast *Caterer* ▽ 23 | 22 | 26 | E

Park Slope | 284 Prospect Park W. (bet. 17th & 18th Sts.) | Brooklyn | 718-965-2900 | www.mfcatering.com
By appointment only

An "easy-to-work-with", "accommodating and resourceful mother-son team" is the force behind this veteran Park Slope catering company that can help orchestrate every stage of an event from invite design to the final "spectacular" sit-down or buffet bash; they're the in-house caterer for the Prospect Park Boathouse, but the feast can be moved, with the same "delicious", internationally accented food and "good value" ensured at any venue.

Murray's Bagels ● *Bagels* 26 | 19 | 19 | M

Chelsea | 242 Eighth Ave. (bet. 22nd & 23rd Sts.) | 646-638-1335
G Village | 500 Sixth Ave. (bet. 12th & 13th Sts.) | 212-462-2830
www.murraysbagelschelsea.com

"Plump", "crispy on the outside, fluffy on the inside" rounds "exactly as a bagel should be" ignite carb cravings at these Village-Chelsea twins, which also supply "all the schmears you can think of" and "fine" smoked fish; "quick service" keeps "out-the-door" lines moving on weekends – so "the only sad thing" is that "they won't toast."

☑ Murray's Cheese Shop ▭ *Cheese/Dairy* 29 | 26 | 25 | E

E 40s | Grand Central Mkt. | Lexington Ave. (43rd St.) | 212-922-1540 ●
W Village | 254 Bleecker St. (Cornelia St.) | 212-243-3289
888-692-4339 | www.murrayscheese.com

Among the city's top destinations "for all things cheesy", this West Village "mecca" – "complete with worshiping crowds" – lays out a "ridiculously expansive" lactic array, from Appenzeller to Zimbro, plus "fabulous" charcuterie and deli items, pastas, bread, nuts, chocolates and more; patrons praise "patient", "knowledgeable" staffers (they're "generous with the samples") and cite the in-house "caves", "classroom" and catering menu as more reasons to ignore your "cardiologist" and sing "cheese, glorious cheese"; P.S. the Grand Central annex is a boon to fromage-seeking "commuters."

☑ Murray's Sturgeon ▭ *Caviar/Smoked Fish* 28 | 20 | 23 | E

W 80s | 2429 Broadway (bet. 89th & 90th Sts.) | 212-724-2650 | www.murraysturgeon.com

The "stalwart sturgeon surgeons" at this "old-time" (since 1946) Upper Westsider serve up "excellent-quality" smoked fish, pickled herring, sturgeon and lox, plus kosher deli meats and other "Jewish soul food at its best" (the "chopped liver is to die for – and of!"); regulars rave these "real"-deal goods are "worth every dollar you spend", especially given the bonus of "wonderful, reliable" service and pleasing "throwback-to-old-NY" digs – just "how do they get so much great stuff into such a small store?"

	QUALITY	DISPLAY	SERVICE	COST

Myers of Keswick 🔲 *Specialty Shop* — 25 | 20 | 22 | M

W Village | 634 Hudson St. (bet. Horatio & Jane Sts.) |
212-691-4194 | www.myersofkeswick.com

"British expats and Anglophiles" hankering for "edible memories"
flock to this "quaint" West Village shop, a "jolly good showcase"
chockablock with "veddy" English specialties "of all sorts", from "top-
notch" "household foods" to key "treats you can't live without";
whether you're "stocking up" on imports "in tins and packets" ("get
your marmite fix") or "guilty pleasures" like "housemade bangers",
"Scotch eggs, sausage rolls and pork pies", with "so many" "favorites in one place" it's the "best thing barring a trip to London."

Nancy's–Wines For Food ◑ *Wine/Liquor* — 24 | 21 | 24 | M

W 70s | 313 Columbus Ave. (75th St.) | 212-877-4040 |
www.aocfinewines.com

"Almost under the radar", this "friendly" Upper West Side wine
store comes "highly recommended" by locals who love the food-
friendly "reasonably priced" selections (each of which has "its own
very thoughtful description") and the "big array of Rieslings" and
other cool-climate options; "super-helpful" service and free shipping
in NYC, Westchester and Fairfield, CT, please a "loyal clientele."

Napoli Bakery ✄ *Baked Goods* — ∇ 28 | 20 | 22 | I

Williamsburg | 616 Metropolitan Ave. (bet. Leonard & Lorimer Sts.) |
Brooklyn | 718-384-6945 | www.napolibakery.com

"Convenient" for locals who live by bread alone, this old-line
Williamsburg bakery's hard-working brick oven emits "some of the
best Italian" loaves and focaccia in "divine", ultrafresh varieties like
country white, rosemary, semolina, sourdough, whole wheat and
many more; just "don't expect to find" much else, other than service
from a "friendly" couple and "great prices."

Natural Frontier Market *Health* — 22 | 17 | 17 | M

E 80s | 1424 Third Ave. (bet. 80th & 81st Sts.) | 212-794-0922 ◑
Gramercy | 325 Third Ave. (bet. 24th & 25th Sts.) | 212-228-9133 ◑
Ditmas Park | 1102 Cortelyou Rd. (Stratford Rd.) | Brooklyn |
718-284-3593 ◑
LIC | 12-01 Jackson Ave. (bet. 47th Rd. & 48th Ave.) | Queens |
718-937-9399
www.naturalfrontiermarket.net

"Just about anything you need to stay healthy" can be had at
these cross-borough natural food marts, which are "crammed"
with "competitively priced" "vitamins and supplements", "gluten-
free" and organic items, "packaged goods" and other products
"supermarkets don't have"; juice bars and prepared foods also
figure, but beware of "narrow aisles" that "can resemble a maze"
and "not-so-nice salespeople."

Nature's Gifts ◑ *Specialty Shop* — ∇ 19 | 17 | 18 | M

E 80s | 1297 Lexington Ave. (bet. 87th & 88th Sts.) | 212-289-6283
Healthy fare puts on a Greek accent at this "reliable" Upper
Eastsider, for three decades a "consistent" source of healthy pre-

QUALITY DISPLAY SERVICE COST

Nespresso Boutique 🖃 *Coffee/Tea*   27 | 27 | 24 | E
E 60s | 761 Madison Ave. (65th St.)
SoHo | 504 Broadway, 2nd fl. (bet. Broome & Spring Sts.)
SoHo | 92 Prince St. (Mercer St.)
W 50s | 306 W. 57th St. (8th Ave.)
800-562-1465 | www.nespresso.com
"Take your coffee experience to a whole new level" at these "beautiful" branches of a global outfit, "pleasingly elite" oases for java "junkies" to "splurge" on "little sachets" of "out-of-this-world" espresso and pick up state-of-the-art machines to brew them in; it's also a "sit-down" "respite" for "delish" snacks and "luxe" cuppas, though even "tony" habitués say it's "difficult paying their prices."

Neuchatel Chocolates 🖃 *Candy/Nuts*   ▽ 28 | 28 | 26 | VE
E 50s | Park Ave. Plaza | 55 E. 52nd St. (bet. Madison & Park Aves.) |
212-759-1388 | 800-597-0759 | www.neuchatelchocolates.com
"Now this is chocolate!" declare devotees of the "excellent truffles" and other "amazingly smooth", "sinful" Swiss confections that are the specialty of this East Side shop; naturally, such "fabulous" treats are costly, so you need to be "feeling flush", but those willing to "splurge" report that, "once inside", you'll "never want to leave."

Neuhaus Chocolate   26 | 25 | 23 | E
Boutique 🖃 *Candy/Nuts*
E 40s | Grand Central Terminal | main concourse (42nd St. & Vanderbilt Ave.) | 212-972-3740
E 50s | 569 Lexington Ave. (bet. 50th & 51st Sts.) | 212-593-0848
www.neuhaus.be
Leave it to the "Belgians to fashion" the kind of "delicious", "decadent" chocolates on offer at these "charming" East Side outposts of the Brussels-based chain, where "rich", "high-end" truffles and other confections come "in familiar as well as unusual flavors" ("the chocolate-covered potato chips are unbelievable"); they're predictably "expensive" and service can be "snobby" at times, but that's "worth putting up with" given their "made-to-order" assortments and "impressive" packaging "perfect for a special gift."

New Amsterdam   28 | 23 | 25 | M
Market ⊭ *Specialty Shop*
Seaport | 100 Peck Slip (South St.) | 212-766-8688 |
www.newamsterdammarket.org
"Such a great concept", this outdoor market on the old Fulton Fish Market site is a "locavore and gastronome heaven" with stalls specializing in a "wide variety" of "artisanal foods" from area providers, including "excellent produce", cheeses, pasture-raised meats, baked goods, ice cream and more; it's becoming a "favorite" of foodies in the know and shoppers in search of "something new and different."

	QUALITY	DISPLAY	SERVICE	COST

New Beer *Beer*
▽ 26 | 15 | 19 | I

LES | 167 Chrystie St. (bet. Delancey & Rivington Sts.) |
212-260-4360 | www.newbeerdistributors.com

It's a beer bonanza at this family-owned LES "warehouse" stocking
some 1,000 domestic and international brews including rare and
hard-to-find ones (arcane local bottlings to New Zealand imports);
sudsophiles say "new" brews "will show up here before they do anywhere else", and prices are "fair", so never mind the "no-frills setup."

New York Cake & Baking
25 | 14 | 13 | M

Distributor *Cookware*

Flatiron | 56 W. 22nd St. (bet. 5th & 6th Aves.) | 212-675-2253 |
www.nycake.com

"Paradise" both for "professional pastry chefs" and "hobbyists" who
want to "indulge" their "Food Network–wannabe dreams", this
Flatiron phenom boasts "everything you could possibly need to bake
a cake", plus tools you "didn't even know existed"; while the trepi-
dacious caution it "looks like a disaster" and is manned by staffers
who're "knowledgeable" but "cranky", even the unenthused concede it's the "only place to get certain things" for baking.

New York Vintners *Wine/Liquor*
▽ 28 | 23 | 25 | E

TriBeCa | 21 Warren St. (bet. B'way & Church St.) | 212-812-3999 |
www.newyorkvintners.com

Educating wine lovers and vending collectible bottles at fair market
values are the twin goals of this capacious TriBeCa merchant, where
shoppers will find everything from an under-the-radar Sauvignon
Blanc for $20 to a rare champagne costing major ka-ching; tastings
are held on weekend afternoons, and customers can purchase tick-
ets to the store's signature 'Wine Basics' classes and other events
through the website.

New York
▽ 25 | 21 | 21 | E

Wine Exchange ◑ *Wine/Liquor*

Financial District | 9 Broadway (bet. Battery Pl. & Morris St.) |
212-422-2222 | www.nywineexchange.com

Located in an "area that could use a drink", this Financial District
wine-and-spirits shop caters to Wall Street workers looking to "grab
a bottle before going home", offering a well-diversified portfolio including California Cabernets and Merlots, an increasing allotment
of Hungarian, Uruguayan, Portuguese and Israeli wines, plus a ro-
bust range of spirits; "high prices" are part of the deal.

Nordic Delicacies *Specialty Shop*
▽ 28 | 23 | 28 | M

Bay Ridge | 6909 Third Ave. (bet. Bay Ridge & Ovington Aves.) |
Brooklyn | 718-748-1874 | 800-346-6734 | www.nordicdeli.com

"One of the few Scandinavian grocery stores left in Brooklyn", this Bay
Ridge outpost is a "real treat" for "delicious" Nordic "specialties you
can't find anywhere else", whether imported jams, cheeses and pickled herring or fresh baked goods and other traditional comestibles like
"homemade *polse*, liver *postei* and *julekake*"; it also can be counted
on for clothing and gifts, and everything's tended by "helpful" fφlks.

#1 Farmers Market ● *Produce* | 23 | 21 | 21 | M |

E 70s | 1458 Second Ave. (76th St.) | 212-396-2626

A "bumper crop" of "garden-fresh" veggies and fruit is available day and night at this Upper Eastsider, along with a "first-rate" assortment of imported and kosher products, flowers, cookies, cheese and "many more goodies"; the 24/7 convenience, "cordial service" and "pleasing displays" are so "welcome" "in the 'hood", most are inclined to excuse what some call "East Side prices."

Nunu Chocolates ●🔲 *Candy/Nuts* | ▽ 25 | 20 | 23 | M |

Downtown Bklyn | 529 Atlantic Ave. (bet. 3rd & 4th Aves.) | Brooklyn | 917-776-7102 | www.nunuchocolates.com

Brooklynites are "falling in love with chocolate all over again" thanks to this "micro shop" on the Downtown–Boerum Hill border producing "amazing" varieties like "gourmet" ganaches filled with fruit purée, tea or liquor, as well as "scrumptious" caramels, all made on-site (you can watch the magic happen through a window in the kitchen); those who agree that pairing beer and chocolate is a "win-win" can sit and sample one of the "hard-to-find" "craft brews" with their bonbons.

Nut Box ●🔲 *Candy/Nuts* | 24 | 23 | 22 | M |

Chelsea | Chelsea Mkt. | 75 Ninth Ave. (bet. 15th & 16th Sts.) | 212-243-2325
G Village | 49 E. Eighth St. (University Pl.) | 212-933-1018
Cobble Hill | 163 Smith St. (Wyckoff St.) | Brooklyn | 347-689-9948
www.thenutbox.com

Whether you hit the Cobble Hill original or the "wonderful" Chelsea Market and Village outposts, these nut emporiums are "fun to discover" given their "quality" selection, mostly from the U.S., which come plain, salted, roasted, honeyed or chocolate-covered; "excellent" dried fruits, including unusual and organic choices, plus ready-made and make-your-own trail mixes, seeds, granola, spices, colorful candies and house-roasted coffee beans round out the offerings, with "amazing prices" as the dried cherry on top.

🄯 NYC Icy ⌇ *Ice Cream* | 29 | 15 | 23 | I |

E Village | 100 Ave. A (bet. 6th & 7th Sts.) | no phone
Kensington | 905 Church Ave. (10th St.) | Brooklyn | 347-789-1849
www.nycicy.com

Italian ice fanciers "wish it were warm all year" now that this seasonal (April–October) outfit has popped up in the East Village, peddling the "freshest" sorbet and gelato in an "ever-changing" assortment of "delightful flavors", including the "unusual" likes of "mango basil, purple carrot and Earl Grey"; the Kensington location is geared to wholesale operations, but it does limited retail business as well.

O&CO. 🔲 *Specialty Shop* | 27 | 25 | 23 | E |

E 40s | Grand Central Terminal | main concourse, Graybar Passage (42nd St. & Vanderbilt Ave.) | 212-973-1472 | 877-828-6620
NEW **W 60s** | Shops at Columbus Circle | 10 Columbus Circle (bet. 58th & 60th Sts.) | 212-757-9877 ●

(continued)

O&CO.

W Village | 249 Bleecker St. (bet. 6th & 7th Aves.) | 212-463-7710 | 877-828-6620
www.oliviersandco.com

"Truly an olive oil mecca", these specialists in "spectacular" oleaginous imports offer a "wonderful selection" with variations for cooking or "dipping" curated by "friendly" staffers who'll let you "test your palate" to explore "subtle differences"; "lovely packaging" makes for "fabulous gifts", and the "highest quality" extends to its aged "balsamic vinegar", tapenades and accessories, so though the tab "can get pretty pricey" it's "well worth the cost."

Obika   *Cheese/Dairy*   ∇ 27 | 20 | 21 | E

W 50s | IBM Bldg. | 590 Madison Ave. (56th St.) | 212-355-2217 | www.obika.it

If you can't book a trip to Milan, this sleek "mozzarella bar" in the atrium of the IBM building will "transport you to Italia" with its creamy, high-quality collection of freshly flown-in mozz – five types in all – plus artisanal charcuterie; all of the goods can be purchased at the retail counter for at-home sampling, and the "pleasant, helpful" service folk are amenable to making recommendations.

Once Upon A Tart . . .   *Baked Goods*   25 | 20 | 19 | M

SoHo | 135 Sullivan St. (bet. Houston & Prince Sts.) | 212-387-8869 | www.onceuponatart.com

SoHo's baked-goods buffs have a storybook rapport with this endearing "treasure" and its "yummy sweet and savory tarts", made from scratch in "tasty combinations" like pear-almond, walnut-chocolate, spinach-and-mushroom and tomato Provençal; it's also a "standby for sandwiches, pastries", scones, cupcakes and cookies, and sipping "coffee is super nice" at its cozy cafe tables.

❷ One Girl Cookies ▣ *Baked Goods*   27 | 26 | 23 | E

Cobble Hill | 68 Dean St. (bet. Boerum Pl. & Smith St.) | Brooklyn | 212-675-4996
NEW **Dumbo** | 33 Main St. (Water St.) | Brooklyn | 347-338-1268
www.onegirlcookies.com

"Definitely one girl who knows how to bake", this "adorable" Cobble Hill shop-cum-espresso bar (with a new Dumbo offshoot) has a flair for "teeny", "exquisite-looking" cookies crafted in a mix of "delish" flavors (e.g. "to-die-for Whoopie Pie") that "really make you want more"; its cupcakes and brownies are "top-notch" too, and the "friendly" staffers can also create upscale event favors and gift boxes; P.S. wedding cakes are another specialty.

One Lucky Duck ◗▣ *Health Food*   ∇ 25 | 19 | 21 | E

Chelsea | Chelsea Mkt. | 75 Ninth Ave. (bet. 15th & 16th Sts.) | 212-255-4300
Gramercy | 125 E. 17th St. (Irving Pl.) | 212-477-7151
www.oneluckyduck.com

Eco-conscious eaters seeking "raw food at its finest" luck out at this Chelsea Market-Gramercy take-out "secret" from owner and cookbook author Sarma Melngailis (of the like-minded restaurant Pure Food and Wine), whose vegan and organic ingredients and ovenless preparations ensure the "flavors really stand out" in her salads, juice-bar blends and treats; "your wallet will feel it", but "when you just have to go raw it can't be beat."

☑ The Orchard 🖃 Specialty Shop   28 | 21 | 23 | E

Midwood | 1367 Coney Island Ave. (bet. Ave. J & Cary Ct.) | Brooklyn | 718-377-1799 | 800-222-0240 | www.orchardfruit.com
"Perfect for every occasion", this Midwood kosher "fixture" dates to 1955 as a purveyor of "fantastic" gourmet fruit in "huge, fresh baskets" filled out with chocolates and preserves, or "fabulous" platters incorporating smoked fish and cheese; prices can quickly add up to "breathtaking" levels, but "when you really want to impress", its "beautiful arrangements" rank with "the very best."

Oren's Daily Roast 🖃 Coffee/Tea   24 | 19 | 21 | M

E 40s | 1440 Broadway (bet. 40th & 41st Sts.) | 646-291-2090
E 40s | Grand Central Mkt. | Lexington Ave. (43rd St.) | 212-338-0014 ●
E 50s | 830 Third Ave. (51st St.) | 212-308-2148
E 70s | 1144 Lexington Ave. (bet. 79th & 80th Sts.) | 212-472-6830
E 70s | 985 Lexington Ave. (71st St.) | 212-717-3907
E 80s | 1574 First Ave. (bet. 81st & 82nd Sts.) | 212-737-2690
G Village | 31 Waverly Pl. (bet. Greene St. & University Pl.) | 212-420-5958
Murray Hill | 434 Third Ave. (bet. 30th & 31st Sts.) | 212-779-1241
W 100s | 2882 Broadway (bet. 112th & 113th Sts.) | 212-749-8779 ●
888-348-5400 | www.orensdailyroast.com
"An all-around caffeine winner", this local chain "can be relied on" for a "decent" "eye-opener" owing to "top-notch" coffee "roasted in small batches" on weekdays and offered "with good humor" by "fun" staffers who offer pointers on "how to make" a good brew and "how to store the beans"; its solid blends "make for a wonderful cup", and "don't forget about" the "fresh" baked goods, including Doughnut Plant holes at some branches.

Orwasher's Bakery Baked Goods   26 | 20 | 22 | M

E 70s | 308 E. 78th St. (bet. 1st & 2nd Aves.) | 212-288-6569 | www.orwasherbakery.com
It "smells amazing even before you go in" at this circa-1916 UES "throwback", a kosher bakery "standout" where the brick oven is "still going strong" producing "memorable" Jewish-style breads ("love that raisin-pumpernickel") in a "no-frills" "neighborhood" setting; between the "old-time feel", "genial" service and "absolute quality", you "can't really go wrong" – "thank heaven it's still here."

☑ Ottomanelli & Sons Meat/Poultry   28 | 22 | 26 | E

W Village | 285 Bleecker St. (bet. Jones St. & 7th Ave.) | 212-675-4217
Woodside | 61-05 Woodside Ave. (61st St.) | Queens | 718-651-5544
"This is what a real butcher shop is" opine "old-fashioned" fans of these "longtime" Italian "landmarks" in the West Village and Woodside, separately run "family operations" famed for "superior", "well-marbled meat" both "common and exotic", all "perfectly

trimmed" with a "smile" by a "terrific" counter staff that "will provision, educate and charm you"; with a "wide" variety from dry-aged beef and homemade sausage to "game meats" like venison and kangaroo, they're worth "a special trip."

☑ Ottomanelli's

| | 28 | 24 | 25 | E |

Prime Meats 🖻 *Meat/Poultry*

Flushing | 190-21 Union Tpke. (192nd St.) | Queens | 718-468-2000 | www.ottomanellibros.com

"Love these guys!" gush Flushing fanciers of this local meat market, where the "fresh" "prime" cuts range from steaks, veal and poultry to exotic game like pheasant, alligator, boar, deer, buffalo, ostrich – "you name it"; add a "wonderful" prepared foods lineup featuring Italian favorites like chicken parm and baked ziti, and there's "something for everyone", even if it is on the "pricey" side.

Our Daily Bread 🌭 *Baked Goods*

| | 25 | 20 | 22 | I |

Location varies | 518-392-9852

Leaven lovers laud this "quality" Greenmarket vendor providing some of the "most flavorful bread in the city" as it plies artisanal loaves with a crisp crust and light center in a variety that extends from traditional rye to sunflower millet flax, challah and cranberry pecan sourdough; it also hits the sweet spot with scones, cookies and brownies, all produced in its Chatham, NY, bakery/cafe home base.

Ovando 🖻 *Flowers*

| ▽ | 29 | 29 | 24 | VE |

W Village | 337 Bleecker St. (bet. Christopher & W. 10th Sts.) | 212-924-7848 | www.ovandony.com

With a "unique" aesthetic among NYC's floral shops (think "architecture in a vase"), this "amazing" West Village store "displays its wares like no other", sporting an all-black decor scheme and "theatrical lighting" that allows its colorful blooms to be the star of the show; clients also "love" the outfit's "innovative", "super-cool" designs (a European–South American fusion of styles often featuring orchids and cacti), which are admittedly "for the chic set" – alas, this kind of "exquisite" "doesn't come cheap."

Paffenroth Gardens 🌭 *Produce*

| ▽ | 28 | 26 | 25 | I |

Location varies | 845-258-2539

A "must" for produce partialists, this Greenmarket "star" is "the place to go for root vegetables" given its "vibrant" panoply of parsnips, onions, "multicolored carrots" and more, fortified by an "incredibly diverse selection of greens" for devotees of "the cruciferous and the leafy"; the "fantastic" flora are shipped "extremely fresh" from the Orange County, NY, farmstead of Alex Paffenroth, a grower with "luster" who's "always reliable for something different."

Pain D'Avignon *Baked Goods*

| ▽ | 24 | 20 | 21 | M |

LES | Essex Street Mkt. | 120 Essex St. (bet. Delancey & Rivington Sts.) | 212-673-4950 | www.paindavignon-nyc.com

"Totally addictive" to breadheads, this retail outlet of a Long Island City-based bakery (by way of a Cape Cod original) packs its Essex

Street Market berth to the rafters with a "wonderful line" of some 50 European-style variations on the staff of life; expect "fresh and tasty" French baguettes, seven-grain, caraway rye and cranberry-pecan, rounded out by croissants and brioche.

Paneantico Bakery & Café ● *Baked Goods* | 26 | 23 | 21 | M |

Bay Ridge | 9124 Third Ave. (92nd St.) | Brooklyn | 718-680-2347 | www.paneanticobakerycafe.com

Among the "best reasons to go out to Bay Ridge", this Italian bakery/cafe (and Royal Crown Pastry Shop sidekick) "gem" is prized for its "fresh" house-baked breads, but it also boasts an "excellent variety" of pastries and prepared foods, not to mention "wonderful sandwiches"; according to "the locals" lingering over espresso, "anything you get, you know it's going to be delicious."

Panya ● *Baked Goods* | ▽ 21 | 19 | 18 | I |

E Village | 8-10 Stuyvesant St. (bet. 9th St. & 3rd Ave.) | 212-777-1930

"After the extensive renovation", East Villagers are "so very glad" this Japanese bakery "came back" "bigger than ever" but with the "quality and flavor" intact in its lineup of authentic breads (red bean, curry, tuna, melon) and desserts; there's now a "cafe attached" with an "expanded" menu of sushi, salads and specialty foods, plus Franco "fusion" fare like baguette sandwiches and croissants.

Papabubble ●▣ *Candy/Nuts* | ▽ 23 | 23 | 21 | M |

Little Italy | 380 Broome St. (bet. Mott & Mulberry Sts.) | 212-966-2599 | www.papabubbleny.com

Demonstrating "the definition of eye candy", artisans at this lablike Little Italy confectioner work in view, stretching and rolling molten sugar in a "rainbow" of colors to sculpt "fun", "unique shapes with unusual flavors" from the fruit and herbal oils they use; the result is "sophisticated" hard sweets that make it a "go-to" for gifts, even "cool, customized" ones – that is "if you can resist eating them all" yourself.

☑ Park Avenue Liquor Shop ▣ *Wine/Liquor* | 27 | 20 | 25 | E |

E 40s | 292 Madison Ave. (bet. 40th & 41st Sts.) | 212-685-2442 | www.parkaveliquor.com

Just the place "to pick up that special bottle" before "taking Metro-North to the 'burbs", this "old-world" Midtown wine seller near Grand Central includes rare-vintage Burgundies and Bordeaux among its "stacked-to-the-ceiling" inventory, and it's also home to one of the "best selections of single-malt scotches" outside "Scotland" (400 labels); what's more, service is "helpful" and "without attitude" – no wonder tabs are so "pricey."

Park East Kosher Butchers & Fine Foods ▣ *Meat/Poultry* | 24 | 16 | 20 | E |

E 80s | 1623 Second Ave. (bet. 84th & 85th Sts.) | 212-737-9800 | www.parkeastkosher.com

"The gold standard" of UES glatt purveyors and "priced to match" ("oy vey!"), this "classic" kosher butcher/specialty market is a "ma-

	QUALITY	DISPLAY	SERVICE	COST

jor" source of "superb" meat, poultry and game trimmed by a "kind and helpful" staff; it's also "fab" for prepared "Jewish cooking" and fine foods like smoked fish and imported cheese, but "lots of patience is required" for the "complete chaos" "around holiday time"; P.S. closes before sundown on Friday and all day Saturday.

Party Rental Ltd. *Party Rentals*

| 22 | 16 | 22 | M |

Chelsea | 261 Fifth Ave., 16th fl. (29th St.) | 201-727-4700
Bridgehampton | 7 Tradesman Path (Butter Ln.), NY | 631-537-4477
Teterboro | 275 North St. (Green St.), NJ | 201-727-4700
www.partyrentalltd.com
By appointment only

"Hey, you gotta love that pink hippo" say enthusiasts of this area-wide party rental titan and its rosy logo, known "for years" as a "reliable" rigger of shindigs with countless items shipped from its 350,000-sq.-ft. warehouse, whether flatware and linens or tables and dance floors (but no tents); there's a $500 minimum, but the "timely" delivery and "efficient" service are a lifesaver "when you have more than you can handle."

Party Time *Party Rentals*

| ∇ 20 | 18 | 20 | M |

Elmhurst | 82-33 Queens Blvd. (bet. 51st Ave. & Van Loon St.) | Queens | 718-639-9105 | 877-865-1122
Festivity fundamentals are the inventory at this Elmhurst party-supply place whose array of rental and purchase choices ranges from the typical (chairs, tables, coat racks, stemware, dance floors) to the more specialized (jukeboxes, popcorn machines, raffle drums, frankfurter wagons), offered at wallet-friendly prices; delivery service in the five boroughs and Westchester is another cause to celebrate.

☒ Pastosa Ravioli ⌷ *Pasta*

| 27 | 22 | 24 | M |

Bronx | 3812 E. Tremont Ave. (Lamport Pl.) | 718-822-2800
Bensonhurst | 7425 New Utrecht Ave. (75th St.) | Brooklyn | 718-236-9615
Mill Basin | 5223 Ave. N (53rd St.) | Brooklyn | 718-258-1002
Ozone Park | 132-10 Cross Bay Blvd. (Sutter Ave.) | Queens | 718-835-6240
Staten Island | 1076 Richmond Rd. (Columbus Ave.) | 718-667-2194
Staten Island | 3817 Richmond Ave. (Wilson Ave.) | 718-356-4600
Staten Island | 764 Forest Ave. (B'way) | 718-420-9000
800-457-2786 | www.pastosa.com

"Creamy, light" ravioli is "king" at this Bensonhurst "landmark" and its separately owned offshoots, but the "excellent breads, pastas" (including "gluten-free options"), sausages, "fresh housemade mozzarella" and a "wide selection" of Italian products also "don't disappoint"; it's a "real experience", and service is "on the money", "just like in the old Brooklyn days"; P.S. the Forest Avenue locale distinguishes itself with a "terrific" range of cheeses.

Pastrami Queen ● *Deli*

| 22 | 13 | 17 | M |

E 70s | 1125 Lexington Ave. (bet. 78th & 79th Sts.) | 212-734-1500 | www.pastramiqueen.com
Although somewhat "unsung", this "old-style kosher deli" on the UES is a provider of "delish" pastrami, brisket, corned beef and

other "comforting" Jewish staples; while the grub "still goes down easy" ("bring Tums"), "pricey" tabs, "tired" digs and merely "adequate" service have critics claiming it's "not quite like" when it was the Pastrami King, its '50s forerunner in Queens.

Patel Brothers ◐◻ *Specialty Shop*   22 | 14 | 14 | I

Flushing | 42-92 Main St. (bet. Blossom & Cherry Aves.) | Queens | 718-661-1112

Jackson Heights | 37-27 74th St. (37th Ave.) | Queens | 718-898-3445
www.patelbrothersusa.com

"Guaranteed to get a 'wow'", these Indian-Pakistani markets in Jackson Heights and Flushing are "one-stop wonderlands" where the "comprehensive selection of imports" includes "wondrous" fruits and veggies "you never imagined" plus "spices galore" and "endless" shelves of rice, yogurts, chutneys and the like, all at "bargain" prices; they're "crowded" as a "bazaar in Karachi" and manned by "indifferent" staffers, but "if you don't find it here, you don't need it."

Patisserie Claude ⊟ *Baked Goods*   26 | 16 | 19 | M

W Village | 187 W. Fourth St. (bet. 6th & 7th Aves.) | 212-255-5911

"Just as good as when Claude was the baker", this veteran Village pâtisserie – now run by the retired namesake's "longtime assistant" – remains a "master" of "spectacular" "buttery, flaky croissants" and "excellent basic French pastries"; combining a "low-key" milieu with "very high quality", it's "totally addictive" despite hints of "attitude" – this is "a true slice of Paris", after all.

Penn Wine & Spirits ◻ *Wine/Liquor*   ▽ 26 | 24 | 23 | M

Garment District | LIRR Level, Penn Station | 234 W. 31st St. (8th Ave.) | 212-630-0219 | www.pennwineandspirits.com

"Location is key" to the success of this "convenient" "underground" Penn Station shop that's just the ticket when you're in a "hurry" to "grab some wine and a train", thanks to a surprisingly "vast array" of "affordable" choices (some 900 labels) from around the globe, including spirits; there's always an "attentive" sales rep "willing to share an opinion", and evening wine tastings Wednesday-Friday make a "nice way to pass the time" when your ride home is "delayed."

People's Pops ◐⊟ *Ice Cream*   ▽ 26 | 21 | 25 | M

Chelsea | Chelsea Mkt. | 75 Ninth Ave. (bet. 15th & 16th Sts.) | 347-850-2388 | www.peoplespops.com

"Who knew so much could be done to a pop?" marvel people pleased with this April–October Chelsea Market stand, a popular pick for popsicles and shaved ice in "the most amazing flavors" (e.g. raspberry-basil, strawberry-rhubarb, sour cherry, pear-ginger) employing seasonal fruit from local farmers; it's also a "favorite stop" after a warm-weather stroll "along the Highline", and it pops up at the New Amsterdam Market and Brooklyn Flea too.

	QUALITY	DISPLAY	SERVICE	COST

☑ Perelandra

26 | 21 | 20 | M

Natural Food Center ◐ *Health*

Brooklyn Heights | 175 Remsen St. (bet. Clinton & Court Sts.) | Brooklyn | 718-855-6068 | www.perelandranatural.com

Obliging Brooklyn Heights with a "wide array" of wholesome staples since 1976, this "wonderful" health haven is "well stocked" with "fresh" organic produce, the "best selection of bulk natural foods in the area" and a "wide array" of "non-mass market brands", "nutritional supplements" and "vegan deli" items and prepared foods; run by a "helpful", "committed" staff, it's "a bit pricey" but often offers "good sale prices."

Pescatore Seafood ◐▣ *Seafood*

25 | 24 | 22 | E

E 40s | Grand Central Mkt. | Lexington Ave. (43rd St.) | 212-557-4466 | www.allfreshseafood.com

The "perfect stop" for fish "on the way home from work", this Grand Central vendor suits "all your seafood needs" with "pristine" marine cuisine "whether pre-prepared or raw" and "enough selection" that "you can go there every day"; it's manned by the "nicest folks", and though critics crab they "could lower prices a bit", "some of their specials are terrific values."

Pete Milano's Discount

▽ 25 | 22 | 24 | M

Wine & Liquor Supermarket *Wine/Liquor*

Staten Island | 1441 Forest Ave. (Marianne St.) | 718-447-2888

"Well known" in Staten Island for its "large selection" of wines from "around the world" plus all you need to supply the "liquor cabinet", this 4,000-sq.-ft. emporium is also toasted by surveyors for its "reasonable" rates and "treat-you-like-family" service overseen by second-generation owners; other bonuses include a 10% case discount (including mixed bottles) and open-Sunday hours.

Peter Pan

▽ 24 | 19 | 21 | I

Donut & Pastry Shop ⌻ *Baked Goods*

Greenpoint | 727 Manhattan Ave. (bet. Meserole & Norman Aves.) | Brooklyn | 718-389-3676

A "hallmark of Greenpoint" is this "old-timey" Manhattan Avenue shop that's been selling "cheap", "delicious" donuts in a "crazy" array of flavors for more than six decades; maybe its "traditional" goods "don't have the sophistication" of some newer-fangled sinkers around town, but you're bound to find plenty to "catch your eye and tantalize your taste buds" – though addicts warn these babies are "like crack – be careful!"

Petrossian

27 | 25 | 24 | VE

Boutique & Cafe ▣ *Caviar/Smoked Fish*

W 50s | 911 Seventh Ave. (bet. 57th & 58th Sts.) | 212-245-2217 | 800-828-9241 | www.petrossian.com

For "special occasions" or a "totally decadent splurge", fish-egg fanciers converge on the "crème de la crème" of "caviar purveyors" near Carnegie Hall to "lust after" "sublime" roe, smoked fish, foie gras, jarred comestibles and other "high-end" "delicacies" at "stratospheric prices"; there are also "mouthwatering" French breads and pastries, which, assuming your wallet is up to the task, complete the "simply splendid" experience.

Phil-Am *Specialty Shop* | - | - | - | I |

Woodside | 7002 Roosevelt Ave. (70th St.) | Queens | 718-899-1797
Cooks hankering for chicken adobo, fried lumpia and other flavors of Manila find many of the ingredients at this small, basic Woodside grocer specializing in hard-to-find Filipino foods – fresh, prepared and frozen – including traditional longanisa sausages and the brioche-like sweet rolls called ensaymada; low prices are another appeal.

Picada y Vino ◑ *Wine/Liquor* | ▽ 26 | 25 | 27 | M |

Park Slope | 327 Fifth Ave. (bet. 3rd & 4th Sts.) | Brooklyn | 718-499-2392 | www.picadayvino.com
There's a "friendly" "community feel" at this "great little" Park Slope wine outlet where "inventive" selections and "excellent" labels "you won't find elsewhere" stand out among a stockpile that's "not huge" but emphasizes small producers and organic and biodynamic picks; "hip" staffers, green business practices and "decent prices" are more reasons to say cheers.

Pick a Bagel ◑ *Bagels* | 21 | 16 | 17 | I |

E 70s | 1101 Lexington Ave. (77th St.) | 212-517-6590
E 70s | 1475 Second Ave. (bet. 76th & 77th Sts.) | 212-717-4662
Financial District | 102 North End Ave. (West Side Hwy.) | 212-786-9200
Gramercy | 297 Third Ave. (bet. 22nd & 23rd Sts.) | 212-686-1414
"Hot, fresh" bagels "as big as your head" slathered with "every spread known to the Western world" plus deli-case salads "any way you like" are the main attractions at these "easy-in-easy-out" nosheries around town; "service is just ok", but "fairly cheap" checks explain the "always-bustling" atmosphere – in short, "works if it's convenient."

☒ Pickle Guys ▤ *Specialty Shop* | 27 | 19 | 23 | I |

LES | 49 Essex St. (bet. Grand & Hester Sts.) | 212-656-9739
Midwood | 1364 Coney Island Ave. (bet. Aves. J & K) | Brooklyn | 718-677-0639
888-474-2553 | www.pickleguys.com
"Pucker up" for "the real thing" at this LES "favorite" (and its Midwood outpost) producing "the freshest", most "mouthwatering" "traditional Jewish pickles" cured "the way God intended" and dispensed "direct from the barrel" with a "good-size helping of New York attitude" from a staff of "jocular" "characters"; it "packs a pungent punch" with varieties like full- and half-sour, sweet gherkin and horseradish, "along with other pickled items" – connoisseurs of fine brines "wouldn't buy them anywhere else."

☒ Pickles, Olives Etc. ▤ *Specialty Shop* | 25 | 18 | 25 | M |

E 80s | 1647 First Ave. (86th St.) | 212-717-8966 | www.picklesandolives.com
"Like the name says", this "very friendly" Upper Eastsider "can't be beat" for "barrels" full of "fantastic pickles" in diverse styles "with

just the right pucker", plus olives "of every type" including "delicacies" "stuffed with goat cheese, blue cheese, lemon rind, garlic", etc.; plus, when you're in a "pre-party shopping" pickle, "you can round out your appetizers" with "fresh baba ghanoush", hummus, grape leaves and more.

☑ Piemonte Ravioli ▣ *Pasta*   27 | 18 | 26 | I

Little Italy | 190 Grand St. (bet. Mott & Mulberry Sts.) | 212-226-0475 | www.piemonteravioli.com

The "easiest way to make a restaurant-quality meal at home" is to head for this "old-fashioned" Little Italy stalwart and pick up some "pillow-soft gnocchi", squid-ink noodles or other "quality" pasta in a myriad of shapes, including filled versions like "top-notch" tortellini, ravioli or cannelloni (it's one of the "only places" around for those tasty cylinders), plus "cheeses to go with"; whatever your choice, it'll be dispensed by a "helpful" staff, but be warned: it's all "so good", you may "never want to eat dried noodles again."

pinkberry *Ice Cream*   22 | 20 | 19 | M

Chelsea | 170 Eighth Ave. (bet. 18th & 19th Sts.) | 212-488-2510 ●
E 50s | 1039 Second Ave. (bet. 54th & 55th Sts.) | 212-223-1918
E 80s | 1577 Second Ave. (82nd St.) | 212-861-0574 ●
E Village | 24 St. Marks Pl. (bet. 2nd & 3rd Aves.) | 212-228-0373
Garment District | 7 W. 32nd St. (bet. 5th & 6th Aves.) | 212-695-9631 ●
Murray Hill | 350 Third Ave. (bet. 25th & 26th Sts.) | 212-685-4301 ●
NoLita | 41 Spring St. (bet. Mott & Mulberry Sts.) | 212-274-8883 ●
W 50s | 330 W. 58th St. (bet. 8th & 9th Aves.) | 212-397-0412
W 70s | 313 Columbus Ave. (75th St.) | 212-874-1280 ●
W 100s | 2873 Broadway (bet. 111th & 112th Sts.) | 212-222-0195 ●
888-757-2331 | www.pinkberry.com
Additional locations throughout the NY area

"Be warned", this "ubiquitous" LA chain's "awesomely" "tangy" fro-yo is a "deliciously addicting" fusion of "refreshing" flavors with a "wide variety" of "excellent fresh fruit" and other "inventive" toppings ("try it with mochi") that "feels a lot more indulgent than it really is"; the treats are swirled by "nice young people" in "cute", "bright" quarters, and though naysayers knock an "overhyped" "fad" that's "not cheap" "for what you get", it draws "ridiculously long" summertime lines of loyalists who declare "this is the dessert of the decade."

Pino Prime Meats ⊅ *Meat/Poultry*   ▽ 29 | 21 | 28 | M

SoHo | 149 Sullivan St. (bet. Houston & Prince Sts.) | 212-475-8134

Pino Cinquemani is the "epitome of the neighborhood butcher", and his "old-school" SoHo shop "takes you back to a better time" with "excellent cuts" of the "freshest possible meat" including prime beef, homemade sausage, salami and game such as venison, wild boar and pheasant; citing "reliable" quality, "friendly" countermen who take "a personal interest" and "great prices to boot", locals and those in the know "love, love, love this place."

	QUALITY	DISPLAY	SERVICE	COST

☒ Pisacane Midtown *Seafood* | 28 | 20 | 24 | E |

E 50s | 940 First Ave. (bet. 51st & 52nd Sts.) | 212-752-7560

Ichthyophagous Eastsiders say "no one can hold a candle to" the "outstanding quality and freshness" at this "superb" family-run fish market, awash with a wide lineup of "impeccable" seafood overseen by an "excellent" crew who'll hospitably "tell you what to order"; the "prepared dishes to go" are "quite good" too, though not surprisingly such "top" offerings are on the "pricey" side.

☒ PJ Wine ◗☑ *Wine/Liquor* | 27 | 17 | 20 | M |

Inwood | 4898 Broadway (bet. 204th & 207th Sts.) | 212-567-5500 | www.pjwine.com

You "can spend hours" at this "massive" (15,000-sq.-ft.) Inwood wine-and-spirits store that scores points for its "good values" on a "vast selection" of bottles "from all over", with a particular concentration on Spanish producers plus a growing number of Chileans and Argentineans; throw in "competitive" delivery rates, and it's "worth the slog" up there, although surveyors encourage anyone who "can't make the trip" to visit its "great website."

Plaza Florists *Flowers* | - | - | - | E |

E 60s | 944 Lexington Ave. (bet. 69th & 70th Sts.) | 212-744-0936 | www.plazafloristsnyc.com

Third-generation owner Alexandra Plaissay presides over this East Side florist, where the "friendly staff" will offer "a crash course" in matching "charming" flowers to any setting (home decor is their specialty), and "you can actually use the word 'budget' without feeling gauche"; they'll go full-service for events, outsourcing for everything from linens to lighting.

☒ Pomegranate ☑ *Specialty Shop* | 26 | 27 | 20 | E |

Midwood | 1507 Coney Island Ave. (Ave. L) | Brooklyn | 718-951-7112 | www.thepompeople.com

"If you're kosher, you owe it to yourself to peruse" the "extraordinary selection" at this "huge, upscale" Midwood supermarket offering an enormous array of staple groceries, prime meats, fish, dairy, "fresh fruits and veggies" and a "lovely assortment" of prepared foods and baked goods from their three kitchens; "the price scale is higher" than some, but with such "impressive" quality "in so many categories", "if you can't find it here, you'd be hard-pressed to find it anywhere."

Popbar *Ice Cream* | 22 | 25 | 23 | M |

W Village | 5 Carmine St. (bet. Bleecker St. & 6th Ave.) | 212-255-4874 | www.pop-bar.com

"Deliciousness on a stick" sums up this "cute, trendy" West Villager, which upgrades the common popsicle by using all-natural gelato made with fresh fruit in 40 "fun" flavors and custom-dipping in chocolate, nuts, coconut and other toppings ("yum!"); the brightly "inviting" space is staffed by "knowledgeable" sorts, and if the concept is "a bit of a gimmick", the "creativity" and "high quality" make it worth popping by all the same.

	QUALITY	DISPLAY	SERVICE	COST

2 Porto Rico Importing Co. 🖃 *Coffee/Tea* | 27 | 22 | 22 | I |

E Village | 40½ St. Marks Pl. (bet. 1st & 2nd Aves.) | 212-533-1982
G Village | 201 Bleecker St. (bet. MacDougal St. & 6th Ave.) |
212-477-5421 | 800-453-5908●
LES | Essex Street Mkt. | 120 Essex St. (bet. Delancey & Rivington Sts.) |
212-677-1210
Williamsburg | 636 Grand St. (bet. Leonard St. & Manhattan Ave.) |
Brooklyn | 718-782-1200
www.portorico.com

"They're serious" about "java beans" at this "well-worn and well-loved" Village "classic" and its offshoots, which cater to "discerning caffeine addicts" with an "incredible selection" of "fresh" roasts "from around the world" displayed in "giant" "burlap sacks", along with a "comparably large" lineup of loose-leaf teas; the "heavenly" "aromas" alone are "intoxicating" ("can this be legal?"), and there's the "added bonus" of "bargain" prices and a staff that "would make a sommelier jealous."

Poseidon Bakery *Baked Goods* | 25 | 18 | 23 | I |

W 40s | 629 Ninth Ave. (bet. 44th & 45th Sts.) | 212-757-6173
"Fresh-made phyllo dough" earns "kudos" for this "funky, little" fourth-generation family-owned bakery in Hell's Kitchen, a "bastion of Greek goodies" turning out "flaky" "delicacies" "both savory and sweet", e.g. "stellar baklava" and "delicious spanakopita"; with service as "charming" as the goods are "authentic", admirers are "so glad" it's around to spare them the "schlep to Astoria."

2 Pour ●🖃 *Wine/Liquor* | 24 | 27 | 28 | M |

W 70s | 321 Amsterdam Ave. (75th St.) | 212-501-7687 |
www.pourwines.com
Oenophiles pour on the praise for this near-"perfect neighborhood wine store" on the UWS that's refreshingly "non-intimidating" thanks to "superb service" from "chilled-out" salespeople who have a flair for "helping you pair wine with food"; "high-end" and hard-to-find spirits share floor space with "value" selections in "beautiful displays" in which "every bottle's a winner"; P.S. daily tastings.

Premier Cru 🖃 *Wine/Liquor* | ▽ 25 | 25 | 26 | E |

E 80s | 1163 Madison Ave. (bet. 85th & 86th Sts.) | 212-534-6709 |
www.premiercruwine.com
This Upper Eastsider, owned by a pair of certified sommeliers, is appreciated locally for its "fabulous" vintages, "convenient location" and "courteous" assistance; maybe the offerings are "limited", but what's there is "carefully chosen" with a focus on French and Italian growers and specialty Burgundies, while somewhat steep prices come with the elite territory.

Props for Today *Party Rentals* | ▽ 20 | 16 | 18 | M |

Garment District | 330 W. 34th St., 12th fl. (bet. 8th & 9th Aves.) |
212-244-9600 | www.propsfortoday.com
For more than 30 years, party planners and members of the film and television industry have flocked to the showrooms of this Garment

District prop rentals company for everything from chalkboards and cigarette machines to tapestries and taxidermy; it's probably the only place in the city you can rent both Harry Potter and bordello modern-themed furniture collections, though if you need a less-exotic sectional sofa, they'll gladly supply that too.

Prospect Wine Shop ◐ ▣ *Wine/Liquor* | ▽ 25 | 22 | 24 | M |

Park Slope | 322 Seventh Ave. (bet. 8th & 9th Sts.) | Brooklyn | 718-768-1232 | www.prospectwine.com

Park Slope sippers raise a glass to the "surprisingly great selection" of "wonderful" wines at this go-to on the Seventh Avenue strip, which specializes in small old-world producers and organic options, and also carries a selection of spirits; other pluses are "extremely knowledgeable" staffers, "fun tastings" on Saturdays (held in the attached garden in summer), moderate prices and open-Sunday hours.

NEW Puddin' by Clio ● *Baked Goods* | ▽ 29 | 25 | 25 | M |

E Village | 102 St. Marks Pl. (bet. Ave. A & 1st Ave.) | 212-477-3537 | www.puddinnyc.com

Sweet tooths rejoice – this nook "dedicated to puddin'" has arrived on St. Marks Place, and admirers say the proof is in the "fantastic" creamy house specialty, which early-goers call just about "the best you can find"; owner/pastry chef Clio Goodman gives the star sweet a sophisticated turn via quality ingredients (organic dairy, high-end dark chocolate), an array of flavors from banana cream to caramel macchiato, plus "yummy" toppings to seal the deal.

Puro Chile *Specialty Shop* | - | - | - | M |

Little Italy | 221 Centre St. (bet. Grand & Howard Sts.) | 212-217-9362 | www.puro-chile.com

Puro Wine ▣ *Wine/Liquor*

Little Italy | 161 Grand St. (bet. Centre & Lafayette Sts.) | 212-925-0090 | www.puro-wine.com

A "piece of Chilean culture" set down "in the middle of" Little Italy, these side-by-side arrivals seek to offer the best of the South American country's exports, in "gorgeous" mod quarters designed by a Santiago architect; on one side are comestibles like olive oil, honey and jam, housewares (including traditional clay pots and tableware) and more, and next door are some 150 impressively displayed wines, ranging from affordable Valle Central labels to hard-to-find collectors' bottles, with tastings held on Fridays and Saturdays to help you get to know them all better.

⊿ Quattro's Game & Poultry Farm ⇆ *Meat/Poultry* | 28 | 18 | 23 | M |

Location varies | 845-635-2018

Fowl fanciers "have yet to find a better big-bird source" than this Pleasant Valley farm's Saturday nest at the Union Square Greenmarket, where the "fabulous" roster of "top-quality poultry" includes "wonderful pheasant, duck and geese" (fresh or "smoked"), plus "terrific" sausage, "wild game" and venison; order ahead for "special offerings" in season, like "heritage turkey" for Thanksgiving.

Queen Ann Ravioli *Pasta* `25` `17` `21` `M`

Bensonhurst | 7205 18th Ave. (bet. 72nd & 73rd Sts.) | Brooklyn | 718-256-1061

The "tasty, housemade ravioli" from this Bensonhurst veteran is a longtime "Sunday family favorite" for loyal subjects who also gobble up its other "excellent-quality" pastas and prepared dishes "like nonna used to make"; supreme "freshness" and "friendly and generous" service secure its reign as a "Brooklyn staple."

Radiance Tea House ● *Coffee/Tea* `∇ 24` `24` `23` `M`

W 50s | 158 W. 55th St. (bet. 6th & 7th Aves.) | 212-217-0442 | www.radiancetea.com

An Asian-influenced tea menu is the attraction at this bookshelf-lined shop and cafe in Midtown with "lovely, quiet" Zen vibes and a "nice" retail section stocked with high-quality teas, many of them 'wellness' blends with roots in traditional Chinese medicine; those who get hungry while sipping Sweet Dragon Eye brew can order "light" bites like dumplings, noodles and salads, plus housemade ice creams, while private Chinese tea ceremonies, tastings and other events can be booked separately.

☑ Raffetto's 📋 ⇗ *Pasta* `28` `21` `24` `I`

G Village | 144 W. Houston St. (bet. MacDougal & Sullivan Sts.) | 212-777-1261

"You can still watch the old-style pasta cutting" machine in action at this circa-1906 "NYC treasure", where loading up on "fantastic fresh pasta in a multitude of shapes and flavors" at "entirely fair prices" is a cherished "Village tradition"; in addition to the noodles ("so tender, so delicate"), ravioli and other filled versions "just like grandma's" and "dry pastas imported from Italy", there are "cheeses, sauces, bread" and prepared dishes (meatballs, lasagna, etc.) so "wonderful", you may be tempted to "claim them as your own."

Ralph's Famous Italian Ices *Ice Cream* `25` `16` `20` `I`

NEW **Murray Hill** | 144 E. 24th St. (bet. Lexington & 3rd Aves.) | 212-533-5333

Bayside | 214-13 41st Ave. (Bell Blvd.) | Queens | 718-428-4578 ● ⇗

Floral Park | 264-21 Union Tpke. (bet. 264th & 265th Sts.) | Queens | 718-343-8724 ● ⇗

Whitestone | 12-48 Clintonville St. (12th Rd.) | Queens | 718-746-1456 ● ⇗

Staten Island | 2361 Hylan Blvd. (bet. Bryant & Otis Aves.) | 718-351-8133

Staten Island | 3285 Richmond Ave. (Gurley Ave.) | 718-967-1212

Staten Island | 4212 Hylan Blvd. (bet. Armstrong & Robinson Aves.) | 718-605-5052 ●

Staten Island | 501 Port Richmond Ave. (Catherine St.) | 718-273-3675 ●

Staten Island | 6272 Amboy Rd. (Bloomingdale Rd.) | 718-605-8133 ●

Staten Island | 890 Huguenot Ave. (bet. Amboy & Drumgoole Rds.) | 718-356-8133

www.ralphsices.com

"So many flavors", "so little time" is the refrain at this Staten Island Italian ice "institution" (the Port Richmond Avenue original opened in 1949) and its multiple offshoots, where "endless" lines form in summer for a rainbow of "refreshing" frozen treats that encompasses not only ices but also ice cream, sherbet, shakes and even "sugar-free choices"; "on a hot day, you can't go wrong", especially given the "affordable" tabs.

Randazzo's Seafood *Seafood*   26 | 21 | 24 | M

Bronx | 2327 Arthur Ave. (bet. 183rd & 187th Sts.) | 718-367-4139 | www.randazzoseafood.com

"If you're looking for fresh seafood", it's "worth the trip to Arthur Avenue" to be dazzo'd by this longtime fishmonger's "superb quality", "excellent selection" (it's "great for shellfish" too) and service "of yesteryear" from family owners who "know their fish"; it specializes in "imported sardines and other ocean goodies from different regions of Italy", and "you can even eat clams standing on the sidewalk" at their raw bar out front.

Ready to Eat ● *Prepared Food*   ▽ 23 | 15 | 17 | M

W Village | 525 Hudson St. (bet. Charles & 10th Sts.) | 212-229-1013 | www.readytoeat.net

"When you're in a hurry" and "ready to eat", this West Village caterer's a whiz at homestyle American prepared dishes, from sandwiches at lunch to standards like pot pie and stuffed turkey for dinner; on top of the "good quality", "you get a lot of food for your money."

⊉ Red Hook Lobster Pound *Seafood*   27 | 18 | 22 | M

Red Hook | 284 Van Brunt St. (bet. Verona St. & Visitation Pl.) | Brooklyn | 718-858-7650 | www.redhooklobsterpound.com

"Save the drive" north courtesy of husband-and-wife owners who "travel to Maine themselves" every week to haul back "fresh live lobsters" for this "tiny" Red Hook "treasure"; the "basic" storefront sports two 700-pound water tanks filled with "the best of the best" crustaceans, and there's now "a space next door with picnic tables" where clawstrophiles can munch "heavenly lobster rolls" (which are also available via its new food truck).

Red Jacket Orchards ▣ *Produce*   26 | 20 | 22 | M

Location varies | 315-781-2749 or 800-828-9410 | www.redjacketorchards.com

Fruit fanciers partial to "fresh" pickings "can't live without" fall apples trucked in "numerous varieties" from this Finger Lakes orchard and sold "with a smile" at its Greenmarket stand, which shifts in summer to "wonderful" pitted pleasures like apricots, plums and peaches; it's a "refreshing" vendor of "fantastic" juices, nectars and ciders to boot, also accessible via Fresh Direct, Whole Foods and other retailers.

Red Mango *Ice Cream*   22 | 19 | 19 | M

Chelsea | 63 W. 14th St. (bet. 5th & 6th Aves.) | 212-414-3009 ●
E 40s | 45 E. 45th St. (bet. Madison & Vanderbilt Aves.) | 212-697-1666
NEW **Financial District** | 111 Fulton St. (bet. Nassau & William Sts.) | 212-321-3210
Garment District | 234 W. 34th St. (bet. 7th & 8th Aves.) | 212-244-0101
LES | 145 Allen St. (Rivington St.) | 212-933-0399 ●

QUALITY DISPLAY SERVICE COST

(continued)

Red Mango

W 60s | 113 W. 60th St. (bet. Amsterdam & Columbus Aves.) | 212-636-6067

Astoria | 30-58 Steinway St. (bet. 30th & 31st Aves.) | Queens | 347-738-4197 🌢

NEW **Bayside** | 42-23 Bell Blvd. (bet. 42nd & 43rd Aves.) | Queens | 718-352-5000

Fresh Meadows | 61-47 188th St. (bet. Horace Harding Expwy. & 64th Ave.) | Queens | 718-264-8881 🌢

NEW **Rego Park** | 6101 Junction Blvd. (62nd Dr.) | Brooklyn | 718-760-7100

www.redmangousa.com

Additional locations throughout the NY area

Depending on which fro-yo fanatic you ask, this mini-chain is either "superior" to the competition or a close "runner-up", but all agree it dispenses "rich, creamy", "delicious" frozen product that's "just the right amount of sweet and tart"; it comes in a "cool" "diversity of flavors" (green tea, seasonal pumpkin spice) embellished with "fresh fruit" and other "great toppings" – although those "add-ons" sure do "add to" the bottom line.

Red, White & Bubbly 🌢 ▣ *Wine/Liquor*   26 | 23 | 24 | M |

Park Slope | 211-213 Fifth Ave. (bet. President & Union Sts.) | Brooklyn | 718-636-9463 | www.redwhiteandbubbly.com

"Spreading love of wine" seems to be the mission of this "pleasant" Park Slope wine-and-liquor mart that's locally appreciated for its "tremendous finds" at "reasonable" prices and "friendly" staffers who make "suggestions that turn out well" (you'll "try a bottle and come back for a case"); other enticements are regular discounts, wine classes for all levels and online ordering.

Rice to Riches 🌢 ▣ *Baked Goods*   24 | 25 | 22 | M |

NoLita | 37 Spring St. (bet. Mott & Mulberry Sts.) | 212-274-0008 | www.ricetoriches.com

"Who knew rice pudding could be hip?" marvel mavens of this "fabulous" NoLita "emporium", which turns "a once-overlooked dessert" into a "self-indulgent" "must-try" with "countless" "wonderfully inventive flavors" like cheesecake, chocolate-hazelnut and mascarpone with cherries ("ask for tastes") dished up in "plastic spaceship" bowls; those who flock to the "cool-looking", "*Jetsons*"-style venue to "savor every grain" of "creamy" "ambrosia" call it "a total crowd-pleaser" – so "why aren't there more" around town?

Rick's Picks ▣ *Specialty Shop*   ▽ 26 | 18 | 20 | M |

Location varies | 212-358-0428 | www.rickspicksnyc.com

"Any pickle lover" should "definitely seek out" this Greenmarket "favorite", which will "rock your world" with all-natural specialties handmade in small batches and spiced up with "great flavor combos" like Phat Beets (pickled beets), the People's Pickle (garlic dills), Smokra (okra with paprika) and Hottie (crinkle-cuts with habanero); once you've had a chance to relish the "right-on" taste, "you'll be hooked"; P.S. the jars are also available at upscale retailers like Murray's Cheese, Whole Foods and Spuyten Duyvil.

Robicelli's ▭ *Baked Goods* ▽ 26 | 23 | 26 | I

Location varies | Brooklyn | 917-509-6048 | robicellis.tumblr.com

"Foodies who want an adventure when satisfying their sweet tooths" seek out the "scrumptious"-yet-"inventive" cupcakes turned out by this Sunset Park–based husband-and-wife team, who sell their wares via markets around town and at the DeKalb Market; the rotating "crazy-amazing" varieties – think chicken 'n' waffles, Sixpoint Brownstone, banana-flavored Elvis with candied bacon – earn "an 'A' on the creative scale", though there are "more tame, but never boring", options too; P.S. the goods can be catered for weddings and events.

Rocco's Pastry Shop ◐▭ *Baked Goods* 25 | 24 | 21 | M

W Village | 243 Bleecker St. (bet. Carmine & Leroy Sts.) | 212-242-6031 | www.roccospastry.com

"Some things simply can't be improved upon" say supporters sweet on this "real-deal" West Village Italian bakery/cafe, a "reliable" "1970s holdout" where the "tempting display" features a "plethora" of "top-quality" "traditional" pastries showcasing cannoli "piped fresh" "the way it should be" plus sfogliatelle and "homemade" gelato and ices in summer; the staff is "always friendly", and even if it gets "busy" with "hordes of tourists", locals still come to "relax over good coffee" "without spending a fortune."

Ronaldo Maia *Flowers* ▽ 24 | 23 | 19 | VE

E 90s | 1143 Park Ave. (bet. 91st & 92nd Sts.) | 212-288-1049

"The beautiful windows" of this veddy posh Upper East Side florist offer a hint of the equally lovely arrangements within, where the eponymous Brazilian-born floral designer creates innovative-yet-natural bouquets using a single flower or a glorious array of unusual blossoms; all are custom-created (no mail order or catalogs) and come in unusual vases or containers, many of which are part of a limited house line of decorative objets and gifts.

Ron Ben-Israel Cakes *Baked Goods* ▽ 27 | 25 | 25 | VE

SoHo | 42 Greene St., 5th fl. (bet. Broome & Grand Sts.) | 212-625-3369 | www.weddingcakes.com
By appointment only

Ron Ben-Israel "is a true artist" say admirers of his top-tier SoHo custom bakery, which focuses on "exquisite" wedding and other special-occasion cakes adorned with spun-sugar florets that are "almost too pretty to eat" but too "delicious" to resist; the maestro will "work closely" with clients to realize their "vision", and although it's certainly "not cheap", all agree the results are "amazing."

Roni-Sue's Chocolates ▭ *Candy/Nuts* ▽ 24 | 20 | 24 | M

LES | Essex Street Mkt. | 120 Essex St. (bet. Delancey & Rivington Sts.) | 212-260-0421 | www.roni-sue.com

The Lower East Side's "queen of chocolatiers", Rhonda Kave reigns over her "tiny" realm "hidden" away in the Essex Street Market, where her "imaginative" handmade treats run from "rich" classic truffles "to die for" to "interesting choices" like her "famous chocolate-covered bacon"; the "service is as sweet" as the goodies, and honestly, "how can you pass by" a place that can "marry pork and cocoa to perfection"?; P.S. you can also place and pick up orders here for First Prize Pies, made by Kave's daughter.

Ronnybrook Milk Bar *Cheese/Dairy*   26 | 20 | 20 | M

Chelsea | Chelsea Mkt. | 75 Ninth Ave. (bet. 15th & 16th Sts.) | 212-741-6455 | 800-772-6455 | www.ronnybrook.com

This "dairy godmother" in the Chelsea Market is a wish-come-true for milk-lovers who are udderly delighted by the "exceptional" offerings in its "farmhouse"-inspired storefront, including many types of milk and cream, butter, "delicious" yogurt drinks and ice cream, plus "thick, frothy" milkshakes, sundaes and such are available at the counter; it's always a "fun" stop "for families and couples alike", but the cream-of-the-crop lineup is also on offer at the Greenmarket and in gourmet stores citywide.

Rosa Rosa *Flowers*   ∇ 24 | 21 | 22 | M

E 60s | 831A Lexington Ave. (bet. 63rd & 64th Sts.) | 212-935-4706 | www.rosarosaflowers.com

Given the name, it's no surprise that "terrific-quality" roses are the best-known buds at this East Side blossom boutique that gets near-daily shipments of the blooms from the Netherlands and Ecuador, and also vends tasteful arrangements of tulips, orchids and other floral fare for weddings and corporate events; pleasingly reasonable prices, online ordering and local and national delivery also help it stand out from the bunch.

Rosenthal Wine Merchant *Wine/Liquor* ∇ 29 | 23 | 26 | E

E 80s | 318 E. 84th St. (bet. 1st & 2nd Aves.) | 212-249-6650

You "feel like you're part of a club" when you step into the brownstone that houses this "old-school" Upper East Side wine shop, where there's "always an interesting selection" of small, artisanal French and Italian producers and other "fine wines you can't get anyplace else", all imported by merchant Neal Rosenthal (who has no official affiliation with the store); "flawless" guidance will lead you to bottles "you've never heard of" yet "love from the first taste" – just know that help from the "best palates" doesn't come cheap.

Royal Crown Pastry Shop *Baked Goods*   26 | 23 | 23 | M

Bensonhurst | 6512 14th Ave. (bet. 65th & 66th Sts.) | Brooklyn | 718-234-1002 | www.newyorkitalianmarket.com

The "real brick-oven" output is "fit for royalty" at this Bensonhurst Italian bakery, which "ranks at the top of the bread basket" for bequeathing "heavenly crusted" loaves ("be sure to try" the "special varieties" like chocolate and fig-and-walnut) at "reasonable prices"; the pastries and other "beautiful" baked goods "can't be underestimated either."

	QUALITY	DISPLAY	SERVICE	COST

Z Russ & Daughters 🍽 *Caviar/Smoked Fish* | 29 | 24 | 25 | E |

LES | 179 E. Houston St. (bet. Allen & Orchard Sts.) |
212-475-4880 | 800-787-7229 | www.russanddaughters.com

This family-run LES "landmark" dating to 1914 is in a "class by it-self" thanks to the "new generation" there that's "keeping up the quality" with "drool-worthy displays" of "legendary offerings", nota-bly sable and "lox to dream of", "herring perfection", "top-quality" caviar and more, from bagels and babka to dried fruits and choco-late; it's always a "mad scene", especially at holidays ("oy vey!"), but the counter folk are "super helpful", so "take a number" – "it's worth the lines" and "expensive" tab to "order some of the best" with a side of "history."

Russo Mozzarella & Pasta *Cheese/Dairy* | 26 | 19 | 22 | M |

E Village | 344 E. 11th St. (bet. 1st & 2nd Aves.) | 212-254-7452
Park Slope | 363 Seventh Ave. (bet. 10th & 11th Sts.) | Brooklyn |
718-369-2874 🍽

Italian cuisine fiends express their *amore* for this "hole-in-the-wall" East Village "old-time holdout" (circa 1908), as well as its Park Slope annex, both of which vend "superb" housemade fresh mozza-rella "made daily", plus a line of "inventive fresh pastas" and sauces whose "taste brings you back" to The Boot; it's all offered at pleas-ingly "moderate" prices, and the Brooklyn outpost adds prepared foods to the mix (try the "amazing" roasted artichokes).

Ruthy's Bakery & Cafe 🍽 *Baked Goods* | 20 | 19 | 17 | M |

Chelsea | Chelsea Mkt. | 75 Ninth Ave. (bet. 15th & 16th Sts.) |
212-463-8800 | 888-729-8800 | www.ruthys.com

"My, they have some very tasty treats" at this Chelsea Market bakery/cafe, which specializes in cheesecake and "delicious ru-galach" as well as customized cakes, including a line with cute themes for "children's birthdays"; but while well-wishers "can't get enough", detractors discern "nothing jaw-dropping"; P.S. they ship nationwide and deliver in Manhattan below 96th Street.

Z Sable's | 27 | 19 | 23 | E |
Smoked Fish 🍽 *Caviar/Smoked Fish*

E 70s | 1489 Second Ave. (bet. 77th & 78th Sts.) | 212-249-6177 |
www.sablesnyc.rapidorders.com

"You can't get out" of this "swimmingly good" UES smoked-fish ba-zaar without being offered a "generous" sample of the signature whitefish or lobster salad as you troll the "cramped" quarters for "wonderful appetizing" and other "high-quality" "Sunday morning" fixings; it's "worth the extra" coinage you pay for this level of "qual-ity and freshness", but just "don't forget to bring your gold bullion."

Z Sahadi's 🍽 *Specialty Shop* | 28 | 22 | 22 | I |

Brooklyn Heights | 187 Atlantic Ave. (bet. Clinton & Court Sts.) |
Brooklyn | 718-624-4550 | www.sahadis.com

"It doesn't get any better" for seekers of "Middle Eastern provisions" than this "long-established" Brooklyn Heights "labyrinth" of "ex-otic" "delights", an "institution to be treasured" for its "vast inventory" of "traditional" staples including nuts, dried fruits, spices, olives, coffee, grains, oils, jams, fresh cheeses and "excellent" prepared foods such as "hummus, grape leaves, etc." – in short, "everything you need"; it's a "zoo" at "peak times" ("get ready to take a number"), but with "efficient" service and "unbeatable prices", it's "worth the hassle" even if you're "schlepping from Manhattan"; P.S. an expansion is in the works.

Sakaya *Wine/Liquor*   ▽ 28 | 26 | 28 | M

E Village | 324 E. Ninth St. (bet. 1st & 2nd Aves.) | 212-505-7253 | www.sakayanyc.com

Sake sippers swear by this "well-kept secret" in the East Village, a "jewel box of a store" chock-full of "amazing choices" imported from Japan, including a locally "unmatched" selection of some 100 varieties of rice wine plus a smaller sampling of the distilled spirit shochu; ultra-"helpful" salesclerks are primed to "educate", and there are also weekly in-store tastings as well as offsite ones that can be arranged at customers' homes.

Sal & Dom's *Baked Goods*   ▽ 28 | 23 | 21 | M

Bronx | 1108 Allerton Ave. (Laconia Ave.) | 718-515-3344 | www.salanddoms.com

"Near the top of the list" for Bronx cannoli and biscotti buffs, this "been-around-for-years" Italian bakery in Williamsbridge is a "neighborhood gem" prized for its "great pastries", cookies and cakes; the high quality and traditional style make it a "family favorite", especially around holidays when the ovens issue the seasonal likes of struffoli, Easter bread and zeppole for St. Joseph's Day.

Salumeria Biellese ▣ *Deli*   26 | 16 | 20 | M

Chelsea | 378 Eighth Ave. (29th St.) | 212-736-7376 | www.salumeriabiellese.com

This 1925-vintage Chelsea salumeria is prized for its "terrific Italian-style cured meats" and "outstanding fresh sausage", housemade "with care" from "farm-raised" stock in 40-plus variations spanning "the usual" to the unique; the products turn up at "forbidding" upscale restaurants like Daniel Boulud's and Jean-Georges Vongerichten's, but those coming straight to the source note the price tag "isn't haute"; P.S. they also offer prepared foods, imported prosciutto and a full line of sandwiches.

⊠ Salumeria Rosi   28 | 24 | 23 | E
Parmacotto ▣ *Specialty Shop*

W 70s | 283 Amsterdam Ave. (bet. 73rd & 74th Sts.) | 212-877-4800 | www.salumeriarosi.com

"Like a little piece of Italy on the UWS", this "spectacular" salumeria/cafe is a "tiny" "gem" where chef Cesare Casella oversees an "eclectic selection" showcasing "wonderful" cured meats (think "authentic" salamis and prosciutto di Parma) "flown in daily" from the old country along with "delicious cheeses", pastas, oils and other "lovely" "specialty foods"; the "super-educated staff" also mans an eating area "crowded" with cognoscenti sampling "tapas dishes", and while it's admittedly "high-priced", the "superior taste is worth every penny"; P.S. a new East Side branch is in the works at 903 Madison Avenue.

Z **S&S Cheesecake** ⌨🚫 *Baked Goods*

| 28 | 14 | 20 | M |

Bronx | 222 W. 238th St. (bet. Bailey Ave. & B'way) | 718-549-3888 | www.sscheesecake.com

Theirs is "the cheesecake you dream about" promise partisans of this "still-incredible" Bronx bakery – "nothing comes close" to the legendarily "rich" "manna" that's the "ultimate" "calorie splurge"; even if you "need your GPS" to find its "no-frills" facility (open Monday–Friday till 3PM), it's worth "the trip from anywhere" – though the wares can also be had at "many fancy NY restaurants" like Morton's and Bobby Van's.

Sant Ambroeus ● *Ice Cream*

| 26 | 25 | 22 | VE |

E 70s | 1000 Madison Ave. (bet. 77th & 78th Sts.) | 212-570-2211
W Village | 259 W. Fourth St. (Perry St.) | 212-604-9254
www.santambroeus.com

"Scenesters, socialites and locals" all know this chichi pair of Italian cafes on the Upper East Side and in the West Village are *the* places to travel for "heavenly" gelato, "out-of-this-world" pastries, "outstanding" espresso and a taste of la dolce vita; "how can price matter" when the bill is "much less" than "airfare" "to Milan"?

Sarabeth's ⌨ *Baked Goods*

| 24 | 21 | 20 | E |

Chelsea | Chelsea Mkt. | 75 Ninth Ave. (bet. 15th & 16th Sts.) | 212-989-2424
E 90s | 1295 Madison Ave. (bet. 92nd & 93rd Sts.) | 212-410-7335 ●
Garment District | Lord & Taylor | 424 Fifth Ave., 5th & 6th fls. (bet. 38th & 39th Sts.) | 212-827-5068
NEW **TriBeCa** | 339 Greenwich St. (bet. Harrison & Jay Sts.) | 212-966-0421
W 80s | 423 Amsterdam Ave. (bet. 80th & 81st Sts.) | 212-496-6280 ●
800-773-7378 | www.sarabeth.com

"Long a local favorite" and "weekend necessity" for "stroller moms and prep parents", these "sweet" bakery/cafes are "tried-and-true" for "simple" pleasures like fresh-made muffins and scones, "jazzed-up jams" and rustic "charm" that's the "perfect escape" for a "midday break"; it's "worth paying a little extra for" the "wonderfully consistent" performance, and they host a "Sunday brunch to get up for" if you're willing to "wait with all of NY for a seat."

Sarge's Deli ●⌨ *Deli*

| 22 | 16 | 19 | M |

Murray Hill | 548 Third Ave. (bet. 36th & 37th Sts.) | 212-679-0442 | www.sargesdeli.com

Noshers "in the mood for old-school Jewish" standards snap a salute to this 24/7 "Murray Hill staple", a "solid choice" "across the board" for "mounds" of "delicious" pastrami, smoked fish, matzo ball soup and plenty more; the "dog-eared" digs are "not the most glamorous", but it's as "authentic" as the "more well-known" competition "without the tourist hordes" – plus there's delivery "whenever you may be pining."

	QUALITY	DISPLAY	SERVICE	COST

Z Saxelby Cheesemongers *Cheese/Dairy* | 29 | 24 | 27 | E |

LES | Essex Street Mkt. | 120 Essex St. (bet. Delancey & Rivington Sts.) | 212-228-8204 | www.saxelbycheese.com

This "lovely little" "American-only" cheese stall in the Essex Street Market is "locavore" heaven given its "small but superb" selection of "regional" artisanal cheeses with a spotlight on those from the Northeast as well as local "milk, yogurt, butter, eggs and bread"; it's all overseen by "very caring owners" Anne Saxelby and Benoit Breal, whose "fun" demeanor adds to the enjoyment and helps compensate for "costly" price tags; P.S. it hosts occasional "field trips" to dairy farms in LI, Upstate and Vermont.

Z Schaller & Weber *Meat/Poultry* | 28 | 22 | 23 | M |

E 80s | 1654 Second Ave. (bet. 85th & 86th Sts.) | 212-879-3047 | 800-847-4115 | www.schallerweber.com

"Danke schön!" cry thankful fans of this "remnant of the old Yorkville", a "real treasure" that "still sets the standard" with a "wide range" of the "finest" "old-world German" wursts, wieners and meats tendered by "butchers who know their trade"; it's also "a mini-grocery well stocked" with "excellent" imported sundries, and while it's "not cheap", for "hands-down" "authentic" goods "this is the spot" – may it "stay there forever."

Z Schatzie's Prime Meats *Meat/Poultry* | 27 | 22 | 24 | E |

W 80s | 555 Amsterdam Ave. (87th St.) | 212-410-1555 | www.schatziethebutcher.com

"He moved" directly across the park from Madison Avenue a couple of years back, but "neighborhood butcher" and "great character" Tony Schatzie remains a "surefire" supplier of "fabulous" beef, poultry and game now that his century-old shop's taken up residence on the UWS; given his singularly personal service – with meat cut and cooked to order when you need to "feed the family in a jiffy" – locals are "so glad" to "welcome" him "to the 'hood"; P.S. there's now an expanded selection of prepared foods.

Schick's Bakery *Baked Goods* | ▽ 23 | 18 | 21 | M |

Borough Park | 4710 16th Ave. (bet. 47th & 48th Sts.) | Brooklyn | 718-436-8020 | www.schicksbakery.com

A "classic kosher bakery" and an "old Brooklyn gem" (since 1943), this Borough Park pastry shop specializes in nondairy baked goods including challah bread and babka, drawing "lines" of "regulars" "every Passover" for flourless cakes like bubby "used to make"; during the rest of the year it offers quintessential "Jewish goods", including kashruth wedding cakes, as well as some French-style sweets; P.S. closed Saturday.

Scratch Bread *Baked Goods* | ▽ 27 | 21 | 25 | M |

Bed-Stuy | 1069 Bedford Ave. (Lexington Ave.) | Brooklyn | no phone | www.scratchbread.com

Founded by baker Matthew Tilden, this "friendly" Bed-Stuy bakery is best known for its "really scrumptious" rustic artisanal breads – made from scratch, natch – like Stuyvesant sour, cacio e peppe and

QUALITY DISPLAY SERVICE COST

hands boulle, until now available mainly at stores and restaurants around town; however, Tilden's focus recently shifted to his on-site Noshery retail window, now offering Stumptown coffee, juices and hearty to-go foods, as well as fresh bread sold retail; P.S. there are also classes, a tasting menu once a month at the shop and even a to-go-style brunch on Sundays.

Screme *Ice Cream* 24 | 21 | 24 | E

NEW E 40s | 47 E. 42nd St. (bet. Madison & Park Aves.) | 212-867-7141
W 60s | 2030 Broadway (bet. 69th & 70th Sts.) | 212-362-2111
W 90s | 176 W. 94th St. (Amsterdam Ave.) | 212-663-1362 ◗
www.screme.com

Everybody scremes for the "delicious" "innovative flavors" and "generous" "sampling" policy at these "gourmet" gelato triplets, branches of an Israeli chain whose creamy scoops are certified kosher; the "ultrapremium" goods are matched by "ultrapremium prices" and seating is lacking, but "if you need a treat" it more than fills the bill.

Sea Breeze *Seafood* ▽ 21 | 16 | 17 | I

W 40s | 541 Ninth Ave. (40th St.) | 212-563-7537

Shopping for "serious fish" is a breeze thanks to this family-run Hell's Kitchen fixture, which flaunts an "awesome" selection of "truly fresh seafood" at some of the "cheapest" prices around; the very basic setup ("wear your waders") is offset by "knowledgeable" service from an on-site owner and "helpful" staffers who "sell you what you need, not what they want to sell."

Seaport Flowers *Flowers* ▽ 27 | 26 | 24 | E

Brooklyn Heights | 309 Henry St. (bet. Atlantic Ave. & State St.) | Brooklyn | 718-858-6443 | www.seaportflowers.com

This stylish Brooklyn Heights florist is known for "absolutely" "beautiful" blooms imported fresh from around the world and garnished with artichokes, grapes, berries and other seasonal flourishes – and planning events of any size; it fits the bill for a "lovely" bouquet when "only the best will do", though wallet-watchers warn "unless you walk in with a Benjamin" a "sniff" is "about all you can afford."

Sensuous Bean ▣ *Coffee/Tea* 25 | 21 | 23 | E

W 70s | 66 W. 70th St. (bet. Columbus Ave. & CPW) | 212-724-7725 | 800-238-6845 | www.sensuousbean.com

A "small shop" steeped in "wonderful" "UWS atmosphere", this '70s-era coffee merchant globally sources "high-quality beans" for its "sensuous" signature blends, along with a similarly "superb" assortment of teas; according to loyalists who "enjoy the neighborhood interactions" and "cluttered space" filled with "unique gifts", it's "comforting in a lot of ways" that this stalwart still "beats the big guys."

S. Feldman Housewares ▣ *Cookware* 26 | 20 | 25 | E

E 90s | 1304 Madison Ave. (bet. 92nd & 93rd Sts.) | 212-289-7367 | 800-359-8558 | www.sfeldmanhousewares.com

"It's unbelievable what they stock" for "such a tiny store" marvel admirers of this UES housewares store that has "just about everything you could ever need" to stock your kitchen and put forth fine meals, from cookware and appliances to Alessi tabletop items, all overseen by a staff that's "so accommodating"; if a few balk at the "chaotic", "expensive" "jumble of stuff", for locals it's a "truly convenient" godsend – "why can't every neighborhood have a place like this?"

NEW Shelsky's
Smoked Fish *Caviar/Smoked Fish*

24	19	25	E

Boerum Hill | 251 Smith St. (bet. Degraw & Douglass Sts.) | Brooklyn | 718-855-8817 | www.shelskys.com

Ready to meet "all your smoked fish emergencies", Boerum Hill's new old-style Jewish appetizing store is "the place" for those who "love a good sturgeon", whitefish, pickled herring or other "scrumptious" classic; add traditional schmears and spreads, not to mention bagels and bialys from Kossar's and bread from Orwasher's, and most happily overlook prices on the "expensive" side – hey, it beats "schlepping" to Manhattan, and the service with "direct-from-Brooklyn humor" comes free.

Z Sherry-Lehmann 🖃 *Wine/Liquor*

29	26	25	E

E 50s | 505 Park Ave. (59th St.) | 212-838-7500 | www.sherry-lehmann.com

The "gold standard" for "well-rounded" wine emporiums, this Midtown imbiber's "Eden" makes it a "pleasure to shop" for vintages and liquor of all kinds "in person", "online" or from the mail-order "catalog" – a bacchanal's "dream book" – given the "superlative selection" of "high-end" libations (some 6,500 labels), "engaged", "knowledgeable" sales reps, "fast" delivery and in-house "educational seminars"; loads of glassware and accessories are also on hand, and if your sales slip is sky-high, at least you "get what you pay for."

Sigmund Pretzel Shop *Baked Goods*

▽ 26	22	23	I

E Village | 29 Ave. B (bet. 2nd & 3rd Sts.) | 646-410-0333 | www.sigmundnyc.com

Devoted to new twists on traditional soft pretzels, this East Villager has tasters tying themselves in happy knots over its hand-braided creations, made from organic flour, with "fresh" ingredient combos like olive-feta, cinnamon-raisin and the "genius" bacon-scallion ("munchies, anyone?"); dunk one into the dips on offer – goat cheese, Nutella – and you'll never be satisfied with the "ballpark" variety again.

Silver Moon Bakery *Baked Goods*

26	22	22	M

W 100s | 2740 Broadway (105th St.) | 212-866-4717 | www.silvermoonbakery.com

"Breads and pastries that transport you to Paris" are the specialty of this "superior" UWS French bakery whose "delicious delights" – from baguettes to challah, cakes to macarons and frangipane tarts – always seem "fresh" "out of the oven"; locals who nearly "jump over the moon" as the "smells waft out to Broadway" warn "don't be put off by cramped quarters" and "weekend crowds" – just join the fray and try to "get noticed" by the counter crew.

QUALITY | DISPLAY | SERVICE | COST

Z Simchick, L. *Meat/Poultry*   `29` `19` `25` `VE`

E 50s | 988 First Ave. (bet. 54th & 55th Sts.) | 212-888-2299
With an "emphasis on top quality and personal service", this East Side "real old-fashioned butcher" supplies "high-end" meats that are simply "the finest", housemade sausages and "oven-ready" specialties including marinated steaks and roasts; naturally "you pay" for such "superb" stock, but it comes courtesy of "knowledgeable and friendly" staffers who dependably "deliver."

16 Handles *Ice Cream*   `24` `22` `20` `I`

E 80s | 1569 Second Ave. (bet. 81st & 82nd Sts.) |
646-863-2522 ●
E Village | 153 Second Ave. (bet. 9th & 10th Sts.) |
212-260-4414 ●
NEW Garment District | Madison Sq. Garden | 4 Pennsylvania Plaza, 6th fl. (bet. 7th & 8th Aves.)
G Village | 498 Sixth Ave. (bet. 12th & 13th Sts.) | 646-524-5904 ●
W 70s | 325 Amsterdam Ave. (bet. 75th & 76th Sts.) |
646-861-1281 ●
NEW Midwood | 1651 Coney Island Ave. (Ave. J) | Brooklyn |
718-676-9889 ●
NEW Astoria | 37-07 30th Ave. (bet. 37th & 38th Sts.) | Queens |
347-527-1050
www.16handles.com
"Weigh, pay, eat, smile" is the deal at this green-minded "favorite" where the "help-yourself" format features a "constantly rotating" selection of 16 "fantastic" fro-yo flavors on tap plus a "buffet-style" array of "every topping imaginable", making for "happy faces galore"; sure, those "ounces really mount up" on the scale and you may have to "fight hordes" on "disorganized" lines, but "nothing satisfies" like this taste of "heaven in a cup."

67 Wine & Spirits ●□ *Wine/Liquor*   `25` `21` `23` `M`

W 60s | 179 Columbus Ave. (68th St.) | 212-724-6767 |
888-671-6767 | www.67wine.com
Westsiders laud this "wine-lover's mecca" whose "remarkable", "competitively priced" 10,000-label inventory includes every "imbibement" imaginable, from "everyday" bottles to rare vintages "for your collection", all sold by a "superb", "no-attitude" staff; a relatively "user-friendly" layout, "frequent tastings" and a "terrific" delivery policy further enhance its rep as a "neighborhood" "treasure."

Skyview Discount   `26` `20` `21` `M`
Wines & Liquors ●□ *Wine/Liquor*

Bronx | Skyview Shopping Ctr. | 5681 Riverdale Ave. (259th St.) |
718-601-8222 | www.skyviewwines.com
The "go-to place" when you need "kosher wine" and "want something different" from the usual, this Riverdale supplier carries some 500 options, in addition to a full selection of "regular" wine and liquor at "reasonable" prices; instrumental advice from "knowledgeable salespeople", free delivery ($150 minimum) and online ordering put this place "in the plus column" for the neighborhood.

	QUALITY	DISPLAY	SERVICE	COST

Slavin, M. & Sons Ltd. ⌐ *Seafood* ▽ 28 | 18 | 22 | M

Hunts Point-Longwood | Hunts Point Mkt. | 800 Food Center Dr.
(Farragut St.) | Bronx | 718-495-2200 | www.mslavin.com
When you "want fresh fish", this family-owned, long-running (since
1920) importer/wholesaler is *the* place to go" given its online oce-
anic catalog featuring 4,000-odd sorts of seafood that land on refrigerated "trucks delivering around the city", typically to leading
eateries; newly relocated to Hunts Point, its flagship retails fillets
cut to order by an "excellent" staff, leaving finatics "very happy, as
they are the best."

Slope Cellars ◐⌐ *Wine/Liquor* ▽ 26 | 22 | 26 | M

Park Slope | 436 Seventh Ave. (bet. 14th & 15th Sts.) | Brooklyn |
718-369-7301 | www.slopecellars.com
Park Slopers hail this "cool" wine outlet as the "perfect neighborhood shop" where shoppers can find a "great selection" of bottles
color-coded by price, participate in a nifty frequent-buyer program
(make a dozen purchases, and the next bottle is 99¢) and browse a
solid "selection of boutique spirits" too; "smart", amicable staffers
ensure that you "always find" something good at "any price range."

Smith & Vine ◐⌐ *Wine/Liquor* 25 | 24 | 22 | M

Cobble Hill | 268 Smith St. (bet. Degraw & Sackett Sts.) | Brooklyn |
718-243-2864 | www.smithandvine.com
The "small" but "highly selective" (and "idiosyncratic") collection of
wines and spirits at this "picture-perfect" Cobble Hiller on the Smith
Street strip has tipplers testifying that labels "show up here that you
won't find anywhere else", while its staff will steer you to those "little gems" that won't "break the bank" – and the tendency to "educate" is evident all the way to the back tasting room; in sum: "the
receipt says 'we love you' and the feeling is mutual."

NEW Soft Serve Fruit Co. ◐⌐ *Ice Cream* 23 | 19 | 20 | M

Union Sq | 25 E. 17th St. (B'way) | 212-675-0550
E 70s | 1371 Third Ave. (78th St.) | 212-794-2200
www.softservefruitco.com
A "health-geek's paradise", these alternative-to-ice-cream start-ups
use only fruit, cane sugar and filtered water to concoct "awesome",
dairy-free sundaes in "classic flavors" with "creative toppings"
(think banana with pretzels, peanut butter and chocolate chips); in-
teriors decorated with reclaimed apple crates create an "inviting" (if
"slightly corny") farmstand-esque backdrop for the "simply amazing"
"treats", which are surprisingly "creamy", as well as "all-natural",
"gluten-free, cholesterol-free", vegan, kosher and "low-cal" – "put a
cherry on top of that."

☑ Soutine ⌐ *Baked Goods* 27 | 19 | 23 | E

W 70s | 104 W. 70th St. (bet. B'way & Columbus Ave.) |
212-496-1450 | 888-806-2253 | www.soutine.com
For "fabulous" pastries, breads, "the most delicious" tarte Tatin and
other "mouthwatering treats", locals say you "can't do better" in the
area than at this "tiny" UWS "boutique bakery"; its "extraordinary"

goods, including "terrific special-occasion cakes", are "prepared with the best ingredients" and "attention to detail", so most don't mind much if prices are on the high side.

Spice Corner *Herbs/Spices*   23 | 19 | 21 | M

Murray Hill | 135 Lexington Ave. (29th St.) | 212-689-5182 | www.spicecorner29.com

Binge on "bargains galore" at this "small", "bodega-style" Murray Hill Indian food market, a "go-to" for "all sorts of" Mideastern and South Asian spices (cardamom, masala, tamarind, curry powders et al.) and "high-quality" groceries including rice, beans, nuts, dates, chutney and Bengali confections; run by staffers who "couldn't be friendlier", it keeps savvy shoppers in its corner with "better prices" and a "warmer welcome" than most.

NEW Spices & Tease *Herbs/Spices*   ▽ 25 | 24 | 26 | M

E 40s | Grand Central Mkt. | Lexington Ave. (43rd St.)
W 90s | 2580 Broadway (bet. 97th & 98th Sts.) | 347-470-8327 www.spicesandtease.com

Now bringing its "heavenly aromas" to the UWS and Grand Central Market, this merchant offers the same "plethora" of "interesting teas" and "fresh spices" (including 30 housemade blends) that have drawn raves at street markets for years; expect some 180 loose-leaf teas, including exotics like strawberry-rhubarb, plus an assortment of dried herbs, flavored sugars, salts and peppers, all overseen by a staff willing to "guide you" if the choices seem "overwhelming"; P.S. it serves brewed tea and pastries at the West 90s location.

Spoon *Caterer*   ▽ 25 | 21 | 21 | M

Flatiron | 17 W. 20th St. (bet. 5th & 6th Aves.) | 646-230-7000 | 888-776-6604 | www.spoonnyc.com

Celebrated for "outstanding" catering built on local and organic ingredients "fresh from the farm", this Flatiron outfit also runs a specialty shop supplying "wonderful" homemade baked goods, direct-trade coffee, salads and panini to the workday crowd; house-brand jams, baking mixes and gift baskets are available too, and you can sit down to a "perfect brunch" in the spiffy storefront cafe, Tbsp.

NEW Sprinkles Cupcakes *Baked Goods*   26 | 25 | 25 | M

E 60s | 780 Lexington Ave. (bet. 60th & 61st Sts.) | 212-207-8375 | www.sprinkles.com

A leader in the "cupcake craze", this Beverly Hills bakery has "finally made its way to NYC" via this East Side outpost offering 14 daily changing varieties of the "melt-in-your-mouth", "moist, soft", "flavorful" "indulgences" topped with "fun decorations"; an "enthusiastic" crew oversees the "adorable" quarters, and although a been-there-done-that few yawn that these "chic", "calorific" concoctions are "not up to the hype", those who appreciate the "no-gimmicks-or-goop" "quality" suggest you "invoke your inner baker by bringing home their mixes."

	QUALITY	DISPLAY	SERVICE	COST

☑ Staubitz Market ▣ *Meat/Poultry* — 29 | 25 | 26 | E

Cobble Hill | 222 Court St. (bet. Baltic & Warren Sts.) | Brooklyn | 718-624-0014 | www.staubitz.com

A "wonderful throwback" "that can't be duplicated", this Cobble Hill "neighborhood" "classic" has "been around forever" (since 1917) and still perches near the "top of the butcher list" with its "fantastic" cuts of beef, pork, poultry and game, including a "terrific range of organic" meats; the prices may be "some of the highest" around, but "everything is prime" and "you can taste the difference"; P.S. "order early for Thanksgiving" and other holidays.

Steve's Authentic — 26 | 13 | 17 | M
Key Lime Pies *Baked Goods*

Red Hook | Pier 41 | 204-207 Van Dyke St. (bet. Conover & Ferris Sts.) | Brooklyn | 718-858-5333 | 888-450-5463 | www.stevesauthentic.com

Yes, there's essentially "only one thing" on offer, but when it comes to "delicious Key lime pie" you should "get it here" according to acolytes of this eccentric dessert wholesaler that's seriously "out of the way" on a Red Hook pier but resoundingly voted "worth the search"; you'll swear you "can see the sun setting" over the Florida Keys when "you take a bite" of its "delicious" sweet-tart treats, including the Swingle, a frozen version on a "popsicle stick dipped in chocolate" that's as "insane" as you imagine.

Steve's Craft Ice Cream *Ice Cream* — 22 | 20 | 23 | M

E 40s | 4 E. 42nd St. (5th Ave.)

NEW **Boerum Hill** | 420 Atlantic Ave. (bet. Bond & Nevins Sts.) | Brooklyn | no phone | www.stevesicecream.com

There's nothing plain-vanilla about this sophisticated scooper with locations in East Midtown and Boerum Hill, which prides itself on churning out "creamy, smooth" ice cream in "revolutionary" flavors (boozy apple cobbler, Mexican chile-chocolate, salted caramel); it divides its product line into three categories – dairy, dairy-free coconut and sorbet – allowing you to be "as decadent or detoxing as you wanna be."

☑ Stinky Bklyn ▣ *Cheese/Dairy* — 27 | 22 | 25 | M

Cobble Hill | 215 Smith St. (bet. Baltic & Butler Sts.) | Brooklyn | 718-522-7425 | www.stinkybklyn.com

This slice of "cheese heaven" in Cobble Hill emits "the best stench around" thanks to its "wonderful selection" of fromage in "peak-ripe" condition, plus an assortment of "good crusty breads" and "amazing" charcuterie to "go with"; the sharp, "friendly" staffers know their stuff, but they just might "make fun of you if you ask for Havarti."

Stogo ● *Ice Cream* — ∇ 25 | 24 | 24 | E

E Village | 159 Second Ave. (10th St.) | 212-677-2301 | www.stogonyc.com

When you've gotta have "dairy-free" "vegan" ice cream and you're "avoiding sugar", this virtuous frozen-dessert stop in the East Village "is the place for you", as its "excellent" scoops in fascinating flavors (salted caramel with pecan, bananas Foster) are all sweetened with agave; vegan cookies and cupcakes are also on offer, but keep in mind that too much of this clean living may also clean out your wallet.

Stokes Farm 🖃 *Produce*　　　26 | 23 | 22 | M

Location varies | 201-768-3931 | www.stokesfarm.com

"Walk over and you can smell" the "intensely fresh herbs" that have Greenmarket-goers stoked about this seasonal "regular", a "destination" since 1976 where faithful patrons "always look for" "top-quality" heirloom tomatoes, bedding plants and herbal wreaths at holiday time; the outgrowth of a fifth-generation family farm in Bergen County, NJ, it's run by "sunny people" led by "helpful" grower-in-chief Ron Binaghi, Jr.

☑ Stork's Pastry Shop *Baked Goods*　　25 | 25 | 21 | M

Whitestone | 12-42 150th St. (12th Rd.) | Queens | 718-767-9220 | www.storkspastry.com

"There's a reason" this "iconic" German bakery in Whitestone has "been around forever" (since 1954) say "loyalists" and "lifelong customers" who keep coming back for the "work-of-art" pastries and "phenomenal" cakes, cookies and breads that make this "little gem" "really stand out from the rest"; "try it once, and you'll be hooked."

Streit's Matzo Co. 🖃🗗 *Baked Goods*　　27 | 14 | 19 | I

LES | 148-154 Rivington St. (bet. Clinton & Suffolk Sts.) | 212-475-7000 | www.streitsmatzos.com

You can "watch the matzo being made" at this "wonderful" Lower East Side "holdover", a fifth-generation family business and factory turning out "authentic" "fresh-baked" unleavened crackers and vending a variety of kosher goods, from macaroons to matzo-ball-soup mix; it's a prime destination come Passover, and to such a "historical spot" surveyors say *"l'chaim!"*

Stuffed Artisan Cannolis *Baked Goods*　▽ 23 | 19 | 23 | M

Location varies | 212-995-2266 | www.stuffedcannoli.com

The "traditional" Italian cannoli gets its groove back at this mobile confectionary that brings "novel" fillings to the genre – 12-15 presented daily, 70 rotated throughout the year – including the likes of banana cream pie, s'mores, cherry cola and a line of liquor-based flavors; the owners began by selling their "inventive treats" at the Feast of San Gennaro, and discovered that the "gimmick is a good one."

Sugar Room *Cookware*　　　　　- | - | - | M

Sunnyside | 44-21 Queens Blvd. (45th St.) | Queens | 718-707-2900 | www.sugarroom.com

Part cake-decorating school, part baking-supplies market, this Sunnyside bastion of buttercream is the creation of high-end pastry chef Juan Arache; students can learn to make a traditional Dominican cake or study the art of piping icing into flowers, while shoppers can peruse shelves filled with candy molds, cookie cutters and other bakewares, plus ready-to-use fondant, cake fillings and more.

	QUALITY	DISPLAY	SERVICE	COST

Sugar Sweet Sunshine ❶ ▣ *Baked Goods* | 26 | 20 | 23 | I |

LES | 126 Rivington St. (bet. Essex & Norfolk Sts.) | 212-995-1960 |
www.sugarsweetsunshine.com

Prepared with "love", the "awesome", "homemade-iest" cupcakes at this LES bakery are worth "daydreaming" over given their "moist, flavorful" base and "wonderful" icing "reminiscent of childhood birthdays", and there are also full-size cakes, cookies, bars and "to-die-for banana pudding"; factor in "cheap" prices that make for an affordable "fix", and this contender "simply outshines the rest" in the neighborhood.

Sullivan Street Bakery *Baked Goods* | 27 | 21 | 21 | M |

W 40s | 533 W. 47th St. (bet. 10th & 11th Aves.) | 212-265-5580 |
www.sullivanstreetbakery.com

"Bless you, Jim Lahey" swoon disciples of the no-knead "master" baker operating out of this Hell's Kitchen "storefront", where he fires up "a variety of artisanal loaves" with a "beautiful crust", "thin, crunchy" pizzas that "transport you to Rome" and an "outstanding" lineup of "rolls, sandwiches, little pies, cakes" and more; sure, the location is "almost in New Jersey", but a trip to "bread heaven" is "worth the walk every time" – and of course the "divine" goods are also on offer at restaurants and gourmet markets around town.

Sundaes & Cones ❶ *Ice Cream* | 25 | 23 | 23 | M |

E Village | 95 E. 10th St. (bet. 3rd & 4th Aves.) | 212-979-9398 |
www.sundaescones.com

"Exotic flavors" like "taro, honeydew and guava" are on the roster at this "high-class" ice cream "joint" in the East Village with a "focus on Asian fusion" combinations that are "offbeat" without being "totally weird", with "rich and creamy" taste bespeaking "superior quality"; there are "standard" flavors too for less-adventurous eaters, but word to the wise: "the ginger is brilliant."

Sunrise Mart ❶ *Specialty Shop* | 23 | 16 | 18 | M |

E 40s | 12 E. 41st St. (bet. 5th & Madison Aves.) | 646-380-9280
E Village | 4 Stuyvesant St., 2nd fl. (3rd Ave.) | 212-598-3040
SoHo | 494 Broome St. (bet. W. B'way & Wooster St.) |
212-219-0033

It's "amazing how many items they fit" into these real-deal "Japanese food marts", where the "great variety" of rising-sun sundries includes "all of the necessary groceries", "amazing green teas" and "traditional" prepared foods like sushi and bento boxes made "fresh" on-site; the "mini" locations in the East Village and Midtown can be an "ordeal" when "crowded", but the SoHo branch boasts "more room."

Sunset Beer Distributor *Beer* | ∇ 24 | 18 | 21 | M |

Sunset Park | 969 Third Ave. (37th St.) | Brooklyn | 718-788-8000 |
888-319-6407 | www.sunsetbeer.com

If you're "having a kegger", head for this beer-and-beverage showroom in Sunset Park, a "frat-guy's dream" stocking 700 kinds of suds from bar basics to "top-notch microbrews" and imports "from ev-

QUALITY DISPLAY SERVICE COST

erywhere", in addition to potables like soda and water; that it's a "great place to save" is another impetus to make the trek.

Super Wang Bakery ⊅ *Baked Goods* | ∇ 21 | 14 | 15 | I |

Chinatown | 42 Mott St. (bet. Bayard & Pell Sts.) | 212-732-3886

Hong Kong comes a-calling at this small, hidden Chinatown bakery, which proffers "excellent Chinese" pies, tarts and "good-quality", "not-too-sweet" pastries, along with "amazing little sponge cakes"; there are also savories like roast pork buns and "other Asian delicacies" that bring the East closer West, not to mention bubble teas and sweet coconut-milk drinks.

☑ Sur La Table ⬛ *Cookware* | 27 | 25 | 22 | E |

E 70s | 1320 Third Ave. (bet. 75th & 76th Sts.) | 646-843-7984
SoHo | 75 Spring St. (bet. Crosby & Lafayette Sts.) | 212-966-3375
NEW **W 50s** | 306 W. 57th St. (8th Ave.) | 212-574-8334
www.surlatable.com

A "cook's delight" "chock-full" of "anything you could want for a well-equipped kitchen", these links of the Seattle-based chain are perfect for stocking up on "creative culinaryware", "high-tech" "workhorse" electrics, "basic" "tools of the trade" and every "gadget imaginable"; the "colorful displays" always boast the "latest trends" from "upscale" brands, making it "so much fun to rummage around", plus the cooking classes are "awesome"; P.S. "frequent sales and discounts" take the edge off kinda "high" prices.

Surroundings *Flowers* | ∇ 27 | 26 | 22 | VE |

W 100s | 1351 Amsterdam Ave. (bet. 125th & 126th Sts.) | 212-580-8982 | 800-567-7007 | www.surroundingsflowers.com

"Gorgeous work for many years" qualifies this high-end florist as a "favorite" of Upper Westsiders aiming to class up their surroundings with "traditionally" "exquisite" arrangements of ultra-"fresh" flora enhanced by "artistic" input from an on-site horticulturalist who can "create something from your imagination"; big-spending sorts "can always depend on them" for "excellent" results.

Sutton Wine Shop ◑⬛ *Wine/Liquor* | 22 | 19 | 23 | E |

E 50s | 403 E. 57th St. (1st Ave.) | 212-755-6626 | www.suttonwine.com

It's a "pleasure to shop" this "small", high-end, family-run wine shop in Sutton Place whose "good variety" of wines (some 2,000 labels in all) highlights Italian producers; perhaps not surprising given "the zip code", the "prices are high", but "friendly" service with a "mom-and-pop" approach compensates.

NEW Sweetery *Baked Goods* | ∇ 23 | 19 | 22 | M |

Garment District | 433 W. 34th St. (Dyer St.) | 212-207-8133 | www.herbnpeach.com

This Garment District bakery aims to reinvent kitschy pastries of the past – magic squares, red-velvet brownies, peaches 'n' cream 'Jell-O' – with "cute", "awesome" results; the goods are all baked on the premises and served by a "friendly staff", and there's also an array of coffee drinks to chase the sugar.

	QUALITY	DISPLAY	SERVICE	COST

The Sweet Life ▣ *Candy/Nuts* ▽ 27 | 25 | 26 | M

LES | 63 Hester St. (Ludlow St.) | 212-598-0092 | 800-692-6887 |
www.sweetlifeny.com

This "tiny" Lower East Side candy shop is "overflowing with temptations of the best quality", from old-time treats like licorice, gummies, caramels and lollipops to "fresh", housemade chocolate products ("try the marshmallow"); imports include an array of honey, syrups, spreads, nuts and halvah, while the health-conscious declare the assortment of dried fruits is a "delicious way to increase your fiber intake."

Sweet Melissa Patisserie ● *Baked Goods* 25 | 23 | 20 | E

Park Slope | 175 Seventh Ave. (bet. 1st & 2nd Sts.) | Brooklyn |
718-788-2700 | www.sweetmelissapatisserie.com

If you "need a sugar fix" in the form of "special" cakes, "elegant pastries", "amazing cookies", housemade ice cream and "everything in between", this "precious" Park Slope bakery/cafe fills the bill; most find "quality and taste reign supreme" here, but "be prepared to pay" for the privilege – theirs may be "the smallest $3 cupcake in NY."

Sweet Revenge ● *Baked Goods* ▽ 25 | 23 | 23 | M

W Village | 62 Carmine St. (Bedford St.) | 212-242-2240 |
www.sweetrevengenyc.com

All "delicious things on the planet unite" at this West Village dessert-and-wine bar where "amazing cupcakes" are "matched", pairings-style, with a "spot-on" selection of wines and beers, making it a "perfect date place" and just right for "chilling with friends"; such a "genius" concept makes "indulging easy" – "sweet revenge on skeptics, indeed."

☑ Sylvia Weinstock Cakes ⊄ *Baked Goods* 29 | 27 | 27 | VE

TriBeCa | 273 Church St. (bet. Franklin & White Sts.) |
212-925-6698 | www.sylviaweinstock.com
By appointment only

When you need the "wedding cake to end all wedding cakes" or a special-occasion number that exhibits "artistry at the highest level", gateau "queen" Sylvia Weinstock's TriBeCa atelier can be counted on for a "swoon"-worthy creation that'll "defy your imagination" and "taste out-of-this-world" too; true, it may cost as much "as the honeymoon", but brides for whom "money is no object" say such frosted fabulousness is "worth every penny."

Tai Pan Bakery Inc. ⊄ *Baked Goods* 21 | 17 | 14 | I

Chinatown | 194 Canal St. (bet. Mott & Mulberry Sts.) |
212-732-2222 | 888-919-8282 ●
Flushing | 37-25 Main St. (bet. 37th & 38th Aves.) | Queens |
718-461-8668
Flushing | 42-05 Main St. (Maple St.) | Queens | 718-460-8787
www.taipanbakeryonline.com

"You'll be coming again and again" just to "try all the different types" of "sweet and savory" baked goods at these Chinese triplets in

Flushing and C-town, where surveyors give special shout-outs to the "wonderful" pork buns and egg tarts; "everything is unbelievably cheap", which may explain why these "joints" are constantly "packed" and service sometimes slips.

Takahachi Bakery *Baked Goods* ▽ 23 | 23 | 22 | M

Financial District | 25 Murray St. (bet B'way & Church Sts.) | 212-791-5550

From the owner of the same-named East Village and TriBeCa eateries, this "super-cute" Japanese bakery in the Financial District has developed a fan base for its "authentic", handmade soft-style breads and buns (some 60 varieties), pastries and sandwiches prepared with "unique" Nipponese "twists", all declared "so good and fresh"; its "courteous" staff and all-around agreeable "energy" are other reasons neighbors hail it as a fine "addition to the neighborhood."

Tal Bagels *Bagels* 22 | 17 | 17 | M

E 50s | 977 First Ave. (54th St.) | 212-753-9080 ●
E 80s | 1228 Lexington Ave. (83rd St.) | 212-717-2080
E 80s | 333 E. 86th St. (bet. 1st & 2nd Aves.) | 212-427-6811 ●
W 90s | 2446 Broadway (bet. 90th & 91st Sts.) | 212-712-0171 ●
www.talbagels.info

Good for "giant", "chewy" bagels, nice Nova and other "delicatessen faves", these quadruplets can be counted on when you need to grab a rolled hole at a "reasonable price" and require "swift" service to get you on your way in a "NY minute"; "no vibe" at all and "assembly-line" service are part of the bargain.

Tarallucci e Vino ● *Baked Goods* 24 | 23 | 21 | M

E Village | 163 First Ave. (10th St.) | 212-388-1190
Flatiron | 15 E. 18th St. (bet. B'way & 5th Ave.) | 212-228-5400
W 80s | 475 Columbus Ave. (83rd St.) | 212-362-5454
www.taralluccievino.net

These Italian bakeries/cafes are primo places to grab a *delizioso* pastry, panino or scoop of housemade gelato ("who needs a long flight to Italy?"), plus they "pull the best espresso" to go with; the East Village original has a "comfortable" lived-in vibe, while the flashier Flatiron and Upper West Side offshoots turn into "too-hip" enotecas as breakfast and lunch crowds are traded for nighttime diners and imbibers.

Tarzian West *Cookware* 22 | 15 | 17 | E

Park Slope | 194 Seventh Ave. (2nd St.) | Brooklyn | 718-788-4213 | www.tarzian-west.com

Boasting "lovely" "upscale" kitchenware ("with prices to match") from boldface names like Cuisinart, Emile Henry and Le Creuset, all overseen by a "helpful staff", this "long-standing" Park Slope standby remains a "key resource for the neighborhood"; the "crammed"-full displays are "more vertical than anything else", but "how else to pack such a broad selection into such a tiny" space?

	QUALITY	DISPLAY	SERVICE	COST

⚡ Tastings by Payard ● *Caterer/Events*   25 | 25 | 21 | VE

E 60s | 52 E. 66th St. (bet. Madison & Park Aves.) | 212-744-4422 |
www.tastingsnyc.com
By appointment only

The catering arm of "master baker" François Payard's patisseries
(FPB, François Chocolate Bar), this impeccably tasteful, full-service
affiliate goes off-site to indulge events of all magnitudes with "excellent" French cuisine and famously "imaginative cakes and pastries";
their planners provide for everything from personalized menus to
"wonderful" service, and though it's seriously "expensive", the "consistently high quality" is "worth the money" – at least "once in a while."

Tea & Honey Store 🍵 *Coffee/Tea*   ▽ 29 | 28 | 26 | E

E 60s | 828 Lexington Ave. (63rd St.) | 212-355-2812 |
www.theteaandhoneystore.com

This mod, honeycomb-shelved East 60s store has enthusiasts
"humming like a bee" over its "incredible selection" of "flavorful
teas" – including "unusual" imports – offered alongside "the best
honeys" for an even sweeter deal, plus accoutrements if "you don't
have a pot to brew in"; the staff is unwaveringly "helpful", and the
goods make standout gifts "when you want to bring something other
than a bottle of wine."

⚡ Teitel Brothers 🍵 *Specialty Shop*   27 | 19 | 22 | M

Bronx | 2372 Arthur Ave. (186th St.) | 718-733-9400 |
800-850-7055 | www.teitelbros.com

The "heart and soul of Arthur Avenue" when it comes to "specialty
Italian items", this circa-1915 "local" grocery is "crowded" to overflowing (the "sidewalk included") with "all sorts of" imports, embracing "hard-to-find" cheeses, "cured meats, dried pastas", olive
oils and "anything else you need" for an old-world "feast"; despite
occasionally "pushy" service, *amici* who feel entEItled to a "varied
selection" at "fair prices" agree it's "worth a trip to the Bronx."

Ten Ren Tea & Ginseng Co. 🍵 *Coffee/Tea*   25 | 21 | 18 | M

Chinatown | 75 Mott St. (bet. Bayard & Canal Sts.) | 212-349-2286 |
800-292-2049 | www.tenrenusa.com

A "dream come true" for the "aficionado of Chinese tea", this "atmospheric" C-town stalwart stocks an "amazing selection" of loose-
leaf "exotics" imported in "many grades", with "prices based on the
quality" – from "decent" to "eye-popping" – to guarantee a brew "for
every budget", plus there are also elegant tea sets and accessories;
it couldn't be more "authentic", and the staffers "know their stuff."

Terhune Orchards 🍐 *Produce*   24 | 21 | 21 | M

Location varies | no phone

"The best of what's in season" can be found at the Greenmarket stall
of this Dutchess County family orchard, which rates "tops" for "fabulous peaches" and apples trucked "fresh" from Upstate, along with
berries, asparagus, pies and "cider to die for"; the "charming" vendors are quick with "knowledgeable recommendations", and fructi-
vore followers can only say "thank you."

	QUALITY	DISPLAY	SERVICE	COST

Terrace Bagels ●⌿ *Bagels* | 25 | 18 | 21 | I |

Windsor Terrace | 224 Prospect Park W. (Windsor Pl.) | Brooklyn | 718-768-3943

The bagels at this Windsor Terrace shop may be "enormous" and "fluffy" (they could double as "pillows"), but their delightfully "crusty and chewy" qualities make them some of the "best in Brooklyn", especially when paired with "fabulous" flavored cream cheeses and other "fixings"; the line is "always a mile long" but the "friendly" attendants "keep things organized."

☑ Terranova Bakery ⌿ *Baked Goods* | 28 | 20 | 22 | I |

Bronx | 691 E. 187th St. (bet. Beaumont & Cambreleng Aves.) | 718-733-3827 | www.terranovabakery.com

Seekers of "fabulous" crusty Italian bread "go no further" than this "friendly" Arthur Avenue–area bakery whose "excellent" loaves, rolls, baguettes, focaccia, "the very best *pane di casa*" and other "fabulous" baked goods keep emerging "fresh" from the coal-fired brick oven "all day"; a pasta factory on the premises adds to the carb-tastic offerings, while nominal prices mean it won't set you back too much dough.

☑ Teuscher Chocolates of Switzerland ▭ *Candy/Nuts* | 29 | 27 | 25 | VE |

W 40s | 620 Fifth Ave. (bet. 49th & 50th Sts.) | 212-246-4416
E 60s | 25 E. 61st St. (bet. Madison & Park Aves.) | 212-751-8482
www.teuscher-newyork.com

Despite "new competition" in recent years, the "luxurious", "eye-pleasingly packed" Swiss chocolates dispensed by this twosome "still reign supreme", and are rated "sensational" enough to "unlock the grumpiest of hearts"; yes, "you gotta pay" "heavily" and "put up with" occasional attitude from the capable staff, but that all melts away when you bite into one of those "divine champagne truffles" – "if you don't swoon, you're dead."

☑ 3-Corner Field Farm ▭ *Cheese/Dairy* | 27 | 22 | 26 | E |

Location varies | 518-854-9695 | www.dairysheepfarm.com

"Everything you could possibly want from a sheep" derives from this Southern Adirondacks farm's grass-fed, hormone- and antibiotic-free flocks, making it a "great source" for "delicious" cheeses, "top-quality" lamb and mutton, yogurt, sausage and extras like lambskin, sheep's-milk and tallow soaps and yarn, all on offer at the Greenmarket (Union Square and Grand Army Plaza); given the "wonderful specialties" and "friendly" "advice on use", it's "delightful to do business with them" even if it's no baa-gain.

Three Guys from Brooklyn ● *Produce* | 23 | 20 | 18 | I |

Bay Ridge | 6502 Ft. Hamilton Pkwy. (65th St.) | Brooklyn | 718-748-8340 | www.3guysfrombrooklyn.com

"Get whatever you need whenever you need it" at this "busy" Bay Ridge produce market, a "feast for your eyes" where an "amazing" "abundance" of fruit and vegetables encompassing "diverse" "ethnic varieties" is on offer 24/7 at "fell-off-a-truck"-level prices; the "hectic" weekend crowds ("like the League of Nations") can be "challenging", so "bring patience" – the "savings make it well worth it."

Three Tarts 🖃 *Baked Goods* ▽ 26 | 26 | 25 | M

Chelsea | 164 Ninth Ave. (20th St.) | 212-462-4392 | www.3tarts.com
"Beautiful sweets and treats" come in "small sizes" at this "cute" Chelsea confectioner/bakery that vends bite-size tarts, pretty petits fours, "the best" homemade marshmallows (some 30 flavors) and other "mini-indulgences" sold in optional tins, jars and trays; these diminutive treats "always impress", making them ideal "to bring to a party or give as gifts"; P.S. there are a few seats for on-site snacking.

Times Square Bagels ◑ *Bagels* 24 | 15 | 14 | I

W 40s | 200 W. 44th St. (bet. B'way & 8th Ave.) | 212-997-7300
An "oasis of authenticity" in a "vortex of artifice" is how bagel and bialy mavens describe this "better-than-it-needs-to-be" Times Square shop selling "sublime" real-deal-NY rolled holes "in the land of neon"; discerning locals, "Broadway stagehands" and "overeager tourists" alike flock here, especially since the "clueless" service is balanced by surprisingly "decent" prices, at least given the location.

Tinto Fino ◑ *Wine/Liquor* ▽ 25 | 19 | 26 | M

E Village | 85 First Ave. (bet. 5th & 6th Sts.) | 212-254-0850 | www.tintofino.com
Anyone with a "passion" for "Spanish wine from all regions" should make for this "tiny shop" in the East Village, "a real gem" housing 300-plus types of vino, sherry and cava from Andalucía to Zamora; it's all sold by staffers who "know their merchandise" and dispense "great advice" – add "affordable" prices and everyone's shouting *olé!*

Titan Foods ◑🖃 *Specialty Shop* 26 | 22 | 20 | M

Astoria | 2556 31st St. (bet. Astoria Blvd. & 28th Ave.) | Queens | 718-626-7771 | www.titanfood.com
The "mother ship" of "all things Greek", this Astoria specialty supermarket is a "phenomenal" source of all that "you could wish for" in the way of "real-deal" imports, offering "outstanding" cheeses (including some 15 types of feta), "wonderful olives", baked goods and other "finds" at a "very fair" price; "don't expect much service", but Hellenists with time to "browse" "really don't have to go anywhere else."

Todaro Brothers ◑🖃 *Specialty Shop* 25 | 20 | 21 | E

Murray Hill | 555 Second Ave. (bet. 30th & 31st Sts.) | 212-532-0633 | 877-472-2767 | www.todarobros.com
A Murray Hill "lifesaver" "year after year", this "classic neighborhood" fixture is a "go-to" for "top-quality" Italian "gourmet" goods that packs "as much as possible" into a "limited space", including a "wide variety of meat and fish", "fresh fruits and vegetables", "some of the best cheeses", pastas, olive oils and "excellent prepared foods" and sandwiches; the aisles are "sometimes very crowded", but the "informed" staff is "a big plus" – local seekers of "authentic" edibles "can't ask for more."

NEW Tompkins Square Bagels 🍴 *Bagels*   ▽ 25 | 25 | 25 | M

E Village | 165 Ave. A (bet. 10th & 11th Sts.) | 646-351-6520

"Way good" hand-rolled, kettle-boiled bagels "right in the heart of the East Village" draw locals to this narrow, brick-walled shop; although muffins and salads are also on the menu, it's the namesake rolled holes that earn plaudits – loyalists decree them "the best in the neighborhood" – and as a bonus, they come with "interesting people-watching on Sunday mornings."

Trader Joe's ● *Major Market*   23 | 20 | 22 | I

Chelsea | 675 Sixth Ave. (21st St.) | 212-255-2106
E 70s | 2073 Broadway (72nd St.) | 212-799-0028
Union Sq | 142 E. 14th St. (bet. 3rd & 4th Aves.) | 212-529-4612
Brooklyn Heights | 130 Court St. (Atlantic Ave.) | Brooklyn | 718-246-8460
Rego Park | 90-30 Metropolitan Ave. (Woodhaven Blvd.) | Queens | 718-275-1791
www.traderjoes.com

Like a "breath of fresh air", this Left Coast chain has "taken NY by storm" as a "cheap fix for foodies" and average Joes "thrilled" by the "abundance of interesting" gourmet goods and "healthy alternatives" (the store brand "rocks"), not to mention "fab prices" and staffers on "happy pills"; the "idiosyncratic selection" runs to "solid" produce, "tempting" frozen foods with "adventurous" international accents, "first-rate" fresh meats, cheeses "you can't refuse" and "excellent" organic fare, and while it's a "victim of its own success", devotees declare even "epic lines" are "worth the hassle."

Trader Joe's Wine Shop ● *Wine/Liquor*   23 | 21 | 22 | I

Union Sq | 138 E. 14th St. (bet. Irving Pl. & Union Sq. E.) | 212-529-6326 | www.traderjoes.com

"Long live" this "awesome source for cheap wines" in Union Square, an adjunct to the main store where "decent wines" are sold at "rotgut prices" (exhibit A: "three-buck-chuck"), offering an excuse to "experiment" and "discover new treasures" even if you don't have a "Gordon Gecko budget"; the vibe is non-elitist and you even see "wine snobs" joining the "mob scene on weekends" – happily, "the lines move quickly" and the "bargain prices" really are "the ultimate buzz."

Treats Truck 🍴 *Baked Goods*   23 | 19 | 24 | I

Location varies | 212-691-5226 | www.treatstruck.com

This "mobile sweets haven" emits a siren call to sugar-lovers who rave about its "wonderful" homestyle baked goods (rice crispy treats, chocolate brownies, etc.) made in small batches "with obvious care and affection" – what a "perfect antidote" to the day's stresses; add in a "super-charming owner", low prices and lots of giveaway "samples" and your day is sure to "brighten."

Tribeca Treats 🖃 *Baked Goods*   ▽ 21 | 20 | 19 | M

TriBeCa | 94 Reade St. (bet. Church St. & W. B'way) | 212-571-0500 | www.tribecatreats.com

From cookies to brownies, whoopie pies to birthday cakes, this trendy TriBeCa bakery has dessert devotees declaring they're "addicted to its treats – especially "those who love frosting" will be in clover; a few naysayers believe the goods have taken a turn for the "average", but they're outvoted by those who're in "love"; P.S. it accepts custom orders for special-occasion creations including wedding cakes.

Trois Pommes Patisserie ▭ *Baked Goods*

▽ 27 | 24 | 24 | M

Park Slope | 260 Fifth Ave. (bet. Carroll St. & Garfield Pl.) | Brooklyn | 718-230-3119 | www.troispommespatisserie.com

"Lovely and intimate", this Park Slope patisserie incorporates Greenmarket ingredients into a "delicious" lineup of cookies, cupcakes and ice cream, as well as "new takes on old favorites" (e.g. housemade 'Oreos' and red-velvet 'Twinkies'); "seasonal offerings", "personal and personable" service and "great-value" prices are other highlights; P.S. it also does special-order birthday and wedding cakes.

Tu-Lu's Gluten-Free Bakery ⬤▭ *Baked Goods*

▽ 25 | 24 | 23 | M

E Village | 338 E. 11th St. (bet. 1st & 2nd Aves.) | 212-777-2227 | www.tu-lusbakery.com

"Who needs gluten anyway?" muse mavens of this "much-needed" East Village niche bakery that devotes its entire menu to wheat- and gluten-free breads, brownies, cookies, cupcakes, muffins and panini, and they "taste great" – "wow"; the impressive options extend to custom cakes (including wedding versions) that can also be prepared to suit dairy-free or vegan predilections.

Two for the Pot ▭⊱ *Coffee/Tea*

▽ 26 | 22 | 26 | M

Brooklyn Heights | 200 Clinton St. (bet. Atlantic Ave. & State St.) | Brooklyn | 718-855-8173

For Brooklyn Heights 'hoodies, this durable little shop may be "the best" choice around for premium coffees and "fantastic" "imported teas", quaintly curated by a "charming" owner who creates his own "custom-blended" brews; also chockablock with an "exotic" variety of spices and herbs, select specialty items, British pantry staples and "beautiful" accessories ("want a teapot?"), "this place has it all" as long as you have "plenty of cash, as they don't take cards."

Two Little Red Hens *Baked Goods*

26 | 23 | 22 | E

E 80s | 1652 Second Ave. (bet. 85th & 86th Sts.) | 212-452-0476 | www.twolittleredhens.com

Surveyors crow with delight over this "absolutely charming" Upper East Side bakery adored for its "gorgeous" "top-quality" cakes and cupcakes in "superlative flavors", which are "exquisitely decorated" and "delicious to eat" (a troublingly "rare combination"); it also proffers pies, and while some cry fowl over "steep" prices, "gracious" service helps tip the scale to "worth every penny" – just be sure to order "well ahead" for the holidays.

Union Market ⬤ *Major Market*

25 | 23 | 22 | E

Cobble Hill | 288 Court St. (bet. Degraw & Douglass Sts.) | Brooklyn | 718-709-5100

(continued)

(continued)

Union Market

Park Slope | 402 Seventh Ave. (bet. 12th & 13th Sts.) | Brooklyn | 718-499-4026
Park Slope | 754-756 Union St. (6th Ave.) | Brooklyn | 718-230-5152
www.unionmarket.com

"When you need everything in one place", these "lovely" Brooklyn markets fill the bill with an "incredible array" highlighting natural and organic goods, all organized into "pretty displays" featuring breads from artisanal bakeries, craft cheeses, "quality" meats and fish as well as "top-notch" produce; they're an "interesting work in progress", and while prices run "high", when your "appetite is stimulated" "convenience sometimes trumps cost"; P.S. a new East Village branch at 240 East Houston Street is on tap.

☑ Union Square Events   *Caterer/Events*   `26` `25` `23` `M`

Chelsea | 640 W. 28th St., 8th fl. (bet. 11th & 12th Aves.) | 212-488-1500 | www.unionsquareevents.com
By appointment only

The catering arm of culinary kingpin Danny Meyer (Union Square Cafe, Gramercy Tavern, the Modern, Maialino, Shake Shack, North End Grill, etc.), this outfit based in Chelsea's Hudson Yards is known for its "excellent", varied fare made with seasonal, local ingredients, whipped up for occasions ranging from intimate dinners to black-tie galas and corporate functions at the Whitney, New York Public Library and other tony venues to outdoor events for up to 17,000.

Union Square   `25` `23` `22` `E`
Wines & Spirits ●◰ *Wine/Liquor*

Union Sq | 140 Fourth Ave. (13th St.) | 212-675-8100 | www.unionsquarewines.com

Vinophiles return "again and again" to the "super" and "superbly edited" selection (some 2,500 labels) at this "spacious", "classy" wine emporium off Union Square that has earned a loyal following among "frequent buyers" who can "rack up points with purchases" and use "Enomatic wine cards" to get "free tastings"; some report "gouge"-level prices, but others citing "case discounts", a "well-educated" staff and "amazing events" chide "no wine-ing"; P.S. its wines can also be ordered through Fresh Direct.

United Meat Market   *Meat/Poultry*   `26` `20` `23` `M`

Windsor Terrace | 219 Prospect Park W. (bet. 16th St. & Windsor Pl.) | Brooklyn | 718-768-7227

A "wonderful" resource for the "neighborhood" and "way beyond", this "old-style" (since 1950) Italian butcher in Windsor Terrace still unites locals behind the "unbelievable quality" of its "always-fresh" meat, poultry and housemade sausage purveyed "with a smile" by a "lovely" staff; there's also "quite a large" lineup of premade faves (lasagna, veal parm, the "best meatballs") and primo imports like "excellent" cheeses, oils and salumi, so it's always a "treat to browse" whether for a "family feast or just a midweek dinner."

	QUALITY	DISPLAY	SERVICE	COST

The Upper Crust *Caterer/Events* ▽ 21 | 21 | 20 | M

G Village | 91 Horatio St. (bet. Washington & West Sts.) |
212-691-4570 | www.theuppercrust.com
By appointment only

As the name suggests, this established events and weddings planner in Greenwich Village courts an upper-crust crowd of corporate clients and cream-of-the-crop couples who seek full-service catering as well as creative party-production assistance for bashes of up to 3,000 guests; founder Dan Fehlig, an alum of the Four Seasons and the '21' Club, oversees the shindig strategizing.

NEW Valley Shepherd ▽ 28 | 24 | 25 | M
Creamery *Cheese/Dairy*

Park Slope | 211 Seventh Ave. (bet. 3rd & 4th Sts.) | Brooklyn |
347-889-5508 | www.valleyshepherd.com

It's all about ewe, ewe, ewe, at this "locavore"-approved sheep-cheese monger in Park Slope (plus at the Greenmarket and other markets), a retail outlet of an NJ dairy that locals say is the next best thing to having "a farm in the neighborhood" given its lactic lineup of more than 30 "extremely delicious" fromages, alongside butter, yogurt, lamb meat, bread and specialty goods; "helpful" counter folk doling out "samples" will keep you coming baaack; P.S. the ewe-nique owners also conduct cheese-making classes at the farm.

☑ Van Leeuwen 26 | 19 | 23 | M
Artisan Ice Cream ●⇄ *Ice Cream*

NEW E Village | 48-1/2 E. Seventh St. (2nd Ave.) | no phone
Boerum Hill | 81 Bergen St. (Smith St.) | Brooklyn |
347-763-2979
Greenpoint | 632 Manhattan Ave. (bet. Bedford & Nassau Aves.) |
Brooklyn | 718-701-1630
www.vanleeuwenicecream.com

An outgrowth of the city's flourishing "truck phenomenon", this artisanal ice cream purveyor's "simply amazing" scoops made with "quality" ingredients in "clean, clear flavors" are available at storefronts in Brooklyn and the East Village in addition to the familiar "adorable yellow" lorries around town; a few shrug "doesn't live up to the hype", but even they concede its coffee from Intelligentsia is "surprisingly good", and now there are housemade pastries too.

Varsano's ▭ *Candy/Nuts* ▽ 29 | 27 | 28 | M

W Village | 172 W. Fourth St. (bet. 6th & 7th Aves.) |
212-352-1171 | 800-414-4718 | www.varsanos.com

The "sweet" proprietor of this West Village bonbon shop is "always experimenting" with new "housemade specialties" to complement such popular signatures as caramel pretzel rods, chocolate-covered potato chips, "the best truffles" and "dark chocolate malted milk balls that will change your life"; even the "sugar-free selections are delicious", while the wide array of novelty molds include Porsches, tools, boxing gloves and other guy-friendly shapes along with ballet slippers and blow-dryers for the ladies.

	QUALITY	DISPLAY	SERVICE	COST

Veniero's ●�𝄖 *Baked Goods* | 25 | 23 | 19 | M |

E Village | 342 E. 11th St. (bet. 1st & 2nd Aves.) | 212-674-7070 | www.venierospastry.com

The line outside "says it all" at this "venerable" Italian bakery, a "superior" pasticceria and East Village "fixture" since 1894 that's famed for its "amazing selection" of "authentic" cannoli, cheesecakes, rainbow cookies and other "old-school" favorites "made with love"; "reasonable prices" add to the "joyful experience" – no wonder diehards say it's a "must-go" for every sweet tooth.

NEW Victory Garden *Ice Cream* ∇ 28 | 25 | 26 | M |

W Village | 31 Carmine St. (bet. Bedford & Bleecker Sts.) | 212-206-7273 | www.victorygardennyc.com

"Don't let the words 'goat milk' turn you away" from this "cute", "friendly" new West Villager whose "unique twist on soft-serve ice cream" is that the "delicious", "creamy concoctions" are made from the dairy output of locally raised goats; amiable staffers are generous with the samples, and the "fresh" flavors are "like a walk through the meadow" for your taste buds – in short, it's "worth a try", especially "if you've soured on the whole frozen-yogurt trend"; P.S. it also vends soups and sandwiches.

⧉ Villabate-Alba Pasticceria ●�𝄖𝄖 *Baked Goods* | 27 | 28 | 23 | M |

Bensonhurst | 7001 18th Ave. (70th St.) | Brooklyn | 718-331-8430 | www.villabate.net

"Each item is a work of art" at this Bensonhurst "Italian pastry emporium" where many of the ingredients are imported from Sicily and the "attention to detail" is "evident" in all manner of "to-die-for" cakes, cannoli, cookies and whimsically shaped marzipan in presentations so "beautiful", it's voted No. 1 for Display in NYC; no surprise this "year-round favorite" has a line "out the door at Christmas" – and "don't forget the housemade gelato" in warmer months – "if you're Italian or want to be", this is "the place."

Vincent's Meat Market 𝄖 *Meat/Poultry* ∇ 29 | 25 | 29 | M |

Bronx | 2374 Arthur Ave. (bet. 186th & 187th Sts.) | 718-295-9048

Choosy carnivores "wouldn't visit Arthur Avenue without a stop" at this "accommodating" "Italian-style" meat market, a local "favorite" since the '50s for the "wonderful quality" of its "traditional" cuts of beef, veal rollatini, baby lamb, homemade sausage and game, which share the "squeaky clean" space with imported cheeses, oils and dry goods; the "moderate" cost also includes "tip-top" service from an "extremely helpful" gang of "the nicest butchers ever."

Vinyl Wine Shop ●𝄖 *Wine/Liquor* | - | - | - | I |

E 90s | 1491 Lexington Ave. (bet. 96th & 97th Sts.) | 646-370-4100 | www.vinylwineshop.com

With wood paneling, a pro stereo system and posters on the wall showing Rod Stewart and other rockers drinking wine, this new East

Harlem arrival is an artfully casual, 1970s-inspired version of a wine shop; it takes its product seriously, though, with an inventory revolving around organic selections – they make up 80% of the offerings – with prices deliberately kept in the affordable range ($10–$25).

☑ Vosges Haut Chocolat ⌐ *Candy/Nuts*

27 | 26 | 23 | E

E 80s | 1100 Madison Ave. (bet. 82nd & 83rd Sts.) | 212-717-2929
SoHo | 132 Spring St. (bet. Greene & Wooster Sts.) | 212-625-2929
888-301-9866 | www.vosgeschocolate.com

"Adventurous" chocoholics "looking for something unusual" hit these SoHo-Upper East Side boutique confectioners where the "fantastic" creations feature unexpected "spices" and "extraordinary flavor combinations" (think bittersweet with Taleggio cheese or "wowza bacon bar"); "sleek" purple packaging and "haute prices" add to the "air of exclusivity", and though a few skeptics sigh it's all a little "over-the-top", even they admit you've "got to give points for gutsy" "innovation."

VSF *Flowers*

∇ 27 | 26 | 24 | E

W Village | 204 W. 10th St. (bet. Bleecker & 4th Sts.) | 212-206-7236 | www.vsfnyc.com

"Nobody does it better" sigh smitten patrons of this "truly special" West Village florist, long known for working with "very high-quality" seasonal blooms in signature 'Flemish-garden style' to yield "simply gorgeous" arrangements that "last a good amount of time"; the "friendly" team of "real professionals" provides service with "no stress" to ensure a "great response" whether for gifts, weddings or corporate events, so few fret when their wallet "takes a dent."

Wafels & Dinges ⌐ *Baked Goods*

24 | 18 | 22 | M

Location varies | 866-429-7329 | www.wafelsanddinges.com

Waffle worshipers "drool" for the "crisp, buttery", hot Belgian wafels topped with "mouthwatering" dinges (that's 'toppings' to "the novitiate"), "sinful blisses" such as ice cream, hot fudge and even pulled pork – "be careful or you will get addicted"; the "real-deal" treats are apportioned by "extremely pleasant" peeps, so the only "downside" is that "there aren't more trucks"; P.S. it caters too.

Warehouse Wines & Spirits ● *Wine/Liquor*

25 | 17 | 19 | I

G Village | 735 Broadway (bet. 8th St. & Waverly Pl.) | 212-982-7770

Dubbed a "house of bargains" with an "incredible selection", this 6,000-sq.-ft. Village mega-store is the "place to go when stocking up" on "excellent" "low-end" wine or "booze for a party", although you'll need "time to search" the shelves ("good stuff arrives in small quantities") and willingness to brave so-so service and a "confusing layout" – "skipping renovations" must be what has "kept prices so low."

Westerly Natural Market ●🗹 *Health* | 23 | 16 | 18 | M |

W 50s | 913 Eighth Ave. (54th St.) | 212-586-5262 |
www.westerlynaturalmarket.com

Ever "reliable", this Hell's Kitchen vet enthuses "health nuts" with a "huge selection" that's "worth exploring" for all kinds of "affordable" natural necessities, including "bulk grains", "fresh" organic produce, "excellent" raw foods, "unusual herbs and supplements" and "delicious" housemade soups and prepared items for lunch hour; those who fret about "ridiculously narrow aisles" should know that it recently (post-Survey) underwent a complete renovation.

Westside Market *Major Market* | 21 | 18 | 16 | M |

Chelsea | 77 Seventh Ave. (bet. 14th & 15th Sts.) |
212-807-7771 ●
W 70s | 2171 Broadway (bet. 76th & 77th Sts.) | 212-595-2536
🆕 **W 90s** | 2589 Broadway (bet. 97th & 98th Sts.) |
212-316-0222 ●
W 100s | 2840 Broadway (bet. 110th & 111th Sts.) |
212-222-3367 ●
www.wmarketnyc.com

"Basic" but "reliable", this "Columbia neighborhood" "staple" and its West 70s and Chelsea follow-ups cover "all your daily" marketing needs with "particularly good" produce, an "array" of "wonderful cheeses", "delicious" deli staples, a "sprinkling of gourmet items" and "an emphasis on" "fresh and tasty" prepared dishes; "whatever the shortcomings", they're "less hectic than" their big-name rivals and always "convenient" for "last-minute shopping", especially since the Uptowners are "open 24/7" (the Chelsea branch closes at midnight).

Whisk 🗹 *Cookware* | - | - | - | M |

Williamsburg | 231 Bedford Ave. (4th St.) | Brooklyn |
718-218-7230 | www.whisknyc.com

This "lovely", "well-lit" kitchenware haven exudes an exuberant "neighborhood feel", making it the perfect fit for the "Billyburg scene"; local home chefs confide it's "my go-to for picking up things" like Staub titanium pots, Calphalon pans, "cooking gadgets", cleavers, barware, cocktail provisions, cookbooks and "some unusual items" too – in fact, it's full of "surprises"; P.S. a roomier Flatiron outpost is in the works at 933 Broadway.

🆕 Whiskey Shop *Wine/Liquor* | ▽ 27 | 27 | 25 | E |

Williamsburg | 44 Berry St. (on N. 11th St., bet. Berry St. & Wythe Ave.) |
Brooklyn | 718-384-7467 | www.whiskeyshopbrooklyn.com

"No normal liquor store", this Williamsburg nook from the owners of the next-door bar Whiskey Brooklyn really "should be called whiskey heaven" given its "unbelievable selection" (a rotating mix of 99 labels) lined up on tall shelves, spanning scotch, bourbon, rye and more, with an emphasis on domestic and local distillers; there are also a few wines in stock, and it's all overseen by "super-friendly" staffers who "know their stuff", meaning this place offers just about "everything a booze-lover needs."

Whole Foods Market ◐ *Major Market*

| 25 | 25 | 21 | E |

Chelsea | 250 Seventh Ave. (24th St.) | 212-924-5969
LES | 95 E. Houston St. (Bowery) | 212-420-1320
TriBeCa | 270 Greenwich St. (bet. Murray & Warren Sts.) |
212-349-6555
Union Sq | 4 Union Square S. (bet. B'way & University Pl.) |
212-673-5388
W 50s | Shops at Columbus Circle | 10 Columbus Circle (bet. 58th &
60th Sts.) | 212-823-9600
W 90s | 808 Columbus Ave. (bet. 97th & 100th Sts.) | 212-222-6160
888-746-7936 | www.wholefoodsmarket.com

"Up there at the top of the food chain", these "big, beautiful"
branches of an "eco-friendly" Texas empire "delight" with the "superior
quality" and "amazing breadth" of their "wholesome" provisions,
notably "fantastic" produce displayed like a "still life", a
"treasure chest" of "fabulous" cheeses, coffee and tea, "choice"
meats and poultry, "exceptional" seafood, "fresh" baked goods, an
"excellent" beer selection heavy on "regional microbrews" and a
"gazillion" "awesome" prepared foods; the "spacious aisles" and
"organized check-out" will "make your day", and if the price tag "can
be hefty", a "splurge" "doesn't get much better than this"; P.S. a new
UES store is expected at 250 East 57th Street in late 2012.

Wild Edibles ◐ 🖃 *Seafood*

| 24 | 22 | 20 | E |

E 40s | Grand Central Mkt. | Lexington Ave. (43rd St.) | 212-687-4255
Murray Hill | 535 Third Ave. (bet. 35th & 36th Sts.) | 212-213-8552
www.wildedibles.com

Seafood savants turn to this East Side twosome, where the "great
selection" of fish is "so fresh it'll jump at you" and the variety of prepared
options are "delicious" "every time"; still, even those who
concede the "quality is high" are less wild about wares that "should
be gold-plated for what they charge"; P.S. the Murray Hill branch offers
"the added plus of eating in."

William Greenberg Jr.
Desserts 🖃 *Baked Goods*

| 25 | 22 | 22 | E |

E 80s | 1100 Madison Ave. (bet. 82nd & 83rd Sts.) | 212-744-0304 |
www.wmgreenbergdesserts.com

Though no longer in the Greenberg family, this "old-time" UES bakery
continues its "long history" of rolling out "classy", "delicious"
kosher baked goods that are perfect "for that special occasion", including
"fabulous" black-and-white cookies, schnecken, babka and
brownies; these days, it's perhaps best known for its "unbelievable
architectural" wedding cakes deemed "worth" the significant price
and the "zillions of calories" – bring on the "butter."

☑ William Poll *Prepared Food*

| 26 | 21 | 23 | VE |

E 70s | 1051 Lexington Ave. (bet. 74th & 75th Sts.) | 212-288-0501 |
800-951-7655 | www.williampoll.com

An Upper Eastsider's "only place to go when company is coming",
this boutique kitchen is a "well-established" source of "the best-
tasting gourmet" prepared dishes, notably "wonderful" tea

sandwiches, house-smoked fish, pot pies, canapés and housemade potato thins and dips; it's a longtime "family business" that "takes pride" in "extremely professional and gracious" service – yes, it's also seriously "expensive", but it's "worth every penny" to know "your worries are over."

⚁ Williams-Sonoma ▭ Cookware — 27 | 27 | 23 | E

Chelsea | 110 Seventh Ave. (bet. 16th & 17th Sts.) | 212-633-2203 ●
E 50s | 121 E. 59th St. (bet. Lexington & Park Aves.) | 917-369-1131
E 80s | 1175 Madison Ave. (86th St.) | 212-289-6832
W 50s | Shops at Columbus Circle | 10 Columbus Circle (bet. 58th & 60th Sts.) | 212-823-9750 ●
www.williams-sonoma.com

It's so "well curated" it could "inspire" even the neophyte who's "never boiled an egg" to "completely outfit a kitchen" say supporters of this chain that's a "trusty, albeit expensive, bet" for the "caviar" of cookware, "hard-to-find culinary" tools and "esoteric morsels" too; whether you want to "ogle the All-Clad" or find a "bridal registry" or "last-minute" "foodie gift", the "knowledgeable" staff is "always at the ready" – no wonder shoppers insist that this culinary "enterprise" is a "must for all entertainers and domestic divas."

Windfall Farms � Produce — ▽ 29 | 28 | 22 | VE

Location varies | 845-457-5988 | www.windfallfarms.com

A year-round windfall for fanciers of "top-quality produce", this staple of the Union Square Greenmarket brings in "consistently" "gorgeous", "honestly healthy" produce from a Montgomery, NY, farm "as the seasons change"; specializing in "fresh and delicious" arugula, mesclun, microgreens and various "interesting" vegetables "for the culinary adventurer", it's "expensive" but worth the lettuce, especially when "nobody else has most of the items" it offers.

Windsor Florist ▭ Flowers — ▽ 24 | 22 | 22 | E

E 70s | 1118 Lexington Ave. (78th St.) | 212-734-4540
E 70s | 1382 Second Ave. (71st St.) | 212-734-4524
800-234-3761 | www.thewindsorflorist.com

High traditional style is the trademark of this standby florist (dating to 1936) with two Upper East Side locations, which fashions the finest handpicked blooms into arrangements that favor the conventional over the cutting-edge; it's resolutely old-school, but whether for events, weddings, home adornment or gifts for any occasion, its steadfast followers are "always satisfied."

Wines at Whole Foods ● Wine/Liquor — 23 | 22 | 21 | M

W 90s | 808 Columbus Ave. (97th St.) | 212-222-6160 | www.wholefoodsmarket.com

Upper Westsiders say it's "awfully handy" to have this "dependable" wine shop annexed to the Columbus Avenue Whole Foods store, especially given its surprisingly "moderately priced" inventory ("no Whole Paycheck here!"), which encompasses everything from European to NY State vintages plus kosher and organic picks; the idea is to grab a bottle to "go with the ingredients you just bought for dinner", and "enthusiastic" employees are there to help you do so – in short, "for convenience", this place "works."

Won Chuen Fish Market ⌦ *Seafood* | 22 | 18 | 19 | M |
(fka 131 Fish Market)

Chinatown | 131 Mott St. (bet. Grand & Hester Sts.) | 212-925-0970
Insiders trawling for a "varied selection" of fresh seafood cite this basic Chinatown fish mart for an "excellent" piscatorial panoply that spans tilapia to shellfish, shrimp, squid and beyond; "if you want to make the effort", the price tag is "definitely worth the trip" – especially for first dibs on the daily haul.

Wright & Goebel *Wine/Liquor* | ▽ 28 | 27 | 28 | M |
Downtown Bklyn | 147 Flatbush Ave. Ext. (bet. Johnson & Tillary Sts.) | Brooklyn | 646-495-1520 | www.wrightandgoebel.com
A "thoughtfully curated selection" with particular strength in biodynamic and sustainable vintages, overseen by "polite", "nonjudgmental" staffers who are generous with their "plethora of knowledge", has already made this "quality" wine-and-spirits shop a "go-to" for Downtown Brooklyn locals; the sleek, "handsome", "easy-to-navigate" premises are home to "both popular and harder-to-find" labels offered at "reasonable prices", leading early-goers to call it "Wright on the money"; P.S. it offers tastings Thursday–Saturday.

🆕 Xocolatti ⌑ *Candy/Nuts* | ▽ 22 | 21 | 19 | E |
SoHo | 172 Prince St. (Thompson St.) | 212-256-0332 | www.xocolatti.com
Adventurous chocolate connoisseurs head to this sleek new SoHo confectioner, a small but deluxe shop with candy box–covered walls that specializes in housemade truffles, clusters and crumbles offered in "delicious" exotic flavors (think passion fruit, sake, pomegranate), along with gelato and hot chocolate; yes, the goods are "expensive", but they make a "great gift option" for "special occasions."

Yi Mei Fung Bakery ⌦ *Baked Goods* | 19 | 17 | 17 | I |
Flushing | 135-38 Roosevelt Ave. (Main St.) | Queens | 718-886-6820 ⌑
Woodside | 8126 Broadway (bet. 81st & 82nd Sts.) | Queens | 718-898-8005
"Delicious moon cakes" are among the standout offerings at these separately owned Flushing-Woodside bakeries, where the "specialty Chinese pastries" like stuffed buns are joined by cookies, gelato, breads and cakes by special order; locals say the "high turnover of products" ensures they're "always fresh", while the prices "can't be beat."

Yogo Monster ● *Ice Cream* | 22 | 18 | 20 | I |
Park Slope | 90 Seventh Ave. (bet. Berkeley Pl. & Union St.) | Brooklyn | 718-230-7107
Forest Hills | 70-19 Austin St. (67th Rd.) | Queens | 718-261-0661 www.yogomonster.com
These "cute" and contemporary Park Slope-Forest Hills twins generate "yummy little" nonfat fro-yo "creations" piled with "lots of dif-

ferent fresh fruit toppings" – "perfect" when you crave a "healthy snack" but lust after a "tasty treat"; maybe they're in the "Pinkberry" knockoff realm, but they're probably a little easier on the "wallet."

Yonah Schimmel Knish Bakery ⌐ *Baked Goods*

| 24 | 11 | 16 | I |

LES | 137 E. Houston St. (bet. 1st & 2nd Aves.) | 212-477-2858 | www.yonahschimmel.com

"A knish is still a knish" at this "one-and-only" LES "legend", a "vestige" of the old neighborhood that has been dispensing "heavy, calorie-filled" Jewish "comfort food" for more than a century, notably "melt-in-your-mouth" knishes "of every variety", plus "great kugel and pickles" and "egg creams too"; aestheticswise it's on the "shabby"-"shoddy" side, and you can "forget about service", but remember you're here "for a blast of old NY" – just "nosh!"

Yorkshire Wines & Spirits ◐⌐ *Wine/Liquor*

| 24 | 19 | 20 | M |

E 80s | 1646 First Ave. (85th St.) | 212-717-5100 | www.yorkshirewines.com

"Budget"-watchers praise this UES merchant for its "moderately priced" stock of "quality" wines – with emphasis on French, Italian and Californian producers – meaning it's the place to "find the perfect midweek bottle" rather than, say, an "expensive vintage wine"; if the displays seem "somewhat cluttered", look to the "helpful" staffers to discern the "method to its madness."

Yorkville Meat Emporium *Meat/Poultry*

| – | – | – | M |

E 80s | 1560 Second Ave. (81st St.) | 212-628-5147 | www.hungarianmeatmarket.com

There's "a reason" this circa-1948 Hungarian butcher is a hardy survivor "from the old Yorkville", namely its "delicious" porcine panoply of smoked sausage, bacon and ham; plus, if you're after "more than meat", the "quality" extends to Magyar "specialties" like genuine paprika (natch), Eastern European breads and "housemade prepared foods such as cherry soup, goulash" and fresh-baked linzertortes and strudel.

Yura on Madison *Baked Goods*

| 24 | 20 | 19 | E |

E 90s | 1292 Madison Ave. (92nd St.) | 212-860-1598 | www.yuraonmadison.com

"Chic" "moms in running outfits" and their "uniformed" "school kids" congregate at this "unassuming" cafe, an Upper East Side "standby" appreciated for its "fresh, first-rate" baked goods and "après-school snacks" to eat in or take out; prices border on "ridiculous" and seating is "limited", but at least this is "good eavesdropping territory"; P.S. it also caters.

ⓩ Zabar's ⌐ *Major Market*

| 27 | 21 | 21 | E |

W 80s | 2245 Broadway (bet. 80th & 81st Sts.) | 212-787-2000 | www.zabars.com

It's worth a "move to the UWS to be near" this "iconic" one-stop gourmet "extravaganza", still proffering a "plethora" of "unbeat-

	QUALITY	DISPLAY	SERVICE	COST

able" goods, from the legendarily "exceptional" smoked fish ("brave the lines" and "get it hand-cut") to "terrific baked goods", a "glorious", "mind-boggling" cheese selection, "outstanding coffee", a "wow" of a deli, "divine" prepared foods, a recently added seafood section plus "discount" cookware and gadgets "cluttered" together upstairs; it's a "jammed" "maze" that's "not for the faint of heart", but the experience "cannot be imitated" so "sharpen your elbows and jump in."

Zeytuna ● *Major Market* 　　　| 20 | 20 | 18 | E |

Financial District | 59 Maiden Ln. (William St.) | 212-742-2436 | www.zeytuna.com

Though "on the small side", this gourmet "oasis in the desert" of the Financial District "surprisingly has a lot of the stuff you need", including the "neatly displayed" likes of "fresh" produce, meat and fish, "satisfactory" baked goods, "high-quality" cheeses and a "smorgasbord" of "fantastic sandwiches" and "ready-made" Turkish "lunch delights" for a "quick" on-site or carry-out bite; nayzeyers claim it's "too expensive" for "hit-or-miss" goods and service, but those "there for the convenience" counter it's "perfect for its location."

☒ Zezé *Flowers* 　　　| 27 | 27 | 25 | VE |

E 50s | 938 First Ave. (bet. 51st & 52nd Sts.) | 212-753-7767 | www.zezeflowers.com

When "you want to wow", "no one compares" to this "superior" East Side "botanical fantasy" for "artistic" use of "beautiful" high-grade blooms (rare orchids are a specialty) in "unique" arrangements that please "all the senses" with "such attention to detail" in "every petal" they'd "make Monet paint"; the "superb" work appeals to chi-chi showbiz types who readily swing the "scandalously expensive" cost, since there's "simply no better" choice "and everyone 'in' knows it."

NEW Zucker Bakery ✄ *Baked Goods* 　| 24 | 21 | 23 | M |

E Village | 433 E. Ninth St. (bet. Ave. A & 1st Ave.) | 646-559-8425 | www.zuckerbakery.com

Be prepared to succumb to "delicious aromas" at this "homey, friendly" bakery in the East Village, a recent arrival that pastry pundits already "love" for its "so-delicious" selection of pastries and other delicacies reflecting the owner's Eastern European and Israeli roots, including signature sticky buns (known as 'roses'), rugalach and Friday-only challah; Stumptown coffee and other barista-made beverages that can be enjoyed on the premises seal the deal – this is a "gem worth coming back to."

Zucker's Bagels & 　　　　　| 22 | 18 | 17 | M |
Smoked Fish ▤ *Bagels*

TriBeCa | 146 Chambers St. (W. B'way) | 212-608-5844 | www.zuckersbagels.com

"Mouthwatering bagels" and traditional "appetizing" await at this TriBeCa outpost from the owners of Murray's Bagels; it "fills the bill" when you're shopping for "Sunday brunch" fixings, notably "crispy-on-the-outside, soft-on-the-inside" bagels and all manner of "schmears", though some say the service could "use some warming up"; P.S. it now sells La Colombe coffee by the pound as well as pastries from Trois Pommes.

Z ZuZu's Petals 🖃 *Flowers*　　　　27 | 24 | 23 | E

Park Slope | 374 Fifth Ave. (bet. 5th & 6th Sts.) | Brooklyn | 718-638-0918 | www.zuzuspetalsbklyn.com

Prettifying Park Slope since the '70s and still a local "leader", this "truly special" flower shop is favored for its "terrific service" and "creative" use of "the best quality in flora" to create arrangements of optimum freshness (they use no refrigeration); it also peddles "lovely gifts and decor items" like linens, candles, pottery and soaps, and the seasonal back garden supplies annuals, perennials and shrubs come summer.

Other Noteworthy Sources

CATERERS/EVENT PLANNERS

Catering by Restaurant Associates
Garment District | 330 Fifth Ave. (bet. 32nd & 33rd Sts.) | 212-613-5500 | www.restaurantassociates.com

Colin Cowie Lifestyle 🖂
SoHo | 568 Broadway, Ste. 705 (bet. Houston & Prince Sts.) | 212-396-9007 | www.colincowie.com
By appointment only

David Stark
Design & Production 🖂
Carroll Gardens | 87 Luquer St. (Clinton St.) | Brooklyn | 718-534-6777 | www.davidstarkdesign.com
By appointment only

David Ziff Cooking 🖂
E 90s | 184 E. 93rd St. (bet. Lexington & 3rd Aves.) | 212-289-6199 | www.davidziffcooking.com
By appointment only

Glazier Group on Location
G Village | Twenty Four Fifth | 24 Fifth Ave. (bet. 8th & 9th Sts.) | 212-505-8000
Seaport | Bridgewaters | 11 Fulton St. (bet. Front & South Sts.) | 212-608-7400
www.theglaziergroup.com

Gracious Thyme Catering
Harlem | 2191 Third Ave. (bet. 119th & 120th Sts.) | 212-873-1965 | www.graciousthyme.com

Indiana Market & Catering
Garment District | 333 W. 39th St., Ste. 404 (bet. 8th & 9th Aves.) | 212-736-3531 | www.indiananyc.com

Naturally Delicious
Carroll Gardens | 487 Court St. (bet. Huntington & Nelson Sts.) | Brooklyn | 718-237-3727 | www.naturallydelicious.com
By appointment only

Neuman's
LES | 203 Chrystie St. (bet. Delancey & Stanton Sts.) |
212-228-2444 | www.caterernyc.com

Newman & Leventhal ⌦
W 80s | 45 W. 81st St. (bet. Columbus Ave. & CPW) | 212-362-9400

Olivier Cheng Catering & Events
TriBeCa | 12-16 Vestry St. (Hudson St.) | 212-625-3151 | www.ocnyc.com
By appointment only

Red Table Catering ⌦
Williamsburg | 205 Leonard St. (Maujer St.) | Brooklyn |
917-749-3639 | www.redtablecatering.com
By appointment only

Robbins Wolfe Eventeurs
Gramercy | 25 Waterside Plaza (FDR & 30th St.) | 212-924-6500 |
www.robbinswolfe.com
By appointment only

Simply Divine
W 70s | 334 Amsterdam Ave. (bet. 75th & 76th Sts.) |
212-541-7300 | www.simplydivine.com
By appointment only

FLOWERS

Antony Todd
Garment District | 260 W. 36th St. (bet. 7th & 8th Aves.) |
212-367-7363 | www.antonytodd.com

Banchet Flowers ▣
Meatpacking | 74 Gansevoort St. (Washington St.) |
212-989-1088 | www.banchetflowers.com

Blue Meadow Flowers
E Village | 336 E. 13th St. (bet. 1st & 2nd Aves.) | 212-979-8618 |
www.bluemeadowflowers.com

Castle & Pierpont
NoLita | 29 Prince St. (Mott St.) | 212-244-8668 |
www.castlepierpont.com

Chestnuts in the Tuileries ▣
TriBeCa | 55 Van Dam St., Ste. 801 (bet. Hudson & Varick Sts.) |
212-367-8151 | www.chestnutsnyc.com
By appointment only

DeJuan Stroud
TriBeCa | 433 Washington St. (bet. Desbrosses & Vestry Sts.) |
212-431-9099 | www.dejuanstroud.com
By appointment only

Elizabeth Ryan Floral Design ▣
LES | 178 Norfolk St. (bet. Houston & Stanton Sts.) | 212-995-1111 |
www.erflowers.com
By appointment only

Floralies
E 50s | 122 E. 55th St. (bet. Lexington & Park Aves.) |
212-755-3990 | www.floraliesinc.com

Florisity
Flatiron | 1 W. 19th St. (5th Ave.) | 212-366-0891 |
www.florisity.com

Flowers by Richard 🖃
W 50s | 316 W. 53rd St. (bet. 8th & 9th Aves.) | 212-582-3505 |
www.flowersbyrichardnyc.com

Jane Packer
E 50s | 328 E. 59th St. (bet. 1st & 2nd Aves.) | 212-754-1731 |
www.janepacker.com

Jes Gordon/Proper Fun ♥
Garment District | 120 W. 28th St., Ste. 2B (bet. 6th & 7th Aves.) |
212-229-2165 | www.jesgordon.com
By appointment only

Jonathan Flowers
Chelsea | 224 W. 29th St. (bet. 7th & 8th Aves.) | 212-586-8414
W 50s | 36 W. 56th St. (bet. 5th & 6th Aves.) | 212-586-8414
By appointment only

Katrina Parris Flowers 🖃
Harlem | 1844 Adam Clayton Powell Jr. Blvd. (bet. 111th & 112th Sts.) |
212-222-7030 | www.katrinaparrisflowers.com
By appointment only

LMD Floral Events Interiors
E Village | 437 E. 12th St. (bet. Ave. A & 1st Ave.) | 212-614-2734 |
www.lmdfloral.com

Raquel Corvino
Chelsea | 540 W. 29th St., 2nd fl. (bet. 10th & 11th Aves.) |
212-947-6365

Rebecca Cole Design 🖃
Garment District | 247 W. 30th St. (bet. 7th & 8th Aves.) |
212-216-9492 | www.rebeccacolegrows.com

Renny & Reed
E 50s | 505 Park Ave. (bet. 59th & 60th Sts.) | 212-288-7000 |
www.rennyandreed.com

Spruce ◐🖃
Chelsea | 222 Eighth Ave. (bet. 21st & 22nd Sts.) | 212-206-1025 |
www.spruceup.com

Stonekelly Events & Florals
W 50s | 736 11th Ave. (bet. 51st & 52nd Sts.) | 212-245-6611 |
www.stonekelly.com
By appointment only

PARTY RENTALS

Broadway Party Rentals
SoHo | 137 Grand St., 6th fl. (bet. Crosby & Lafayette Sts.) |
212-269-2666
Williamsburg | 134 Morgan Ave. (bet. Johnson Ave. & Meserole St.) |
Brooklyn | 718-821-4000
www.broadwaypartyrentals.com
By appointment only

Classic Party Rentals
Garment District | 336 W. 37th St. (bet. 8th & 9th Aves.) |
212-752-7661 | www.classicpartyrentals.com
By appointment only

County Chair Party Rentals ✉
Mt. Vernon | 25 Oak St. (Lincoln Ave.), NY | 914-664-5700 |
www.countychair.com

Something Different Party Rental
Paterson | 107-117 Pennsylvania Ave. (Iowa Ave.), NJ |
973-742-1779 | www.somethingdifferentparty.com
By appointment only

Greenmarket Locations

For ratings and reviews, see p. 89. And for the most current information about Greenmarket locations, check www.grownyc.org.

Manhattan

E 40s | Dag Hammarskjold Plaza | 47th St. (2nd Ave.) | Wed., Year-round
E 80s | 82nd St. (bet. 1st & York Aves.) | Sat., Year-round
E 90s | First Ave. (bet. 92nd & 93rd Sts.) | Sun., June–Dec.
E 90s | Mt. Sinai Hospital | 99th St. (bet. Madison & Park Aves.) | Wed., June–Nov.
E Village | St. Mark's Church | 10th St. (2nd Ave.) | Tues., May–Dec.
E Village | Tompkins Sq. | E. Seventh St. (Ave. A) | Sun., Year-round
Financial District | Staten Island Ferry/Whitehall Terminal | 4 South St. | Tues./Fri., Year-round
Financial District | Bowling Green | Broadway (Battery Pl.) | Tues./Thurs., Year-round
Financial District | City Hall Park | Broadway (Chambers St.) | Tues./Fri., March–Dec.
Financial District | South End Ave. (Liberty St.) | Thurs., April–Dec.
Financial District | W. Broadway (bet. Barclay St. & Park Pl.) | Tues., Year-round
Gramercy | Stuyvesant Town Oval | 14th St. Loop (bet. Ave. A & 1st Ave.) | Sun., May–Nov.
Inwood | Isham St. (bet. Cooper St. & Seaman Ave.) | Sat., Year-round
TriBeCa | Greenwich St. (bet. Chambers & Duane Sts.) | Wed./Sat., Year-round
Union Sq. | Union Sq. | Broadway (17th St.) | Mon./Wed./Fri./Sat., Year-round
Washington Heights | 175th St. (bet. B'way & Wadsworth Ave.) | Thurs., June–Nov.
Washington Heights | 168th St. (Fort Washington Ave.) | Tues., June–Nov.
W 40s | Port Authority Bus Terminal | 42nd St. (8th Ave.) | Thurs., Year-round
W 50s | Ninth Ave. (bet. 56th & 57th Sts.) | Wed., May–Dec., Sat., April–Dec.
W 50s | Rockefeller Ctr. | 50th St. (Rockefeller Plaza) | Wed./Thurs./Fri., July–Aug.
W 60s | Columbus Ave. (66th St.) | Thurs./Sat., Year-round
W 70s | Columbus Ave. (bet. 80th & 81st Sts.) | Sun., Year-round
W 90s | 97th St. (bet. Amsterdam & Columbus Aves.) | Fri., Year-round
W Village | Abingdon Sq. | Eighth Ave. & Hudson St. (bet. Bethune & W. 12th Sts.) | Sat., Year-round
W 100s | Columbia | Broadway (bet. 114th & 115th Sts.) | Thurs./Sun., Year-round
W 100s | Stranger's Gate | Central Park W. (106th St.) | Sat., July–Nov.

Bronx

Bronx | Poe Park | 192nd St. (bet. Grand Concourse & Valentine Ave.) | Tues., July–Nov.
Bronx | Bronx Borough Hall | Grand Concourse (bet. 161st & 162nd Sts.) | Tues., June–Dec.

GREENMARKET LOCATIONS

Bronx | New York Botanical Gdn. | Southern Blvd. (bet. Bedford Park Blvd. & Mosholu Pkwy.) | Wed., June–Nov.
Bronx | Lincoln Hospital | 149th St. (bet. Morris & Park Aves.) | Tues./Fri., June–Nov.

Brooklyn
Bay Ridge | 95th St. (3rd Ave.) | Sat., June–Nov.
Borough Park | 14th Ave. (bet. 49th & 50th Sts.) | Thurs., July–Nov.
Carroll Gardens | Carroll Park | Carroll St. (bet. Court & Smith Sts.) | Sun., Year-round
Downtown Bklyn | Brooklyn Borough Hall | Court & Montague Sts. | Tues./Thurs./Sat., Year-round
Flatbush | Cortelyou Rd. (bet. Argyle & Rugby Rds.) | Sun., Year-round
Fort Greene | Fort Greene Park | Washington Park (bet. DeKalb Ave. & Willoughby St.) | Sat., Year-round
Greenpoint | McCarren Park | Union Ave. (bet. Driggs Ave. & 12th St.) | Sat., Year-round
Park Slope | Grand Army Plaza | Prospect Park, NW entrance | Sat., Year-round
Sunset Park | Fourth Ave. (bet. 59th & 60th Sts.) | Sat., June–Nov.
Williamsburg | Havemeyer St. (bet. B'way & Division St.) | Thurs., July–Nov.
Windsor Terrace | Prospect Park W. (15th St.) | Wed., May–Nov.

Queens
Astoria | 14th St. (bet. 31st Ave. & 31st Rd.) | Wed., July–Nov.
Corona | Roosevelt Ave. (103rd St.) | Fri., July–Nov.
Douglaston | 41st Ave. (235th St.) | Sun., July–Nov.
Elmhurst | 41st Ave. (bet. 80th & 81st Sts.) | Tues., July–Nov.
Glendale | Atlas Park | Cooper Ave. (80th St.) | Sat., June–Nov.
Jackson Heights | 34th Ave. (77th St.) | Sun., Year-round
LIC | Socrates Sculpture Park | Vernon Blvd. (B'way) | Sat., June–Nov.
Sunnyside | Skillman Ave. (bet. 42nd & 43rd Sts.) | Sat., June–Dec.

Staten Island
Staten Island | St. George at Borough Hall | St. Mark's St. (Hyatt St.) | Sat., May–Nov.
Staten Island | Staten Island Mall | Richmond Ave. (main parking lot) | Sat., June–Nov.

Green Glossary

As the New York City Greenmarket system continues to flourish – and upstart markets like the New Amsterdam sprout up around town – more and more New Yorkers are seeking out locally grown and produced foods rather than those trucked in from afar, and opting for sustainably raised choices whenever possible. But as the green/local movement has come into bloom, so has a thicket of terminology surrounding it, which can make shopping a confusing experience. What does 'free range' really mean? What is the difference between 'natural' and 'organic'? Herewith is our attempt to explain these and other terms in this ever-evolving lexicon.

Carbon footprint: The total amount of carbon dioxide and other greenhouse gases emitted over the life of a product or service.

Fair Trade: A social movement that promotes standards for international labor and strives to help workers gain economic self-sufficiency through fair wages and viable employment opportunities. Fair Trade principles include fair prices, fair labor conditions, direct trade, democratic and transparent organizations, community development and environmental sustainability, including the promotion of sustainable farming methods.

Food miles: A measure of the distance food has traveled from field to plate.

Free range/free roaming: A method of livestock/poultry husbandry in which animals are permitted to graze or forage rather than being confined to a feedlot. The term is defined by the USDA only for poultry (not for eggs), and requires that outdoor access be provided for an unspecified period each day.

Genetically Modified Organisms (GMOs): Plants, animals or micro-organisms that have been altered through the use of genetic engineering techniques, with the aim of enhancing growth, nutritional value or pest resistance. The use of GMOs in agriculture is controversial due to concerns about potential adverse environmental and health consequences.

Grass-fed/pasture-raised: Beef that has been raised almost exclusively on grass rather than grain or commercially produced cattle feed. Grass-fed or pasture-raised livestock have had continuous access to pasture throughout their lives and have never been confined to a feedlot where movement is limited.

Green building/design: A green building is designed to conserve resources – energy, water, building materials, land – and reduce negative impact on the environment. Green buildings may use one or more renewable energy systems for heating and cooling, such as solar electric, solar hot water, geothermal or bio mass.

Natural food: Ideally, food that has been minimally processed and remains as close as possible to its original state. No standard definition for this term exists except when applied to meat and poultry products. The USDA defines "natural" meat and poultry as free from artificial flavoring, colors, chemical preservatives or synthetic ingredients, but the claim does not have to be verified.

Organic farming: A form of agriculture that relies on ecosystem management and attempts to reduce or eliminate external agricultural inputs, such as synthetic pesticides and fertilizers, and bans the use of animal by-products, antibiotics and sewage sludge, among other practices.

Organic food (certified): Food that has been certified as organic by a certification agency recognized by the USDA. In general, food that has been certified as organic has been grown without synthetic chemicals such as fertilizers, pesticides, antibiotics or GMOs. Producers of certified organic foods must undergo periodic on-site inspections. Note that the USDA has not yet set standards for organic seafood.

Slow Food: A social movement that began in Italy in the 1980s as a protest against the proliferation of fast-food restaurants. Now operating worldwide, the organization works primarily to preserve local culinary traditions by identifying foods and techniques that are on the verge of extinction and finding ways to help the people who produce them.

Sustainable agriculture: Farming practices that are healthy for workers and the environment, humane to animals and profitably produce food relying primarily on natural ecological controls rather than pesticides and other chemicals.

Party Sites

The figures below showing room capacity (cap) and, for multiple spaces, the maximum capcity of the largest available space (max cap) are only guidelines. Call ahead for pricing, and remember that most sites will negotiate.

Museums & Other Spaces

Alger House | *rooms: 2* | *max cap: 110*
G Village | 45 Downing St. (bet. Bedford & 7th Ave.) | 212-627-8838 | www.algerhouse.com

Alice Tully Hall | *rooms: 4* | *max cap: 900*
W 60s | Lincoln Ctr. | 1941 Broadway (bet. 65th & 66th Sts.) | 212-875-5037 | www.lincolncenter.org/yourevent

Altman Building | *rooms: 2* | *max cap: 600*
Chelsea | 135 W. 18th St. (bet. 6th & 7th Aves.) | 212-741-3400 | www.altmanbldg.com

American Museum of Natural History | *rooms: 45* | *max cap: 3000*
W 70s | 79th St. & CPW | 212-769-5350 | www.amnh.org

Americas Society | *rooms: 3* | *max cap: 200*
E 60s | 680 Park Ave. (68th St.) | 212-249-8950 | www.americas-society.org

Angel Orensanz Foundation | *rooms: 1* | *cap: 650*
LES | 172 Norfolk St. (bet. Houston & Stanton Sts.) | 212-529-7194 | www.orensanzevents.com

The Art Farm | *rooms: 4* | *max cap: 35*
E 90s | 419 E. 91st St. (bet. 1st & York Aves.) | 212-410-3117 | www.theartfarms.org

Astor Center | *rooms: 4* | *max cap: 200*
SoHo | 399 Lafayette St. (4th St.) | 212-674-7501 | rentals.astorcenternyc.com

Astra | *rooms: 1* | *cap: 300*
E 50s | 979 Third Ave., 14th fl. (bet. 58th & 59th Sts.) | 212-644-9394 | www.charliepalmerny.com

Avery Fisher Hall | *rooms: 4* | *max cap: 1000*
W 60s | Lincoln Ctr. | 10 Lincoln Ctr. (B'way) | 212-875-5037 | www.lincolncenter.org/yourevent

Bateaux New York | *rooms: 2* | *max cap: 300*
Chelsea | Chelsea Piers | Pier 61 (West Side Hwy.) | 212-727-7768 | www.bateauxnewyork.com

Bohemian National Hall | *rooms: 6* | *max cap: 300*
E 70s | Czech Ctr. | 321 E. 73rd St. (bet. 1st & 2nd Aves.) | 646-422-3318 | www.bohemianbenevolent.org

Bourne Townhouse | *rooms: 3* | *max cap: 100*
Clinton Hill | 137 Clinton Ave. (bet. Myrtle & Park Aves.) | Brooklyn | www.thebournetownhouse.com

Bridgewaters | *rooms: 3* | *max cap: 2000*
Seaport | 11 Fulton St. (bet. East River Piers & Seaport Plaza) |
212-608-7400 | www.theglaziergroup.com

Bronx Zoo | *rooms: 6* | *max cap: 5000*
Bronx | 2300 Southern Blvd. (Fordham Rd.) | 718-741-3836 |
www.bronxzoo.com

**Brooklyn Botanic Garden,
Palm House** | *rooms: 1* | *cap: 400*
Prospect Heights | 1000 Washington Ave. (Montgomery St.) |
Brooklyn | 718-398-2400 | www.palmhouse.com

Brooklyn Masonic Temple | *rooms: 3* | *max cap: 500*
Fort Greene | 317 Clermont Ave. (Lafayette Ave.) | Brooklyn |
718-638-1256 | www.brooklynmasonictemple.com

Brooklyn Museum of Art | *rooms: 6* | *max cap: 1000*
Prospect Heights | 200 Eastern Pkwy. (Washington Ave.) |
Brooklyn | 718-638-5000 | www.brooklynmuseum.org

Brooklyn Winery | *rooms: 6* | *max cap: 250*
Williamsburg | 213 N. Eighth St. (bet. Driggs Ave. & Roebling St.) |
Brooklyn | 347-763-1506 | www.bkwinery.com

Capitale | *rooms: 2* | *max cap: 1200*
Little Italy | 130 Bowery (bet. Broome & Grand Sts.) | 212-334-5500 |
www.capitaleny.com

Carnegie Hall Dining Rooms | *rooms: 4* | *max cap: 300*
W 50s | 154 W. 57th St. (bet. 6th & 7th Aves.) | 212-903-9647 |
www.carnegiehall.org

Center 548 | *rooms: 4* | *max cap: 1000*
Chelsea | 548 W. 22nd St. (11th Ave.) | 646-398-9100 |
www.center548.com

Center for Architecture | *rooms: 4* | *max cap: 276*
G Village | 536 LaGuardia Pl. (Bleecker St.) | 212-683-0023 |
www.aiany.org

Central Park Zoo | *rooms: 4* | *max cap: 1500*
E 60s | 830 Fifth Ave. (64th St.) | 718-741-3836 |
www.centralparkzoo.com

Chelsea Piers Lighthouse | *rooms: 5* | *max cap: 1000*
Chelsea | Chelsea Piers | Pier 61 (23rd St. & West Side Hwy.) |
212-336-6144 | www.piersixty.com

Chelsea Piers, Pier 60 | *rooms: 6* | *max cap: 2000*
Chelsea | Chelsea Piers | Pier 60 (23rd St. & West Side Hwy.) |
212-336-6144 | www.piersixty.com

**Children's Museum of
Manhattan** | *rooms: 1* | *cap: 170*
W 80s | 212 W. 83rd St. (bet. Amsterdam Ave. & B'way) | 212-721-1223 |
www.cmom.org

**Cooper Classics
Collection** | *rooms: 2* | *max cap: 400*
G Village | 137 Perry St. (bet. Greenwich & Washington Sts.) |
212-929-3909 | www.cooperclassiccars.com

Council on Foreign Relations:
Harold Pratt House/ Peterson Hall | *rooms: 7 | max cap: 250*
E 60s | 58 E. 68th St. (bet. Madison & Park Aves.) | 212-434-9576 |
www.pratthouse.com

Culinary Loft | *rooms: 1 | cap: 70*
SoHo | 515 Broadway (bet. Broome & Spring Sts.) | 212-431-7425 |
www.culinaryloft.com

Damrosch Park Tent, Lincoln Ctr. | *rooms: 1 | cap: 2000*
W 60s | Lincoln Ctr. | W. 62nd St. (bet. Amsterdam & Columbus Aves.) |
212-875-5037 | www.lincolncenter.org/yourevent

David Rubenstein Atrium, Lincoln Ctr. | *rooms: 1 | cap: 250*
W 60s | Lincoln Ctr. | 61 W. 62nd St. (bet. Amsterdam & Columbus Aves.) |
212-875-5037 | www.lincolncenter.org/yourevent

Delegates Dining Room | *rooms: 2 | max cap: 900*
E 40s | United Nations Secretariat Building 414 | 1st Ave. & 46th St. |
212-963-7099 | www.un.org/events

Desmond Tutu Center | *rooms: 1 | cap: 300*
Chelsea | 180 10th Ave. (bet. 20th & 21st Sts.) | 212-929-3888 |
www.acc-tutuconferencecenter.com

Downtown Community Television
Center | *rooms: 2 | max cap: 300*
Chinatown | 87 Lafayette St. (bet. Walker & White Sts.) |
212-966-4510 | www.dctvny.org

Drive In Studios | *rooms: 3 | max cap: 350*
Chelsea | 443 W. 18th St. (bet. 9th & 10th Aves.) | 212-645-2244 |
www.driveinstudios.com

Edison Ballroom | *rooms: 3 | max cap: 1200*
W 40s | 240 W. 47th St. (bet. B'way & 8th Ave.) | 212-201-7650 |
www.edisonballroom.com

Elevated Acre | *rooms: 1 | cap: 800*
Financial District | 55 Water St. (bet. Coenties Slip & Hanover Sq.) |
212-963-7029 | www.elevatedacre.com

Ellis Island
Immigration Museum | *rooms: 3 | max cap: 1200*
Ellis Island | Ellis Island | 212-344-0996 |
www.thestatueofliberty.com

espace | *rooms: 2 | max cap: 1200*
W 40s | 635 W. 42nd St. (bet. 11th & 12th Aves.) | 212-967-7003 |
www.espaceny.com

Explorers Club | *rooms: 3 | max cap: 250*
E 70s | 46 E. 70th St. (bet. Madison & Park Aves.) | 212-396-1008 |
www.manhattaneventsny.com

Eyebeam | *rooms: 1 | cap: 640*
Chelsea | 540 W. 21st St. (bet. 10th & 11th Aves.) | 212-340-4792 |
www.eyebeam.org

The Foundry | *rooms: 1 | cap: 200*
LIC | 42-38 Ninth St. (bet. 43rd Ave. & Queens Plaza S.) | Queens |
718-786-7776 | www.thefoundry.info

Frick Collection | *rooms: 4* | *max cap: 450*
E 70s | 1 E. 70th St. (5th Ave.) | 212-288-0700 | www.frick.org

Georgian Suite | *rooms: 1* | *cap: 150*
E 70s | 1A E. 77th St. (5th Ave.) | 212-734-1468

The Glasshouses | *rooms: 2* | *max cap: 200*
Chelsea | Chelsea Arts Tower | 545 W. 25th St., 14th & 21st fls.
(bet. 10th & 11th Aves.) | 212-242-7800 | www.theglasshouses.com

Grand Central Terminal,
Vanderbilt Hall | *rooms: 1* | *cap: 900*
E 40s | 42nd St. & Park Ave. | 212-340-3404 |
www.grandcentralterminal.com

House of the Redeemer | *rooms: 3* | *max cap: 125*
E 90s | 7 E. 95th St. (bet. 5th & Madison Aves.) | 212-289-0399 |
www.houseoftheredeemer.org

Industria | *rooms: 5* | *max cap: 350*
G Village | 775 Washington St. (bet. Jane & 12th Sts.) |
212-366-1114 | www.industrianyc.com

Institute of
Culinary Education | *rooms: 6* | *max cap: 90*
Chelsea | 50 W. 23rd St. (bet. 5th & 6th Aves.) | 212-847-0707 |
www.iceculinary.com

Intrepid Sea, Air & Space
Museum | *rooms: 12* | *max cap: 5000*
Chelsea | Pier 86 (46th St. & 12th Ave.) | 646-381-5301 |
www.intrepidmuseum.org

Italian Wine Merchants | *rooms: 3* | *max cap: 115*
Union Sq | 108 E. 16th St. (bet. Irving Pl. & Union Sq. E.) | 212-473-2323 |
www.italianwinemerchant.com

Landmark on the Park | *rooms: 2* | *max cap: 500*
W 70s | 160 Central Park W. (bet. 75th & 76th Sts.) | 212-595-1658 |
www.landmarkonthepark.org

Little Owl - The Venue | *rooms: 1* | *cap: 70*
W Village | 93 Greenwich Ave. (bet. Bank & 12th Sts.) | 212-741-4695 |
www.littleowlthevenue.tumblr.com

Lower East Side
Tenement Museum | *rooms: 2* | *max cap: 175*
LES | 103 Orchard St. (Delancey St.) | 212-431-0233 |
www.tenement.org

Lucky Strike Lanes | *rooms: 1* | *cap: 300*
W 40s | 624-660 W. 42nd St. (12th Ave.) | 646-829-0170 |
www.bowlluckystrike.com

Madame Tussaud's | *rooms: 5* | *max cap: 1200*
W 40s | 234 W. 42nd St. (bet. 7th & 8th Aves.) | 212-512-9600 |
www.nycwax.com

Manhattan Center Studios | *rooms: 2* | *max cap: 3500*
Garment District | 311 W. 34th St. (bet. 8th & 9th Aves.) |
212-279-7740 | www.mcstudios.com

Manhattan Penthouse on
Fifth Avenue | *rooms: 2* | *max cap: 200*
Flatiron | 80 Fifth Ave., 17th fl. (bet. 13th & 14th Sts.) |
212-627-8838 | www.manhattanpentouse.com

Merchant's House Museum | *rooms: 3* | *max cap: 125*
G Village | 29 E. Fourth St. (bet. Bowery & Lafayette St.) |
212-777-1089 | www.merchantshouse.org

Metropolitan Museum of Art | *rooms: 4* | *max cap: 650*
E 80s | 1000 Fifth Ave. (82nd St.) | 212-570-3773 |
www.metmuseum.org

Metropolitan Pavilion | *rooms: 4* | *max cap: 1565*
Flatiron | 125 W. 18th St. (bet. 6th & 7th Aves.) | 212-463-0071 |
www.metropolitanevents.com

Michelson Studio | *rooms: 1* | *cap: 350*
G Village | 163 Bank St. (bet. Washington St. & West Side Hwy.) |
212-633-1111 | www.michelsonstudio.com

Milk Studios | *rooms: 10* | *max cap: 650*
Chelsea | 450 W. 15th St., 1st fl. (bet. 9th & 10th Aves.) |
212-645-2797 | www.milkstudios.com

Morgan Library & Museum | *rooms: 6* | *max cap: 800*
Murray Hill | 225 Madison Ave. (bet. 36th & 37th Sts.) |
212-685-0008 | www.morganlibrary.org

Morris-Jumel Mansion | *rooms: 3* | *max cap: 200*
Washington Heights | 65 Jumel Terrace (bet. 160th & 162nd Sts.) |
212-923-8008 | www.morrisjumel.org

Mount Vernon Hotel, Museum & Garden and the
Abigail Adams Smith Auditorium | *rooms: 5* | *max cap: 200*
E 60s | 417-421 E. 61st St. (bet. 1st & York Aves.) | 212-838-5489 |
www.colonialdamesofamerica.org

Museum of Arts and Design | *rooms: 3* | *max cap: 200*
W 50s | 2 Columbus Circle (bet. B'way & 8th Ave.) | 212-299-7729 |
www.madmuseum.org

Museum of Jewish Heritage | *rooms: 7* | *max cap: 500*
Financial District | Battery Park City | 36 Battery Pl. (Little West St.) |
646-437-4206 | www.mjhnyc.org

Museum of the City of New York | *rooms: 3* | *max cap: 500*
E 90s | 1220 Fifth Ave. (103rd St.) | 212-534-1672, ext. 3327 |
www.mcny.org

Nansen Park/A Taste of Honey | *rooms: 2* | *max cap: 1100*
Staten Island | 3465 Victory Blvd. (Signs Rd.) | 718-983-0464 |
www.tasteofhoney.com

National Academy Museum | *rooms: 10* | *max cap: 200*
E 80s | 1083 Fifth Ave. (bet. 89th & 90th Sts.) | 212-369-4880 |
www.nationalacademy.org

National Museum of the American
Indian | *rooms: 9* | *max cap: 1500*
Financial District | 1 Bowling Green (State St.) | 212-514-3820 |
www.americanindian.si.edu

NBC Experience Store | *rooms: 1 | cap: 200*
W 40s | 30 Rockefeller Plaza (bet. 49th & 50th Sts.) | 212-664-3700 |
www.nbcstudiotour.com

New Museum | *rooms: 3 | max cap: 400*
LES | 235 Bowery (Prince St.) | 212-219-1222 |
www.newmuseum.org

New York Academy of Sciences | *rooms: 4 | max cap: 300*
Financial District | 7 World Trade Ctr. | 250 Greenwich St.
(bet. Barclay & Vesey Sts.) | 212-298-8615 | www.nyas.org

New York Aquarium | *rooms: 7 | max cap: 5000*
Coney Island | 602 Surf Ave. (W. 8th St.) | Brooklyn | 718-741-3836 |
www.nyaquarium.com

New York Botanical Garden | *rooms: 2 | max cap: 300*
Bronx | Southern Blvd. & 200th St. | 718-220-0300 |
www.abigailkirsch.com

New York City Bar Association | *rooms: 12 | max cap: 450*
W 40s | 42 W. 44th St. (bet. 5th & 6th Aves.) | 212-382-6637 |
www.nycbar.org

New York City Fire Museum | *rooms: 1 | cap: 300*
SoHo | 278 Spring St. (bet. Hudson & Varick Sts.) | 212-691-1303 |
www.nycfiremuseum.org

New-York Historical Society | *rooms: 7 | max cap: 500*
W 70s | 170 Central Park W. (bet. 76th & 77th Sts.) | 212-485-9294 |
www.nyhistory.org

New York Public Library | *rooms: 7 | max cap: 750*
E 40s | Fifth Ave. & 42nd St. | 212-930-0730 | www.nypl.org/spacerental

New York Stock Exchange | *rooms: 4 | max cap: 800*
Financial District | 11 Wall St. (Nassau St.) | 212-656-6190 |
www.nyx.com/eventrental

91 – The Upper Crust | *rooms: 1 | cap: 200*
G Village | 91 Horatio St. (bet. Washington St. & West Side Hwy.) |
212-691-4570 | www.theuppercrust.com

Party Loft | *rooms: 1 | cap: 80*
Flatiron | 73 Fifth Ave. (15th St.) | 212-620-0622 |
www.thepartyloft.com

Pasanella & Son, Vintners | *rooms: 1 | cap: 75*
Seaport | 115 South St. (bet. Beekman St. & Peck Slip) | 212-233-8383 |
www.pasanellaandson.com

Picnic Housein Prospect Park | *rooms: 1 | cap: 250*
Park Slope | 95 Prospect Park W. (5th St.) | Brooklyn | 646-391-9031, ext. 2 |
www.prospectpark.org

Pratt Mansions | *rooms: 2 | max cap: 200*
E 80s | 1027 Fifth Ave. (bet. 83rd & 84th Sts.) | 212-744-4486, ext. 173 |
www.prattmansions.org

Radio City Music Hall | *rooms: 15 | max cap: 5900*
W 50s | 1260 Sixth Ave. (bet. 50th & 51st Sts.) | 212-465-6106 |
www.radiocity.com

Reception House | *rooms: 3 | max cap: 250*
Flushing | 167-17 Northern Blvd. (167th St.) | Queens | 718-463-1600 |
www.thereceptionhouse.com

Scandinavia House | *rooms: 6 | max cap: 250*
Murray Hill | 58 Park Ave. (bet. 37th & 38th Sts.) | 212-847-9719 |
www.scandinaviahouse.org

632 on Hudson | *rooms: 1 | cap: 150*
W Village | 632 Hudson St. (Horatio St.) | 212-620-7631 |
www.632onhudson.com

Skylight | *rooms: 1 | cap: 1000*
W Village | 275 Hudson St. (Dominick St.) | 212-736-6200 |
www.skylightnyc.com

South Oxford Space | *rooms: 1 | cap: 74*
Fort Greene | 138 S. Oxford St. (bet. Atlantic Ave. & Fulton St.) |
Brooklyn | 718-398-3078 | www.art-newyork.org

Spirit Cruises | *rooms: 2 | max cap: 600*
Chelsea | Chelsea Piers | Pier 61 (23rd St. & West Side Hwy.) |
866-483-3866 | www.spiritcruises.com

Splashlight Studios | *rooms: 4 | max cap: 450*
SoHo | One Hudson Sq. | 75 Varick St. (bet. Canal & Watts St.) |
212-268-7247 | www.splashlight.com

**Stanley H. Kaplan
Penthouse** | *rooms: 1 | cap: 300*
W 60s | Lincoln Ctr. | 70 Lincoln Ctr. (bet. Amsterdam Ave. & B'way) |
212-857-5037 | www.lincolncenter.org/yourevent

**St. Bartholomew's
Church** | *rooms: 6 | max cap: 350*
E 50s | 325 Park Ave. (50th St.) | 212-378-0254 |
www.stbarts.org

Studio 450 | *rooms: 1 | cap: 300*
Garment District | 450 W. 31st St. (bet. 9th & 10th Aves.) |
212-871-0940 | www.studio450ny.com

Tribeca Rooftop | *rooms: 1 | cap: 500*
TriBeCa | 2 Desbrosses St. (bet. Greenwich & Hudson Sts.) |
212-625-2600 | www.tribec.com

Twenty Four Fifth | *rooms: 1 | cap: 250*
G Village | 24 Fifth Ave. (bet. 9th & 10th Sts.) | 212-505-8000 |
www.theglaziergroup.com | French

**Ukrainian Institute
of America** | *rooms: 6 | max cap: 300*
E 70s | 2 E. 79th St. (bet. 5th & Madison Aves.) | 212-288-8660 |
www.ukrainianinstitute.org

Union Ballroom | *rooms: 1 | cap: 200*
W 100s | 3041 Broadway (121st St.) | 212-280-1301 |
www.utsnyc.edu

Union Square Ballroom | *rooms: 2 | max cap: 400*
Union Sq | 27 Union Sq. W. (bet. 15th & 16th Sts.) | 212-645-1802 |
www.unionsquareballroom.com

Union Square Events | *rooms: 2 | max cap: 225*
Chelsea | Hudson Yards | 640 W. 28th St., 8th fl. (bet. 11th Ave. & West Side Hwy.) | 212-488-1500 | www.unionsquareevents.com

Union Square
Wines & Spirits | *rooms: 1 | cap: 60*
Union Sq | 140 Fourth Ave. (13th St.) | 212-675-8100 | www.unionsquarewines.com

Villa Barone | *rooms: 2 | max cap: 600*
Bronx | 737 Throgs Neck Expwy. (bet. Philip & Randall Aves.) | 718-892-3500 | www.villabaronemanor.com

Whitney Museum | *rooms: 4 | max cap: 500*
E 70s | 945 Madison Ave. (bet. 74th & 75th Sts.) | 212-606-0388 | www.whitney.org

World Yacht Restaurant | *rooms: 4 | max cap: 500*
W 40s | Pier 81 (41st St. & West Side Hwy.) | 212-630-8800 | www.worldyacht.com

Hotels

Ace Hotel | *rooms: 3 | max cap: 200*
Chelsea | 20 W. 29th St. (bet. B'way & 5th Ave.) | 212-679-2222 | www.acehotel.com/newyork

Alex Hotel | *rooms: 1 | cap: 50*
E 40s | 205 E. 45th St. (3rd Ave.) | 212-850-6302 | www.thealexhotel.com

Andaz 5th Avenue | *rooms: 5 | max cap: 500*
W 40s | 485 Fifth Ave. (41st St.) | 212-601-1234 | www.andaz.com

Andaz Wall Street | *rooms: 11 | max cap: 200*
Financial District | 75 Wall St. (Water St.) | 212-590-1234 | www.andaz.com

Beekman Tower | *rooms: 3 | max cap: 150*
E 40s | 3 Mitchell Pl. (49th St.) | 212-224-0920 | www.thebeekmanhotel.com

Bowery Hotel | *rooms: 3 | max cap: 600*
LES | 335 Bowery (Great Jones St.) | 212-505-9100 | www.theboweryhotel.com

Bryant Park | *rooms: 4 | max cap: 300*
W 40s | 40 W. 40th St. (bet. 5th & 6th Aves.) | 212-869-0100 | www.bryantparkhotel.com

Carlton | *rooms: 9 | max cap: 700*
Gramercy | 88 Madison Ave. (bet. 28th & 29th Sts.) | 212-889-7100 | www.carltonhotelny.com

Carlyle | *rooms: 5 | max cap: 225*
E 70s | 35 E. 76th St. (Madison Ave.) | 212-570-7106 | www.thecarlyle.com

Chatwal New York | *rooms: 3 | max cap: 125*
W 40s | 130 W. 44th St. (bet. 6th & 7th Aves.) | 212-997-5262 | www.thechatwalny.com

Crosby Street Hotel | *rooms: 3 | max cap: 250*
SoHo | 79 Crosby St. (bet. Prince & Spring Sts.) | 212-226-6400 |
www.crosbystreethotel.com

Crowne Plaza Times Square | *rooms: 25 | max cap: 700*
W 50s | 1605 Broadway (bet. 48th & 49th Sts.) | 212-315-6126 |
www.manhattan.crowneplaza.com

DoubleTree Guest Suites | *rooms: 9 | max cap: 200*
W 40s | 1568 Broadway (47th St.) | 212-719-1600 |
www.nyc.doubletreehotels.com

Dream Hotel | *rooms: 3 | max cap: 300*
W 50s | 210 W. 55th St. (bet. B'way & 7th Ave.) | 212-974-1934 |
www.dreamny.com

Eventi Hotel | *rooms: 9 | max cap: 330*
Chelsea | 851 Sixth Ave. (30th St.) | 212-564-4567 |
www.eventihotel.com

Flatotel | *rooms: 3 | max cap: 200*
W 50s | 135 W. 52nd St. (bet. 6th & 7th Aves.) | 212-887-9515 |
www.flatotel.com

Gansevoort | *rooms: 4 | max cap: 350*
Meatpacking | 18 Ninth Ave. (13th St.) | 212-206-6700 |
www.hotelgansevoort.com

Gansevoort Hotel Park Ave. | *rooms: 5 | max cap: 580*
Flatiron | 420 Park Ave. S. (bet. 28th & 29th Sts.) | 212-317-2900 |
www.gansevoortpark.com

Giraffe | *rooms: 1 | cap: 100*
Gramercy | 365 Park Ave. S. (26th St.) | 212-894-0497 |
www.hotelgiraffe.com

Grand Hyatt New York | *rooms: 40 | max cap: 1800*
E 40s | 109 E. 42nd St. (Park Ave.) | 646-213-6640 |
www.grandnewyork.hyatt.com

Helmsley Park Lane | *rooms: 6 | max cap: 400*
W 50s | 36 Central Park S. (bet. 5th & 6th Aves.) | 212-521-6210 |
www.helmsleyparklane.com

Hilton New York and Towers | *rooms: 39 | max cap: 3300*
W 50s | 1335 Sixth Ave. (bet. 53rd & 54th Sts.) | 212-586-7000 |
www.hiltonfamilynewyork.com

The Hotel on Rivington | *rooms: 5 | max cap: 250*
LES | 107 Rivington St. (bet. Essex & Ludlow Sts.) | 212-475-2600 |
www.hotelonrivington.com

Hudson Hotel | *rooms: 16 | max cap: 600*
W 50s | 356 W. 58th St. (bet. 8th & 9th Aves.) | 212-554-6128 |
www.morganshotelgroup.com

Ink 48 | *rooms: 5 | max cap: 300*
W 40s | 653 11th Ave. (48th St.) | 212-757-0088 |
www.ink48.com

Inn at Irving Place | *rooms: 4 | max cap: 60*
Union Sq | 56 Irving Pl. (bet. 17th & 18th Sts.) | 212-533-4466 |
www.innatirving.com

Inter-Continental, NY Barclay | *rooms: 18* | *max cap: 550*
E 40s | 111 E. 48th St. (bet. Lexington & Park Aves.) | 212-906-3110 |
www.intercontinentalnybarclay.com

James New York | *rooms: 2* | *max cap: 75*
SoHo | 27 Grand St. (bet. 6th Ave. & Thompson St.) | 212-465-2000 |
www.jameshotels.com

Jumeirah Essex House | *rooms: 12* | *max cap: 500*
W 50s | 160 Central Park S. (bet. 6th & 7th Aves.) | 212-484-5144 |
www.jumeirahessexhouse.com

The Kitano | *rooms: 1* | *cap: 146*
Murray Hill | 66 Park Ave. (38th St.) | 212-885-7017 | www.kitano.com

Le Parker Meridien | *rooms: 7* | *max cap: 300*
W 50s | 119 W. 56th St. (bet. 6th & 7th Aves.) | 212-708-7450 |
www.parkermeridien.com

Library Hotel | *rooms: 1* | *cap: 150*
E 40s | 299 Madison Ave. (41st St.) | 212-983-4500 | www.libraryhotel.com

Loews Regency | *rooms: 3* | *max cap: 200*
E 60s | 540 Park Ave. (61st St.) | 212-759-4100 | www.loewsregency.com

The Lowell | *rooms: 1* | *cap: 75*
E 60s | 28 E. 63rd St. (bet. Madison & Park Aves.) | 212-605-6825 |
www.lowellhotel.com

Mandarin Oriental | *rooms: 2* | *max cap: 650*
W 60s | Time Warner Ctr. | 80 Columbus Circle (60th St.) |
212-805-8857 | www.mandarinoriental.com

Maritime Hotel | *rooms: 3* | *max cap: 800*
Chelsea | 363 W. 16th St. (bet. 8th & 9th Aves.) | 212-242-4300 |
www.themaritimehotel.com

The Mark | *rooms: 3* | *max cap: 22*
E 70s | 25 E. 77th St. (bet. 5th & Madison Aves.) | 212-606-4511 |
www.themarkhotel.com

Millennium Broadway | *rooms: 15* | *max cap: 700*
W 40s | 145 W. 44th St. (bet. B'way & 6th Ave.) | 212-768-4400 |
www.millenniumhotels.com

Millennium UN Plaza | *rooms: 7* | *max cap: 300*
E 40s | 1 United Nations Plaza (1st Ave. & 44th St.) | 212-758-7041 |
www.millenniumhotels.com

Morgans | *rooms: 1* | *cap: 75*
Murray Hill | 237 Madison Ave. (bet. 37th & 38th Aves.) |
212-686-0300 | www.morganshotelgroup.com

The Muse | *rooms: 5* | *max cap: 120*
W 40s | 130 W. 46th St. (bet. 6th & 7th Aves.) | 212-485-2736 |
www.themusehotel.com

New York Marriott Downtown | *rooms: 12* | *max cap: 450*
Financial District | 85 West St. (Albany St.) | 212-385-4900 |
www.nymarriottdowntown.com

New York Marriott Marquis | *rooms: 67* | *max cap: 2800*
W 40s | 1535 Broadway (bet. 45th & 46th Sts.) | 212-704-8775 |
www.nymarriottmarquis.com

New York Palace | *rooms: 13 | max cap: 300*
E 50s | 455 Madison Ave. (bet. 50th & 51st Sts.) | 212-888-7000 |
www.newyorkpalace.com

Night Hotel | *rooms: 1 | cap: 100*
W 40s | 132 W. 45th St. (bet. 6th & 7th Aves.) | 212-835-9600 |
www.nighthotelny.com

Omni Berkshire Place | *rooms: 10 | max cap: 128*
E 50s | 21 E. 52nd St. (bet. 5th & Madison Aves.) | 212-753-5800 |
www.omnihotels.com

Paramount | *rooms: 2 | max cap: 350*
W 40s | 235 W. 46th St. (bet. B'way & 8th Ave.) | 212-764-5500 |
www.nycparamount.com

The Peninsula | *rooms: 6 | max cap: 180*
E 50s | 700 Fifth Ave. (55th St.) | 212-903-3861 |
www.peninsula.com

The Pierre | *rooms: 6 | max cap: 1500*
E 60s | 2 E. 61st St. (5th Ave.) | 212-940-8111 |
www.tajhotels.com

Plaza Athénée | *rooms: 4 | max cap: 150*
E 60s | 37 E. 64th St. (bet. Madison & Park Aves.) | 212-606-4663 |
www.plaza-athenee.com

The Plaza Hotel | *rooms: 10 | max cap: 1000*
W 50s | 768 Fifth Ave. (bet. 58th & 59th Sts.) | 212-549-0550 |
www.theplaza.com

Ritz-Carlton, Battery Park | *rooms: 7 | max cap: 600*
Financial District | 2 West St. (bet. Battery Pl. & South St.) |
917-790-2400 | www.ritzcarlton.com

Ritz-Carlton, Central Park | *rooms: 4 | max cap: 150*
W 50s | 50 Central Park S. (bet. 5th & 6th Aves.) | 212-521-6051 |
www.ritzcarlton.com

Setai Fifth Avenue | *rooms: 3 | max cap: 250*
Flatiron | 400 Fifth Ave. (bet. 36th & 37th Sts.) | 212-613-8736 |
www.setaififthavenue.com

70 Park Avenue | *rooms: 3 | max cap: 110*
Murray Hill | 70 Park Ave. (38th St.) | 212-973-2437 |
www.70parkave.com

60 Thompson | *rooms: 4 | max cap: 225*
SoHo | 60 Thompson St. (bet. Broome & Spring Sts.) | 212-219-2000 |
www.60thompson.com

Smyth Tribeca Hotel | *rooms: 5 | max cap: 150*
TriBeCa | 85 W. Broadway (bet. Chambers & Warren Sts.) |
212-587-7000 | www.thompsonhotels.com

Soho Grand | *rooms: 7 | max cap: 300*
SoHo | 310 W. Broadway (bet. Canal & Grand Sts.) | 212-519-6666 |
www.sohogrand.com

Standard Hotel | *rooms: 6 | max cap: 350*
Chelsea | 848 Washington St. (13th St.) | 212-645-4646 |
www.standardhotels.com

St. Regis | *rooms: 10* | *max cap: 250*
E 50s | 2 E. 55th St. (bet. 5th & Madison Aves.) | 212-339-6776 |
www.stregis.com

Tribeca Grand | *rooms: 6* | *max cap: 375*
TriBeCa | 2 Sixth Ave. (Church St.) | 212-519-6666 |
www.tribecagrand.com

Trump Soho | *rooms: 5* | *max cap: 400*
SoHo | 246 Spring St. (Varick St.) | 212-842-5500 |
www.trumpsohohotel.com

Waldorf-Astoria | *rooms: 40* | *max cap: 1700*
E 40s | 301 Park Ave. (bet. 49th & 50th Sts.) | 212-872-4700 |
www.waldorfnewyork.com

Westin Times Square | *rooms: 30* | *max cap: 350*
W 40s | 270 W. 43rd St. (8th Ave.) | 212-841-6615 |
www.westinny.com

W Hotel Downtown | *rooms: 4* | *max cap: 120*
Financial District | 123 Washington St. (bet. Albany & Carlisle Sts.) |
212-841-6615 | www.starwoodhotels.com

W New York | *rooms: 12* | *max cap: 375*
E 50s | 541 Lexington Ave. (bet. 49th & 50th Sts.) | 212-841-6615 |
www.starwoodhotels.com

W Times Square | *rooms: 6* | *max cap: 130*
W 40s | 1567 Broadway (47th St.) | 212-841-6615 |
www.starwoodhotels.com

W Union Square | *rooms: 6* | *max cap: 240*
Union Sq | 201 Park Ave. S. (17th St.) | 212-841-6615 |
www.starwoodhotels.com

Nightclubs/Bars

For additional listings, see Zagat NYC Nightlife.

The Ainsworth | *rooms: 1* | *cap: 565*
Chelsea | 122 W. 26th St. (bet. 6th & 7th Aves.) | 212-741-0646 |
www.ainsworthnyc.com

Ajna Bar | *rooms: 1* | *cap: 800*
Meatpacking | 25 Little W. 12th St. (bet. 9th Ave. & Washington St.) |
646-416-6002 | www.ajnabarnyc.com

Bacaro | *rooms: 3* | *max cap: 95*
Chinatown | 136 Division St. (east of Orchard St.) | 212-941-5060 |
www.bacaronyc.com

Bell House | *rooms: 2* | *max cap: 500*
Gowanus | 149 Seventh St. (bet. 2nd & 3rd Aves.) | Brooklyn |
718-369-3310, ext. 10 | www.thebellhouseny.com

Blue Owl | *rooms: 2* | *max cap: 120*
E Village | 196 Second Ave. (bet. 12th & 13th Sts.) | 212-505-2583 |
www.blueowlnyc.com

Bowlmor | *rooms: 3* | *max cap: 1000*
G Village | 110 University Pl. (bet. 12th & 13th Sts.) |
212-255-8188 | www.bowlmor.com

Bowlmor Times Square | *rooms: 9 | max cap: 1500*
W 40s | 222 W. 44th St. (bet. 7th & 8th Aves.) | 212-680-0012 |
www.bowlmor.com

Brooklyn Bowl | *rooms: 1 | cap: 600*
Williamsburg | 61 Wythe Ave. (bet. 11th & 12th Sts.) | Brooklyn |
718-963-3369 | www.brooklynbowl.com

Butter | *rooms: 2 | max cap: 300*
G Village | 415 Lafayette St. (bet. Astor Pl. & 4th St.) | 212-253-2828 |
www.butterrestaurant.com

Campbell Apartment | *rooms: 1 | cap: 125*
E 40s | Grand Central Terminal | 15 Vanderbilt Ave. (bet. 42nd &
43rd Sts.) | 212-980-9476 | www.hospitalityholdings.com

Canal Room | *rooms: 1 | cap: 450*
SoHo | 285 W. Broadway (Canal St.) | 212-941-8100 |
www.canalroom.com

Carnegie Club | *rooms: 1 | cap: 150*
W 50s | 156 W. 56th St. (bet. 6th & 7th Aves.) | 212-980-9476 |
www.hospitalityholdings.com

Cotton Club | *rooms: 1 | cap: 175*
Harlem | 656 W. 125th St. (12th Ave.) | 212-663-7980 |
www.cottonclub-newyork.com

Empire Hotel Rooftop | *rooms: 1 | cap: 700*
W 60s | 44 W. 63rd St., 12th fl. (B'way) | 212-265-7400 |
www.empirehotelnyc.com

Empire Room | *rooms: 1 | cap: 250*
Flatiron | Empire State Bldg. | 350 Fifth Ave. (bet. 33rd & 34th Sts.) |
212-643-5400 | www.hospitalityholdings.com

Galapagos | *rooms: 1 | cap: 250*
Dumbo | 16 Main St. (Water St.) | Brooklyn | 718-222-8500 |
www.galapagosartspace.com

Hudson Terrace | *rooms: 2 | max cap: 800*
W 40s | 621 W. 46th St. (bet. 11th & 12th Aves.) | 212-315-9400 |
www.hudsonterracenyc.com

Lani Kai | *rooms: 2 | max cap: 100*
SoHo | 525 Broome St. (bet. Sullivan & Thompson Sts.) | 646-596-8778 |
www.lanikainy.com

Latitude | *rooms: 4 | max cap: 300*
W 40s | 783 Eighth Ave. (bet. 47th & 48th Sts.) | 212-245-3034 |
www.latitudebarnyc.com

Los Feliz | *rooms: 3 | max cap: 250*
LES | 109 Ludlow St. (bet. Delancey & Rivington Sts.) | 212-228-8383 |
www.losfeliznyc.com

Mercury Lounge | *rooms: 2 | max cap: 250*
LES | 217 E. Houston St. (bet. Essex & Ludlow Sts.) | 212-260-4700 |
www.mercuryloungenyc.com

Penny Farthing | *rooms: 1 | cap: 75*
E Village | 103 Third Ave. (13th St.) | 212-387-7300 |
www.thepennyfarthingnyc.com

Providence/Triumph Room | *rooms: 3 | max cap: 1200*
W 50s | 311 W. 57th St. (bet. 8th & 9th Aves.) | 212-307-0062 |
www.metronomenyc.com

PS 450 | *rooms: 3 | max cap: 350*
Murray Hill | 450 Park Ave. S. (bet. 30th & 31st Sts.) | 212-532-1519 |
www.ps450.com

Ravel Rooftop | *rooms: 1 | cap: 400*
LIC | Ravel Hotel | 8-08 Queens Plaza (Vernon Blvd.) | Queens |
718-289-6118 | www.penthouse808rooftop.com

Roseland Ballroom | *rooms: 1 | cap: 3200*
W 50s | 239 W. 52nd St. (bet. B'way & 8th Ave.) | 212-489-8350 |
www.roselandballroom.com

S.O.B.'s | *rooms: 2 | max cap: 400*
Hudson Square | 204 Varick St. (Houston St.) | 212-645-2577 |
www.sobs.com

Spice Market | *rooms: 7 | max cap: 20*
Meatpacking | 403 W. 13th St. (9th Ave.) | 646-747-8380 |
www.spicemarketnewyork.com

230 Fifth | *rooms: 3 | max cap: 1200*
Flatiron | 230 Fifth Ave., penthouse (bet. 26th & 27th Sts.) |
212-725-4300 | www.230-fifth.com

Webster Hall | *rooms: 5 | max cap: 1500*
E Village | 125 E. 11th St. (bet. 3rd & 4th Aves.) | 212-353-1600 |
www.websterhall.com

World Bar | *rooms: 1 | cap: 125*
E 40s | Trump World Tower | 845 United Nations Plaza (48th St.) |
212-980-9476 | www.hospitalityholdings.com

Private Clubs

Members only, or nonmembers with sponsorship

National Arts Club | *rooms: 7 | max cap: 300*
Gramercy | 15 Gramercy Park S. (Irving Pl.) | 212-475-3424 |
www.nationalartsclub.org

Players Club | *rooms: 6 | max cap: 350*
Union Sq | 16 Gramercy Park S. (Irving Pl.) | 212-475-6116 |
www.theplayersnyc.org

Yale Club | *rooms: 11 | max cap: 350*
E 40s | 50 Vanderbilt Ave. (bet. 44th & 45th Sts.) | 212-716-2122 |
www.yaleclubnyc.org

Restaurants

For additional listings, see Zagat NYC Restaurants.

Adour | *rooms: 3 | max cap: 16*
E 50s | St. Regis Hotel | 2 E. 55th St. (bet. 5th & Madison Aves.) |
212-710-2279 | www.adour-stregis.com | French

American Girl Place Cafe | *rooms: 2 | max cap: 150*
E 40s | 609 Fifth Ave. (49th St.) | 212-371-2220 |
www.americangirlplace.com | American

Aroma
Kitchen & Winebar | *rooms: 2* | *max cap: 36*
NoHo | 36 E. Fourth St. (bet. Bowery & Lafayette St.) | 212-375-0100 | www.aromanyc.com | Italian

Aureole | *rooms: 1* | *cap: 125*
W 40s | Bank of America Tower | 135 W. 42nd St. (bet. B'way & 6th Ave.) | 646-392-9172, ext. 20 | www.charliepalmerny.com | American

Bar Americain | *rooms: 2* | *max cap: 50*
W 50s | 152 W. 52nd St. (bet. 6th & 7th Aves.) | 212-265-9701 | www.baramericain.com | American

Barbetta | *rooms: 6* | *max cap: 200*
W 40s | 321 W. 46th St. (bet. 8th & 9th Aves.) | 212-246-9171 | www.barbettarestaurant.com | Italian

Bar Boulud | *rooms: 3* | *max cap: 100*
W 60s | 1900 Broadway (bet. 63rd & 64th Sts.) | 212-595-9604, ext. 161 | www.danielnyc.com | French

Battery Gardens | *rooms: 2* | *max cap: 500*
Financial District | Battery Park (opp. 17 State St.) | 212-809-5508 | www.batterygardens.com | American/Continental

Bayard's | *rooms: 8* | *max cap: 1000*
Financial District | 1 Hanover Sq. (bet. Pearl & Stone Sts.) | 212-514-9454 | www.bayards.com | American

Beacon | *rooms: 4* | *max cap: 400*
W 50s | 25 W. 56th St. (bet. 5th & 6th Aves.) | 212-332-0500 | www.beaconnyc.com | American

Becco | *rooms: 4* | *max cap: 100*
W 40s | 355 W. 46th St. (bet. 8th & 9th Aves.) | 212-397-7597 | www.becconyc.com | Italian

Benoit | *rooms: 4* | *max cap: 120*
W 50s | 60 W. 55th St. (bet. 5th & 6th Aves.) | 646-943-7378 | www.benoitny.com | French

Bill's
Bar & Burger | *rooms: 1* | *cap: 125*
W 50s | 16 W. 51st St. (bet. 5th & 6th Aves.) | 212-705-8510 | www.billsbarandburger.com | Burgers

BLT Bar & Grill | *rooms: 1* | *cap: 50*
Financial District | W Hotel Downtown | 123 Washington St. (bet. Albany & Carlisle Sts.) | 646-826-8668 | www.bltrestaurants.com | American

BLT Fish | *rooms: 1* | *cap: 125*
Flatiron | 21 W. 17th St. (bet. 5th & 6th Aves.) | 212-691-8888 | www.bltfish.com | Seafood

BLT Prime | *rooms: 1* | *cap: 75*
Gramercy | 111 E. 22nd St. (bet. Lexington Ave. & Park Ave S.) | 212-995-8500 | www.bltprime.com | American

BLT Steak | *rooms: 1* | *cap: 20*
E 50s | 106 E. 57th St. (bet. Lexington & Park Aves.) | 212-752-4411 | www.bltsteak.com | American/Steak

PARTY SITES – RESTAURANTS

Blue Fin | *rooms: 3* | *max cap: 500*
W 40s | W Hotel Times Square | 1567 Broadway (bet. 47th & 48th Sts.) | 212-331-0328 | www.brguesthospitality.com | Seafood

Blue Hill | *rooms: 1* | *cap: 16*
G Village | 75 Washington Pl. (bet. 6th Ave. & Washington Sq. W.) | 212-539-1776 | www.bluehillfarm.com | American

Blue Water Grill | *rooms: 2* | *max cap: 115*
Union Sq | 31 Union Sq. W. (16th St.) | 212-331-0328 | www.brguesthospitality.com | Seafood

Boathouse | *rooms: 1* | *cap: 500*
E 70s | Central Park | E. 72nd St. (Central Park Dr. N.) | 212-517-2233 | www.thecentralparkboathouse.com | American

Bottega del Vino | *rooms: 2* | *max cap: 193*
E 50s | 7 E. 59th St. (bet. 5th & Madison Aves.) | 212-223-3028 | www.bottegadelvinonyc.com | Italian

Bouley | *rooms: 3* | *max cap: 75*
TriBeCa | 163 Duane St. (Hudson St.) | 917-237-3205 | www.davidbouley.com | French

Brasserie Julien | *rooms: 1* | *cap: 7*
E 80s | 1422 Third Ave. (bet. 80th & 81st Sts.) | 212-744-6327 | www.brasseriejulien.com | French

Breslin | *rooms: 2* | *max cap: 185*
Chelsea | Ace Hotel | 16 W. 29th St. (bet. B'way & 5th Ave.) | 212-679-1939 | www.thebreslin.com | British

Bryant Park Grill/Cafe | *rooms: 3* | *max cap: 800*
W 40s | 25 W. 40th St. (bet. 5th & 6th Aves.) | 212-206-8815 | www.arkrestaurants.com | American

Buddakan | *rooms: 1* | *cap: 60*
Meatpacking | 75 Ninth Ave. (bet. 15th & 16th Sts.) | 212-989-6699 | www.buddakannyc.com | Asian

Cafe Fiorello | *rooms: 2* | *max cap: 220*
W 60s | 1900 Broadway (63rd St.) | 212-265-0100 | www.cafefiorello.com | Italian

Calle Ocho | *rooms: 3* | *max cap: 150*
W 80s | 45 W. 81st St. (bet. Columbus Ave. & CPW) | 212-873-5025 | www.calleochonyc.com | Nuevo Latino

Ça Va | *rooms: 3* | *max cap: 225*
W 40s | InterContinental NY Times Sq. | 310 W. 44th St. (8th Ave.) | 212-803-4545 | www.cavatoddenglish.com | French

Cellini | *rooms: 2* | *max cap: 125*
E 50s | 65 E. 54th St. (bet. Madison & Park Aves.) | 212-751-1555 | www.cellinirestaurant.com | Italian

Chin Chin | *rooms: 2* | *max cap: 54*
E 40s | 216 E. 49th St. (bet. 2nd & 3rd Aves.) | 212-888-4555 | www.chinchinny.com | Chinese

Cipriani Wall Street | *rooms: 2* | *max cap: 140*
Financial District | 55 Wall St. (bet. Hanover & Williams Sts.) | 212-699-4096 | www.cipriani.com | Italian

City Hall | *rooms: 3* | *max cap: 415*
TriBeCa | 131 Duane St. (bet. Church St. & W. B'way) |
212-964-4118 | www.cityhallnewyork.com | American

City Winery | *rooms: 4* | *max cap: 500*
SoHo | 155 Varick St. (Vandam St.) | 212-608-0555 |
www.citywinery.com | Mediterranean

Colicchio & Sons | *rooms: 1* | *cap: 65*
Chelsea | 85 10th Ave. (bet. 15th & 16th Sts.) | 212-400-6699 |
www.colicchioandsons.com | American

Convivium Osteria | *rooms: 3* | *max cap: 90*
Park Slope | 68 Fifth Ave. (bet. Bergen St. & St. Marks Ave.) |
Brooklyn | 718-857-1833 | www.conviviumosteria.com |
Mediterranean

Cowgirl | *rooms: 4* | *max cap: 230*
G Village | 519 Hudson St. (10th St.) | 212-633-1133 |
www.cowgirlnyc.com | Southwestern

Daniel | *rooms: 2* | *max cap: 150*
E 50s | 60 E. 65th St. (bet. Madison & Park Aves.) | 212-933-5261 |
www.danielnyc.com | French

Del Frisco's | *rooms: 4* | *max cap: 85*
W 40s | 1221 Sixth Ave. (49th St.) | 212-575-5129 |
www.delfriscos.com | Steak

Del Posto | *rooms: 5* | *max cap: 1200*
Meatpacking | 85 10th Ave. (bet. 15th & 16th Sts.) |
646-278-0800 | www.delposto.com | Italian

Dos Caminos
rooms: 3 | *max cap: 300*
E 50s | 825 Third Ave. (50th St.) | 212-331-0328
rooms: 2 | *max cap: 100*
Gramercy | 373 Park Ave. S. (bet. 26th & 27th Sts.) |
212-331-0328
www.brguesthospitality.com | Mexican

Dovetail | *rooms: 1* | *cap: 20*
W 70s | 103 W. 77th St. (Columbus Ave.) | 212-362-3800 |
www.dovetailnyc.com | American

Eleven Madison Park | *rooms: 2* | *max cap: 50*
Flatiron | 11 Madison Ave. (24th St.) | 212-889-0905 |
www.elevenmadisonpark.com | French

Eli's Vinegar Factory | *rooms: 1* | *cap: 300*
E 90s | 431 E. 91st St. (bet. 1st & York Aves.) | 212-987-0885 |
www.elizabar.com | American

Elmo | *rooms: 1* | *cap: 100*
Chelsea | 156 Seventh Ave. (bet. 19th & 20th Sts.) | 212-337-8000 |
www.elmorestaurant.com | American

EN Japanese Brasserie | *rooms: 7* | *max cap: 300*
W Village | 435 Hudson St. (Leroy St.) | 212-647-9196 |
www.enjb.com | Japanese

PARTY SITES – RESTAURANTS

Felidia | *rooms: 4 | max cap: 150*
E 50s | 243 E. 58th St. (bet. 2nd & 3rd Aves.) | 212-758-1479 |
www.felidianyc.com | Italian

FireBird | *rooms: 6 | max cap: 325*
W 40s | 365 W. 46th St. (bet. 8th & 9th Aves.) | 212-586-0244 |
www.firebirdrestaurant.com | Russian

5 Ninth | *rooms: 1 | cap: 60*
Meatpacking | 5 Ninth Ave. (bet. Gansevoort & Little W. 12th Sts.) |
212-929-9460 | www.fiveninth.com | American

Four Seasons | *rooms: 5 | max cap: 475*
E 50s | 99 E. 52nd St. (bet. Lexington & Park Aves.) | 212-754-9494 |
www.fourseasonsrestaurant.com | American

Frankies Spuntino | *rooms: 1 | cap: 75*
Carroll Gardens | 457 Court St. (bet. 4th Pl. & Lucquer St.) |
Brooklyn | 718-403-0033 | www.frankiesspuntino.com | Italian

Fraunces Tavern | *rooms: 6 | max cap: 350*
Financial District | 54 Pearl St. (Broad St.) | 212-968-1776 |
www.frauncestavern.com | American

Fred's at Barneys NY | *rooms: 1 | cap: 40*
E 60s | 660 Madison Ave., 9th fl. (bet. 60th & 61st Sts.) |
212-833-2200 | American/Italian

Freemans | *rooms: 3 | max cap: 250*
LES | Freeman Alley (off Rivington St., bet. Bowery & Chrystie St.) |
212-420-0012 | www.freemansrestaurant.com | American

Fresco by Scotto | *rooms: 2 | max cap: 120*
E 50s | 34 E. 52nd St. (bet. Madison & Park Aves.) | 212-935-3434 |
www.frescobyscotto.com | Italian

Girasole | *rooms: 1 | cap: 40*
E 80s | 151 E. 82nd St. (bet. Lexington & 3rd Aves.) | 212-772-6690 |
www.girasolerestaurantnyc.com | Italian

Golden Unicorn | *rooms: 2 | max cap: 500*
Chinatown | 18 E. Broadway (Catherine St.) | 212-941-0911 |
www.goldenunicornrestaurant.com | Chinese

Gramercy Tavern | *rooms: 1 | cap: 22*
Flatiron | 42 E. 20th St. (bet. B'way & Park Ave. S.) | 212-477-0777 |
www.gramercytavern.com | American

Guastavino's | *rooms: 1 | cap: 2000*
E 50s | 409 E. 59th St. (bet. 1st & York Aves.) | 212-980-2711 |
www.guastavinos.com | American

The Harrison | *rooms: 1 | cap: 24*
TriBeCa | 355 Greenwich St. (Harrison St.) | 212-274-9310 |
www.theharrison.com | American

Hurricane Club | *rooms: 6 | max cap: 150*
Flatiron | 360 Park Ave. S. (26th St.) | 212-951-7111 |
www.thehurricaneclub.com | Polynesian

Ici | *rooms: 1 | cap: 100*
Fort Greene | 246 DeKalb Ave. (bet. Clermont & Vanderbilt Aves.) |
Brooklyn | 718-789-2778 | www.icirestaurant.com | American/French

Il Buco | *rooms: 2* | *max cap: 25*
NoHo | 47 Bond St. (bet. Bowery & Lafayette St.) | 212-533-1932 | www.ilbuco.com | Italian/Mediterranean

Il Buco Alimentari/Vineria | *rooms: 1* | *cap: 55*
NoHo | 53 Great Jones St. (bet. Bowery & Lafayette St.) | 212-8372622 | www.ilbucovineria.com | Italian/Mediterranean

Ilili | *rooms: 3* | *max cap: 300*
Chelsea | 236 Fifth Ave. (bet. 27th & 28th Sts.) | 212-481-1840 | www.ililinyc.com | Lebanese

Insieme | *rooms: 1* | *cap: 150*
W 50s | Michelangelo Hotel | 777 Seventh Ave. (bet. 50th & 51st Sts.) | 212-582-1310 | www.restaurantinsieme.com | Italian

I Trulli | *rooms: 4* | *max cap: 160*
Gramercy | 122 E. 27th St. (bet. Lexington Ave. & Park Ave. S.) | 212-481-7372 | www.itrulli.com | Italian

Jean Georges | *rooms: 1* | *cap: 30*
W 60s | Trump Int'l Hotel | 1 Central Park W. (bet. 60th & 61st Sts.) | 212-299-3900 | www.jean-georges.com | French

Keens Steakhouse | *rooms: 2* | *max cap: 125*
Garment District | 72 W. 36th St. (bet. 5th & 6th Aves.) | 212-268-5056 | www.keens.com | Steak

La Esquina | *rooms: 2* | *max cap: 35*
SoHo | 114 Kenmare St. (bet. Cleveland Pl. & Lafayette St.) | 646-613-7100 | www.esquinanyc.com | Mexican

Landmarc | *rooms: 2* | *max cap: 125*
W 60s | Time Warner Ctr. | 10 Columbus Circle, 3rd fl. (60th St.) | 212-823-6123 | www.landmarc-restaurant.com | French

Le Bernardin | *rooms: 3* | *max cap: 80*
W 50s | 155 W. 51st St. (bet. 6th & 7th Aves.) | 212-554-1108 | www.le-bernardin.com | French/Seafood

Le Cirque | *rooms: 2* | *max cap: 85*
E 50s | One Beacon Court | 151 E. 58th St. (bet. Lexington & 3rd Aves.) | 212-405-5095 | www.lecirque.com | French

Le Perigord | *rooms: 2* | *max cap: 100*
E 50s | 405 E. 52nd St. (bet. FDR Dr. & 1st Ave.) | 212-755-6244 | www.leperigord.com | French

Lincoln | *rooms: 1* | *cap: 142*
W 60s | Lincoln Ctr. | 142 W. 65th St. (bet. Amsterdam Ave. & B'way) | 212-359-6500 | www.lincolnristorante.com | Italian

The Lion | *rooms: 1* | *cap: 12*
G Village | 62 W. Ninth St. (bet. 5th & 6th Aves.) | 212-353-8400 | www.thelionnyc.com | American

Locanda Verde | *rooms: 1* | *cap: 60*
TriBeCa | 377 Greenwich St. (Moore St.) | 212-925-3797 | www.locandeverdenyc.com | Italian

Lupa | *rooms: 1* | *cap: 30*
G Village | 170 Thompson St. (bet. Bleecker & Houston Sts.) | 212-982-5089 | www.luparestaurant.com | Italian

PARTY SITES - RESTAURANTS

Lure Fishbar | *rooms: 1* | *cap: 30*
SoHo | 142 Mercer St., downstairs (Prince St.) | 212-431-7676 | www.lurefishbar.com | Seafood

Maialino | *rooms: 1* | *cap: 24*
Gramercy | Gramercy Park Hotel | 2 Lexington Ave. (21st St.) | 212-777-2410 | www.maialinonyc.com | Italian

Marea | *rooms: 3* | *max cap: 35*
W 50s | 240 Central Park S. | 212-582-5100 | www.marea-nyc.com | Italian/Seafood

Mas | *rooms: 2* | *max cap: 24*
W Village | 39 Downing St. (bet. Bedford & Varick Sts.) | 212-255-1790 | www.masfarmhouse.com | American

Megu | *rooms: 3* | *max cap: 100*
TriBeCa | 62 Thomas St. (bet. Church St. & W. B'way) | 212-964-7777 | www.megurestaurants.com | Japanese

Megu Midtown | *rooms: 2* | *max cap: 50*
E 40s | Trump World Tower | 845 United Nations Plaza (1st Ave. & 47th St.) | 212-644-0777 | www.megurestaurants.com | Japanese

Michael Jordan's
The Steak House NYC | *rooms: 3* | *max cap: 500*
E 40s | Grand Central Terminal | West Balcony (42nd St. & Vanderbilt Ave.) | 212-608-7400 | www.thegalziergroup.com | Steak

Mickey Mantle's | *rooms: 3* | *max cap: 300*
W 50s | 42 Central Park S. (bet. 5th & 6th Aves.) | 212-688-7777 | www.mickeymantles.com | American

Millesime | *rooms: 3* | *max cap: 600*
Murray Hill | Carlton Hotel | 92 Madison Ave., 2nd fl. (29th St.) | 212-889-7100 | www.millesimerestaurant.com | Seafood

The Modern | *rooms: 1* | *cap: 64*
W 50s | Museum of Modern Art | 9 W. 53rd St. (bet. 5th & 6th Aves.) | 212-408-6641 | www.themodernnyc.com | American/French

Moran's Chelsea | *rooms: 4* | *max cap: 500*
Chelsea | 146 10th Ave. (19th St.) | 212-627-3030 | www.moransrestaurant.com | American

Morimoto | *rooms: 2* | *max cap: 350*
Chelsea | 88 10th Ave. (16th St.) | 212-989-8883 | www.morimotonyc.com | Japanese

Mr. Chow Tribeca | *rooms: 1* | *cap: 60*
TriBeCa | 121 Hudson St. (Moore St.) | 212-965-9500 | www.mrchow.com | Chinese

Nobu | *rooms: 1* | *cap: 200*
TriBeCa | 105 Hudson St. (Franklin St.) | 212-219-8095 | www.noburestaurants.com | Japanese

Nobu 57 | *rooms: 6* | *max cap: 300*
W 50s | 40 W. 57th St. (bet. 5th & 6th Aves.) | 212-757-3000 | www.noburestaurants.com | Japanese

Oceana | *rooms: 6 | max cap: 120*
W 40s | McGraw Hill Bldg. | 120 W. 49th St. (bet. 6th & 7th Aves.) |
212-759-5941 | www.oceanarestaurant.com | American/Seafood

Ocean Grill | *rooms: 3 | max cap: 199*
W 70s | 384 Columbus Ave. (bet. 78th & 79th Sts.) | 212-579-2300 |
www.oceangrill.com | Seafood

Old Homestead | *rooms: 4 | max cap: 75*
Chelsea | 56 Ninth Ave. (bet. 14th & 15th Sts.) | 212-242-9040 |
www.theoldhomesteadsteakhouse.com | Steak

One if by Land,
Two if by Sea | *rooms: 3 | max cap: 125*
G Village | 17 Barrow St. (bet. 7th Ave. & W. 4th St.) | 646-496-6433 |
www.oneifbyland.com | American

Opia | *rooms: 3 | max cap: 150*
E 50s | Renaissance Hotel 57 | 130 E. 57th St. (Lexington Ave.) |
212-688-3939 | www.opiarestaurant.com | French

Palma | *rooms: 2 | max cap: 22*
W Village | 28 Cornelia St. (bet. Bleecker & W. 4th Sts.) |
212-691-8842 | www.palmanyc.com | Italian

The Park | *rooms: 5 | max cap: 1000*
Chelsea | 118 10th Ave. (bet. 17th & 18th Sts.) | 212-352-3313 |
www.theparknyc.com | Mediterranean

Patroon | *rooms: 6 | max cap: 400*
E 40s | 160 E. 46th St. (bet. Lexington & 3rd Aves.) | 212-973-1022 |
www.patroonrestaurant.com | American

Periyali | *rooms: 3 | max cap: 125*
Flatiron | 35 W. 20th St. (bet. 5th & 6th Aves.) | 212-463-7890 |
www.periyali.com | Greek

Per Se | *rooms: 2 | max cap: 60*
W 60s | Time Warner Ctr. | 10 Columbus Circle, 4th fl. (60th St.) |
212-823-9349 | www.perseny.com | American/French

Picholine | *rooms: 2 | max cap: 22*
W 60s | 35 W. 64th St. (bet. B'way & CPW) | 212-724-8585 |
www.picholinenyc.com | French/Mediterranean

Pop Burger
rooms: 2 | max cap: 200
E 50s | 14 E. 58th St. (bet. 5th & Madison Aves.) | 212-991-6644
rooms: 1 | cap: 200
Meatpacking | 58-60 Ninth Ave. (bet. 14th & 15th Sts.) |
212-414-8686
www.popburger.com | Burgers

Prune | *rooms: 1 | cap: 9*
E Village | 54 E. First St. (bet. 1st & 2nd Aves.) | 212-677-6221 |
www.prunerestaurant.com | American

Public | *rooms: 4 | max cap: 120*
NoLita | 210 Elizabeth St. (bet. Prince & Spring Sts.) | 212-343-7011 |
www.public-nyc.com | Eclectic

Quality Meats | *rooms: 2 | max cap: 40*
W 50s | 57 W. 58th St. (bet. 5th & 6th Aves.) | 212-360-0438 |
www.qualitymeatsnyc.com | American/Steak

Redeye Grill | *rooms: 3 | max cap: 125*
W 50s | 890 Seventh Ave. (bet. 56th & 57th Sts.) | 212-265-0100 |
www.redeyegrill.com | American/Seafood

Re Sette | *rooms: 1 | cap: 50*
W 40s | 7 W. 45th St. (bet. 5th & 6th Aves.) | 212-221-7530 |
www.resette.com | Italian

River Café | *rooms: 1 | cap: 100*
Dumbo | 1 Water St. (bet. Furman & Old Fulton Sts.) | Brooklyn |
718-522-5200 | www.rivercafe.com | American

Riverpark | *rooms: 3 | max cap: 575*
Murray Hill | 450 E. 29th St. (1st Ave.) | 212-729-9790 |
www.riverparknyc.com | American

Rosa Mexicano | *rooms: 2 | max cap: 70*
W 60s | 61 Columbus Ave. (62nd St.) | 212-977-7700 |
www.rosamexicano.com | Mexican

Rosie O'Grady's Manhattan Club | *rooms: 1 | cap: 300*
W 50s | 800 Seventh Ave. (52nd St.) | 212-489-9595 |
www.rosieogradys.com | American/Steak

Rouge Tomate | *rooms: 3 | max cap: 400*
E 60s | 10 E. 60th St. (bet. 5th & Madison Aves.) | 646-237-8963 |
www.rougetomatenyc.com | American

Ruby Foo's | *rooms: 1 | cap: 300*
W 40s | 1626 Broadway (49th St.) | 212-331-0328 |
www.brguesthospitality.com | Asian

SD26 | *rooms: 5 | max cap: 600*
Murray Hill | 19 E. 26th St. (bet. 5th & Madison Aves.) |
646-448-0973 | www.sd26ny.com | Italian

SHO Shaun Hergatt | *rooms: 3 | max cap: 60*
Financial District | 40 Broad St., 2nd fl. (Exchange Pl.) | 212-809-3993 |
www.shoshaunhergatt.com | French

Shun Lee Palace | *rooms: 1 | cap: 124*
E 50s | 155 E. 55th St. (bet. Lexington & 3rd Aves.) | 212-371-8844 |
www.shunleepalace.com | Chinese

Sidecar | *rooms: 2 | max cap: 60*
Park Slope | 560 Fifth Ave. (bet. 15th & 16th Sts.) | Brooklyn |
718-369-0077 | www.sidecarbrooklyn.com | American

Smith & Wollensky | *rooms: 4 | max cap: 200*
E 40s | 797 Third Ave. (49th St.) | 212-360-0438 |
www.smithandwollenskynyc.com | Steak

South Gate | *rooms: 1 | cap: 80*
W 50s | Jumeirah Essex Hse. | 154 Central Park S. (bet. 6th & 7th Aves.) |
212-484-5120 | www.154southgate.com | American

Spotted Pig | *rooms: 1 | cap: 50*
W Village | 314 W. 11th St. (Greenwich St.) | 212-620-0393 |
www.thespottedpig.com | European

Stanton Social | *rooms: 5 | max cap: 120*
LES | 99 Stanton St. (bet. Ludlow & Orchard Sts.) | 212-995-0099 | www.thestantonsocial.com | Eclectic

SushiSamba
rooms: 3 | max cap: 150
Flatiron | 245 Park Ave. S. (bet. 19th & 20th Sts.) | 212-475-9377
rooms: 2 | max cap: 230
G Village | 87 Seventh Ave. S. (bet. Bleecker & W. 4th Sts.) | 212-691-7885
www.sushisamba.com | Brazilian/Japanese

Taj II | *rooms: 2 | max cap: 350*
Flatiron | 48 W. 21st St. (bet. 5th & 6th Aves.) | 212-620-3033 | www.tajlounge.com | American/Indian

Tamarind | *rooms: 1 | cap: 30*
TriBeCa | 99 Hudson St. (bet. Franklin & Harrison Sts.) | 212-775-9000 | www.tamarinde22.com | Indian

Tao | *rooms: 1 | cap: 26*
E 50s | 42 E. 58th St. (bet. Madison & Park Aves.) | 212-399-3097 | www.taorestaurant.com | Asian

Thalassa | *rooms: 2 | max cap: 200*
TriBeCa | 179 Franklin St. (bet. Greenwich & Hudson Sts.) | 212-941-7661 | www.thalassanyc.com | Greek/Seafood

Tocqueville | *rooms: 2 | max cap: 102*
Union Sq | 1 E. 15th St. (bet. 5th Ave. & Union Sq. W.) | 212-647-1515 | www.tocquevillerestaurant.com | American/French

Trattoria Dell'Arte | *rooms: 5 | max cap: 125*
W 50s | 900 Seventh Ave. (bet. 56th & 57th Sts.) | 212-265-0100 | www.trattoriadellarte.com | Italian

Tribeca Grill | *rooms: 2 | max cap: 500*
TriBeCa | 375 Greenwich St. (Franklin St.) | 212-941-3905 | www.myriadrestaurantgroup.com | American

21 Club | *rooms: 10 | max cap: 200*
W 50s | 21 W. 52nd St. (bet. 5th & 6th Aves.) | 212-582-1400, ext. 7214 | www.21club.com | American

Txikito | *rooms: 2 | max cap: 65*
Chelsea | 240 Ninth Ave. (bet. 24th & 25th Sts.) | 212-242-4730 | www.txikitonyc.com | Spanish

Valbella | *rooms: 5 | max cap: 130*
Meatpacking | 421 W. 13th St. (bet. 9th Ave. & Washington St.) | 212-645-7777 | www.valbellanyc.com | Italian

Villa Pacri | *rooms: 1 | cap: 200*
Meatpacking | 55 Gansevoort St. (bet. Greenwich & Washington Sts.) | 212-924-5559 | www.villapacri.com | Italian

Vinegar Hill House | *rooms: 1 | cap: 20*
Vinegar Hill | 72 Hudson Ave. (Water St.) | Brooklyn | 718-522-1018 | www.vinegarhillhouse.com | American

Wall & Water | *rooms: 6 | max cap: 550*
Financial District | Andaz Wall St. | 75 Wall St. (Water St.) | 212-699-1700 | www.wallandwaterny.com | American

PARTY SITES – RESTAURANTS

Wallsé | *rooms: 1* | *cap: 35*
G Village | 344 W. 11th St. (Washington St.) | 212-352-2300 |
www.kg-ny.com | Austrian

Water Club | *rooms: 3* | *max cap: 1000*
Murray Hill | 500 E. 30th St. (East River & FDR Dr., enter via E. 23rd St.) |
212-545-1155 | www.thewaterclub.com | American

Water's Edge | *rooms: 2* | *max cap: 350*
LIC | 44th Dr. (East River & Vernon Blvd.) | Queens | 718-482-0033 |
www.watersedgenyc.com | American/Seafood

Zengo | *rooms: 3* | *max cap: 400*
E 40s | 622 Third Ave. (40th St.) | 212-808-8110 |
www.richardsandoval.com | Pan-Latin

NYC SOURCES
INDEXES

Special Features

Listings cover the best in each category and include source names, locations and Quality ratings.

ADDITIONS

(Properties added since the last edition of the book)

Amorino	**G Vill**	25
Ample Hills	**Prospect Hts**	28
Ann Clair's Salum.	**Bronx**	25
Baconery	**Chelsea**	25
Bagels by Park	**Carroll Gdns**	23
Bagel Store	**W'burg**	24
Bake City Bagels	**Gravesend**	28
Bakeri	**W'burg**	22
B&B Empire	**Boerum Hill**	17
Beecher's Cheese	**Flatiron**	27
Bee Desserts	**W Vill**	24
Beer Table Pantry	**E 40s**	26
Berry Fresh Farm	**Astoria**	25
Bien Cuit	**Cobble Hill**	23
Blossom Bakery	**Chelsea**	26
Blue Sky	**Park Slope**	27
Brooklyn Brew Shop	**Location Varies**	26
Brooklyn Cupcake	**W'burg**	27
Christian Vautier Le Concept	**LES**	–
Cork & Bottle	**E 60s**	23
Court Street Grocers	**Carroll Gdns**	29
Cupcake Kings	**Sheepshead**	24
DavidsTea	**multi.**	28
Dolce Vizio	**W Vill**	25
Dominique Ansel	**SoHo**	27
Donna Bell's	**W 40s**	24
Donut Pub	**Chelsea**	22
Dragonland Bakery	**Chinatown**	25
East Village Wines	**E Vill**	26
Eli's Bread	**E 40s**	26
Elm Health	**Chelsea**	24
Family Health Foods	**SI**	22
Fleisher's Grassfed	**Park Slope**	29
Heritage Meat Shop	**LES**	27
Holey Cream	**W 50s**	21
Hot Bagels & Bialys	**Midwood**	25

Ice Cream House	**multi.**	24
Il Buco Alimentari	**NoHo**	25
Kosher Bagel	**Flatbush**	27
La Cremeria	**L Italy**	22
London Candy Co.	**E 90s**	25
ⓩ Maison Ladurée	**E 70s**	28
Mille-Feuille	**G Vill**	25
Mitchel London	**E 60s**	25
Penn Wine/Spirits	**Garment**	26
Peter Pan Donut	**Greenpt**	24
Puddin' by Clio	**E Vill**	29
Shelsky's Smoked Fish	**Boerum Hill**	24
Soft Serve Fruit	**multi.**	23
Spices/Tease	**W 90s**	25
Sprinkles	**E 60s**	26
Sweetery	**Garment**	23
Tompkins Sq. Bagels	**E Vill**	25
The Upper Crust	**G Vill**	21
Valley Shepherd	**Park Slope**	28
Victory Garden	**W Vill**	28
Whiskey Shop	**W'burg**	27
Wright/Goebel	**Downtown Bklyn**	28
Xocolatti	**SoHo**	22
Yi Mei Fung	**multi.**	19
Zucker Bakery	**E Vill**	24

BAGELS & BIALYS

ⓩ Absolute Bagels	**W 100s**	26
Bagel Bob's	**multi.**	23
Bagel Hole	**Park Slope**	25
Bagel Oasis	**Fresh Meadows**	25
Bagels/Co.	**multi.**	21
Bagels by Park	**Carroll Gdns**	23
Bagels on Sq.	**W Vill**	20
Bagel Store	**W'burg**	24
Bagelworks	**E 60s**	26
Bake City Bagels	**Gravesend**	28
NEW B&B Empire	**Boerum Hill**	17
ⓩ Barney Greengrass	**W 80s**	27
Bergen Bagels	**multi.**	23

Catskill Bagel | **Ditmas Pk** 22

Corrado | **E 70s** 22

Daniel's Bagels | **Murray Hill** 24

David's Bagels | **Gramercy** 25

East Side Bagel | **E 70s** 21

Eli's Manhattan | **E 80s** 25

Eli's Vinegar | **E 90s** 24

Ess-a-Bagel | **multi.** 26

Good/Plenty | **W 40s** 21

Gourmet Garage | **multi.** 20

H & H Midtown | **E 80s** 25

Hot Bagels & Bialys | **Midwood** 25

Hot Bialys & Bagels | **Forest Hills** 23

Kosher Bagel | **Flatbush** 27

Z Kossar's | **LES** 26

La Bagel | **multi.** 22

Lenny's Bagels | **W 90s** 21

Leo's Bagels | **Financial** 24

Moishe's | **E Vill** 23

Montague St. | **Bklyn Hts** 23

Murray's Bagels | **multi.** 26

Z Murray's Sturgeon | **W 80s** 28

Pick/Bagel | **multi.** 21

NEW Shelsky's Smoked Fish | **Boerum Hill** 24

Tal Bagels | **multi.** 22

Terrace Bagels | **Windsor Terr** 25

Times Sq. Bagels | **W 40s** 24

NEW Tompkins Sq. Bagels | **E Vill** 25

Yonah Schimmel | **LES** 24

Z Zabar's | **W 80s** 27

Zucker's Bagels | **TriBeCa** 22

BAKED GOODS

(See also Bagels & Bialys, Cakes & Cupcakes, Cookies, Pies/Tarts)

Z Addeo Bakery | **Bronx** 28

Agata/Valentina | **E 70s** 25

Almondine | **multi.** 26

Amish Mkt. | **multi.** 22

Amy's Bread | **multi.** 26

Andre's | **multi.** 24

AQ Kafé | **W 50s** 23

Z Artopolis | **Astoria** 27

Artuso Pastry | **Bronx** 24

Astor Bake Shop | **Astoria** 23

Aunt Butchie's | **multi.** 26

BabyCakes | **LES** 24

Baconery | **Chelsea** 25

Z Baked | **Red Hook** 26

Baked/Melissa | **multi.** 24

Balady Foods | **Bay Ridge** -

Z Balthazar Bakery | **SoHo** 27

Battery Place Mkt. | **Financial** 27

Bay Ridge Bake | **Bay Ridge** 25

Z Bedford Cheese | **W'burg** 27

Bee Desserts | **W Vill** 24

Betty Bakery | **Boerum Hill** 26

NEW Bien Cuit | **Cobble Hill** 23

Billy's Bakery | **multi.** 24

Birdbath | **multi.** 23

Bis.Co.Latte | **W 40s** 24

Bisous, Ciao | **LES** 25

Z Black Hound | **E Vill** 26

NEW Blossom Bakery | **Chelsea** 26

Z Blue Apron | **Park Slope** 28

Blue Ribbon | **W Vill** 26

Blue Sky | **Park Slope** 27

Blue Smoke | **Murray Hill** 25

Bomboloni | **W 60s** 22

Bonsignour | **W Vill** 27

Z Bouchon Bakery | **W 60s** 27

Bread Alone | **Boiceville** 25

Brooklyn Cupcake | **W'burg** 27

Brooklyn Fare | **Downtown Bklyn** 26

Brooklyn Flea | **Ft Greene** 22

Bruno/Pasticceria | **multi.** 24

Butcher Block | **Sunnyside** 27

Buttercup | **E 50s** 22

Butter Lane Cupcakes | **E Vill** 25

Caffé Roma | **L Italy** 22

Cake Chef Bakery | **SI** 28

Cake Man | **Ft Greene** 24

Cannelle Patisserie | **Jackson Hts** 29

Z Caputo | **Carroll Gdns** 27

Carrot Top | **multi.** 23

Carry On Tea | **W Vill** 25

Cathcart/Reddy | **LES** 25

Ceci-Cela | **L Italy** 26

Cheryl Kleinman | **Boerum Hill**	28
ChikaLicious | **E Vill**	25
Choco Bolo | **NoLita**	21
Choice Greene/Mkt. | **Clinton Hill**	27
Choux Factory | **multi.**	23
NEW Christian Vautier Le Concept | **LES**	–
Cipriani | **E 40s**	26
Citarella | **multi.**	26
City Bakery | **Flatiron**	25
Clinton St. Baking | **LES**	26
Colette's | **W Vill**	27
Colson | **Park Slope**	24
Cookie Jar | **SI**	27
Corner Café | **E 90s**	23
Corrado | **multi.**	22
Costco | **Harlem**	23
Court Pastry | **Cobble Hill**	26
Cousin John's | **Park Slope**	22
Crespella | **Park Slope**	–
Crumbs | **multi.**	22
Cupcake Cafe | **W 40s**	24
Cupcake Kings | **Sheepshead**	24
Damascus | **Bklyn Hts**	26
Dean/DeLuca | **multi.**	26
Delillo Pastry | **Bronx**	25
De Robertis | **E Vill**	23
NEW Dolce Vizio | **W Vill**	25
NEW Dominique Ansel | **SoHo**	27
Donna Bell's | **W 40s**	24
Donut Pub | **Chelsea**	22
Dough | **Bed-Stuy**	26
Doughnut Plant | **multi.**	27
Dragonland Bakery | **Chinatown**	25
Duane Pk. | **TriBeCa**	25
E.A.T. | **E 80s**	24
Z Eataly | **Flatiron**	27
Egidio Pastry | **Bronx**	25
Eileen's Cheesecake | **NoLita**	25
Eleni's Cookies | **Chelsea**	22
Eli's Bread | **E 40s**	26
Eli's Manhattan | **E 80s**	25
Eli's Vinegar | **E 90s**	24
Empire Cake | **Chelsea**	26
Fairway | **multi.**	25
Fay Da | **multi.**	20
Ferrara Bakery | **L Italy**	22
Financier Patisserie | **multi.**	25
Foragers City Grocer | **multi.**	26
Z Fortunato | **W'burg**	27
Four/Twenty Blackbirds | **Gowanus**	26
FPB | **multi.**	27
FreshDirect | **LIC**	23
Fulton Stall Mkt. | **Financial**	25
Garden/Eden | **multi.**	23
Glaser's Bake | **E 80s**	24
Good/Plenty | **W 40s**	21
Gourmet Garage | **multi.**	20
Grab Specialty | **Park Slope**	26
Grace's Market | **E 70s**	25
Grandaisy | **multi.**	25
Greenmarket | **Union Sq**	29
Güllüoglu | **multi.**	23
Hester Street Fair | **LES**	21
Holey Cream | **W 50s**	21
Hungarian Pastry | **W 100s**	23
Il Cantuccio | **W Vill**	26
Insomnia Cookies | **G Vill**	22
Joyce Bake | **Prospect Hts**	25
Junior's | **multi.**	21
Z Kalustyan's | **Murray Hill**	27
Koryodang | **Garment**	22
La Bergamote | **multi.**	26
La Boîte à Epice | **W 50s**	–
Z L.A. Burdick Handmade Chocolates | **Flatiron**	28
Z Ladybird | **Park Slope**	27
Z Lady M | **E 70s**	29
La Guli | **Astoria**	27
La Maison/Macaron | **Chelsea**	28
Lamarca | **Gramercy**	26
Led Zeppole | **E Vill**	22
Le Pain Quotidien | **multi.**	23
Z Levain Bakery | **multi.**	28
Lily O'Brien's | **W 40s**	22
Little Brown | **E 80s**	21
Little Cupcake | **multi.**	23
Little Pie | **W 40s**	24

NYC SOURCES

SPECIAL FEATURES

Whole Foods	**multi.**	25
William Greenberg	**E 80s**	25
Yi Mei Fung	**multi.**	19
Yonah Schimmel	**LES**	24
Yorkville Meat	**E 80s**	–
🆉 Zabar's	**W 80s**	27
Zeytuna	**Financial**	20
NEW Zucker Bakery	**E Vill**	24

BEER SPECIALISTS

Amer. Beer	**Cobble Hill**	26
NEW Beer Table Pantry	**E 40s**	26
Bierkraft	**Park Slope**	27
Brooklyn Beer/Soda	**Prospect-Lefferts Gardens**	25
Brooklyn Brew Shop	**Location Varies**	26
Brooklyn Fare	**Downtown Bklyn**	26
Brouwerij Ln.	**Greenpt**	28
Costco	**multi.**	23
Eagle Provisions	**Greenwood Hts**	23
Eastern District	**Greenpt**	–
🆉 Eataly	**Flatiron**	27
Fairway	**multi.**	25
Filling Station	**Chelsea**	25
Good Beer	**E Vill**	27
Grab Specialty	**Park Slope**	26
Grace's Market	**E 70s**	25
Greene Grape	**Ft Greene**	27
New Beer	**LES**	26
Sunrise Mart	**E 40s**	23
Sunset Beer	**Sunset Pk**	24
Trader Joe's	**multi.**	23
Whole Foods	**multi.**	25

BREAD

🆉 Addeo Bakery	**Bronx**	28
Amy's Bread	**multi.**	26
🆉 Artopolis	**Astoria**	27
Astor Bake Shop	**Astoria**	23
Balady Foods	**Bay Ridge**	–
🆉 Balthazar Bakery	**SoHo**	27
Battery Place Mkt.	**Financial**	27
🆉 Bedford Cheese	**W'burg**	27
NEW Bien Cuit	**Cobble Hill**	23

🆉 Blue Apron	**Park Slope**	28
Blue Ribbon	**W Vill**	26
🆉 Bouchon Bakery	**W 60s**	27
Bread Alone	**Boiceville**	25
Cannelle Patisserie	**Jackson Hts**	29
🆉 Caputo	**Carroll Gdns**	27
Citarella	**multi.**	26
Corrado	**multi.**	22
Damascus	**Bklyn Hts**	26
Dean/DeLuca	**multi.**	26
E.A.T.	**E 80s**	24
🆉 Eataly	**Flatiron**	27
Eli's Bread	**E 40s**	26
Eli's Manhattan	**E 80s**	25
Eli's Vinegar	**E 90s**	24
Fairway	**multi.**	25
Foragers City Grocer	**multi.**	26
FreshDirect	**LIC**	23
Fulton Stall Mkt.	**Financial**	25
Grab Specialty	**Park Slope**	26
Grandaisy	**multi.**	25
Greenmarket	**Union Sq**	29
Il Cantuccio	**W Vill**	26
🆉 Kalustyan's	**Murray Hill**	27
Koryodang	**Garment**	22
Lamarca	**Gramercy**	26
Le Pain Quotidien	**multi.**	23
🆉 Levain Bakery	**multi.**	28
Madonia Bakery	**Bronx**	26
M & I	**Brighton Bch**	22
Market	**Ditmas Pk**	24
Mazzola Bakery	**Carroll Gdns**	27
Moishe's	**E Vill**	23
Momofuku Milk Bar	**multi.**	25
🆉 Mona Lisa	**Bensonhurst**	24
Mother's Bake	**Bronx**	20
🆉 Murray's Cheese	**W Vill**	29
Napoli	**W'burg**	28
🆉 New Amsterdam Mkt.	**Seaport**	28
Orwasher's	**E 70s**	26
Our Daily Bread	**Chatham**	25
Pain D'Avignon	**LES**	24
Paneantico	**Bay Ridge**	26
Panya	**E Vill**	21

216

Petrossian | **W 50s**	27	Caffé Roma | **L Italy**	22
🅔 Pomegranate | **Midwood**	26	Cake Chef Bakery | **SI**	28
Royal Crown | **Bensonhurst**	26	Cake Man | **Ft Greene**	24
🅔 Saxelby Cheese | **LES**	29	Cannelle Patisserie | **Jackson Hts**	29
Schick's | **Borough Pk**	23	Carrot Top | **multi.**	23
Scratch Bread | **Bed-Stuy**	27	Ceci-Cela | **L Italy**	26
NEW Shelsky's Smoked Fish | **Boerum Hill**	24	Cheryl Kleinman | **Boerum Hill**	28
		ChikaLicious | **E Vill**	25
Silver Moon | **W 100s**	26	Choco Bolo | **NoLita**	21
🅔 Soutine | **W 70s**	27	Cipriani | **E 40s**	26
🅔 Stinky Bklyn | **Cobble Hill**	27	Colette's | **W Vill**	27
🅔 Stork's Pastry | **Whitestone**	25	Corner Café | **E 90s**	23
Sullivan St. Bakery | **W 40s**	27	Corrado | **multi.**	22
Takahachi | **Financial**	23	Court Pastry | **Cobble Hill**	26
🅔 Terranova | **Bronx**	28	Crumbs | **multi.**	22
Trader Joe's | **E 70s**	23	Cupcake Cafe | **W 40s**	24
Tu-Lu's GF | **E Vill**	25	Cupcake Kings | **Sheepshead**	24
Union Mkt. | **multi.**	25	Dean/DeLuca | **multi.**	26
🅔 Villabate | **Bensonhurst**	27	Delillo Pastry | **Bronx**	25
Whole Foods | **multi.**	25	De Robertis | **E Vill**	23
Yorkville Meat | **E 80s**	-	**NEW** Dolce Vizio | **W Vill**	25
		NEW Dominique Ansel | **SoHo**	27
CAKES & CUPCAKES		Donna Bell's | **W 40s**	24
(See also Wedding Cakes)		Duane Pk. | **TriBeCa**	25
Amy's Bread | **multi.**	26	E.A.T. | **E 80s**	24
Andre's | **multi.**	24	Egidio Pastry | **Bronx**	25
🅔 Artopolis | **Astoria**	27	Eileen's Cheesecake | **NoLita**	25
Artuso Pastry | **Bronx**	24	Eli's Manhattan | **E 80s**	25
Astor Bake Shop | **Astoria**	23	Eli's Vinegar | **E 90s**	24
Aunt Butchie's | **multi.**	26	Empire Cake | **Chelsea**	26
BabyCakes | **LES**	24	Fay Da | **multi.**	20
🅔 Baked | **Red Hook**	26	Ferrara Bakery | **L Italy**	22
Baked/Melissa | **multi.**	24	Financier Patisserie | **E 50s**	25
🅔 Balthazar Bakery | **SoHo**	27	F. Monteleone | **Carroll Gdns**	29
Bay Ridge Bake | **Bay Ridge**	25	FPB | **G Vill**	27
Bee Desserts | **W Vill**	24	Glaser's Bake | **E 80s**	24
Betty Bakery | **Boerum Hill**	26	Grace's Market | **E 70s**	25
Billy's Bakery | **multi.**	24	Joyce Bake | **Prospect Hts**	25
🅔 Black Hound | **E Vill**	26	Junior's | **multi.**	21
Blue Sky | **Park Slope**	27	La Bergamote | **multi.**	26
Blue Smoke | **Murray Hill**	25	🅔 Ladybird | **Park Slope**	27
Brooklyn Cupcake | **W'burg**	27	🅔 Lady M | **E 70s**	29
Bruno/Pasticceria | **multi.**	24	Little Cupcake | **multi.**	23
Buttercup | **E 50s**	22	Little Pie | **W 40s**	24
Butter Lane Cupcakes | **E Vill**	25		

Lloyd's Carrot Cake | **Bronx**	29
Lung Moon | **Chinatown**	20
Magnolia Bakery | **multi.**	21
Make My Cake | **Harlem**	26
Margot Pâtisserie | **W 70s**	23
Martha's Bakery | **multi.**	22
Mast Brothers | **W'burg**	25
🆕 Mille-Feuille | **G Vill**	25
Momofuku Milk Bar | **multi.**	25
Mother Mousse | **SI**	25
Mother's Bake | **Bronx**	20
🅩 One Girl | **Cobble Hill**	27
Paneantico | **Bay Ridge**	26
Patisserie Claude | **W Vill**	26
Robicelli's | **Location Varies**	26
Rocco's Pastry | **W Vill**	25
Ron Ben-Israel | **SoHo**	27
Royal Crown | **Bensonhurst**	26
Ruthy's Bakery | **Chelsea**	20
Sal/Dom's | **Bronx**	28
🅩 S&S Cheesecake | **Bronx**	28
Sarabeth's | **multi.**	24
Schick's | **Borough Pk**	23
Silver Moon | **W 100s**	26
🅩 Soutine | **W 70s**	27
🆕 Sprinkles | **E 60s**	26
🅩 Stork's Pastry | **Whitestone**	25
Sugar Sweet | **LES**	26
Super Wang Bakery | **Chinatown**	21
Sweet Melissa | **Park Slope**	25
Sweet Revenge | **W Vill**	25
🅩 Sylvia Weinstock | **TriBeCa**	29
Tai Pan Bakery | **multi.**	21
Takahachi | **Financial**	23
Tribeca Treats | **TriBeCa**	21
Trois Pommes | **Park Slope**	27
Tu-Lu's GF | **E Vill**	25
Two/Red Hens | **E 80s**	26
Veniero's | **E Vill**	25
🅩 Villabate | **Bensonhurst**	27
Whole Foods | **multi.**	25
William Greenberg | **E 80s**	25
Yi Mei Fung | **Flushing**	19
🅩 Zabar's | **W 80s**	27

CANDY & NUTS

Aji Ichiban | **Chinatown**	22
Baruir's Coffee | **Sunnyside**	27
🅩 Black Hound | **E Vill**	26
🅩 Blue Apron | **Park Slope**	28
Bond St. Choc. | **E Vill**	27
Brooklyn Flea | **Ft Greene**	22
Bruno/Pasticceria | **G Vill**	24
Charbonnel/Walker | **E 40s**	23
Chelsea Baskets | **Chelsea**	23
Chocolate Bar | **W Vill**	25
Chocolate Rm. | **multi.**	25
Chocolat Michel | **W 40s**	27
🆕 Christian Vautier Le Concept | **LES**	-
Citarella | **multi.**	26
Cocoa Bar | **multi.**	21
Dean/DeLuca | **multi.**	26
🅩 Dylan's Candy | **E 60s**	23
🅩 Eataly | **Flatiron**	27
Economy Candy | **LES**	25
Eggers Ice Cream | **SI**	26
Eli's Manhattan | **E 80s**	25
Eli's Vinegar | **E 90s**	24
Fairway | **multi.**	25
Fifth Ave. Choc. | **E 40s**	25
FPB | **G Vill**	27
FreshDirect | **LIC**	23
Godiva | **multi.**	23
Grab Specialty | **Park Slope**	26
Gustiamo | **Bronx**	-
Hershey's | **W 40s**	21
Hester Street Fair | **LES**	21
Hinsch's | **Bay Ridge**	22
Integral Yoga | **W Vill**	23
🅩 Jacques Torres | **multi.**	28
JoMart Choc. | **Marine Pk**	28
🅩 Kalustyan's | **Murray Hill**	27
🅩 Kee's Choc. | **multi.**	28
🅩 L.A. Burdick Handmade Chocolates | **Flatiron**	28
🅩 La Maison/Choc. | **multi.**	29
Leonidas | **multi.**	26
Liddabit Sweets | **Location Varies**	25
Li-Lac Choc. | **multi.**	26

Lily O'Brien's | **W 40s**	22
Lindt | **W 50s**	25
Little Brown | **E 80s**	21
NEW London Candy Co. | **E 90s**	25
M&M's World | **W 40s**	21
⛉ Manhattan Fruitier | **Murray Hill**	25
Martine's Choc. | **multi.**	25
Mast Brothers | **W'burg**	25
Max Brenner | **G Vill**	22
Meadow | **W Vill**	29
Minamoto | **W 40s**	29
Mondel Choc. | **W 100s**	24
⛉ Murray's Cheese | **W Vill**	29
Neuchatel Choc. | **E 50s**	28
Neuhaus Choc. | **E 40s**	26
⛉ New Amsterdam Mkt. | **Seaport**	28
Nunu Choc. | **Downtown Bklyn**	25
Nut Box | **multi.**	24
Papabubble | **L Italy**	23
Petrossian | **W 50s**	27
Roni-Sue's | **LES**	24
⛉ Russ/Daughters | **LES**	29
⛉ Sahadi's | **Bklyn Hts**	28
⛉ Stork's Pastry | **Whitestone**	25
Sweet Life | **LES**	27
Sweet Melissa | **Park Slope**	25
⛉ Teuscher Choc. | **multi.**	29
Trader Joe's | **multi.**	23
Tribeca Treats | **TriBeCa**	21
Varsano's | **W Vill**	29
⛉ Vosges | **multi.**	27
Whole Foods | **multi.**	25
NEW Xocolatti | **SoHo**	22
⛉ Zabar's | **W 80s**	27

CARRIAGE TRADE

Abigail Kirsch | **multi.**	26
⛉ Acker Merrall | **W 70s**	28
Agata/Valentina | **E 70s**	25
Alessi | **SoHo**	26
Belle Fleur | **Flatiron**	28
Bond St. Choc. | **E Vill**	27
Butterfield/Baked | **E 70s**	25
Calvisius Caviar | **E 50s**	29
Castle/Pierpont | **NoLita**	–

Caviar Russe | **E 50s**	26
Citarella | **multi.**	26
Dean/DeLuca | **multi.**	26
Eli's Manhattan | **E 80s**	25
Eli's Vinegar | **E 90s**	24
Fellan Florist | **E 60s**	24
Glorious Food | **E 70s**	26
Grace's Market | **E 70s**	25
Jane Packer | **E 50s**	–
Japan Premium Beef | **NoHo**	29
⛉ Lady M | **E 70s**	29
⛉ La Maison/Choc. | **multi.**	29
⛉ Lobel's Meats | **E 80s**	28
L'Olivier | **E 70s**	27
⛉ Lorenzo/Maria's | **E 80s**	27
⛉**NEW** Maison Ladurée | **E 70s**	28
Maison Prive | **Location Varies**	–
⛉ Manhattan Fruitier | **Murray Hill**	25
Marché Madison | **E 70s**	21
Morrell & Co. | **W 40s**	26
O&CO. | **multi.**	27
Petrossian | **W 50s**	27
Renny/Reed | **E 50s**	–
Ronaldo Maia | **E 90s**	24
Ron Ben-Israel | **SoHo**	27
⛉ Sherry-Lehmann | **E 50s**	29
⛉ Sylvia Weinstock | **TriBeCa**	29
⛉ Teuscher Choc. | **multi.**	29
⛉ Vosges | **SoHo**	27
Wild Edibles | **E 40s**	24
William Greenberg | **E 80s**	25
⛉ William Poll | **E 70s**	26
⛉ Zezé | **E 50s**	27

CATERERS

(See also Event Planners and Office Catering; * listed in Other Noteworthy Sources on p. 178)

Abigail Kirsch | **multi.**	26
Agata/Valentina | **E 70s**	25
Amanda Smith | **W 80s**	27
Ann Clair's Salum. | **Bronx**	25
Arthur Ave. | **Bronx**	23
Barbarini | **Financial**	25
Ben's Kosher | **multi.**	22
Between/Bread | **W 50s**	23

☑ Bklyn Larder | **Park Slope**	27
Blue Smoke | **Murray Hill**	25
Brooklyn Fare | **Downtown Bklyn**	26
Butterfield/Baked | **E 70s**	25
Carnegie Deli | **W 50s**	23
Catering/Rest. Assoc.* | **Garment**	21
Ceriello | **multi.**	24
Cer té | **W 50s**	23
Citarella | **multi.**	26
City Bakery | **Flatiron**	25
Cleaver Co. | **Chelsea**	27
Cucina | **E 40s**	22
Cucina Vivolo | **E 70s**	22
David Burke | **E 50s**	21
David Ziff* | **E 90s**	-
Dean/DeLuca | **multi.**	26
Dishes | **E 40s**	24
E.A.T. | **E 80s**	24
Edible Arrange | **multi.**	22
Eli's Vinegar | **E 90s**	24
Fairway | **Red Hook**	25
Family Store | **Bay Ridge**	24
Financier Patisserie | **Financial**	25
Foremost RAM Caterers | **Moonachie**	23
Garden/Eden | **multi.**	23
Glazier Group* | **multi.**	-
Glorious Food | **E 70s**	26
Good/Plenty | **W 40s**	21
Grace's Market | **E 70s**	25
☑ Great Performances | **Hudson Square**	26
Iavarone Bros. | **Maspeth**	26
Indiana Mkt.* | **Garment**	-
Katz's Deli | **LES**	25
Kosher Bagel | **Flatbush**	27
Lassen/Hennigs | **Bklyn Hts**	25
☑ Lorenzo/Maria's | **E 80s**	27
Maison Prive | **Location Varies**	-
Mangia | **multi.**	23
Mauzone | **Flushing**	21
Miss Mamie's/Maude's | **Harlem**	20
Mitchel London | **E 60s**	25
Movable Feast | **Park Slope**	23

Neuman's* | **LES**	-
Newman/Leventhal* | **W 80s**	-
Nordic Delicacies | **Bay Ridge**	28
Olivier Cheng* | **TriBeCa**	-
☑ Pomegranate | **Midwood**	26
Ready to Eat | **W Vill**	23
Robbins Wolfe* | **Gramercy**	-
Russo Mozz. | **Park Slope**	26
Ruthy's Bakery | **Chelsea**	20
Simply Divine* | **W 70s**	-
Spoon | **Flatiron**	25
☑ Tastings/Payard | **E 60s**	25
☑ Union Sq. Events | **Chelsea**	26
The Upper Crust | **G Vill**	21
Whole Foods | **W 90s**	25
Wild Edibles | **multi.**	24
Zeytuna | **Financial**	20

CAVIAR & SMOKED FISH

Acme Fish | **Greenpt**	25
Agata/Valentina | **E 70s**	25
☑ Barney Greengrass | **W 80s**	27
☑ Blue Apron | **Park Slope**	28
☑ Blue Moon Fish | **Mattituck**	28
Calvisius Caviar | **E 50s**	29
Caviar Russe | **E 50s**	26
Citarella | **multi.**	26
Dean/DeLuca | **multi.**	26
Dorian's Seafood | **E 80s**	26
E.A.T. | **E 80s**	24
Eli's Manhattan | **E 80s**	25
Eli's Vinegar | **E 90s**	24
Fairway | **multi.**	25
Gustiamo | **Bronx**	-
Leonard's Market | **E 70s**	26
M & I | **Brighton Bch**	22
Murray's Bagels | **multi.**	26
☑ Murray's Sturgeon | **W 80s**	28
Park E. Kosher | **E 80s**	24
Petrossian | **W 50s**	27
☑ Russ/Daughters | **LES**	29
☑ Sable's | **E 70s**	27
NEW Shelsky's Smoked Fish | **Boerum Hill**	24

Todaro Bros. | **Murray Hill**	25
Trader Joe's | **multi.**	23
Union Mkt. | **Park Slope**	25
Whole Foods | **multi.**	25
Wild Edibles | **multi.**	24
🗷 William Poll | **E 70s**	26
🗷 Zabar's | **W 80s**	27
Zeytuna | **Financial**	20
Zucker's Bagels | **TriBeCa**	22

CHARCUTERIE

Agata/Valentina | **E 70s**	25
Ann Clair's Salum. | **Bronx**	25
Bari Pork | **multi.**	26
Battery Place Mkt. | **Financial**	27
🗷 Bedford Cheese | **W'burg**	27
Belfiore Meats | **SI**	25
🗷 Bklyn Larder | **Park Slope**	27
🗷 Blue Apron | **Park Slope**	28
BuonItalia | **Chelsea**	26
Butcher Block | **Sunnyside**	27
🗷 Calabria Pork | **Bronx**	27
Carolina Country | **Brownsville**	–
🗷 Casa Della | **Bronx**	29
Ceriello | **multi.**	24
Cheese/World | **Forest Hills**	26
Christos Steak | **Astoria**	25
Citarella | **multi.**	26
Dean/DeLuca | **multi.**	26
🗷 Despaña | **multi.**	27
🗷 Dickson's Farmstand | **Chelsea**	28
🗷 Di Palo Dairy | **L Italy**	29
Durso's Pasta | **Flushing**	26
Eagle Provisions | **Greenwood Hts**	23
Eastern District | **Greenpt**	–
East Vill. Meat | **E Vill**	26
🗷 Eataly | **Flatiron**	27
Eli's Manhattan | **E 80s**	25
Eli's Vinegar | **E 90s**	24
Empire Mkt. | **College Pt**	23
🗷 Esposito/Sons Pork | **Carroll Gdns**	27
🗷 Esposito Meat | **Garment**	27
Faicco's Pork | **multi.**	28
Fairway | **multi.**	25

🆕 Fleisher's Grassfed | **Park Slope**	29
Foragers City Grocer | **multi.**	26
🗷 Formaggio | **LES**	27
Grab Specialty | **Park Slope**	26
Grace's Market | **E 70s**	25
Heights Meats | **Bklyn Hts**	27
Hudson Valley Foie Gras | **Ferndale**	29
Iavarone Bros. | **Maspeth**	26
🆕 Il Buco Alimentari | **NoHo**	25
Jubilat Provisions | **Greenwood Hts**	–
Katz's Deli | **LES**	25
Lamarca | **Gramercy**	26
Les Halles | **Murray Hill**	23
🗷 Lioni Fresh Mozz. | **Bensonhurst**	27
Los Paisanos | **Cobble Hill**	26
Malaysia Beef Jerky | **Chinatown**	25
🗷 Marlow/Daughters | **W'burg**	28
Meat Hook | **W'burg**	27
🗷 Murray's Cheese | **multi.**	29
🗷 Ottomanelli/Sons | **multi.**	28
🗷 Ottomanelli's Meats | **Flushing**	28
Petrossian | **W 50s**	27
Salumeria Biellese | **Chelsea**	26
🗷 Salumeria Rosi | **W 70s**	28
🗷 Schaller/Weber | **E 80s**	28
🗷 Simchick | **E 50s**	29
🗷 Stinky Bklyn | **Cobble Hill**	27
Todaro Bros. | **Murray Hill**	25
United Meat | **Windsor Terr**	26
Whole Foods | **multi.**	25
Yorkville Meat | **E 80s**	–
🗷 Zabar's | **W 80s**	27
Zeytuna | **Financial**	20

CHEESE & DAIRY

🗷 Alleva Dairy | **L Italy**	28
Amish Mkt. | **multi.**	22
🗷 Artisanal | **multi.**	27
Barbarini | **Financial**	25
Barnyard Cheese | **E Vill**	26
Battery Place Mkt. | **Financial**	27
🗷 Bedford Cheese | **W'burg**	27
🆕 Beecher's Cheese | **Flatiron**	27
🗷 Bklyn Larder | **Park Slope**	27

⚡ Blue Apron | **Park Slope**	28
Blue Ribbon | **W Vill**	26
Brooklyn Fare | **Downtown Bklyn**	26
Brooklyn Flea | **Ft Greene**	22
BuonItalia | **Chelsea**	26
Butterfield/Baked | **E 70s**	25
Calandra Cheese | **Bronx**	27
⚡ Casa Della | **Bronx**	29
Cheese/World | **Forest Hills**	26
Citarella | **multi.**	26
⚡ Coluccio/Sons | **Borough Pk**	27
Commodities | **E Vill**	25
Costco | **multi.**	23
⚡ D'Amico | **Carroll Gdns**	27
Dean/DeLuca | **multi.**	26
⚡ Despaña | **multi.**	27
⚡ Di Palo Dairy | **L Italy**	29
Durso's Pasta | **Flushing**	26
⚡ D'Vine | **Park Slope**	26
Eastern District | **Greenpt**	-
East Vill. Cheese | **E Vill**	23
E.A.T. | **E 80s**	24
⚡ Eataly | **Flatiron**	27
Eli's Manhattan | **E 80s**	25
Fairway | **multi.**	25
Foragers City Grocer | **multi.**	26
⚡ Formaggio | **LES**	27
FreshDirect | **LIC**	23
Fulton Stall Mkt. | **Financial**	25
Garden/Eden | **multi.**	23
Gourmet Garage | **multi.**	20
Grab Specialty | **Park Slope**	26
Grace's Market | **E 70s**	25
Greenmarket | **Union Sq**	29
Gustiamo | **Bronx**	-
Hawthorne Farm | **Ghent**	28
Hester Street Fair | **LES**	21
Iavarone Bros. | **Maspeth**	26
Ideal Cheese | **E 50s**	27
NEW Il Buco Alimentari | **NoHo**	25
Internat'l Grocery | **W 40s**	24
⚡ Joe's Dairy | **SoHo**	28
Lamarca | **Gramercy**	26
Lamazou | **Murray Hill**	26

Las Palomas | **W 100s**	-
⚡ Lioni Fresh Mozz. | **Bensonhurst**	27
Los Paisanos | **Cobble Hill**	26
Lucy's Whey | **Chelsea**	29
M & I | **Brighton Bch**	22
Market | **Ditmas Pk**	24
Med. Foods | **Astoria**	26
⚡ Murray's Cheese | **multi.**	29
⚡ New Amsterdam Mkt. | **Seaport**	28
Nordic Delicacies | **Bay Ridge**	28
Obika | **W 50s**	27
⚡ Pastosa Ravioli | **multi.**	27
⚡ Pomegranate | **Midwood**	26
Ronnybrook | **Chelsea**	26
Russo Mozz. | **multi.**	26
⚡ Sahadi's | **Bklyn Hts**	28
⚡ Salumeria Rosi | **W 70s**	28
⚡ Saxelby Cheese | **LES**	29
⚡ Staubitz Mkt. | **Cobble Hill**	29
⚡ Stinky Bklyn | **Cobble Hill**	27
⚡ 3-Corner Farm | **Shushan**	27
Titan Foods | **Astoria**	26
Todaro Bros. | **Murray Hill**	25
Trader Joe's | **multi.**	23
Union Mkt. | **multi.**	25
United Meat | **Windsor Terr**	26
NEW Valley Shepherd | **Park Slope**	28
Westside Mkt. | **multi.**	21
Whole Foods | **multi.**	25
⚡ Zabar's | **W 80s**	27
Zeytuna | **Financial**	20

CLASSES

(Call for details)

NEW Ample Hills | **Prospect Hts**	28
Appellation | **Chelsea**	26
⚡ Artisanal | **Garment**	27
Astor Wines | **NoHo**	26
Bloomingdale's | **E 50s**	25
Brooklyn Fare | **Downtown Bklyn**	26
Brooklyn Wine | **Cobble Hill**	25
Bruno/Pasticceria | **G Vill**	24
Butter Lane Cupcakes | **E Vill**	25
Colette's | **W Vill**	27
Cupcake Cafe | **W 40s**	24

Z Dickson's Farmstand | **Chelsea**	28
Z Eataly | **Flatiron**	27
In Pursuit of Tea | **SoHo**	28
Japanese Culinary Ctr. | **E 40s**	24
JoMart Choc. | **Marine Pk**	28
Lucy's Whey | **Chelsea**	29
Make My Cake | **Harlem**	26
Meadow | **W Vill**	29
Meat Hook | **W'burg**	27
Morrell & Co. | **W 40s**	26
Z Murray's Cheese | **W Vill**	29
New York Cake | **Flatiron**	25
New York Vintners | **TriBeCa**	28
Z One Girl | **multi.**	27
Red/White | **Park Slope**	26
Scratch Bread | **Bed-Stuy**	27
Z Stinky Bklyn | **Cobble Hill**	27
Sugar Room | **Sunnyside**	-
Sullivan St. Bakery | **W 40s**	27
Z Sur La Table | **SoHo**	27
NEW Valley Shepherd | **Park Slope**	28

COFFEE & TEA

Agata/Valentina | **E 70s**	25
Alessi | **SoHo**	26
Alice's Tea/Wonderland | **multi.**	22
Amish Mkt. | **multi.**	22
Baruir's Coffee | **Sunnyside**	27
Bell Bates | **TriBeCa**	24
Z Blue Apron | **Park Slope**	28
BuonItalia | **Chelsea**	26
Butcher Block | **Sunnyside**	27
Carry On Tea | **W Vill**	25
Chelsea Baskets | **Chelsea**	23
Citarella | **multi.**	26
Z D'Amico | **Carroll Gdns**	27
NEW DavidsTea | **multi.**	28
Dean/DeLuca | **multi.**	26
Z Eataly | **Flatiron**	27
Eli's Manhattan | **E 80s**	25
Eli's Vinegar | **E 90s**	24
Empire Coffee | **W 40s**	24
Fairway | **multi.**	25
Family Store | **Bay Ridge**	24

FreshDirect | **LIC**	23
Gourmet Garage | **multi.**	20
Gustiamo | **Bronx**	-
Harney & Sons | **SoHo**	28
In Pursuit of Tea | **SoHo**	28
Internat'l Grocery | **W 40s**	24
Java Joe | **Park Slope**	-
Z Kalustyan's | **Murray Hill**	27
Katagiri | **E 50s**	23
Kusmi Tea | **E 60s**	26
NEW London Candy Co. | **E 90s**	25
Z McNulty's | **W Vill**	28
Myers/Keswick | **W Vill**	25
Z Nespresso | **E 60s**	27
Nut Box | **multi.**	24
Oren's Roast | **multi.**	24
Z Porto Rico | **multi.**	27
Radiance Tea | **W 50s**	24
Z Sahadi's | **Bklyn Hts**	28
Sensuous Bean | **W 70s**	25
NEW Spices/Tease | **multi.**	25
Tea/Honey | **E 60s**	29
Ten Ren Tea | **Chinatown**	25
Todaro Bros. | **Murray Hill**	25
Trader Joe's | **multi.**	23
Two for the Pot | **Bklyn Hts**	26
Union Mkt. | **Cobble Hill**	25
Whole Foods | **multi.**	25
Z Zabar's | **W 80s**	27

COOKIES

Agata/Valentina | **E 70s**	25
Amy's Bread | **multi.**	26
Andre's | **multi.**	24
Z Artopolis | **Astoria**	27
Astor Bake Shop | **Astoria**	23
Z Baked | **Red Hook**	26
Z Balthazar Bakery | **SoHo**	27
Betty Bakery | **Boerum Hill**	26
Bis.Co.Latte | **W 40s**	24
Bisous, Ciao | **LES**	25
Z Black Hound | **E Vill**	26
Blue Smoke | **Murray Hill**	25
Z Bouchon Bakery | **W 60s**	27
Bruno/Pasticceria | **G Vill**	24

Caffé Roma | **L Italy**	22
Cake Chef Bakery | **SI**	28
Cake Man | **Ft Greene**	24
Cannelle Patisserie | **Jackson Hts**	29
Carry On Tea | **W Vill**	25
Ceci-Cela | **L Italy**	26
City Bakery | **Flatiron**	25
Cookie Jar | **SI**	27
Corner Café | **E 90s**	23
Court Pastry | **Cobble Hill**	26
Crumbs | **multi.**	22
Dean/DeLuca | **multi.**	26
Delillo Pastry | **Bronx**	25
De Robertis | **E Vill**	23
NEW Dominique Ansel | **SoHo**	27
Duane Pk. | **TriBeCa**	25
E.A.T. | **E 80s**	24
Z Eataly | **Flatiron**	27
Eleni's Cookies | **Chelsea**	22
Eli's Manhattan | **E 80s**	25
Eli's Vinegar | **E 90s**	24
Ferrara Bakery | **L Italy**	22
Financier Patisserie | **multi.**	25
F. Monteleone | **Carroll Gdns**	29
Z Fortunato | **W'burg**	27
FPB | **G Vill**	27
Good/Plenty | **W 40s**	21
Grace's Market | **E 70s**	25
Hungarian Pastry | **W 100s**	23
Il Cantuccio | **W Vill**	26
Insomnia Cookies | **G Vill**	22
Joyce Bake | **Prospect Hts**	25
La Bergamote | **multi.**	26
La Boîte à Epice | **W 50s**	-
Z Ladybird | **Park Slope**	27
La Maison/Macaron | **Chelsea**	28
Z Levain Bakery | **multi.**	28
Lily O'Brien's | **W 40s**	22
Little Pie | **W 40s**	24
Macaron Café | **multi.**	24
Madonia Bakery | **Bronx**	26
Magnolia Bakery | **W Vill**	21
Z NEW Maison Ladurée | **E 70s**	28
Margot Pâtisserie | **W 70s**	23

Mast Brothers | **W'burg**	25
Milk/Cookies | **W Vill**	25
Moishe's | **E Vill**	23
Momofuku Milk Bar | **multi.**	25
Mother Mousse | **SI**	25
Mother's Bake | **Bronx**	20
Z One Girl | **Cobble Hill**	27
One Lucky Duck | **multi.**	25
Patisserie Claude | **W Vill**	26
Rocco's Pastry | **W Vill**	25
Ruthy's Bakery | **Chelsea**	20
Sal/Dom's | **Bronx**	28
Sarabeth's | **multi.**	24
Schick's | **Borough Pk**	23
Silver Moon | **W 100s**	26
Z Soutine | **W 70s**	27
Z Stork's Pastry | **Whitestone**	25
Sweet Melissa | **Park Slope**	25
Todaro Bros. | **Murray Hill**	25
Two/Red Hens | **E 80s**	26
Veniero's | **E Vill**	25
Z Villabate | **Bensonhurst**	27
Whole Foods | **multi.**	25
William Greenberg | **E 80s**	25
NEW Zucker Bakery | **E Vill**	24

COOKWARE & SUPPLIES

Alessi | **multi.**	26
Bari Equipment | **LES**	-
Bloomingdale's | **E 50s**	25
Bowery Kitchen | **Chelsea**	23
Broadway Pan. | **G Vill**	26
Brooklyn Kitchen | **W'burg**	25
Z Cook's Companion | **Bklyn Hts**	28
Costco | **multi.**	23
Dean/DeLuca | **SoHo**	26
Z Eataly | **Flatiron**	27
Gracious Home | **multi.**	26
Japanese Culinary Ctr. | **E 40s**	24
Z J.B. Prince | **Murray Hill**	29
Z Kalustyan's | **Murray Hill**	27
Kam Man | **Chinatown**	21
Z Korin | **TriBeCa**	29
Macy's Cellar | **Garment**	23

New York Cake | **Flatiron**	25
O&CO. | **W Vill**	27
S. Feldman | **E 90s**	26
Sugar Room | **Sunnyside**	–
Sunrise Mart | **E Vill**	23
☑ Sur La Table | **multi.**	27
Tarzian West | **Park Slope**	22
Whisk | **W'burg**	–
☑ Williams-Sonoma | **multi.**	27
☑ Zabar's | **W 80s**	27

DELIS

Agata/Valentina | **E 70s**	25
Ann Clair's Salum. | **Bronx**	25
Barbarini | **Financial**	25
Battery Place Mkt. | **Financial**	27
Bell Bates | **TriBeCa**	24
Ben's Best | **Rego Pk**	25
Ben's Kosher | **multi.**	22
☑ Bklyn Larder | **Park Slope**	27
Brooklyn Fare | **Downtown Bklyn**	26
BuonItalia | **Chelsea**	26
Butterfield/Baked | **E 70s**	25
☑ Calabria Pork | **Bronx**	27
Carnegie Deli | **W 50s**	23
Choice Greene/Mkt. | **multi.**	27
Citarella | **multi.**	26
Court Street Grocers | **Carroll Gdns**	29
☑ D'Amico | **Carroll Gdns**	27
☑ Despaña | **multi.**	27
☑ Dickson's Farmstand | **Chelsea**	28
☑ Di Palo Dairy | **L Italy**	29
☑ D'Vine | **Park Slope**	26
Eagle Provisions | **Greenwood Hts**	23
E.A.T. | **E 80s**	24
☑ Eataly | **Flatiron**	27
Eli's Manhattan | **E 80s**	25
Eli's Vinegar | **E 90s**	24
☑ Esposito/Sons Pork | **Carroll Gdns**	27
Fairway | **multi.**	25
Family Health Foods | **SI**	22
Fischer Bros. | **W 70s**	24
Foragers City Grocer | **Dumbo**	26
☑ Formaggio | **LES**	27

Garden/Eden | **multi.**	23
Heights Meats | **Bklyn Hts**	27
Iavarone Bros. | **Maspeth**	26
Jay/Lloyd's Kosher | **Sheepshead**	22
Jubilat Provisions | **Greenwood Hts**	–
Katz's Deli | **LES**	25
Lassen/Hennigs | **Bklyn Hts**	25
Liebman's | **Bronx**	24
☑ Lioni Fresh Mozz. | **Bensonhurst**	27
Los Paisanos | **Cobble Hill**	26
Mangia | **multi.**	23
Mill Basin Kosher | **Mill Basin**	24
☑ Murray's Cheese | **multi.**	29
☑ Murray's Sturgeon | **W 80s**	28
Paneantico | **Bay Ridge**	26
Pastrami Queen | **E 70s**	22
Royal Crown | **Bensonhurst**	26
Russo Mozz. | **Park Slope**	26
Salumeria Biellese | **Chelsea**	26
☑ Salumeria Rosi | **W 70s**	28
Sarge's Deli | **Murray Hill**	22
☑ Stinky Bklyn | **Cobble Hill**	27
Todaro Bros. | **Murray Hill**	25
Union Mkt. | **Cobble Hill**	25
Whole Foods | **multi.**	25
☑ Zabar's | **W 80s**	27

DRIED FRUIT

Aji Ichiban | **Chinatown**	22
Balady Foods | **Bay Ridge**	–
Bell Bates | **TriBeCa**	24
Citarella | **multi.**	26
Commodities | **E Vill**	25
Dean/DeLuca | **multi.**	26
☑ D'Vine | **Park Slope**	26
Economy Candy | **LES**	25
Eli's Manhattan | **E 80s**	25
Eli's Vinegar | **E 90s**	24
Fairway | **multi.**	25
Gourmet Garage | **multi.**	20
Greenwich Produce | **E 40s**	28
Gustiamo | **Bronx**	–
☑ Kalustyan's | **Murray Hill**	27
Manhattan Fruit Ex. | **Chelsea**	25
Nut Box | **multi.**	24

Patel Bros. | multi.	22	Greenwich Produce | E 40s	28
☑ Russ/Daughters | LES	29	Hong Kong | multi.	19
☑ Sahadi's | Bklyn Hts	28	Katagiri | E 50s	23
Sweet Life | LES	27	☑ Keith's Farm | Westtown	29
Trader Joe's | multi.	23	Manhattan Fruit Ex. | Chelsea	25
Whole Foods | multi.	25	Marché Madison | E 70s	21
☑ Zabar's | W 80s	27	☑ Perelandra | Bklyn Hts	26

EVENT PLANNERS

(* listed in Other Noteworthy Sources on p. 178)

Abigail Kirsch | multi.	26	☑ Pomegranate | Midwood	26
Banchet Flowers* | Meatpacking	26	Three Guys | Bay Ridge	23
Between/Bread | W 50s	23	Whole Foods | TriBeCa	25
☑ Bloom | E 50s	27	Zeytuna | Financial	20

FLOWERS

(* listed in Other Noteworthy Sources on p. 178)

Castle/Pierpont* | NoLita	–	Academy Floral | W 100s	22
Chestnuts* | TriBeCa	–	Angelica Flowers | W Vill	24
Cleaver Co. | Chelsea	27	Antony Todd* | Garment	–
Colin Cowie* | SoHo	–	Ariston | multi.	26
David Stark* | Carroll Gdns	–	Banchet Flowers* | Meatpacking	26
DeJuan Stroud* | TriBeCa	–	Belle Fleur | Flatiron	28
Flowers/Reuven | Ft Greene	26	Big Apple Florist | E 40s	27
Glazier Group* | multi.	–	☑ Bloom | E 50s	27
Glorious Food | E 70s	26	Blue Meadow* | E Vill	–
Gracious Thyme* | Harlem	–	Brooklyn Flea | Ft Greene	22
☑ Great Performances | Hudson Square	26	Castle/Pierpont* | NoLita	–
Jes Gordon/Proper Fun* | Garment	–	Chestnuts* | TriBeCa	–
Jonathan Flowers* | multi.	–	Dahlia | multi.	25
L'Olivier | multi.	27	Dean/DeLuca | multi.	26
Movable Feast | Park Slope	23	DeJuan Stroud* | TriBeCa	–
Naturally Delic.* | Carroll Gdns	–	Eli's Manhattan | E 80s	25
Olivier Cheng* | TriBeCa	–	Elizabeth Ryan* | LES	–
Plaza Florists | E 60s	–	Fellan Florist | E 60s	24
Renny/Reed* | E 50s	–	Floralies* | E 50s	–
Seaport Flowers | Bklyn Hts	27	Florisity* | Flatiron	–
☑ Tastings/Payard | E 60s	25	Flowers/Reuven | Ft Greene	26
☑ Union Sq. Events | Chelsea	26	Flowers by Richard* | W 50s	–

EXOTIC PRODUCE

		Flowers/World | multi.	26
Agata/Valentina | E 70s	25	☑ Gramercy Park Flower | multi.	27
Chung Fat | Flushing	22	Greenmarket | Union Sq	29
Dean/DeLuca | E 80s	26	Jane Packer* | E 50s	–
Eli's Manhattan | E 80s	25	Jerome Florists | E 90s	24
Eli's Vinegar | E 90s	24	Jonathan Flowers* | multi.	–
Fairway | multi.	25	Katrina Parris* | Harlem	–
Garden/Eden | multi.	23	LMD Floral* | E Vill	–

L'Olivier | **E 70s**	27
Meadow | **W Vill**	29
Z New Amsterdam Mkt. | **Seaport**	28
Ovando | **W Vill**	29
Plaza Florists | **E 60s**	-
Raquel Corvino* | **Chelsea**	-
Rebecca Cole* | **Garment**	-
Renny/Reed* | **E 50s**	-
Ronaldo Maia | **E 90s**	24
Rosa Rosa | **E 60s**	24
Seaport Flowers | **Bklyn Hts**	27
Spruce* | **Chelsea**	-
Stonekelly* | **W 50s**	-
Surroundings | **W 100s**	27
VSF | **W Vill**	27
Whole Foods | **multi.**	25
Windsor Florist | **E 70s**	24
Z Zezé | **E 50s**	27
Z ZuZu's Petals | **Park Slope**	27

GAME

(May need prior notice)

Agata/Valentina | **E 70s**	25
Z Biancardi Meats | **Bronx**	28
Brooklyn Fare | **Downtown Bklyn**	26
Dean/DeLuca | **multi.**	26
Eagle Provisions | **Greenwood Hts**	23
Eli's Manhattan | **E 80s**	25
Eli's Vinegar | **E 90s**	24
Empire Mkt. | **College Pt**	23
Z Esposito Meat | **Garment**	27
Z Florence Meat | **W Vill**	29
Grace's Market | **E 70s**	25
Greene Grape | **Ft Greene**	27
Heights Meats | **Bklyn Hts**	27
Iavarone Bros. | **Maspeth**	26
Le Marais | **W 40s**	23
Leonard's Market | **E 70s**	26
Les Halles | **Murray Hill**	23
Z Lobel's Meats | **E 80s**	28
Z Ottomanelli/Sons | **multi.**	28
Z Ottomanelli's Meats | **Flushing**	28
Pino Meats | **SoHo**	29
Z Quattro's | **Pleasant Valley**	28
Z Schaller/Weber | **E 80s**	28

Z Schatzie's Meats | **W 80s**	27
Z Simchick | **E 50s**	29
Vincent's Meat | **Bronx**	29
Whole Foods | **multi.**	25

GIFT BASKETS

(All Mail Order index entries as well as most candy and flower shops, plus the following standouts)

Z Acker Merrall | **W 70s**	28
Agata/Valentina | **E 70s**	25
Angelica Flowers | **W Vill**	24
Z Artisanal | **multi.**	27
Z Beth's Farm | **Stuyvesant Falls**	28
Z Bklyn Larder | **Park Slope**	27
Z Black Hound | **E Vill**	26
Z Bloom | **E 50s**	27
Z Blue Apron | **Park Slope**	28
Butterfield/Baked | **E 70s**	25
Caviar Russe | **E 50s**	26
Chelsea Baskets | **Chelsea**	23
Chelsea Wine | **Chelsea**	24
Chocolate Bar | **W Vill**	25
Citarella | **multi.**	26
Costco | **multi.**	23
Dean/DeLuca | **multi.**	26
Z Dylan's Candy | **E 60s**	23
E.A.T. | **E 80s**	24
Z Eataly | **Flatiron**	27
Economy Candy | **LES**	25
Eli's Manhattan | **E 80s**	25
Eli's Vinegar | **E 90s**	24
Fairway | **E 80s**	25
Fat Witch | **Chelsea**	24
Fellan Florist | **E 60s**	24
Fifth Ave. Choc. | **E 40s**	25
Financier Patisserie | **Financial**	25
Garden/Eden | **multi.**	23
Grab Specialty | **Park Slope**	26
Grace's Market | **E 70s**	25
Gustiamo | **Bronx**	-
Harney & Sons | **SoHo**	28
Iavarone Bros. | **Maspeth**	26
In Pursuit of Tea | **SoHo**	28
Z Jacques Torres | **multi.**	28
K & D Wines | **E 90s**	26

L.A. Burdick Handmade Chocolates | Flatiron — 28

Le Pain Quotidien | SoHo — 23

Lily O'Brien's | W 40s — 22

NEW London Candy Co. | E 90s — 25

Z Manhattan Fruitier | Murray Hill — 25

MarieBelle's | SoHo — 26

Market | Ditmas Pk — 24

Max Brenner | G Vill — 22

Minamoto | W 40s — 29

Morrell & Co. | W 40s — 26

Mother Mousse | SI — 25

Z Murray's Cheese | W Vill — 29

Myers/Keswick | W Vill — 25

Neuhaus Choc. | multi. — 26

Nordic Delicacies | Bay Ridge — 28

Nut Box | multi. — 24

O&CO. | multi. — 27

Once Upon/Tart | SoHo — 25

Z One Girl | Cobble Hill — 27

Z Orchard | Midwood — 28

Oren's Roast | multi. — 24

Plaza Florists | E 60s — –

Red Jacket | Geneva — 26

Z Russ/Daughters | LES — 29

Z Sahadi's | Bklyn Hts — 28

Sarabeth's | multi. — 24

Z Sherry-Lehmann | E 50s — 29

Z Soutine | W 70s — 27

Spoon | Flatiron — 25

Surroundings | W 100s — 27

Three Tarts | Chelsea — 26

Tribeca Treats | TriBeCa — 21

Z Vosges | SoHo — 27

Whole Foods | multi. — 25

Wild Edibles | multi. — 24

William Greenberg | E 80s — 25

Z William Poll | E 70s — 26

Z Zabar's | W 80s — 27

Z Zezé | E 50s — 27

GIFT IDEAS

(See also Gift Baskets)

Alessi | SoHo — 26

Alice's Tea/Wonderland | W 70s — 22

Baked/Melissa | multi. — 24

Bee Desserts | W Vill — 24

Bisous, Ciao | LES — 25

Bloomingdale's | E 50s — 25

Broadway Pan. | G Vill — 26

Dean/DeLuca | SoHo — 26

Z Eataly | Flatiron — 27

FPB | multi. — 27

Güllüoglu | E 50s — 23

Z Korin | TriBeCa — 29

Kusmi Tea | E 60s — 26

Z L.A. Burdick Handmade Chocolates | Flatiron — 28

Liddabit Sweets | Location Varies — 25

Macaron Café | E 50s — 24

Z **NEW** Maison Ladurée | E 70s — 28

MarieBelle's | SoHo — 26

Meadow | W Vill — 29

Minamoto | W 40s — 29

Nordic Delicacies | Bay Ridge — 28

Nut Box | multi. — 24

Papabubble | L Italy — 23

Sensuous Bean | W 70s — 25

Z Sur La Table | multi. — 27

Tea/Honey | E 60s — 29

Whisk | W'burg — –

Z Williams-Sonoma | multi. — 27

NEW Xocolatti | SoHo — 22

Z ZuZu's Petals | Park Slope — 27

GINGERBREAD HOUSES

Amish Mkt. | W 40s — 22

Bruno/Pasticceria | G Vill — 24

Dean/DeLuca | multi. — 26

Egidio Pastry | Bronx — 25

Garden/Eden | multi. — 23

Z Ladybird | Park Slope — 27

La Guli | Astoria — 27

Todaro Bros. | Murray Hill — 25

Two/Red Hens | E 80s — 26

HARD-TO-FIND INGREDIENTS

Agata/Valentina | E 70s — 25

Asia Mkt. | Chinatown — 20

Balady Foods | Bay Ridge — –

Bangkok Grocery | **Chinatown** 24

Citarella | **multi.** 26

Dean/DeLuca | **multi.** 26

Z Despaña | **multi.** 27

Eagle Provisions | **Greenwood Hts** 23

Z Eataly | **Flatiron** 27

Eli's Manhattan | **E 80s** 25

Eli's Vinegar | **E 90s** 24

Fairway | **multi.** 25

Foods/India | **Murray Hill** 23

Grace's Market | **E 70s** 25

H Mart | **multi.** 22

Internat'l Grocery | **W 40s** 24

Japanese Culinary Ctr. | **E 40s** 24

Z Kalustyan's | **Murray Hill** 27

Kam Man | **Chinatown** 21

Katagiri | **E 50s** 23

M & I | **Brighton Bch** 22

Nordic Delicacies | **Bay Ridge** 28

Patel Bros. | **multi.** 22

Phil-Am | **Woodside** -

Z Sahadi's | **Bklyn Hts** 28

Spice Corner | **Murray Hill** 23

NEW Spices/Tease | **multi.** 25

Sunrise Mart | **multi.** 23

Z Teitel Bros. | **Bronx** 27

Titan Foods | **Astoria** 26

Two for the Pot | **Bklyn Hts** 26

Whole Foods | **Chelsea** 25

Z Zabar's | **W 80s** 27

HEALTH & NATURAL FOODS

(See also Organic)

A Matter/Health | **E 70s** 23

BabyCakes | **LES** 24

Back/Land | **Park Slope** 24

Bell Bates | **TriBeCa** 24

Birdbath | **multi.** 23

NEW Blossom Bakery | **Chelsea** 26

Commodities | **E Vill** 25

Elm Health | **Chelsea** 24

Fairway | **multi.** 25

Family Health Foods | **SI** 22

NEW Fleisher's Grassfed | **Park Slope** 29

Foragers City Grocer | **multi.** 26

FreshDirect | **LIC** 23

Gary Null's | **W 80s** 20

Health/Harmony | **W Vill** -

Health Nuts | **multi.** 22

NEW Heritage Meat Shop | **LES** 27

Integral Yoga | **W Vill** 23

LifeThyme Mkt. | **G Vill** 22

Natural Frontier | **multi.** 22

Nature's Gifts | **E 80s** 19

One Lucky Duck | **Chelsea** 25

Z Perelandra | **Bklyn Hts** 26

NEW Soft Serve Fruit | **multi.** 23

Stogo | **E Vill** 25

Trader Joe's | **multi.** 23

Tu-Lu's GF | **E Vill** 25

NEW Victory Garden | **W Vill** 28

Westerly Natural | **W 50s** 23

Whole Foods | **multi.** 25

HERBS & SPICES

Asia Mkt. | **Chinatown** 20

Bell Bates | **TriBeCa** 24

Commodities | **E Vill** 25

Dean/DeLuca | **multi.** 26

Z D'Vine | **Park Slope** 26

Fairway | **multi.** 25

Family Store | **Bay Ridge** 24

Foods/India | **Murray Hill** 23

Hester Street Fair | **LES** 21

H Mart | **multi.** 22

Hong Kong | **Chinatown** 19

House/Spices | **Flushing** 26

Integral Yoga | **W Vill** 23

Internat'l Grocery | **W 40s** 24

Z Kalustyan's | **Murray Hill** 27

La Boîte à Epice | **W 50s** -

Las Palomas | **W 100s** -

LIC Market | **LIC** 25

Market | **Ditmas Pk** 24

Nut Box | **multi.** 24

Patel Bros. | **multi.** 22

Phil-Am | **Woodside** -

Puro Chile/Wine | **L Italy** -

Z Sahadi's | **Bklyn Hts** 28

Spice Corner | **Murray Hill** 23

NEW Spices/Tease | **multi.** 25

Stokes Farm | **Old Tappan** 26

Trader Joe's | **multi.** 23

Two for the Pot | **Bklyn Hts** 26

Whole Foods | **W 90s** 25

Z Zabar's | **W 80s** 27

HISTORIC INTEREST
(Year opened)

1820 | Acker Merrall | **W 70s** 28

1888 | Katz's Deli | **LES** 25

1890 | Yonah Schimmel | **LES** 24

1891 | Caffè Roma | **L Italy** 22

1892 | Alleva Dairy | **L Italy** 28

1892 | Ferrara Bakery | **L Italy** 22

1894 | Veniero's | **E Vill** 25

1895 | McNulty's | **W Vill** 28

1898 | Sahadi's | **Bklyn Hts** 28

1900 | Faicco's Pork | **multi.** 28

1900 | Sea Breeze | **W 40s** 21

1902 | Glaser's Bake | **E 80s** 24

1904 | Caputo | **Carroll Gdns** 27

1904 | De Robertis | **E Vill** 23

1906 | Raffetto's | **G Vill** 28

1907 | Katagiri | **E 50s** 23

1907 | Porto Rico | **G Vill** 27

1908 | Anopoli | **Bay Ridge** 24

1908 | Barney Greengrass | **W 80s** 27

1908 | Empire Coffee | **W 40s** 24

1908 | Russo Mozz. | **E Vill** 26

1910 | Eddie's Sweet | **Forest Hills** 25

1910 | Leonard's Market | **E 70s** 26

1910 | Pisacane | **E 50s** 28

1911 | Schatzie's Meats | **W 80s** 27

1912 | Egidio Pastry | **Bronx** 25

1914 | Russ/Daughters | **LES** 29

1915 | Butterfield/Baked | **E 70s** 25

1915 | Cosenza's Fish | **Bronx** 25

1915 | Teitel Bros. | **Bronx** 27

1916 | Orwasher's | **E 70s** 26

1917 | Staubitz Mkt. | **Cobble Hill** 29

1917 | Todaro Bros. | **Murray Hill** 25

1918 | Madonia Bakery | **Bronx** 26

1918 | Mona Lisa | **Bensonhurst** 24

1920 | Piemonte Ravioli | **L Italy** 27

1921 | Empire Mkt. | **College Pt** 23

1921 | William Poll | **E 70s** 26

1922 | Casa Della | **Bronx** 29

1922 | Esposito/Sons Pork | **Carroll Gdns** 27

1923 | Poseidon | **W 40s** 25

1924 | Hinsch's | **Bay Ridge** 22

1925 | Delillo Pastry | **Bronx** 25

1925 | Di Palo Dairy | **L Italy** 29

1925 | Joe's Dairy | **SoHo** 28

1925 | Randazzo's | **Bronx** 26

1925 | Salumeria Biellese | **Chelsea** 26

1925 | Streit's Matzo | **LES** 27

1927 | Iavarone Bros. | **Maspeth** 26

1927 | Mazzola Bakery | **Carroll Gdns** 27

1929 | Addeo Bakery | **Bronx** 28

1930 | Damascus | **Bklyn Hts** 26

1931 | Zabar's | **W 80s** 27

1932 | Biancardi Meats | **Bronx** 28

1932 | Esposito Meat | **Garment** 27

1933 | Cork & Bottle | **E 60s** 23

1933 | East Village Wines | **E Vill** 26

1933 | Eggers Ice Cream | **SI** 26

1933 | In Vino | **E 70s** 22

1935 | Borgatti's | **Bronx** 29

1935 | Kossar's | **LES** 26

1935 | Mount Carmel | **Bronx** 24

1935 | Ottomanelli/Sons | **W Vill** 28

1936 | Florence Meat | **W Vill** 29

1937 | Carnegie Deli | **W 50s** 23

1937 | Economy Candy | **LES** 25

1937 | La Guli | **Astoria** 27

1937 | Schaller/Weber | **E 80s** 28

1938 | Jordan's | **Sheepshead** 24

1943 | Mondel Choc. | **W 100s** 24

1943 | Schick's | **Borough Pk** 23

1944 | Kalustyan's | **Murray Hill** 27

1944 | Lemon Ice | **Corona** 26

1946 | Artuso Pastry | **Bronx** 24

1946 | JoMart Choc. | **Marine Pk** 28

1946 | Murray's Sturgeon | **W 80s** 28

1946 | William Greenberg | **E 80s** 25

1947 | Astor Wines | **NoHo** 26
1947 | Ben's Best | **Rego Pk** 25
1948 | Court Pastry | **Cobble Hill** 26
1948 | D'Amico | **Carroll Gdns** 27
1948 | Morrell & Co. | **W 40s** 26
1948 | Yorkville Meat | **E 80s** ⏤
1949 | Bari Equipment | **LES** ⏤
1949 | Fischer Bros. | **W 70s** 24
1949 | Lassen/Hennigs | **Bklyn Hts** 25
1949 | Peter Pan Donut | **Greenpt** 24
1949 | Ralph's/Ices | **SI** 25
1950 | Junior's | **Downtown Bklyn** 21
1950 | Mauzone | **Flushing** 21
1950 | United Meat | **Windsor Terr** 26
1952 | Calandra Cheese | **Bronx** 27
1952 | Cheese/World | **Forest Hills** 26
1953 | Liebman's | **Bronx** 24
1954 | Acme Fish | **Greenpt** 25
1954 | Ideal Cheese | **E 50s** 27
1954 | Lobel's Meats | **E 80s** 28
1954 | Mother's Bake | **Bronx** 20
1954 | Stork's Pastry | **Whitestone** 25
1954 | Vincent's Meat | **Bronx** 29
1956 | Sal/Dom's | **Bronx** 28
1957 | Beekman Liquors | **E 40s** 24
1957 | Orchard | **Midwood** 28
1958 | Cassinelli Food | **Astoria** 29
1958 | Red Jacket | **Geneva** 26

HORS D'OEUVRES

Agata/Valentina | **E 70s** 25
Between/Bread | **W 50s** 23
Butterfield/Baked | **E 70s** 25
Ceriello | **multi.** 24
Cer té | **W 50s** 23
Citarella | **multi.** 26
David Burke | **E 50s** 21
Dean/DeLuca | **multi.** 26
Dishes | **E 40s** 24
E.A.T. | **E 80s** 24
Eli's Vinegar | **E 90s** 24
Fairway | **multi.** 25
Family Store | **Bay Ridge** 24
Gourmet Garage | **multi.** 20
Grace's Market | **E 70s** 25

Marché Madison | **E 70s** 21
Mitchel London | **E 60s** 25
Nordic Delicacies | **Bay Ridge** 28
Once Upon/Tart | **SoHo** 25
Petrossian | **W 50s** 27
Todaro Bros. | **Murray Hill** 25
Trader Joe's | **multi.** 23
Wild Edibles | **E 40s** 24
🄩 William Poll | **E 70s** 26
🄩 Zabar's | **W 80s** 27

ICE CREAM, ICES & FROZEN YOGURT

NEW Amorino | **G Vill** 25
NEW Ample Hills | **Prospect Hts** 28
Anopoli | **Bay Ridge** 24
Berrywild | **multi.** 21
Big Gay Ice Cream | **E Vill** 27
Blue Marble | **multi.** 26
Bomboloni | **W 60s** 22
Brooklyn Farmacy | **Carroll Gdns** 25
Bruno/Pasticceria | **multi.** 24
Caffé Roma | **L Italy** 22
Chinatown Ice Cream | **Chinatown** 24
Ciao Bella | **multi.** 26
Colson | **Park Slope** 24
🄩 Cones | **W Vill** 27
Court Pastry | **Cobble Hill** 26
De Robertis | **E Vill** 23
Dolly's Ices | **Mill Basin** 25
🄩 Dylan's Candy | **E 60s** 23
🄩 Eataly | **Flatiron** 27
Eggers Ice Cream | **SI** 26
Emack/Bolio | **multi.** 25
Ferrara Bakery | **L Italy** 22
Financier Patisserie | **Financial** 25
F. Monteleone | **Carroll Gdns** 29
🄩 Fortunato | **W'burg** 27
Forty Carrots | **E 50s** 22
Grom | **multi.** 26
Holey Cream | **W 50s** 21
Ice Cream House | **multi.** 24
🄩 Il Laboratorio | **LES** 28
🄩 Jacques Torres | **Dumbo** 28
Koryodang | **Garment** 22

NEW La Cremeria | **L Italy**	22
La Guli | **Astoria**	27
La Newyorkina | **Location Varies**	-
L'Arte/Gelato | **multi.**	25
Z Lemon Ice | **Corona**	26
Momofuku Milk Bar | **multi.**	25
Z NYC Icy | **multi.**	29
People's Pops | **Chelsea**	26
pinkberry | **multi.**	22
Popbar | **W Vill**	22
Ralph's/Ices | **multi.**	25
Red Mango | **multi.**	22
Rocco's Pastry | **W Vill**	25
Ronnybrook | **Chelsea**	26
Sant Ambroeus | **multi.**	26
Screme | **multi.**	24
16 Handles | **E Vill**	24
NEW Soft Serve Fruit | **multi.**	23
Steve's/Ice Cream | **E 40s**	22
Stogo | **E Vill**	25
Sundaes/Cones | **E Vill**	25
Sweet Melissa | **Park Slope**	25
Tarallucci/Vino | **multi.**	24
Z Van Leeuwen | **multi.**	26
NEW Victory Garden | **W Vill**	28
Z Villabate | **Bensonhurst**	27
Z Vosges | **SoHo**	27
Yogo Monster | **multi.**	22

KOSHER

Andre's | **multi.**	24
Bagels/Co. | **multi.**	21
Ben's Best | **Rego Pk**	25
Ben's Kosher | **multi.**	22
Crumbs | **multi.**	22
Eleni's Cookies | **multi.**	22
Eli's Bread | **E 40s**	26
Fifth Ave. Choc. | **E 40s**	25
Fischer Bros. | **W 70s**	24
Foremost RAM Caterers | **Moonachie**	23
H & H Midtown | **E 80s**	25
Ice Cream House | **multi.**	24
Kosher Bagel | **Flatbush**	27
Z Kossar's | **LES**	26

Le Marais | **W 40s**	23
Liebman's | **Bronx**	24
Magnolia Bakery | **multi.**	21
Mauzone | **Flushing**	21
Max/Mina's | **Flushing**	25
Mill Basin Kosher | **Mill Basin**	24
Moishe's | **E Vill**	23
Mother's Bake | **Bronx**	20
Newman/Leventhal | **W 80s**	-
Z Orchard | **Midwood**	28
Orwasher's | **E 70s**	26
Park E. Kosher | **E 80s**	24
Pastrami Queen | **E 70s**	22
Z Pickle Guys | **multi.**	27
Z Pomegranate | **Midwood**	26
Schick's | **Borough Pk**	23
Screme | **multi.**	24
Simply Divine | **W 70s**	-
16 Handles | **multi.**	24
Streit's Matzo | **LES**	27
William Greenberg | **E 80s**	25

MAJOR MARKETS

Agata/Valentina | **E 70s**	25
Amish Mkt. | **multi.**	22
Battery Place Mkt. | **Financial**	27
Brooklyn Fare | **Downtown Bklyn**	26
Citarella | **multi.**	26
Costco | **multi.**	23
Dean/DeLuca | **multi.**	26
Z Eataly | **Flatiron**	27
Eli's Manhattan | **E 80s**	25
Eli's Vinegar | **E 90s**	24
Fairway | **multi.**	25
FreshDirect | **LIC**	23
Garden/Eden | **multi.**	23
Gourmet Garage | **multi.**	20
Grace's Market | **E 70s**	25
Trader Joe's | **multi.**	23
Union Mkt. | **Park Slope**	25
Westside Mkt. | **W 100s**	21
Whole Foods | **multi.**	25
Z Zabar's | **W 80s**	27
Zeytuna | **Financial**	20

MARKET VENDORS/ FOOD TRUCKS

(See also Brooklyn Flea, p. 45;
Fulton Stall Market, p. 84;
Greenmarket, p. 89;
Hester Street Fair, p. 93;
New Amsterdam Market, p. 128)

Berried Treasures | **Roscoe** 29
🔢 Beth's Farm | **Stuyvesant Falls** 28
🔢 Blue Moon Fish | **Mattituck** 28
Bread Alone | **Boiceville** 25
Brooklyn Brew Shop | 26
  Location Varies
Brooklyn Oenology | **Greenpt** ‑
Cathcart/Reddy | **LES** 25
🔢 DiPaola Turkey | **Hamilton** 28
🔢 Flying Pigs | **Shushan** 29
Gorzynski Ornery | 26
  Cochecton Ctr.
Hawthorne Farm | **Ghent** 28
Hudson Valley Foie Gras | **Ferndale** 29
🔢 Keith's Farm | **Westtown** 29
La Newyorkina | **Location Varies** ‑
Liddabit Sweets | **Location Varies** 25
Martin's Pretzels | **Theresa** 26
McClure's Pickles | **Location Varies** 27
Migliorelli Farm | **Tivoli** 25
Our Daily Bread | **Chatham** 25
Paffenroth | **Warwick** 28
People's Pops | **Chelsea** 26
🔢 Quattro's | **Pleasant Valley** 28
Red Jacket | **Geneva** 26
Rick's Picks | **LES** 26
Robicelli's | **Location Varies** 26
Ronnybrook | **Chelsea** 26
Stokes Farm | **Old Tappan** 26
Terhune Orchards | **Salt Pt** 24
🔢 3-Corner Farm | **Shushan** 27
Treats Truck | **Location Varies** 23
🔢 Van Leeuwen | **multi.** 26
Wafels/Dinges | **Location Varies** 24
Windfall Farms | **Montgomery** 29

MEAT & POULTRY

Agata/Valentina | **E 70s** 25
Ann Clair's Salum. | **Bronx** 25
Balady Foods | **Bay Ridge** ‑

Bari Pork | **multi.** 26
Battery Place Mkt. | **Financial** 27
Bayard St. Meat | **multi.** 21
Belfiore Meats | **SI** 25
Best Yet Mkt. | **multi.** 23
🔢 Biancardi Meats | **Bronx** 28
Brooklyn Fare | **Downtown Bklyn** 26
Brooklyn Kitchen | **W'burg** 25
Butcher Block | **Sunnyside** 27
🔢 Calabria Pork | **Bronx** 27
Carolina Country | **Brownsville** ‑
Ceriello | **multi.** 24
Christos Steak | **Astoria** 25
Chung Fat | **Flushing** 22
Citarella | **multi.** 26
Costco | **multi.** 23
Court Street Grocers | **Carroll Gdns** 29
Dean/DeLuca | **multi.** 26
Deluxe Food | **Chinatown** 23
🔢 Dickson's Farmstand | **Chelsea** 28
🔢 DiPaola Turkey | **Hamilton** 28
Eagle Provisions | **Greenwood Hts** 23
East Vill. Meat | **E Vill** 26
🔢 Eataly | **Flatiron** 27
Eli's Manhattan | **E 80s** 25
Eli's Vinegar | **E 90s** 24
Empire Mkt. | **College Pt** 23
🔢 Esposito/Sons Pork | 27
  Carroll Gdns
🔢 Esposito Meat | **Garment** 27
Faicco's Pork | **multi.** 28
Fairway | **multi.** 25
Fischer Bros. | **W 70s** 24
NEW Fleisher's Grassfed | 29
  Park Slope
🔢 Florence Meat | **W Vill** 29
🔢 Flying Pigs | **Shushan** 29
Foragers City Grocer | **multi.** 26
Fulton Stall Mkt. | **Financial** 25
Garden/Eden | **multi.** 23
Grace's Market | **E 70s** 25
GreatWall Supermkt. | **multi.** 19
Greene Grape | **Ft Greene** 27
Greenmarket | **Union Sq** 29

Hawthorne Farm | **Ghent**	28
Heights Meats | **Bklyn Hts**	27
NEW Heritage Meat Shop | **LES**	27
Hester Street Fair | **LES**	21
H Mart | **multi.**	22
Hong Kong | **Chinatown**	19
Hudson Valley Foie Gras | **Ferndale**	29
Iavarone Bros. | **Maspeth**	26
Japan Premium Beef | **NoHo**	29
Jubilat Provisions | **Greenwood Hts**	-
Le Marais | **W 40s**	23
Leonard's Market | **E 70s**	26
Les Halles | **Murray Hill**	23
⊠ Lobel's Meats | **E 80s**	28
Los Paisanos | **Cobble Hill**	26
Malaysia Beef Jerky | **Chinatown**	25
M & I | **Brighton Bch**	22
⊠ Marlow/Daughters | **W'burg**	28
Meat Hook | **W'burg**	27
⊠ New Amsterdam Mkt. | **Seaport**	28
⊠ Ottomanelli/Sons | **multi.**	28
⊠ Ottomanelli's Meats | **Flushing**	28
Park E. Kosher | **E 80s**	24
Pino Meats | **SoHo**	29
⊠ Pomegranate | **Midwood**	26
⊠ Quattro's | **Pleasant Valley**	28
Salumeria Biellese | **Chelsea**	26
⊠ Schaller/Weber | **E 80s**	28
⊠ Schatzie's Meats | **W 80s**	27
⊠ Simchick | **E 50s**	29
⊠ Staubitz Mkt. | **Cobble Hill**	29
Sunrise Mart | **multi.**	23
⊠ 3-Corner Farm | **Shushan**	27
Todaro Bros. | **Murray Hill**	25
Trader Joe's | **multi.**	23
Union Mkt. | **multi.**	25
Vincent's Meat | **Bronx**	29
Whole Foods | **multi.**	25
Yorkville Meat | **E 80s**	-
⊠ Zabar's | **W 80s**	27
Zeytuna | **Financial**	20

OFFBEAT

Aji Ichiban | **Chinatown**	22
Baconery | **Chelsea**	25

Brouwerij Ln. | **Greenpt**	28
Cake Man | **Ft Greene**	24
Choux Factory | **multi.**	23
Doughnut Plant | **multi.**	27
Empire Mkt. | **College Pt**	23
Insomnia Cookies | **G Vill**	22
⊠ Kossar's | **LES**	26
Mast Brothers | **W'burg**	25
Max/Mina's | **Flushing**	25
Max Brenner | **G Vill**	22
Meadow | **W Vill**	29
Meat Hook | **W'burg**	27
Myers/Keswick | **W Vill**	25
Papabubble | **L Italy**	23
Rice/Riches | **NoLita**	24
Rick's Picks | **LES**	26

OFFICE CATERING

(All caterers and delis, plus the following standouts)

Agata/Valentina | **E 70s**	25
Alice's Tea/Wonderland | **multi.**	22
Arthur Ave. | **Bronx**	23
⊠ Balthazar Bakery | **SoHo**	27
Barbarini | **Financial**	25
Bari Pork | **multi.**	26
⊠ Barney Greengrass | **W 80s**	27
Belfiore Meats | **SI**	25
Between/Bread | **W 50s**	23
⊠ Bklyn Larder | **Park Slope**	27
Bonsignour | **W Vill**	27
⊠ Bouchon Bakery | **W 60s**	27
BuonItalia | **Chelsea**	26
Butterfield/Baked | **E 70s**	25
Ceriello | **multi.**	24
Cer té | **W 50s**	23
Cipriani | **E 40s**	26
Citarella | **multi.**	26
City Bakery | **Flatiron**	25
Clinton St. Baking | **LES**	26
Cucina | **multi.**	22
Cucina Vivolo | **multi.**	22
Dean/DeLuca | **multi.**	26
Dishes | **multi.**	24
E.A.T. | **E 80s**	24

Eli's Manhattan | **E 80s**	25
Eli's Vinegar | **E 90s**	24
Fairway | **multi.**	25
Family Store | **Bay Ridge**	24
Financier Patisserie | **Financial**	25
Garden/Eden | **multi.**	23
Good/Plenty | **W 40s**	21
Grace's Market | **E 70s**	25
Iavarone Bros. | **Maspeth**	26
Katz's Deli | **LES**	25
Kosher Bagel | **Flatbush**	27
Le Pain Quotidien | **multi.**	23
☑ Lorenzo/Maria's | **E 80s**	27
Mangia | **multi.**	23
Marché Madison | **E 70s**	21
Melange | **E 60s**	23
Mitchel London | **E 60s**	25
Ready to Eat | **W Vill**	23
Salumeria Biellese | **Chelsea**	26
Sweet Melissa | **Park Slope**	25
Todaro Bros. | **Murray Hill**	25
Wafels/Dinges | **Location Varies**	24
Wild Edibles | **multi.**	24
Yura/Madison | **E 90s**	24
☑ Zabar's | **W 80s**	27
Zeytuna | **Financial**	20

OLIVES & PICKLES

Amish Mkt. | **multi.**	22
Balady Foods | **Bay Ridge**	-
☑ Beth's Farm | **Stuyvesant Falls**	28
☑ Coluccio/Sons | **Borough Pk**	27
Eli's Manhattan | **E 80s**	25
Eli's Vinegar | **E 90s**	24
Fairway | **multi.**	25
NEW Il Buco Alimentari | **NoHo**	25
M & I | **Brighton Bch**	22
McClure's Pickles | **Location Varies**	27
☑ Pickle Guys | **multi.**	27
☑ Pickles/Olives | **E 80s**	25
Rick's Picks | **LES**	26
☑ Sahadi's | **Bklyn Hts**	28
☑ Teitel Bros. | **Bronx**	27

Titan Foods | **Astoria**	26
Todaro Bros. | **Murray Hill**	25
Union Mkt. | **multi.**	25
Whole Foods | **multi.**	25
☑ Zabar's | **W 80s**	27

ONE-STOP SHOPPING

Agata/Valentina | **E 70s**	25
Amish Mkt. | **multi.**	22
Best Yet Mkt. | **multi.**	23
Brooklyn Fare | **Downtown Bklyn**	26
Chung Fat | **Flushing**	22
Citarella | **multi.**	26
Costco | **multi.**	23
Dean/DeLuca | **multi.**	26
Deluxe Food | **Chinatown**	23
☑ Eataly | **Flatiron**	27
Eli's Manhattan | **E 80s**	25
Eli's Vinegar | **E 90s**	24
Fairway | **multi.**	25
FreshDirect | **LIC**	23
Garden/Eden | **multi.**	23
Gary Null's | **W 80s**	20
Gourmet Garage | **multi.**	20
Grace's Market | **E 70s**	25
GreatWall Supermkt. | **multi.**	19
Greene Grape | **Ft Greene**	27
Gustiamo | **Bronx**	-
H Mart | **multi.**	22
Hong Kong | **multi.**	19
Kam Man | **Chinatown**	21
LifeThyme Mkt. | **G Vill**	22
M & I | **Brighton Bch**	22
Patel Bros. | **multi.**	22
☑ Perelandra | **Bklyn Hts**	26
☑ Pomegranate | **Midwood**	26
Sunrise Mart | **multi.**	23
Titan Foods | **Astoria**	26
Todaro Bros. | **Murray Hill**	25
Trader Joe's | **multi.**	23
Union Mkt. | **multi.**	25
Whole Foods | **multi.**	25
☑ Zabar's | **W 80s**	27
Zeytuna | **Financial**	20

OPEN LATE

BAGELS & BIALYS
Z Absolute Bagels | W 100s — 26
Daniel's Bagels | Murray Hill — 24
East Side Bagel | E 70s — 21
Ess-a-Bagel | multi. — 26
H & H Midtown | E 80s — 25
Hot Bagels & Bialys | Midwood — 25
Montague St. | Bklyn Hts — 23
Murray's Bagels | G Vill — 26
Pick/Bagel | multi. — 21
Tal Bagels | multi. — 22
Terrace Bagels | Windsor Terr — 25
Times Sq. Bagels | W 40s — 24

BAKED GOODS
Amy's Bread | multi. — 26
Billy's Bakery | Chelsea — 24
Z Black Hound | E Vill — 26
Bruno/Pasticceria | G Vill — 24
Buttercup | E 50s — 22
Carrot Top | Wash. Hts — 23
Clinton St. Baking | LES — 26
Crumbs | multi. — 22
Donut Pub | Chelsea — 22
Eileen's Cheesecake | NoLita — 25
Fay Da | multi. — 20
Ferrara Bakery | L Italy — 22
Financier Patisserie | Financial — 25
Z Fortunato | W'burg — 27
Güllüoglu | multi. — 23
Hungarian Pastry | W 100s — 23
Insomnia Cookies | multi. — 22
Junior's | multi. — 21
La Guli | Astoria — 27
Led Zeppole | E Vill — 22
Little Brown | E 80s — 21
Magnolia Bakery | multi. — 21
Milk/Cookies | W Vill — 25
NEW Puddin' by Clio | E Vill — 29
Rice/Riches | NoLita — 24
Rocco's Pastry | W Vill — 25
Sarabeth's | multi. — 24
Sugar Sweet | LES — 26
Sweet Melissa | Park Slope — 25

Tai Pan Bakery | Chinatown — 21
Veniero's | E Vill — 25

CANDY & NUTS
Z Dylan's Candy | E 60s — 23
Hershey's | W 40s — 21
Z L.A. Burdick Handmade Chocolates | Flatiron — 28
Lily O'Brien's | W 40s — 22
M&M's World | W 40s — 21
Nut Box | multi. — 24
Papabubble | L Italy — 23

CHEESE & DAIRY
Z Artisanal | Murray Hill — 27
Z Bedford Cheese | W'burg — 27

COFFEE & TEA
Carry On Tea | W Vill — 25
Z McNulty's | W Vill — 28
Two for the Pot | Bklyn Hts — 26

DELIS
Carnegie Deli | W 50s — 23
Katz's Deli | LES — 25
Liebman's | Bronx — 24
Pastrami Queen | E 70s — 22

HEALTH & NATURAL FOODS
Gary Null's | W 80s — 20
Health/Harmony | W Vill — -
Health Nuts | multi. — 22
Integral Yoga | W Vill — 23
LifeThyme Mkt. | G Vill — 22
One Lucky Duck | multi. — 25

ICE CREAM
Ben/Jerry's | multi. — 24
Brooklyn Ice Cream | Dumbo — 25
Chinatown Ice Cream | Chinatown — 24
Z Cones | W Vill — 27
Emack/Bolio | W 70s — 25
Z Fortunato | W'burg — 27
Z Il Laboratorio | LES — 28
L'Arte/Gelato | multi. — 25
Z Lemon Ice | Corona — 26
Max/Mina's | Flushing — 25
People's Pops | Chelsea — 26
Sant Ambroeus | multi. — 26
16 Handles | multi. — 24

Stogo | **E Vill**   25
Sundaes/Cones | **E Vill**   25
Yogo Monster | **Park Slope**   22

MEAT, POULTRY & GAME
Christos Steak | **Astoria**   25
Le Marais | **W 40s**   23
Les Halles | **Murray Hill**   23

PREPARED FOODS
Lamarca | **Gramercy**   26

PRODUCE
Annie's | **E 80s**   20
Manhattan Fruit Ex. | **Chelsea**   25
#1 Farmers Mkt. | **E 70s**   23
Three Guys | **Bay Ridge**   23

SPECIALTY SHOPS
Berry Fresh Farm | **Astoria**   25
Ceriello | **E 40s**   24
Grab Specialty | **Park Slope**   26
Greene Grape | **Ft Greene**   27
H Mart | **multi.**   22
Kam Man | **Chinatown**   21
☑ Marlow/Sons | **W'burg**   27
Nature's Gifts | **E 80s**   22
Patel Bros. | **multi.**   23
Sunrise Mart | **multi.**   23
Todaro Bros. | **Murray Hill**   25

WINES, BEER & LIQUOR
Astor Wines | **NoHo**   26
Beacon Wines | **W 70s**   23
Bierkraft | **Park Slope**   27
Dry Dock Wine | **Red Hook**   28
Garnet Wines | **E 60s**   26
Good Beer | **E Vill**   27
Gotham Wines | **W 90s**   24
Grande Harvest | **E 40s**   22
Grand Wine | **Astoria**   22
Greene Grape | **Ft Greene**   22
☑ Heights Chateau | **Bklyn Hts**   25
K & D Wines | **E 90s**   26
Landmark Wine | **Chelsea**   24
Martin Bros. | **W 100s**   24
McCabes Wines | **E 70s**   22
☑ Moore Bros. | **Flatiron**   28
Mount Carmel | **Bronx**   24

Nancy's-Wines | **W 70s**   24
New York/Exchange | **Financial**   25
Picada/Vino | **Park Slope**   26
☑ PJ Wine | **Inwood**   27
☑ Pour | **W 70s**   24
Prospect Wine | **Park Slope**   25
Red/White | **Park Slope**   26
67 Wine & Spirits | **W 60s**   25
Smith/Vine | **Cobble Hill**   25
Tinto Fino | **E Vill**   25

OPEN SUNDAY

(Except for liquor stores, butchers and fish markets, most places are open Sunday; here are some sources in those hard-to-find categories)

Ambassador Wine | **E 50s**   25
Astor Wines | **NoHo**   26
Bari Pork | **multi.**   26
Bayard St. Meat | **multi.**   21
Beacon Wines | **W 70s**   23
Belfiore Meats | **SI**   25
Best Cellars | **W 80s**   22
Bierkraft | **Park Slope**   27
Brooklyn Liquors | **Sunset Pk**   24
☑ Chambers Wines | **TriBeCa**   27
Chelsea Wine | **Chelsea**   24
Christos Steak | **Astoria**   25
Columbus Circle Wine | **W 50s**   25
☑ Crush Wine | **E 50s**   27
Eagle Provisions | **Greenwood Hts**   23
Empire Mkt. | **College Pt**   23
☑ Esposito/Sons Pork | 27
   Carroll Gdns
Faicco's Pork | **multi.**   28
Garnet Wines | **E 60s**   26
Gotham Wines | **W 90s**   24
Grande Harvest | **E 40s**   22
Greene Grape | **Ft Greene**   22
Harlem Vintage | **Harlem**   27
Jordan's | **Sheepshead**   24
Le Marais | **W 40s**   23
Leonard's Market | **E 70s**   26
Les Halles | **Murray Hill**   23
☑ Lobster Pl. | **Chelsea**   27
McCabes Wines | **E 70s**   22

Mister Wright | **E 80s**	25
Mount Carmel | **Bronx**	24
Nancy's–Wines | **W 70s**	24
Park E. Kosher | **E 80s**	24
Pescatore | **E 40s**	25
Premier Cru | **E 80s**	25
Prospect Wine | **Park Slope**	25
🅉 Quattro's | **Pleasant Valley**	28
Red/White | **Park Slope**	26
67 Wine & Spirits | **W 60s**	25
Slavin/Sons | **Bronx**	28
Slope Cellars | **Park Slope**	26
Smith/Vine | **Cobble Hill**	25
Sutton Wine | **E 50s**	22
Union Sq. Wines | **Union Sq**	25
Warehouse Wines | **G Vill**	25
Wild Edibles | **multi.**	24
Yorkshire Wines | **E 80s**	24
Yorkville Meat | **E 80s**	–

ORGANIC

Ackerson, T.B. | **Ditmas Pk**	25
A Matter/Health | **E 70s**	23
Amish Mkt. | **E 40s**	22
Amy's Bread | **W 40s**	26
Appellation | **Chelsea**	26
BabyCakes | **LES**	24
Back/Land | **Park Slope**	24
Barbarini | **Financial**	25
Battery Place Mkt. | **Financial**	27
Bell Bates | **TriBeCa**	24
Berried Treasures | **Roscoe**	29
Birdbath | **multi.**	23
NEW Blossom Bakery | **Chelsea**	26
Blue Marble | **Prospect Hts**	26
🅉 Bouchon Bakery | **multi.**	27
Bread Alone | **Boiceville**	25
Brooklyn Wine | **Cobble Hill**	25
Butter Lane Cupcakes | **E Vill**	25
🅉 Chambers Wines | **TriBeCa**	27
Choice Greene/Mkt. | **Ft Greene**	27
City Bakery | **Flatiron**	25
Cleaver Co. | **Chelsea**	27
Commodities | **E Vill**	25
Dry Dock Wine | **Red Hook**	28

Elm Health | **Chelsea**	24
Empire Mkt. | **College Pt**	23
Fairway | **multi.**	25
Family Health Foods | **SI**	22
Foragers City Grocer | **multi.**	26
FreshDirect | **LIC**	23
Gourmet Garage | **multi.**	20
Greene Grape | **Ft Greene**	27
Hawthorne Farm | **Ghent**	28
Health/Harmony | **W Vill**	–
Health Nuts | **multi.**	22
Integral Yoga | **W Vill**	23
🅉 Keith's Farm | **Westtown**	29
LifeThyme Mkt. | **G Vill**	22
Little Brown | **E 80s**	21
Los Paisanos | **Cobble Hill**	26
🅉 Marlow/Sons | **W'burg**	27
Milk/Cookies | **W Vill**	25
Natural Frontier | **multi.**	22
Nordic Delicacies | **Bay Ridge**	28
Obika | **W 50s**	27
🅉 Orchard | **Midwood**	28
🅉 Ottomanelli/Sons | **W Vill**	28
🅉 Perelandra | **Bklyn Hts**	26
Picada/Vino | **Park Slope**	26
Pino Meats | **SoHo**	29
🅉 Porto Rico | **multi.**	27
Prospect Wine | **Park Slope**	25
Ronnybrook | **Chelsea**	26
Sensuous Bean | **W 70s**	25
NEW Soft Serve Fruit | **multi.**	23
Stogo | **E Vill**	25
Tea/Honey | **E 60s**	29
Union Mkt. | **multi.**	25
Vinyl Wine | **E 90s**	–
Westerly Natural | **W 50s**	23
Whole Foods | **multi.**	25
Zeytuna | **Financial**	20

PARTY RENTALS

(* listed in Other Noteworthy Sources on p. 178)

Atlas Party | **Mt. Vernon**	25
Broadway Party* | **multi.**	–
Classic Party* | **Garment**	–

County Chair* | **Mt. Vernon** ⌐⌐

Party Rental | **multi.** 22

Party Time | **Elmhurst** 20

Props/Today | **Garment** 20

Something Different* | **Paterson** ⌐⌐

PASTAS

Agata/Valentina | **E 70s** 25

Bari Pork | **multi.** 26

☒ Borgatti's | **Bronx** 29

Brooklyn Fare | **Downtown Bklyn** 26

Bruno Ravioli | **Gramercy** 21

BuonItalia | **Chelsea** 26

Cassinelli Food | **Astoria** 29

Ceriello | **multi.** 24

Citarella | **multi.** 26

☒ Coluccio/Sons | **Borough Pk** 27

Dean/DeLuca | **multi.** 26

☒ Di Palo Dairy | **L Italy** 29

Durso's Pasta | **Flushing** 26

☒ Eataly | **Flatiron** 27

Eli's Manhattan | **E 80s** 25

Eli's Vinegar | **E 90s** 24

Fairway | **multi.** 25

FreshDirect | **LIC** 23

Gourmet Garage | **multi.** 20

Gustiamo | **Bronx** ⌐⌐

Iavarone Bros. | **Maspeth** 26

Los Paisanos | **Cobble Hill** 26

☒ Murray's Cheese | **W Vill** 29

☒ Pastosa Ravioli | **multi.** 27

☒ Piemonte Ravioli | **L Italy** 27

Queen Ann | **Bensonhurst** 25

☒ Raffetto's | **G Vill** 28

Russo Mozz. | **multi.** 26

☒ Teitel Bros. | **Bronx** 27

☒ Terranova | **Bronx** 28

Todaro Bros. | **Murray Hill** 25

Trader Joe's | **multi.** 23

Whole Foods | **multi.** 25

☒ Zabar's | **W 80s** 27

PICNICS

Amanda Smith | **W 80s** 27

Between/Bread | **W 50s** 23

Citarella | **multi.** 26

Dean/DeLuca | **multi.** 26

Eli's Manhattan | **E 80s** 25

Eli's Vinegar | **E 90s** 24

Garden/Eden | **multi.** 23

Grace's Market | **E 70s** 25

Movable Feast | **Park Slope** 23

Todaro Bros. | **Murray Hill** 25

Wild Edibles | **Murray Hill** 24

PIES/TARTS

Andre's | **multi.** 24

Astor Bake Shop | **Astoria** 23

Aunt Butchie's | **multi.** 26

☒ Baked | **Red Hook** 26

☒ Balthazar Bakery | **SoHo** 27

Bay Ridge Bake | **Bay Ridge** 25

NEW Bien Cuit | **Cobble Hill** 23

Birdbath | **SoHo** 23

☒ Black Hound | **E Vill** 26

Blue Smoke | **Murray Hill** 25

☒ Bouchon Bakery | **W 60s** 27

Buttercup | **E 50s** 22

Cake Chef Bakery | **SI** 28

Cannelle Patisserie | **Jackson Hts** 29

Ceci-Cela | **L Italy** 26

City Bakery | **Flatiron** 25

Colson | **Park Slope** 24

Dean/DeLuca | **multi.** 26

Delillo Pastry | **Bronx** 25

NEW Dominique Ansel | **SoHo** 27

Donna Bell's | **W 40s** 24

Duane Pk. | **TriBeCa** 25

Egidio Pastry | **Bronx** 25

Fairway | **multi.** 25

Financier Patisserie | **multi.** 25

Four/Twenty Blackbirds | **Gowanus** 26

FPB | **G Vill** 27

Glaser's Bake | **E 80s** 24

Grace's Market | **E 70s** 25

Grandaisy | **TriBeCa** 25

Hungarian Pastry | **W 100s** 23

Joyce Bake | **Prospect Hts** 25

La Bergamote | **multi.** 26

☒ Ladybird | **Park Slope** 27

La Guli	**Astoria**	27
Little Pie	**W 40s**	24
Magnolia Bakery	**W Vill**	21
Margot Pâtisserie	**W 70s**	23
Martha's Bakery	**Astoria**	22
Momofuku Milk Bar	**multi.**	25
Once Upon/Tart	**SoHo**	25
Patisserie Claude	**W Vill**	26
Petrossian	**W 50s**	27
Sarabeth's	**multi.**	24
Silver Moon	**W 100s**	26
☑ Soutine	**W 70s**	27
Steve's/Key Lime	**Red Hook**	26
☑ Stork's Pastry	**Whitestone**	25
Sugar Sweet	**LES**	26
Super Wang Bakery	**Chinatown**	21
Sweet Melissa	**Park Slope**	25
Three Tarts	**Chelsea**	26
Trois Pommes	**Park Slope**	27
Two/Red Hens	**E 80s**	26
Veniero's	**E Vill**	25
Whole Foods	**TriBeCa**	25
William Greenberg	**E 80s**	25

PREPARED FOODS

(See also Delis and Soups)

Agata/Valentina	**E 70s**	25
Ann Clair's Salum.	**Bronx**	25
Anthi's	**W 80s**	-
AQ Kafé	**W 50s**	23
Barbarini	**Financial**	25
Bari Pork	**multi.**	26
Battery Place Mkt.	**Financial**	27
NEW Beecher's Cheese	**Flatiron**	27
Bell Bates	**TriBeCa**	24
Between/Bread	**W 50s**	23
☑ Bklyn Larder	**Park Slope**	27
☑ Bouchon Bakery	**W 60s**	27
Brooklyn Fare	**Downtown Bklyn**	26
BuonItalia	**Chelsea**	26
Butcher Block	**Sunnyside**	27
Butterfield/Baked	**E 70s**	25
Carry On Tea	**W Vill**	25
Choice Greene/Mkt.	**Clinton Hill**	27
Citarella	**multi.**	26

City Bakery	**Flatiron**	25
Cleaver Co.	**Chelsea**	27
Clinton St. Baking	**LES**	26
Commodities	**E Vill**	25
Corner Café	**E 90s**	23
Costco	**multi.**	23
Court Street Grocers	**Carroll Gdns**	29
Cucina	**multi.**	22
Cucina Vivolo	**multi.**	22
Dean/DeLuca	**multi.**	26
Dishes	**multi.**	24
Dorian's Seafood	**E 80s**	26
Durso's Pasta	**Flushing**	26
☑ D'Vine	**Park Slope**	26
E.A.T.	**E 80s**	24
☑ Eataly	**Flatiron**	27
Eli's Manhattan	**E 80s**	25
Eli's Vinegar	**E 90s**	24
☑ Esposito/Sons Pork	**Carroll Gdns**	27
Faicco's Pork	**multi.**	28
Fairway	**multi.**	25
Family Store	**Bay Ridge**	24
Financier Patisserie	**Financial**	25
Foragers City Grocer	**multi.**	26
Fulton Stall Mkt.	**Financial**	25
Garden/Eden	**multi.**	23
Gary Null's	**W 80s**	20
Gourmet Garage	**multi.**	20
Grace's Market	**E 70s**	25
Health Nuts	**multi.**	22
Heights Meats	**Bklyn Hts**	27
Iavarone Bros.	**Maspeth**	26
Integral Yoga	**W Vill**	23
Internat'l Grocery	**W 40s**	24
☑ Kalustyan's	**Murray Hill**	27
Kam Man	**Chinatown**	21
Katagiri	**E 50s**	23
Lamarca	**Gramercy**	26
Lamazou	**Murray Hill**	26
Leonard's Market	**E 70s**	26
Le Pain Quotidien	**multi.**	23
LIC Market	**LIC**	25
LifeThyme Mkt.	**G Vill**	22

☑ Lobel's Meats | **E 80s** 28
☑ Lobster Pl. | **Chelsea** 27
☑ Lorenzo/Maria's | **E 80s** 27
M & I | **Brighton Bch** 22
Mangia | **multi.** 23
Market | **Ditmas Pk** 24
Max Brenner | **G Vill** 22
Melange | **E 60s** 23
Mitchel London | **E 60s** 25
Myers/Keswick | **W Vill** 25
Natural Frontier | **E 80s** 22
☑ New Amsterdam Mkt. | **Seaport** 28
One Lucky Duck | **Chelsea** 25
☑ Ottomanelli's Meats | **Flushing** 28
Paneantico | **Bay Ridge** 26
Park E. Kosher | **E 80s** 24
Pescatore | **E 40s** 25
☑ Pomegranate | **Midwood** 26
Queen Ann | **Bensonhurst** 25
☑ Raffetto's | **G Vill** 28
Ready to Eat | **W Vill** 23
Russo Mozz. | **Park Slope** 26
☑ Sahadi's | **Bklyn Hts** 28
☑ Schaller/Weber | **E 80s** 28
Scratch Bread | **Bed-Stuy** 27
Sunrise Mart | **multi.** 23
Sweet Melissa | **Park Slope** 25
Todaro Bros. | **Murray Hill** 25
Trader Joe's | **multi.** 23
Union Mkt. | **multi.** 25
United Meat | **Windsor Terr** 26
Westside Mkt. | **multi.** 21
Whole Foods | **multi.** 25
Wild Edibles | **multi.** 24
☑ William Poll | **E 70s** 26
Yonah Schimmel | **LES** 24
Yorkville Meat | **E 80s** -
Yura/Madison | **E 90s** 24
☑ Zabar's | **W 80s** 27

PRODUCE

Agata/Valentina | **E 70s** 25
Amish Mkt. | **multi.** 22
Annie's | **E 80s** 20
Asia Mkt. | **Chinatown** 20

Bell Bates | **TriBeCa** 24
Berried Treasures | **Roscoe** 29
Berry Fresh Farm | **Astoria** 25
Best Yet Mkt. | **multi.** 23
Brooklyn Fare | **Downtown Bklyn** 26
Butterfield/Baked | **E 70s** 25
Chung Fat | **Flushing** 22
Citarella | **multi.** 26
Commodities | **E Vill** 25
Costco | **multi.** 23
Dean/DeLuca | **E 80s** 26
☑ Eataly | **Flatiron** 27
Eli's Manhattan | **E 80s** 25
Eli's Vinegar | **E 90s** 24
Elm Health | **Chelsea** 24
Fairway | **multi.** 25
Foragers City Grocer | **multi.** 26
FreshDirect | **LIC** 23
Fulton Stall Mkt. | **Financial** 25
Garden/Eden | **multi.** 23
Gary Null's | **W 80s** 20
Gorzynski Ornery | **Cochecton Ctr.** 26
Gourmet Garage | **multi.** 20
Grace's Market | **E 70s** 25
GreatWall Supermkt. | **Dumbo** 19
Greene Grape | **Ft Greene** 27
Greenmarket | **Union Sq** 29
Greenwich Produce | **E 40s** 28
Hawthorne Farm | **Ghent** 28
Health/Harmony | **W Vill** -
Health Nuts | **multi.** 22
H Mart | **multi.** 22
Hong Kong | **multi.** 19
Integral Yoga | **W Vill** 23
Katagiri | **E 50s** 23
☑ Keith's Farm | **Westtown** 29
LIC Market | **LIC** 25
LifeThyme Mkt. | **G Vill** 22
Manhattan Fruit Ex. | **Chelsea** 25
☑ Manhattan Fruitier | **Murray Hill** 25
Marché Madison | **E 70s** 21
Migliorelli Farm | **Tivoli** 25
Natural Frontier | **multi.** 22
Nature's Gifts | **E 80s** 19

New Amsterdam Mkt. | **Seaport** 28

#1 Farmers Mkt. | **E 70s** 23

Paffenroth | **Warwick** 28

Perelandra | **Bklyn Hts** 26

Pomegranate | **Midwood** 26

Red Jacket | **Geneva** 26

Stokes Farm | **Old Tappan** 26

Terhune Orchards | **Salt Pt** 24

Three Guys | **Bay Ridge** 23

Trader Joe's | **multi.** 23

Union Mkt. | **multi.** 25

Whole Foods | **multi.** 25

Windfall Farms | **Montgomery** 29

Zabar's | **W 80s** 27

Zeytuna | **Financial** 20

SEAFOOD

Agata/Valentina | **E 70s** 25

Amish Mkt. | **multi.** 22

Asia Mkt. | **Chinatown** 20

Blue Moon Fish | **Mattituck** 28

Brooklyn Fare | **Downtown Bklyn** 26

Chung Fat | **Flushing** 22

Citarella | **multi.** 26

Cosenza's Fish | **Bronx** 25

Costco | **multi.** 23

Dean/DeLuca | **multi.** 26

Dorian's Seafood | **E 80s** 26

Eataly | **Flatiron** 27

Eli's Manhattan | **E 80s** 25

Eli's Vinegar | **E 90s** 24

Fairway | **multi.** 25

Fish Tales | **Cobble Hill** 27

Foragers City Grocer | **Dumbo** 26

FreshDirect | **LIC** 23

Garden/Eden | **multi.** 23

Gourmet Garage | **multi.** 20

GreatWall Supermkt. | **Dumbo** 19

Greene Grape | **Ft Greene** 27

Greenmarket | **Union Sq** 29

H Mart | **multi.** 22

Hong Kong | **multi.** 19

Jordan's | **Sheepshead** 24

Leonard's Market | **E 70s** 26

Lobster Pl. | **Chelsea** 27

New Amsterdam Mkt. | **Seaport** 28

Pescatore | **E 40s** 25

Pisacane | **E 50s** 28

Randazzo's | **Bronx** 26

Red Hook Lobster | **Red Hook** 27

Sea Breeze | **W 40s** 21

Slavin/Sons | **Bronx** 28

Sunrise Mart | **multi.** 23

Todaro Bros. | **Murray Hill** 25

Trader Joe's | **Rego Pk** 23

Union Mkt. | **multi.** 25

Whole Foods | **multi.** 25

Wild Edibles | **Murray Hill** 24

Won Chuen | **Chinatown** 22

SOUPS

Agata/Valentina | **E 70s** 25

Bonsignour | **W Vill** 27

Brooklyn Fare | **Downtown Bklyn** 26

Cipriani | **E 40s** 26

Citarella | **multi.** 26

Dean/DeLuca | **multi.** 26

Dishes | **multi.** 24

Eataly | **Flatiron** 27

Eli's Manhattan | **E 80s** 25

Eli's Vinegar | **E 90s** 24

Fairway | **multi.** 25

Financier Patisserie | **Financial** 25

Good/Plenty | **W 40s** 21

Grace's Market | **E 70s** 25

Iavarone Bros. | **Maspeth** 26

Le Pain Quotidien | **multi.** 23

Pisacane | **E 50s** 28

Todaro Bros. | **Murray Hill** 25

Trader Joe's | **Chelsea** 23

Union Mkt. | **Cobble Hill** 25

Westerly Natural | **W 50s** 23

Whole Foods | **multi.** 25

Zabar's | **W 80s** 27

SPECIALTY SHOPS

Asia Mkt. | **Chinatown** 20

Balady Foods | **Bay Ridge** -

Bangkok Grocery | **Chinatown** 24

Battery Place Mkt. | **Financial** 27

Berry Fresh Farm | **Astoria**	25
Best Yet Mkt. | **multi.**	23
☑ Beth's Farm | **Stuyvesant Falls**	28
☑ Bklyn Larder | **Park Slope**	27
☑ Blue Apron | **Park Slope**	28
Blue Ribbon | **W Vill**	26
Brooklyn Flea | **Ft Greene**	22
BuonItalia | **Chelsea**	26
Butcher Block | **Sunnyside**	27
Butterfield/Baked | **E 70s**	25
Carolina Country | **Brownsville**	–
Ceriello | **multi.**	24
Chelsea Baskets | **Chelsea**	23
Chung Fat | **Flushing**	22
☑ Coluccio/Sons | **Borough Pk**	27
Deluxe Food | **Chinatown**	23
☑ Despaña | **multi.**	27
☑ D'Vine | **Park Slope**	26
Eastern District | **Greenpt**	–
Family Store | **Bay Ridge**	24
Filling Station | **Chelsea**	25
Grab Specialty | **Park Slope**	26
GreatWall Supermkt. | **multi.**	19
Greene Grape | **Ft Greene**	27
Gustiamo | **Bronx**	–
Hester Street Fair | **LES**	21
H Mart | **multi.**	22
Hong Kong | **multi.**	19
NEW Il Buco Alimentari | **NoHo**	25
Internat'l Grocery | **W 40s**	24
☑ Kalustyan's | **Murray Hill**	27
Kam Man | **Chinatown**	21
Katagiri | **E 50s**	23
Las Palomas | **W 100s**	–
LIC Market | **LIC**	25
M & I | **Brighton Bch**	22
☑ Manhattan Fruitier | **Murray Hill**	25
Market | **Ditmas Pk**	24
☑ Marlow/Sons | **W'burg**	27
McClure's Pickles | **Location Varies**	27
Meadow | **W Vill**	29
Med. Foods | **Astoria**	26
Myers/Keswick | **W Vill**	25
Nature's Gifts | **E 80s**	19

☑ New Amsterdam Mkt. | **Seaport**	28
Nordic Delicacies | **Bay Ridge**	28
O&CO. | **multi.**	27
☑ Orchard | **Midwood**	28
Patel Bros. | **multi.**	22
Phil-Am | **Woodside**	–
☑ Pickle Guys | **multi.**	27
☑ Pickles/Olives | **E 80s**	25
☑ Pomegranate | **Midwood**	26
Puro Chile/Wine | **L Italy**	–
Rick's Picks | **LES**	26
☑ Sahadi's | **Bklyn Hts**	28
☑ Salumeria Rosi | **W 70s**	28
Sunrise Mart | **multi.**	23
☑ Teitel Bros. | **Bronx**	27
Titan Foods | **Astoria**	26
Todaro Bros. | **Murray Hill**	25

TRENDY

Alessi | **SoHo**	26
☑ Baked | **Red Hook**	26
☑ Balthazar Bakery | **SoHo**	27
Billy's Bakery | **Chelsea**	24
☑ Bklyn Larder | **Park Slope**	27
Brooklyn Farmacy | **Carroll Gdns**	25
Brooklyn Flea | **Ft Greene**	22
ChikaLicious | **E Vill**	25
Choco Bolo | **multi.**	21
☑ Cones | **W Vill**	27
☑ Eataly | **Flatiron**	27
Empire Cake | **Chelsea**	26
Four/Twenty Blackbirds | **Gowanus**	26
FPB | **multi.**	27
Good Beer | **E Vill**	27
Hester Street Fair | **LES**	21
☑ Il Laboratorio | **LES**	28
☑ Jacques Torres | **Dumbo**	28
Led Zeppole | **E Vill**	22
Lucy's Whey | **Chelsea**	29
☑ **NEW** Maison Ladurée | **E 70s**	28
☑ Marlow/Sons | **W'burg**	27
Momofuku Milk Bar | **multi.**	25
☑ Murray's Cheese | **multi.**	29
☑ NYC Icy | **multi.**	29
NEW Puddin' by Clio | **E Vill**	29

Salumeria Rosi | **W 70s**	28
Scratch Bread | **Bed-Stuy**	27
NEW Sprinkles | **E 60s**	26
Sullivan St. Bakery | **W 40s**	27
Vosges | **SoHo**	27

WEDDING CAKES

Artopolis | **Astoria**	27
Artuso Pastry | **Bronx**	24
BabyCakes | **LES**	24
Balthazar Bakery | **SoHo**	27
Bay Ridge Bake | **Bay Ridge**	25
Betty Bakery | **Boerum Hill**	26
Buttercup | **E 50s**	22
Butter Lane Cupcakes | **E Vill**	25
Caffé Roma | **L Italy**	22
Cake Chef Bakery | **SI**	28
Cake Man | **Ft Greene**	24
Cannelle Patisserie | **Jackson Hts**	29
Ceci-Cela | **L Italy**	26
Cheryl Kleinman | **Boerum Hill**	28
Citarella | **multi.**	26
Colette's | **W Vill**	27
Delillo Pastry | **Bronx**	25
Duane Pk. | **TriBeCa**	25
Egidio Pastry | **Bronx**	25
Empire Cake | **Chelsea**	26
Fay Da | **multi.**	20
Glaser's Bake | **E 80s**	24
La Bergamote | **Chelsea**	26
Ladybird | **Park Slope**	27
Lady M | **E 70s**	29
Margot Pâtisserie | **W 70s**	23
Momofuku Milk Bar | **multi.**	25
Mother Mousse | **SI**	25
One Girl | **Cobble Hill**	27
Paneantico | **Bay Ridge**	26
Patisserie Claude | **W Vill**	26
Rocco's Pastry | **W Vill**	25
Ron Ben-Israel | **SoHo**	27
Royal Crown | **Bensonhurst**	26
Sal/Dom's | **Bronx**	28
Schick's | **Borough Pk**	23
Silver Moon | **W 100s**	26
Soutine | **W 70s**	27

Stork's Pastry | **Whitestone**	25
Sweet Melissa | **Park Slope**	25
Sylvia Weinstock | **TriBeCa**	29
Tribeca Treats | **TriBeCa**	21
Trois Pommes | **Park Slope**	27
Tu-Lu's GF | **E Vill**	25
Two/Red Hens | **E 80s**	26
Veniero's | **E Vill**	25
Villabate | **Bensonhurst**	27
William Greenberg | **E 80s**	25
Yi Mei Fung | **Flushing**	19

WINES & LIQUOR

(* Open Sunday)

Acker Merrall | **W 70s**	28
Ackerson, T.B. | **Ditmas Pk**	25
Ambassador Wine* | **E 50s**	25
Appellation | **Chelsea**	26
Astor Wines* | **NoHo**	26
Beacon Wines* | **W 70s**	23
Beekman Liquors | **E 40s**	24
Best Cellars* | **W 80s**	22
Big Nose | **Park Slope**	24
Botta di Vino | **Red Hook**	24
Bottlerocket | **Flatiron**	25
Bowery/Vine | **LES**	22
Brooklyn Liquors* | **Sunset Pk**	24
Brooklyn Oenology | **Greenpt**	–
Brooklyn Wine | **Cobble Hill**	25
Burgundy | **Chelsea**	28
California Wine | **Financial**	24
Chambers Wines* | **TriBeCa**	27
Chelsea Wine* | **Chelsea**	24
Columbus Circle Wine* | **W 50s**	25
Cork & Bottle | **E 60s**	23
Crush Wine* | **E 50s**	27
Despaña Vinos | **L Italy**	29
Dry Dock Wine | **Red Hook**	28
East Village Wines | **E Vill**	26
Eataly | **Flatiron**	27
Enoteca Di Palo | **L Italy**	27
First Ave. Wines | **Gramercy**	22
Foragers City Grocer | **Chelsea**	26
FreshDirect* | **LIC**	23
Garnet Wines* | **E 60s**	26

Gotham Wines* | **W 90s** _24_

Grande Harvest* | **E 40s** _22_

Grand Wine | **Astoria** _22_

Greene Grape* | **Ft Greene** _22_

Harlem Vintage* | **Harlem** _27_

☒ Heights Chateau | **Bklyn Hts** _25_

In Vino | **E 70s** _22_

☒ Italian Wine | **Union Sq** _29_

K & D Wines | **E 90s** _26_

Landmark Wine | **Chelsea** _24_

☒ Le Dû's Wines | **W Vill** _29_

Martin Bros. | **W 100s** _24_

McCabes Wines* | **E 70s** _22_

Michael-Towne | **Bklyn Hts** _27_

Mister Wright* | **E 80s** _25_

☒ Moore Bros. | **Flatiron** _28_

Morrell & Co. | **W 40s** _26_

Mount Carmel* | **Bronx** _24_

Nancy's–Wines* | **W 70s** _24_

New York Vintners | **TriBeCa** _28_

New York/Exchange | **Financial** _25_

☒ Park Ave. Liquor | **E 40s** _27_

Penn Wine/Spirits | **Garment** _26_

Pete Milano's | **SI** _25_

Picada/Vino | **Park Slope** _26_

☒ PJ Wine | **Inwood** _27_

☒ Pour | **W 70s** _24_

Premier Cru* | **E 80s** _25_

Prospect Wine* | **Park Slope** _25_

Puro Chile/Wine | **L Italy** _–_

Red/White* | **Park Slope** _26_

Rosenthal Wine | **E 80s** _29_

Sakaya | **E Vill** _28_

☒ Sherry-Lehmann | **E 50s** _29_

67 Wine & Spirits* | **W 60s** _25_

Skyview Wines | **Bronx** _26_

Slope Cellars* | **Park Slope** _26_

Smith/Vine* | **Cobble Hill** _25_

Sutton Wine* | **E 50s** _22_

Tinto Fino | **E Vill** _25_

Trader Joe's Wine | **Union Sq** _23_

Union Sq. Wines* | **Union Sq** _25_

Vinyl Wine | **E 90s** _–_

Warehouse Wines* | **G Vill** _25_

NEW Whiskey Shop | **W'burg** _27_

Wines/Whole Foods | **W 90s** _23_

Wright/Goebel | **Downtown Bklyn** _28_

Yorkshire Wines* | **E 80s** _24_

Ethnic Focus

Listings cover the best in each category and include source names, categories and Quality ratings.

AMERICAN

NEW Ample Hills	*Ice Cream*	28
Baconery	*Baked Gds.*	25
Bake City Bagels	*Bagels*	28
NEW Beer Table Pantry	*Beer*	26
Between/Bread	*Caterer*	23
Z Blue Apron	*Spec. Shop*	28
Bonsignour	*Prepared*	27
Buttercup	*Baked Gds.*	22
Carrot Top	*Baked Gds.*	23
City Bakery	*Baked Gds.*	25
Cousin John's	*Baked Gds.*	22
Crumbs	*Baked Gds.*	22
Eddie's Sweet	*Ice Cream*	25
Emack/Bolio	*Ice Cream*	25
Family Health Foods	*Health*	22
Gracious Thyme	*Caterer*	-
Z Great Performances	*Caterer*	26
Hinsch's	*Ice Cream*	22
Indiana Mkt.	*Caterer*	-
Z Jacques Torres	*Candy/Nuts*	28
Joyce Bake	*Baked Gds.*	25
Junior's	*Baked Gds.*	21
Z Ladybird	*Baked Gds.*	27
Little Pie	*Baked Gds.*	24
Lucy's Whey	*Cheese/Dairy*	29
Magnolia Bakery	*Baked Gds.*	21
Market	*Spec. Shop*	24
Martha's Bakery	*Baked Gds.*	22
Mondel Choc.	*Candy/Nuts*	24
Naturally Delic.	*Caterer/Events*	-
Neuman's	*Caterer*	-
Z One Girl	*Baked Gds.*	27
Rick's Picks	*Spec. Shop*	26
Ronnybrook	*Cheese/Dairy*	26
Sarabeth's	*Baked Gds.*	24
Z Saxelby Cheese	*Cheese/Dairy*	29
Spoon	*Caterer*	25
Trois Pommes	*Baked Gds.*	27

Two/Red Hens | *Baked Gds.* | 26
Yura/Madison | *Baked Gds.* | 24

ASIAN

(See also Chinese, Japanese, Korean, Thai and Vietnamese)

Aji Ichiban	*Candy/Nuts*	22
Chinatown Ice Cream	*Ice Cream*	24
Fay Da	*Baked Gds.*	20
Foods/India	*Herbs/Spices*	23
House/Spices	*Herbs/Spices*	26
Z Kalustyan's	*Spec. Shop*	27
Patel Bros.	*Spec. Shop*	22
Phil-Am	*Spec. Shop*	-
Radiance Tea	*Coffee/Tea*	24
Spice Corner	*Herbs/Spices*	23

BELGIAN

Colson	*Baked Gds.*	24
Leonidas	*Candy/Nuts*	26
Le Pain Quotidien	*Baked Gds.*	23
Martine's Choc.	*Candy/Nuts*	25
Neuhaus Choc.	*Candy/Nuts*	26
Wafels/Dinges	*Baked Gds.*	24

BRAZILIAN

Bee Desserts | *Baked Gds.* | 24

CARIBBEAN

Brooklyn Cupcake | *Baked Gds.* | 27

CHINESE

Asia Mkt.	*Spec. Shop*	20
Bayard St. Meat	*Meat/Poultry*	21
Chung Fat	*Spec. Shop*	22
Deluxe Food	*Spec. Shop*	23
Dragonland Bakery	*Baked Gds.*	25
Fay Da	*Baked Gds.*	20
GreatWall Supermkt.	*Spec. Shop*	19
Hong Kong	*Spec. Shop*	19
Kam Man	*Spec. Shop*	21
Lung Moon	*Baked Gds.*	20
Super Wang Bakery	*Baked Gds.*	21

Vote at zagat.com

Tai Pan Bakery | *Baked Gds.* 21

Ten Ren Tea | *Coffee/Tea* 25

Yi Mei Fung | *Baked Gds.* 19

ECLECTIC

(Most caterers and prepared food shops offer a variety of cuisines)

Abigail Kirsch | *Caterer* 26

🆕 Beer Table Pantry | *Beer* 26

Cer té | *Caterer/Events* 23

Court Street Grocers | *Maj. Market* 29

David Ziff | *Caterer* -

Dishes | *Prepared* 24

Gracious Thyme | *Caterer* -

Maison Prive | *Caterers/Events* -

Mitchel London | *Prepared* 25

Movable Feast | *Caterer* 23

Naturally Delic. | *Caterer/Events* -

Neuman's | *Caterer* -

Ready to Eat | *Prepared* 23

Red Table Catering | *Caterer* -

Robbins Wolfe | *Caterer* -

ENGLISH

Butcher Block | *Spec. Shop* 27

Carry On Tea | *Coffee/Tea* 25

Charbonnel/Walker | *Candy/Nuts* 23

🆕 London Candy Co. | *Candy* 25

Myers/Keswick | *Spec. Shop* 25

FRENCH

Almondine | *Baked Gds.* 26

🇿 Balthazar Bakery | *Baked Gds.* 27

🆕 Bien Cuit | *Baked Gds.* 23

Bisous, Ciao | *Baked Gds.* 25

Bonsignour | *Prepared* 27

🇿 Bouchon Bakery | *Baked Gds.* 27

🇿 Burgundy | *Wine/Liquor* 28

Cannelle Patisserie | *Baked Gds.* 29

🇿 Caputo | *Baked Gds.* 27

Ceci-Cela | *Baked Gds.* 26

Chocolat Michel | *Candy/Nuts* 27

🆕 Christian Vautier Le Concept | *Candy/Nuts* -

Colson | *Baked Gds.* 24

🆕 Dominique Ansel | *Baked Gds.* 27

Duane Pk. | *Baked Gds.* 25

Financier Patisserie | *Baked Gds.* 25

FPB | *Baked Gds.* 27

🇿 Jacques Torres | *Candy/Nuts* 28

Joyce Bake | *Baked Gds.* 25

Kusmi Tea | *Coffee/Tea* 26

La Bergamote | *Baked Gds.* 26

🇿 La Maison/Choc. | *Candy/Nuts* 29

La Maison/Macaron | *Baked Gds.* 28

Le Marais | *Meat/Poultry* 23

Le Pain Quotidien | *Baked Gds.* 23

Les Halles | *Meat/Poultry* 23

Macaron Café | *Baked Gds.* 24

🇿🆕 Maison Ladurée | *Baked Gds.* 28

Margot Pâtisserie | *Baked Gds.* 23

🆕 Mille-Feuille | *Baked Gds.* 25

Patisserie Claude | *Baked Gds.* 26

Petrossian | *Caviar/Smoked Fish* 27

Premier Cru | *Wine/Liquor* 25

Silver Moon | *Baked Gds.* 26

Sweet Melissa | *Baked Gds.* 25

🇿 Tastings/Payard | *Caterer/Events* 25

Trois Pommes | *Baked Gds.* 27

GERMAN/AUSTRIAN

Duane Pk. | *Baked Gds.* 25

Empire Mkt. | *Meat/Poultry* 23

Glaser's Bake | *Baked Gds.* 24

🇿 Schaller/Weber | *Meat/Poultry* 28

🇿 Stork's Pastry | *Baked Gds.* 25

GREEK

Anthi's | *Prepared* -

🇿 Artopolis | *Baked Gds.* 27

Christos Steak | *Meat/Poultry* 25

Internat'l Grocery | *Spec. Shop* 24

Med. Foods | *Spec. Shop* 26

Nature's Gifts | *Spec. Shop* 19

Poseidon | *Baked Gds.* 25

Titan Foods | *Spec. Shop* 26

HUNGARIAN

Andre's | *Baked Gds.* 24

Hungarian Pastry | *Baked Gds.* 23

Yorkville Meat | *Meat/Poultry* -

INDIAN

Foods/India | *Herbs/Spices* — 23
House/Spices | *Herbs/Spices* — 26
🅩 Kalustyan's | *Spec. Shop* — 27
Patel Bros. | *Spec. Shop* — 22
Spice Corner | *Herbs/Spices* — 23

ISRAELI

NEW Zucker Bakery | *Baked Gds.* — 24

ITALIAN

🅩 Addeo Bakery | *Baked Gds.* — 28
Agata/Valentina | *Maj. Market* — 25
Alessi | *Cookware* — 26
🅩 Alleva Dairy | *Cheese/Dairy* — 28
NEW Amorino | *Ice Cream* — 25
Ann Clair's Salum. | *Deli* — 25
Arthur Ave. | *Caterer* — 23
Artuso Pastry | *Baked Gds.* — 24
Barbarini | *Prepared* — 25
Bari Pork | *Meat/Poultry* — 26
Belfiore Meats | *Meat/Poultry* — 25
🅩 Biancardi Meats | *Meat/Poultry* — 28
Bis.Co.Latte | *Baked Gds.* — 24
Bomboloni | *Baked Gds.* — 22
🅩 Borgatti's | *Pasta* — 29
Brooklyn Cupcake | *Baked Gds.* — 27
Bruno/Pasticceria | *Baked Gds.* — 24
Bruno Ravioli | *Pasta* — 21
BuonItalia | *Spec. Shop* — 26
Caffé Roma | *Baked Gds.* — 22
🅩 Calabria Pork | *Meat/Poultry* — 27
Calandra Cheese | *Cheese/Dairy* — 27
Calvisius Caviar | *Caviar/Smoked Fish* — 29
🅩 Caputo | *Baked Gds.* — 27
🅩 Casa Della | *Cheese/Dairy* — 29
Cassinelli Food | *Pasta* — 29
Ceriello | *Spec. Shop* — 24
Ciao Bella | *Ice Cream* — 26
Cipriani | *Baked Gds.* — 26
🅩 Coluccio/Sons | *Spec. Shop* — 27
Cosenza's Fish | *Seafood* — 25
Court Pastry | *Baked Gds.* — 26
Crespella | *Baked Gds.* — –
Cucina Vivolo | *Prepared* — 22

🅩 D'Amico | *Coffee/Tea* — 27
Delillo Pastry | *Baked Gds.* — 25
De Robertis | *Baked Gds.* — 23
🅩 Di Palo Dairy | *Cheese/Dairy* — 29
NEW Dolce Vizio | *Baked Gds.* — 25
Durso's Pasta | *Pasta* — 26
🅩 Eataly | *Maj. Market* — 27
Egidio Pastry | *Baked Gds.* — 25
🅩 Enoteca Di Palo | *Wine/Liquor* — 27
🅩 Esposito/Sons Pork | *Meat/Poultry* — 27
🅩 Esposito Meat | *Meat/Poultry* — 27
Faicco's Pork | *Meat/Poultry* — 28
Fay Da | *Baked Gds.* — 20
Ferrara Bakery | *Baked Gds.* — 22
🅩 Florence Meat | *Meat/Poultry* — 29
F. Monteleone | *Baked Gds.* — 29
🅩 Fortunato | *Baked Gds.* — 27
Grandaisy | *Baked Gds.* — 25
Grom | *Ice Cream* — 26
Gustiamo | *Spec. Shop* — –
Iavarone Bros. | *Prepared* — 26
NEW Il Buco Alimentari | *Spec. Shop* — 25
Il Cantuccio | *Baked Gds.* — 26
🅩 Il Laboratorio | *Ice Cream* — 28
🅩 Italian Wine | *Wine/Liquor* — 29
🅩 Joe's Dairy | *Cheese/Dairy* — 28
NEW La Cremeria | *Ice Cream* — 22
La Guli | *Baked Gds.* — 27
Lamarca | *Prepared* — 26
L'Arte/Gelato | *Ice Cream* — 25
Led Zeppole | *Baked Gds.* — 22
🅩 Lemon Ice | *Ice Cream* — 26
🅩 Lioni Fresh Mozz. | *Cheese/Dairy* — 27
Locanda Verde | *Baked Gds.* — 26
Los Paisanos | *Meat/Poultry* — 26
Madonia Bakery | *Baked Gds.* — 26
Mangia | *Prepared* — 23
Mazzola Bakery | *Baked Gds.* — 27
🅩 Mona Lisa | *Baked Gds.* — 24
Mount Carmel | *Wine/Liquor* — 24
Napoli | *Baked Gds.* — 28
Obika | *Cheese/Dairy* — 27

Ottomanelli/Sons | *Meat/Poultry* — 28
Ottomanelli's Meats | *Meat/Poultry* — 28
Paneantico | *Baked Gds.* — 26
Pastosa Ravioli | *Pasta* — 27
Piemonte Ravioli | *Pasta* — 27
Pino Meats | *Meat/Poultry* — 29
Queen Ann | *Pasta* — 25
Raffetto's | *Pasta* — 28
Ralph's/Ices | *Ice Cream* — 25
Randazzo's | *Seafood* — 26
Rocco's Pastry | *Baked Gds.* — 25
Royal Crown | *Baked Gds.* — 26
Russo Mozz. | *Cheese/Dairy* — 26
Sal/Dom's | *Baked Gds.* — 28
Salumeria Biellese | *Deli* — 26
Salumeria Rosi | *Spec. Shop* — 28
Sant Ambroeus | *Ice Cream* — 26
Sullivan St. Bakery | *Baked Gds.* — 27
Tarallucci/Vino | *Baked Gds.* — 24
Teitel Bros. | *Spec. Shop* — 27
Terrace Bagels | *Bagels* — 25
Terranova | *Baked Gds.* — 28
Todaro Bros. | *Spec. Shop* — 25
United Meat | *Meat/Poultry* — 26
Veniero's | *Baked Gds.* — 25
Villabate | *Baked Gds.* — 27
Vincent's Meat | *Meat/Poultry* — 29

JAPANESE

H Mart | *Spec. Shop* — 22
Japanese Culinary Ctr. | *Cookware* — 24
Japan Premium Beef | *Meat* — 29
Katagiri | *Spec. Shop* — 23
Korin | *Cookware* — 29
Landmark Wine | *Wine/Liquor* — 24
Minamoto | *Candy/Nuts* — 29
Panya | *Baked Gds.* — 21
Sakaya | *Wine/Liquor* — 28
Sunrise Mart | *Spec. Shop* — 23
Takahachi | *Baked Gds.* — 23

JEWISH

Acme Fish | *Caviar/Smoked Fish* — 25
Bagels/Co. | *Bagels* — 21

Bagel Store | *Bagels* — 24
Barney Greengrass | *Caviar/Smoked Fish* — 27
Ben's Best | *Deli* — 25
Ben's Kosher | *Deli* — 22
Carnegie Deli | *Deli* — 23
Eli's Bread | *Baked Gds.* — 26
Fischer Bros. | *Meat/Poultry* — 24
Foremost RAM Caterers | *Caterer* — 23
Jay/Lloyd's Kosher | *Deli* — 22
Katz's Deli | *Deli* — 25
Kosher Bagel | *Bagels* — 27
Kossar's | *Bagels* — 26
Liebman's | *Deli* — 24
Mauzone | *Caterer* — 21
Mill Basin Kosher | *Deli* — 24
Moishe's | *Baked Gds.* — 23
Mother's Bake | *Baked Gds.* — 20
Murray's Sturgeon | *Caviar/Smoked Fish* — 28
Orwasher's | *Baked Gds.* — 26
Park E. Kosher | *Meat/Poultry* — 24
Pastrami Queen | *Deli* — 22
Pickle Guys | *Spec. Shop* — 27
Pomegranate | *Spec. Shop* — 26
Russ/Daughters | *Caviar/Smoked Fish* — 29
Sarge's Deli | *Deli* — 22
Schick's | *Baked Gds.* — 23
NEW Shelsky's Smoked Fish | *Caviar/Smoked Fish* — 24
Simply Divine | *Caterer* — -
Streit's Matzo | *Baked Gds.* — 27
Yonah Schimmel | *Baked Gds.* — 24
Zucker's Bagels | *Bagels* — 22

KOREAN

H Mart | *Spec. Shop* — 22
Koryodang | *Baked Gds.* — 22

MEDITERRANEAN

Artopolis | *Baked Gds.* — 27
Balady Foods | *Spec. Shop* — -
Cucina | *Prepared* — 22
Internat'l Grocery | *Spec. Shop* — 24
Mangia | *Prepared* — 23

Melange | *Prepared* 23
O&CO. | *Spec. Shop* 27
Todaro Bros. | *Spec. Shop* 25
Zeytuna | *Maj. Market* 20

MEXICAN

La Newyorkina | *Ice Cream* ‒
Las Palomas | *Spec. Shop* ‒

MIDDLE EASTERN

Balady Foods | *Spec. Shop* ‒
Damascus | *Baked Gds.* 26
Ⓩ D'Vine | *Spec. Shop* 26
Family Store | *Spec. Shop* 24
Ⓩ Kalustyan's | *Spec. Shop* 27
Market | *Spec. Shop* 24
Ⓩ Sahadi's | *Spec. Shop* 28

POLISH

Eagle Provisions | *Meat/Poultry* 23
East Vill. Meat | *Meat/Poultry* 26
Jubilat Provisions | *Meat/Poultry* ‒

RUSSIAN

Caviar Russe | *Caviar* 26
M & I | *Spec. Shop* 22
Petrossian | *Caviar/Smoked Fish* 27

SCANDINAVIAN

AQ Kafé | *Baked Gds.* 23
Nordic Delicacies | *Spec. Shop* 28

SOUTHERN/ SOUL FOOD

Blue Smoke | *Baked Gds.* 25
Cake Man | *Baked Gds.* 24
Carolina Country | *Spec. Shop* ‒
Donna Bell's | *Baked Gds.* 24

Make My Cake | *Baked Gds.* 26
Miss Mamie's/Maude's | *Caterer* 20

SPANISH

Ⓩ Despaña | *Spec. Shop* 27
Despaña Vinos | *Wine/Liquor* 29
Tinto Fino | *Wine/Liquor* 25

SWISS

Lindt | *Candy/Nuts* 25
Neuchatel Choc. | *Candy/Nuts* 28
Ⓩ Teuscher Choc. | *Candy/Nuts* 29

THAI

Asia Mkt. | *Spec. Shop* 20
Bangkok Grocery | *Spec. Shop* 24

TURKISH

Güllüoglu | *Baked Gds.* 23

UKRAINIAN

East Vill. Meat | *Meat/Poultry* 26

VEGETARIAN

(Most prepared food shops and
health food stores offer vegetarian
options, including these standouts)
A Matter/Health | *Health* 23
NEW Blossom Bakery | *Baked Gds.* 26
City Bakery | *Baked Gds.* 25
Fairway | *Maj. Market* 25
Family Health Foods | *Health* 22
Gary Null's | *Health* 20
Integral Yoga | *Health* 23
LifeThyme Mkt. | *Health* 22
One Lucky Duck | *Health* 25
Silver Moon | *Baked Gds.* 26
NEW Soft Serve Fruit | *Ice Cream* 23

Locations

Includes source names, categories and Quality ratings.

Manhattan

CHELSEA

(26th to 30th Sts., west of 5th; 14th to 26th Sts., west of 6th)

Abigail Kirsch | *Caterer* — 26
Amy's Bread | *Baked Gds.* — 26
Appellation | *Wine/Liquor* — 26
Ariston | *Flowers* — 26
Baconery | *Baked Gds.* — 25
Billy's Bakery | *Baked Gds.* — 24
NEW Blossom Bakery | *Baked Gds.* — 26
Bowery Kitchen | *Cookware* — 23
BuonItalia | *Spec. Shop* — 26
☑ Burgundy | *Wine/Liquor* — 28
Chelsea Baskets | *Spec. Shop* — 23
Chelsea Wine | *Wine/Liquor* — 24
Cleaver Co. | *Caterer/Events* — 27
☑ Dickson's Farmstand | *Meat/Poultry* — 28
Donut Pub | *Baked Gds.* — 22
Doughnut Plant | *Baked Gds.* — 27
Eleni's Cookies | *Baked Gds.* — 22
Elm Health | *Health* — 24
Empire Cake | *Baked Gds.* — 26
Fat Witch | *Baked Gds.* — 24
Filling Station | *Specialty Shop* — 25
Foragers City Grocer | *Maj. Market* — 26
Garden/Eden | *Maj. Market* — 23
☑ Gramercy Park Flower | *Flowers* — 27
☑ Jacques Torres | *Candy/Nuts* — 28
Jonathan Flowers | *Flowers* — –
La Bergamote | *Baked Gds.* — 26
La Maison/Macaron | *Baked Gds.* — 28
Landmark Wine | *Wine/Liquor* — 24
L'Arte/Gelato | *Ice Cream* — 25
☑ Lobster Pl. | *Seafood* — 27
L'Olivier | *Flowers* — 27
Lucy's Whey | *Cheese/Dairy* — 29
Manhattan Fruit Ex. | *Produce* — 25
Murray's Bagels | *Bagels* — 26
Nut Box | *Candy/Nuts* — 24

One Lucky Duck | *Health* — 25
Party Rental | *Party Rent.* — 22
People's Pops | *Ice Cream* — 26
pinkberry | *Ice Cream* — 22
Raquel Corvino | *Flowers* — –
Red Mango | *Ice Cream* — 22
Ronnybrook | *Cheese/Dairy* — 26
Ruthy's Bakery | *Baked Gds.* — 20
Salumeria Biellese | *Deli* — 26
Sarabeth's | *Baked Gds.* — 24
Spruce | *Flowers* — –
Three Tarts | *Baked Gds.* — 26
Trader Joe's | *Maj. Market* — 23
☑ Union Sq. Events | *Caterer/Events* — 26
Westside Mkt. | *Maj. Market* — 21
Whole Foods | *Maj. Market* — 25
☑ Williams-Sonoma | *Cookware* — 27

CHINATOWN

(Canal to Pearl Sts., east of B'way)

Aji Ichiban | *Candy/Nuts* — 22
Asia Mkt. | *Spec. Shop* — 20
Bangkok Grocery | *Spec. Shop* — 24
Bayard St. Meat | *Meat/Poultry* — 21
Chinatown Ice Cream | *Ice Cream* — 24
Deluxe Food | *Spec. Shop* — 23
Dragonland Bakery | *Baked Gds.* — 25
Fay Da | *Baked Gds.* — 20
Hong Kong | *Spec. Shop* — 19
Kam Man | *Spec. Shop* — 21
Lung Moon | *Baked Gds.* — 20
Malaysia Beef Jerky | *Meat/Poultry* — 25
Super Wang Bakery | *Baked Gds.* — 21
Tai Pan Bakery | *Baked Gds.* — 21
Ten Ren Tea | *Coffee/Tea* — 25
Won Chuen | *Seafood* — 22

EAST 40s

Amish Mkt. | *Maj. Market* — 22
Ariston | *Flowers* — 26
Baked/Melissa | *Baked Gds.* — 24

Beekman Liquors | *Wine/Liquor* 24
NEW Beer Table Pantry | *Beer* 26
Big Apple Florist | *Flowers* 27
Ceriello | *Spec. Shop* 24
Charbonnel/Walker | *Candy/Nuts* 23
Choux Factory | *Baked Gds.* 23
Ciao Bella | *Ice Cream* 26
Cipriani | *Baked Gds.* 26
Cucina | *Prepared* 22
Dahlia | *Flowers* 25
Dishes | *Prepared* 24
Eli's Bread | *Baked Gds.* 26
Fifth Ave. Choc. | *Candy/Nuts* 25
Financier Patisserie | *Baked Gds.* 25
Godiva | *Candy/Nuts* 23
Grande Harvest | *Wine/Liquor* 22
Greenwich Produce | *Produce* 28
Health Nuts | *Health* 22
Japanese Culinary Ctr. | *Cookware* 24
Junior's | *Baked Gds.* 21
Le Pain Quotidien | *Baked Gds.* 23
Li-Lac Choc. | *Candy/Nuts* 26
Magnolia Bakery | *Baked Gds.* 21
Mangia | *Prepared* 23
Z Murray's Cheese | *Cheese/Dairy* 29
Neuhaus Choc. | *Candy/Nuts* 26
O&CO. | *Spec. Shop* 27
Oren's Roast | *Coffee/Tea* 24
Z Park Ave. Liquor | *Wine/Liquor* 27
Pescatore | *Seafood* 25
Red Mango | *Ice Cream* 22
Screme | *Ice Cream* 24
NEW Spices/Tease | *Herbs/Spices* 25
Steve's/Ice Cream | *Ice Cream* 22
Sunrise Mart | *Spec. Shop* 23
Z Teuscher Choc. | *Candy/Nuts* 29
Wild Edibles | *Seafood* 24

EAST 50s

Ambassador Wine | *Wine/Liquor* 25
Z Bloom | *Flowers* 27
Bloomingdale's | *Cookware* 25
Buttercup | *Baked Gds.* 22
Calvisius Caviar | 29
   Caviar/Smoked Fish

Caviar Russe | *Caviar* 26
Crumbs | *Baked Gds.* 22
Z Crush Wine | *Wine/Liquor* 27
Cucina Vivolo | *Prepared* 22
David Burke | *Caterer/Events* 21
Dishes | *Prepared* 24
Ess-a-Bagel | *Bagels* 26
Financier Patisserie | *Baked Gds.* 25
Floralies | *Flowers* -
Forty Carrots | *Ice Cream* 22
Godiva | *Candy/Nuts* 23
Güllüoglu | *Baked Gds.* 23
Ideal Cheese | *Cheese/Dairy* 27
Jane Packer | *Flowers* -
Katagiri | *Spec. Shop* 23
Leonidas | *Candy/Nuts* 26
Lindt | *Candy/Nuts* 25
Macaron Café | *Baked Gds.* 24
Magnolia Bakery | *Baked Gds.* 21
Martine's Choc. | *Candy/Nuts* 25
Neuchatel Choc. | *Candy/Nuts* 28
Neuhaus Choc. | *Candy/Nuts* 26
Oren's Roast | *Coffee/Tea* 24
pinkberry | *Ice Cream* 22
Z Pisacane | *Seafood* 28
Renny/Reed | *Flowers* -
Z Sherry-Lehmann | *Wine/Liquor* 29
Z Simchick | *Meat/Poultry* 29
Sutton Wine | *Wine/Liquor* 22
Tal Bagels | *Bagels* 22
Z Williams-Sonoma | *Cookware* 27
Z Zezé | *Flowers* 27

EAST 60s

Alessi | *Cookware* 26
Alice's Tea/Wonderland | 22
   Coffee/Tea
Bagelworks | *Bagels* 26
Berrywild | *Ice Cream* 21
Cork & Bottle | *Wine/Liquor* 23
NEW DavidsTea | *Coffee/Tea* 28
Z Dylan's Candy | *Candy/Nuts* 23
Fellan Florist | *Flowers* 24
Garnet Wines | *Wine/Liquor* 26
Godiva | *Candy/Nuts* 23

Gourmet Garage | *Maj. Market* 20
Health Nuts | *Health* 22
Kusmi Tea | *Coffee/Tea* 26
Le Pain Quotidien | *Baked Gds.* 23
Melange | *Prepared* 23
Mitchel London | *Prepared* 25
Z Nespresso | *Coffee/Tea* 27
Plaza Florists | *Flowers* -
Rosa Rosa | *Flowers* 24
NEW Sprinkles | *Baked Gds.* 26
Z Tastings/Payard | *Caterer/Events* 25
Tea/Honey | *Coffee/Tea* 29
Z Teuscher Choc. | *Candy/Nuts* 29

NEW Soft Serve Fruit | *Ice Cream* 23
Z Sur La Table | *Cookware* 27
Trader Joe's | *Maj. Market* 23
Z William Poll | *Prepared* 26
Windsor Florist | *Flowers* 24

EAST 80s

Alice's Tea/Wonderland | *Coffee/Tea* 22
Andre's | *Baked Gds.* 24
Annie's | *Produce* 20
Bagel Bob's | *Bagels* 23
Choco Bolo | *Baked Gds.* 21
Choux Factory | *Baked Gds.* 23
Dean/DeLuca | *Maj. Market* 26
Dorian's Seafood | *Seafood* 26
E.A.T. | *Prepared* 24
Eli's Manhattan | *Maj. Market* 25
Emack/Bolio | *Ice Cream* 25
Fairway | *Maj. Market* 25
Glaser's Bake | *Baked Gds.* 24
H & H Midtown | *Bagels* 25
Insomnia Cookies | *Baked Gds.* 22
Little Brown | *Baked Gds.* 21
Z Lobel's Meats | *Meat/Poultry* 28
Z Lorenzo/Maria's | *Prepared* 27
Martine's Choc. | *Candy/Nuts* 25
Mister Wright | *Wine/Liquor* 25
Natural Frontier | *Health* 22
Nature's Gifts | *Spec. Shop* 19
Oren's Roast | *Coffee/Tea* 24
Park E. Kosher | *Meat/Poultry* 24
Z Pickles/Olives | *Spec. Shop* 25
pinkberry | *Ice Cream* 22
Premier Cru | *Wine/Liquor* 25
Rosenthal Wine | *Wine/Liquor* 29
Z Schaller/Weber | *Meat/Poultry* 28
16 Handles | *Ice Cream* 24
Tal Bagels | *Bagels* 22
Two/Red Hens | *Baked Gds.* 26
Z Vosges | *Candy/Nuts* 27
William Greenberg | *Baked Gds.* 25
Z Williams-Sonoma | *Cookware* 27
Yorkshire Wines | *Wine/Liquor* 24
Yorkville Meat | *Meat/Poultry* -

EAST 70s

Agata/Valentina | *Maj. Market* 25
A Matter/Health | *Health* 23
Bagels/Co. | *Bagels* 21
Butterfield/Baked | *Spec. Shop* 25
Citarella | *Maj. Market* 26
Corrado | *Baked Gds.* 22
Crumbs | *Baked Gds.* 22
Cucina Vivolo | *Prepared* 22
East Side Bagel | *Bagels* 21
Glorious Food | *Caterer* 26
Grace's Market | *Maj. Market* 25
Gracious Home | *Cookware* 26
In Vino | *Wine/Liquor* 22
Z Lady M | *Baked Gds.* 29
Z La Maison/Choc. | *Candy/Nuts* 29
Leonard's Market | *Seafood* 26
Le Pain Quotidien | *Baked Gds.* 23
L'Olivier | *Flowers* 27
Z NEW Maison Ladurée | *Baked Gds.* 28
Marché Madison | *Prepared* 21
McCabes Wines | *Wine/Liquor* 22
#1 Farmers Mkt. | *Produce* 23
Oren's Roast | *Coffee/Tea* 24
Orwasher's | *Baked Gds.* 26
Pastrami Queen | *Deli* 22
Pick/Bagel | *Bagels* 21
Z Sable's | *Caviar/Smoked Fish* 27
Sant Ambroeus | *Ice Cream* 26

EAST 90s & 100s

(90th to 110th Sts.)

Ciao Bella	Ice Cream	26
Corner Café	Baked Goods	23
Corrado	Baked Gds.	22
David Ziff	Caterer	-
Eleni's Cookies	Baked Gds.	22
Eli's Vinegar	Maj. Market	24
Gourmet Garage	Maj. Market	20
Jerome Florists	Flowers	24
K & D Wines	Wine/Liquor	26
Lloyd's Carrot Cake	Baked Gds.	29
NEW London Candy Co.	Candy	25
Ronaldo Maia	Flowers	24
Sarabeth's	Baked Gds.	24
S. Feldman	Cookware	26
Vinyl Wine	Wine/Liquor	-
Yura/Madison	Baked Gds.	24

EAST VILLAGE

(14th to Houston Sts.,
east of B'way, excluding NoHo)

Barnyard Cheese	Cheese/Dairy	26
Big Gay Ice Cream	Ice Cream	27
Birdbath	Baked Gds.	23
Z Black Hound	Baked Gds.	26
Blue Meadow	Flowers	-
Bond St. Choc.	Candy/Nuts	27
Butter Lane Cupcakes	Baked Gds.	25
ChikaLicious	Baked Gds.	25
Commodities	Health	25
De Robertis	Baked Gds.	23
East Vill. Cheese	Cheese/Dairy	23
East Vill. Meat	Meat/Poultry	26
East Village Wines	Wine/Liquor	26
Edible Arrange	Caterer	22
Good Beer	Beer	27
Led Zeppole	Baked Gds.	22
LMD Floral	Flowers	-
Moishe's	Baked Gds.	23
Momofuku Milk Bar	Baked Gds.	25
Z NYC Icy	Ice Cream	29
Panya	Baked Gds.	21
pinkberry	Ice Cream	22
Z Porto Rico	Coffee/Tea	27
NEW Puddin' by Clio	Baked Gds.	29

Russo Mozz.	Cheese/Dairy	26
Sakaya	Wine/Liquor	28
Sigmund Pretzel	Baked Gds.	26
16 Handles	Ice Cream	24
Stogo	Ice Cream	25
Sundaes/Cones	Ice Cream	25
Sunrise Mart	Spec. Shop	23
Tarallucci/Vino	Baked Gds.	24
Tinto Fino	Wine/Liquor	25
NEW Tompkins Sq. Bagels	Bagels	25
Tu-Lu's GF	Baked Gds.	25
Z Van Leeuwen	Ice Cream	26
Veniero's	Baked Gds.	25
NEW Zucker Bakery	Baked Gds.	24

FINANCIAL DISTRICT

(South of Murray St.)

Amish Mkt.	Maj. Market	22
Aunt Butchie's	Baked Gds.	26
Barbarini	Prepared	25
Battery Place Mkt.	Major Mkt.	27
Z Bloom	Flowers	27
Blue Smoke	Baked Gds.	25
California Wine	Wine/Liquor	24
Crumbs	Baked Gds.	22
Financier Patisserie	Baked Gds.	25
Flowers/World	Flowers	26
FPB	Baked Gds.	27
Fulton Stall Mkt.	Produce	25
Godiva	Candy/Nuts	23
Z La Maison/Choc.	Candy/Nuts	29
Leonidas	Candy/Nuts	26
Leo's Bagels	Bagels	24
New York/Exchange	Wine/Liquor	25
Pick/Bagel	Bagels	21
Red Mango	Ice Cream	22
Takahachi	Baked Gds.	23
Zeytuna	Maj. Market	20

FLATIRON

(14th to 26th Sts., 6th Ave. to Park
Ave. S., excluding Union Sq.)

Baked/Melissa	Baked Gds.	24
NEW Beecher's Cheese		27
Cheese/Dairy		
Belle Fleur	Flowers	28

🆉 Bottlerocket | *Wine/Liquor* 25

City Bakery | *Baked Gds.* 25

🆉 Eataly | *Maj. Market* 27

Financier Patisserie | *Baked Gds.* 25

Florisity | *Flowers* -

🆉 L.A. Burdick Handmade 28
   Chocolates | *Candy/Nuts*

Mangia | *Prepared* 23

🆉 Moore Bros. | *Wine/Liquor* 28

New York Cake | *Cookware* 25

Spoon | *Caterer* 25

Tarallucci/Vino | *Baked Gds.* 24

GARMENT DISTRICT

(30th to 40th Sts., west of 5th)

Antony Todd | *Events/Flowers* -

🆉 Artisanal | *Cheese/Dairy* 27

Ben/Jerry's | *Ice Cream* 24

Ben's Kosher | *Deli* 22

Catering/Rest. Assoc. | *Caterer* 21

Classic Party | *Party Rent.* -

Cucina | *Prepared* 22

Edible Arrange | *Caterer* 22

🆉 Esposito Meat | *Meat/Poultry* 27

Fay Da | *Baked Gds.* 20

H Mart | *Spec. Shop* 22

Indiana Mkt. | *Caterer* -

Jes Gordon/Proper Fun | *Flowers* -

Koryodang | *Baked Gds.* 22

Macaron Café | *Baked Gds.* 24

Macy's Cellar | *Cookware* 23

Mangia | *Prepared* 23

Penn Wine/Spirits | *Wine/Liquor* 26

pinkberry | *Ice Cream* 22

Props/Today | *Party Rent.* 20

Rebecca Cole | *Flowers* -

Red Mango | *Ice Cream* 22

Sarabeth's | *Baked Gds.* 24

16 Handles | *Ice Cream* 24

🆕 Sweetery | *Baked Gds.* 23

GRAMERCY PARK

(14th to 23rd Sts., east of Park Ave. S.)

Bruno Ravioli | *Pasta* 21

David's Bagels | *Bagels* 25

Ess-a-Bagel | *Bagels* 26

First Ave. Wines | *Wine/Liquor* 22

🆉 Gramercy Park Flower | *Flowers* 27

Lamarca | *Prepared* 26

Natural Frontier | *Health* 22

One Lucky Duck | *Health* 25

Pick/Bagel | *Bagels* 21

Robbins Wolfe | *Caterer* -

GREENWICH VILLAGE

(Houston to 14th Sts., west of
B'way, east of 6th Ave.)

🆕 Amorino | *Ice Cream* 25

Bagel Bob's | *Bagels* 23

Broadway Pan. | *Cookware* 26

Bruno/Pasticceria | *Baked Gds.* 24

Citarella | *Maj. Market* 26

Crumbs | *Baked Gds.* 22

FPB | *Baked Gds.* 27

Glazier Group | *Caterer* -

Insomnia Cookies | *Baked Gds.* 22

LifeThyme Mkt. | *Health* 22

Max Brenner | *Candy/Nuts* 22

🆕 Mille-Feuille | *Baked Gds.* 25

Murray's Bagels | *Bagels* 26

Nut Box | *Candy/Nuts* 24

Oren's Roast | *Coffee/Tea* 24

🆉 Porto Rico | *Coffee/Tea* 27

🆉 Raffetto's | *Pasta* 28

16 Handles | *Ice Cream* 24

The Upper Crust | *Caterer/Events* 21

Warehouse Wines | *Wine/Liquor* 25

HARLEM/
EAST HARLEM

(110th to 155th Sts., excluding
Columbia U. area)

Best Yet Mkt. | *Spec. Shop* 23

Costco | *Maj. Market* 23

Edible Arrange | *Caterer* 22

Fairway | *Maj. Market* 25

Gracious Thyme | *Caterer* -

Harlem Vintage | *Wine/Liquor* 27

Katrina Parris | *Flowers* -

🆉 Levain Bakery | *Baked Gds.* 28

Make My Cake | *Baked Gds.* 26

Miss Mamie's/Maude's | *Caterer* 20

HUDSON SQUARE

(Canal to Houston Sts.,
west of 6th Ave.)

Z Great Performances | *Caterer* 26

Z Jacques Torres | *Candy/Nuts* 28

LITTLE ITALY

(Canal to Kenmare Sts.,
Bowery to Lafayette St.)

Z Alleva Dairy | *Cheese/Dairy* 28

Bayard St. Meat | *Meat/Poultry* 21

Caffé Roma | *Baked Gds.* 22

Ceci-Cela | *Baked Gds.* 26

Z Despaña | *Spec. Shop* 27

Despaña Vinos | *Wine/Liquor* 29

Z Di Palo Dairy | *Cheese/Dairy* 29

Z Enoteca Di Palo | *Wine/Liquor* 27

Ferrara Bakery | *Baked Gds.* 22

NEW La Cremeria | *Ice Cream* 22

Papabubble | *Candy/Nuts* 23

Z Piemonte Ravioli | *Pasta* 27

Puro Chile/Wine | *Spec. Shop* ─

LOWER EAST SIDE

(Houston to Canal Sts.,
east of Bowery)

BabyCakes | *Baked Gds.* 24

Bari Equipment | *Cookware* ─

Birdbath | *Baked Gds.* 23

Bisous, Ciao | *Baked Gds.* 25

Bowery/Vine | *Wine/Liquor* 22

Cathcart/Reddy | *Baked Gds.* 25

NEW Christian Vautier Le ─
Concept | *Candy/Nuts*

Clinton St. Baking | *Baked Gds.* 26

Cocoa Bar | *Candy/Nuts* 21

Doughnut Plant | *Baked Gds.* 27

Economy Candy | *Candy/Nuts* 25

Elizabeth Ryan | *Flowers* ─

Z Formaggio | *Cheese/Dairy* 27

NEW Heritage Meat Shop | 27
Meat/Poultry

Hester Street Fair | *Spec. Items* 21

Z Il Laboratorio | *Ice Cream* 28

Katz's Deli | *Deli* 25

Z Kossar's | *Bagels* 26

Neuman's | *Caterer* ─

New Beer | *Beer* 26

Pain D'Avignon | *Baked Gds.* 24

Z Pickle Guys | *Spec. Shop* 27

Z Porto Rico | *Coffee/Tea* 27

Red Mango | *Ice Cream* 22

Rick's Picks | *Spec. Shop* 26

Roni-Sue's | *Candy/Nuts* 24

Z Russ/Daughters | 29
Caviar/Smoked Fish

Z Saxelby Cheese | *Cheese/Dairy* 29

Streit's Matzo | *Baked Gds.* 27

Sugar Sweet | *Baked Gds.* 26

Sweet Life | *Candy/Nuts* 27

Whole Foods | *Maj. Market* 25

Yonah Schimmel | *Baked Gds.* 24

MEATPACKING

(Gansevoort to 15th Sts.,
west of 9th Ave.)

Banchet Flowers | *Flowers* 26

MURRAY HILL

(26th to 40th Sts., east of 5th; 23rd to
26th Sts., east of Park Ave. S.)

Z Artisanal | *Cheese/Dairy* 27

Berrywild | *Ice Cream* 21

Blue Smoke | *Baked Gds.* 25

Crumbs | *Baked Gds.* 22

Daniel's Bagels | *Bagels* 24

Foods/India | *Herbs/Spices* 23

Insomnia Cookies | *Baked Gds.* 22

Z J.B. Prince | *Cookware* 29

Z Kalustyan's | *Spec. Shop* 27

Lamazou | *Cheese/Dairy* 26

Les Halles | *Meat/Poultry* 23

Z Manhattan Fruitier | *Spec. Shop* 25

Oren's Roast | *Coffee/Tea* 24

pinkberry | *Ice Cream* 22

Ralph's/Ices | *Ice Cream* 25

Sarge's Deli | *Deli* 22

Spice Corner | *Herbs/Spices* 23

Todaro Bros. | *Spec. Shop* 25

Wild Edibles | *Seafood* 24

NOHO

(Houston to 4th Sts.,
Bowery to B'way)

Astor Wines | *Wine/Liquor* 26

Financier Patisserie | *Baked Gds.* 25

NEW Il Buco Alimentari | *Spec. Shop* — 25

Japan Premium Beef | *Meat* — 29

Le Pain Quotidien | *Baked Gds.* — 23

NOLITA

(Houston to Kenmare Sts.,
Bowery to Lafayette St.)

Billy's Bakery | *Baked Gds.* — 24

Castle/Pierpont | *Flowers* — ⁻

Choco Bolo | *Baked Gds.* — 21

Ciao Bella | *Ice Cream* — 26

Eileen's Cheesecake | *Baked Gds.* — 25

Little Cupcake | *Baked Gds.* — 23

pinkberry | *Ice Cream* — 22

Rice/Riches | *Baked Gds.* — 24

SOHO

(Canal to Houston Sts.,
west of Lafayette St.)

Alessi | *Cookware* — 26

Baked/Melissa | *Baked Gds.* — 24

Z Balthazar Bakery | *Baked Gds.* — 27

Birdbath | *Baked Gds.* — 23

Broadway Party | *Party Rent.* — ⁻

Colin Cowie | *Events* — ⁻

Dean/DeLuca | *Maj. Market* — 26

NEW Dominique Ansel | *Baked Gds.* — 27

Emack/Bolio | *Ice Cream* — 25

Gourmet Garage | *Maj. Market* — 20

Grandaisy | *Baked Gds.* — 25

Harney & Sons | *Coffee/Tea* — 28

In Pursuit of Tea | *Coffee/Tea* — 28

Z Joe's Dairy | *Cheese/Dairy* — 28

Z Kee's Choc. | *Candy/Nuts* — 28

Le Pain Quotidien | *Baked Gds.* — 23

MarieBelle's | *Candy/Nuts* — 26

Z Nespresso | *Coffee/Tea* — 27

Once Upon/Tart | *Baked Gds.* — 25

Pino Meats | *Meat/Poultry* — 29

Ron Ben-Israel | *Baked Gds.* — 27

Sunrise Mart | *Spec. Shop* — 23

Z Sur La Table | *Cookware* — 27

Z Vosges | *Candy/Nuts* — 27

NEW Xocolatti | *Candy/Nuts* — 22

SOUTH STREET SEAPORT

Glazier Group | *Caterer* — ⁻

Z New Amsterdam Mkt. | *Spec. Shop* — 28

TRIBECA

(Canal to Murray Sts.,
west of B'way)

Bell Bates | *Health* — 24

Billy's Bakery | *Baked Gds.* — 24

Birdbath | *Baked Gds.* — 23

Z Chambers Wines | *Wine/Liquor* — 27

Chestnuts | *Flowers* — ⁻

DeJuan Stroud | *Flowers* — ⁻

Duane Pk. | *Baked Gds.* — 25

Grandaisy | *Baked Gds.* — 25

Z Korin | *Cookware* — 29

Locanda Verde | *Baked Gds.* — 26

New York Vintners | *Wine/Liquor* — 28

Olivier Cheng | *Caterer* — ⁻

Sarabeth's | *Baked Gds.* — 24

Z Sylvia Weinstock | *Baked Gds.* — 29

Tribeca Treats | *Baked Gds.* — 21

Whole Foods | *Maj. Market* — 25

Zucker's Bagels | *Bagels* — 22

UNION SQUARE

(14th to 17th Sts., 5th Ave.
to Union Sq. E.)

Garden/Eden | *Maj. Market* — 23

Z Italian Wine | *Wine/Liquor* — 29

NEW Soft Serve Fruit | *Ice Cream* — 23

Trader Joe's | *Maj. Market* — 23

Trader Joe's Wine | *Wine/Liquor* — 23

Union Sq. Wines | *Wine/Liquor* — 25

Whole Foods | *Maj. Market* — 25

Alice's Tea/Wonderland | *Coffee/Tea* — 22

WASHINGTON HTS./ INWOOD

(North of W. 155th St.)

Carrot Top | *Baked Gds.* — 23

Z PJ Wine | *Wine/Liquor* — 27

WEST 40s

Amish Mkt. | *Maj. Market* — 22

Amy's Bread | *Baked Gds.* — 26

Ben/Jerry's | *Ice Cream*	24
Bis.Co.Latte | *Baked Gds.*	24
☑ Bouchon Bakery | *Baked Gds.*	27
Chocolat Michel | *Candy/Nuts*	27
Crumbs | *Baked Gds.*	22
Cucina | *Prepared*	22
Cupcake Cafe | *Baked Gds.*	24
Dahlia | *Flowers*	25
Donna Bell's | *Baked Gds.*	24
Empire Coffee | *Coffee/Tea*	24
Financier Patisserie | *Baked Gds.*	25
Godiva | *Candy/Nuts*	23
Good/Plenty | *Prepared*	21
Hershey's | *Candy/Nuts*	21
Internat'l Grocery | *Spec. Shop*	24
☑ Jacques Torres | *Candy/Nuts*	28
Junior's | *Baked Gds.*	21
☑ Kee's Choc. | *Candy/Nuts*	28
☑ La Maison/Choc. | *Candy/Nuts*	29
Le Marais | *Meat/Poultry*	23
Lily O'Brien's | *Candy/Nuts*	22
Little Pie | *Baked Gds.*	24
Magnolia Bakery | *Baked Gds.*	21
M&M's World | *Candy*	21
Minamoto | *Candy/Nuts*	29
Morrell & Co. | *Wine/Liquor*	26
Poseidon | *Baked Gds.*	25
Sea Breeze | *Seafood*	21
Sullivan St. Bakery | *Baked Gds.*	27
Times Sq. Bagels | *Bagels*	24

WEST 50s

AQ Kafé | *Baked Gds.*	23
Between/Bread | *Caterer*	23
Carnegie Deli | *Deli*	23
Cer té | *Caterer/Events*	23
Columbus Circle Wine | *Wine/Liquor*	25
Edible Arrange | *Caterer*	22
Flowers by Richard | *Flowers*	-
Flowers/World | *Flowers*	26
FPB | *Baked Gds.*	27
Godiva | *Candy/Nuts*	23
Grom | *Ice Cream*	26
Holey Cream | *Ice Cream*	21

Jonathan Flowers | *Flowers*	-
La Bergamote | *Baked Gds.*	26
La Boîte à Epice | *Herbs/Spices*	-
Lindt | *Candy/Nuts*	25
Mangia | *Prepared*	23
Momofuku Milk Bar | *Baked Gds.*	25
☑ Nespresso | *Coffee/Tea*	27
Obika | *Cheese/Dairy*	27
Petrossian | *Caviar/Smoked Fish*	27
pinkberry | *Ice Cream*	22
Radiance Tea | *Coffee/Tea*	24
Stonekelly | *Flowers*	-
☑ Sur La Table | *Cookware*	27
Westerly Natural | *Health*	23
Whole Foods | *Maj. Market*	25
☑ Williams-Sonoma | *Cookware*	27

WEST 60s

Bomboloni | *Baked Gds.*	22
☑ Bouchon Bakery | *Baked Gds.*	27
Gourmet Garage | *Maj. Market*	20
Gracious Home | *Cookware*	26
Le Pain Quotidien | *Baked Gds.*	23
Magnolia Bakery | *Baked Gds.*	21
O&CO. | *Spec. Shop*	27
Red Mango | *Ice Cream*	22
Screme | *Ice Cream*	24
67 Wine & Spirits | *Wine/Liquor*	25

WEST 70s

☑ Acker Merrall | *Wine/Liquor*	28
Alice's Tea/Wonderland | *Coffee/Tea*	22
Bagels/Co. | *Bagels*	21
Beacon Wines | *Wine/Liquor*	23
Choco Bolo | *Baked Gds.*	21
Citarella | *Maj. Market*	26
Crumbs | *Baked Gds.*	22
Emack/Bolio | *Ice Cream*	25
Fairway | *Maj. Market*	25
Fischer Bros. | *Meat/Poultry*	24
Grandaisy | *Baked Gds.*	25
Grom | *Ice Cream*	26
Insomnia Cookies | *Baked Gds.*	22
☑ Jacques Torres | *Candy/Nuts*	28

Le Pain Quotidien | *Baked Gds.* 23
🄴 Levain Bakery | *Baked Gds.* 28
Margot Pâtisserie | *Baked Gds.* 23
Nancy's-Wines | *Wine/Liquor* 24
pinkberry | *Ice Cream* 22
🄴 Pour | *Wine/Liquor* 24
🄴 Salumeria Rosi | *Spec. Shop* 28
Sensuous Bean | *Coffee/Tea* 25
Simply Divine | *Caterer* -
16 Handles | *Ice Cream* 24
🄴 Soutine | *Baked Gds.* 27
Westside Mkt. | *Maj. Market* 21

Ben/Jerry's | *Ice Cream* 24
Crumbs | *Baked Gds.* 22
Garden/Eden | *Maj. Market* 23
Hungarian Pastry | *Baked Gds.* 23
Las Palomas | *Spec. Shop* -
Martin Bros. | *Wine/Liquor* 24
Mondel Choc. | *Candy/Nuts* 24
Oren's Roast | *Coffee/Tea* 24
pinkberry | *Ice Cream* 22
Silver Moon | *Baked Gds.* 26
Surroundings | *Flowers* 27
Westside Mkt. | *Maj. Market* 21

WEST 80s

Amanda Smith | *Caterer/Events* 27
Anthi's | *Prepared* -
🄴 Barney Greengrass | 27
   Caviar/Smoked Fish
Best Cellars | *Wine/Liquor* 22
Gary Null's | *Health* 20
Le Pain Quotidien | *Baked Gds.* 23
Momofuku Milk Bar | *Baked Gds.* 25
🄴 Murray's Sturgeon | 28
   Caviar/Smoked Fish
Newman/Leventhal | *Caterer* -
Sarabeth's | *Baked Gds.* 24
🄴 Schatzie's Meats | *Meat/Poultry* 27
Tarallucci/Vino | *Baked Gds.* 24
🄴 Zabar's | *Maj. Market* 27

WEST 90s

Gotham Wines | *Wine/Liquor* 24
Health Nuts | *Health* 22
Lenny's Bagels | *Bagels* 21
Le Pain Quotidien | *Baked Gds.* 23
Screme | *Ice Cream* 24
🆕 Spices/Tease | *Herbs/Spices* 25
Tal Bagels | *Bagels* 22
Westside Mkt. | *Maj. Market* 21
Whole Foods | *Maj. Market* 25
Wines/Whole Foods | *Wine/Liquor* 23

WEST 100s

(See also Harlem/East Harlem)
🄴 Absolute Bagels | *Bagels* 26
Academy Floral | *Flowers* 22

WEST VILLAGE

(Houston to 14th Sts., west of 6th
Ave., excluding Meatpacking)
Amy's Bread | *Baked Gds.* 26
Angelica Flowers | *Flowers* 24
Bagels on Sq. | *Bagels* 20
Bee Desserts | *Baked Gds.* 24
Blue Ribbon | *Spec. Shop* 26
Bonsignour | *Prepared* 27
Carry On Tea | *Coffee/Tea* 25
Chocolate Bar | *Candy/Nuts* 25
Colette's | *Baked Gds.* 27
🄴 Cones | *Ice Cream* 27
Corrado | *Baked Gds.* 22
🆕 DavidsTea | *Coffee/Tea* 28
🆕 Dolce Vizio | *Baked Gds.* 25
Faicco's Pork | *Meat/Poultry* 28
🄴 Florence Meat | *Meat/Poultry* 29
Gourmet Garage | *Maj. Market* 20
Grom | *Ice Cream* 26
Health/Harmony | *Health* -
Il Cantuccio | *Baked Gds.* 26
Integral Yoga | *Health* 23
L'Arte/Gelato | *Ice Cream* 25
🄴 Le Dû's Wines | *Wine/Liquor* 29
Le Pain Quotidien | *Baked Gds.* 23
Li-Lac Choc. | *Candy/Nuts* 26
Magnolia Bakery | *Baked Gds.* 21
🄴 McNulty's | *Coffee/Tea* 28
Meadow | *Spec. Shop* 29
Milk/Cookies | *Baked Gds.* 25
🄴 Murray's Cheese | *Cheese/Dairy* 29

Myers/Keswick | *Spec. Shop* 25

O&CO. | *Spec. Shop* 27

☑ Ottomanelli/Sons | 28
Meat/Poultry

Ovando | *Flowers* 29

Patisserie Claude | *Baked Gds.* 26

Popbar | *Ice Cream* 22

Ready to Eat | *Prepared* 23

Rocco's Pastry | *Baked Gds.* 25

Sant Ambroeus | *Ice Cream* 26

Sweet Revenge | *Baked Gds.* 25

Varsano's | *Candy/Nuts* 29

NEW Victory Garden | *Ice Cream* 28

VSF | *Flowers* 27

Bronx

Abigail Kirsch | *Caterer* 26

☑ Addeo Bakery | *Baked Gds.* 28

Ann Clair's Salum. | *Deli* 25

Arthur Ave. | *Caterer* 23

Artuso Pastry | *Baked Gds.* 24

☑ Biancardi Meats | *Meat/Poultry* 28

☑ Borgatti's | *Pasta* 29

☑ Calabria Pork | *Meat/Poultry* 27

Calandra Cheese | *Cheese/Dairy* 27

☑ Casa Della | *Cheese/Dairy* 29

Cosenza's Fish | *Seafood* 25

Delillo Pastry | *Baked Gds.* 25

Edible Arrange | *Caterer* 22

Egidio Pastry | *Baked Gds.* 25

Gustiamo | *Spec. Shop* -

Liebman's | *Deli* 24

Lloyd's Carrot Cake | *Baked Gds.* 29

Madonia Bakery | *Baked Gds.* 26

Mother's Bake | *Baked Gds.* 20

Mount Carmel | *Wine/Liquor* 24

☑ Pastosa Ravioli | *Pasta* 27

Randazzo's | *Seafood* 26

Sal/Dom's | *Baked Gds.* 28

☑ S&S Cheesecake | *Baked Gds.* 28

Skyview Wines | *Wine/Liquor* 26

Slavin/Sons | *Seafood* 28

☑ Teitel Bros. | *Spec. Shop* 27

☑ Terranova | *Baked Gds.* 28

Vincent's Meat | *Meat/Poultry* 29

Brooklyn

BAY RIDGE

Anopoli | *Ice Cream* 24

Balady Foods | *Spec. Shop* -

Bay Ridge Bake | *Baked Gds.* 25

Faicco's Pork | *Meat/Poultry* 28

Family Store | *Spec. Shop* 24

Hinsch's | *Ice Cream* 22

Little Cupcake | *Baked Gds.* 23

Nordic Delicacies | *Spec. Shop* 28

Paneantico | *Baked Gds.* 26

Three Guys | *Produce* 23

BEDFORD-STUYVESANT

Dough | *Baked Gds.* 26

Scratch Bread | *Baked Gds.* 27

BENSONHURST

Bari Pork | *Meat/Poultry* 26

☑ Lioni Fresh Mozz. | 27
Cheese/Dairy

☑ Mona Lisa | *Baked Gds.* 24

☑ Pastosa Ravioli | *Pasta* 27

Queen Ann | *Pasta* 25

Royal Crown | *Baked Gds.* 26

☑ Villabate | *Baked Gds.* 27

BOERUM HILL

NEW B&B Empire | *Bagels* 17

Bergen Bagels | *Bagels* 23

Betty Bakery | *Baked Gds.* 26

Cheryl Kleinman | *Baked Gds.* 28

NEW Shelsky's Smoked Fish | 24
Caviar/Smoked Fish

Steve's/Ice Cream | *Ice Cream* 22

☑ Van Leeuwen | *Ice Cream* 26

BOROUGH PARK

☑ Coluccio/Sons | *Spec. Shop* 27

Ice Cream House | *Ice Cream* 24

Schick's | *Baked Gds.* 23

BRIGHTON BEACH

Güllüoglu | *Baked Gds.* 23

M & I | *Spec. Shop* 22

BROOKLYN HEIGHTS

Cook's Companion | *Cookware* 28
Damascus | *Baked Gds.* 26
Garden/Eden | *Maj. Market* 23
Heights Chateau | *Wine/Liquor* 25
Heights Meats | *Meat/Poultry* 27
La Bagel | *Bagels* 22
Lassen/Hennigs | *Caterer* 25
Michael-Towne | *Wine/Liquor* 27
Montague St. | *Bagels* 23
Perelandra | *Health* 26
Sahadi's | *Spec. Shop* 28
Seaport Flowers | *Flowers* 27
Trader Joe's | *Maj. Market* 23
Two for the Pot | *Coffee/Tea* 26

BROOKLYN NAVY YARD

Abigail Kirsch | *Caterer* 26

BROWNSVILLE

Carolina Country | *Spec. Shop* -

CARROLL GARDENS

Bagels by Park | *Bagels* 23
Brooklyn Farmacy | *Ice Cream* 25
Caputo | *Baked Gds.* 27
Court Street Grocers | *Maj. Market* 29
D'Amico | *Coffee/Tea* 27
David Stark | *Caterer/Events* -
Esposito/Sons Pork | 27
  Meat/Poultry
F. Monteleone | *Baked Gds.* 29
Mazzola Bakery | *Baked Gds.* 27
Momofuku Milk Bar | *Baked Gds.* 25
Naturally Delic. | *Caterer/Events* -

CLINTON HILL

Choice Greene/Mkt. | *Prepared* 27

COBBLE HILL

Amer. Beer | *Beer* 26
NEW Bien Cuit | *Baked Gds.* 23
Blue Marble | *Ice Cream* 26
Brooklyn Wine | *Wine/Liquor* 25
Chocolate Rm. | *Candy/Nuts* 25
Court Pastry | *Baked Gds.* 26

Fish Tales | *Seafood* 27
Los Paisanos | *Meat/Poultry* 26
Nut Box | *Candy/Nuts* 24
One Girl | *Baked Gds.* 27
Smith/Vine | *Wine/Liquor* 25
Staubitz Mkt. | *Meat/Poultry* 29
Stinky Bklyn | *Cheese/Dairy* 27
Union Mkt. | *Maj. Market* 25

DITMAS PARK

Ackerson, T.B. | *Wine/Liquor* 25
Catskill Bagel | *Bagels* 22
Market | *Spec. Shop* 24
Natural Frontier | *Health* 22

DOWNTOWN BROOKLYN

Brooklyn Fare | *Maj. Market* 26
Junior's | *Baked Gds.* 21
Nunu Choc. | *Candy/Nuts* 25
Wright/Goebel | *Wine/Liquor* 28

DUMBO

Almondine | *Baked Gds.* 26
Brooklyn Ice Cream | *Ice Cream* 25
Choco Bolo | *Baked Gds.* 21
Foragers City Grocer | *Maj. Market* 26
Gramercy Park Flower | *Flowers* 27
GreatWall Supermkt. | *Spec. Shop* 19
Jacques Torres | *Candy/Nuts* 28
La Bagel | *Bagels* 22
One Girl | *Baked Gds.* 27

DYKER HEIGHTS

Aunt Butchie's | *Baked Gds.* 26

FLATBUSH

Edible Arrange | *Caterer* 22
Ice Cream House | *Ice Cream* 24
Kosher Bagel | *Bagels* 27

FORT GREENE

Bergen Bagels | *Bagels* 23
Brooklyn Flea | *Spec. Items* 22
Cake Man | *Baked Gds.* 24
Choice Greene/Mkt. | *Prepared* 27
Flowers/Reuven | *Flowers* 26

Greene Grape | *Wine/Liquor* 22
Greene Grape | *Spec. Shop* 27
La Bagel | *Bagels* 22

GOWANUS

Four/Twenty Blackbirds | 26
Baked Gds.

GRAVESEND

Bake City Bagels | *Bagels* 28
Bari Pork | *Meat/Poultry* 26

GREENPOINT

Acme Fish | *Caviar/Smoked Fish* 25
Brooklyn Ice Cream | *Ice Cream* 25
Brooklyn Oenology | *Wine/Liquor* –
Brouwerij Ln. | *Beer* 28
Eastern District | *Spec. Shop* –
Peter Pan Donut | *Baked Gds.* 24
Z Van Leeuwen | *Ice Cream* 26

GREENWOOD HEIGHTS

Eagle Provisions | *Meat/Poultry* 23
Jubilat Provisions | *Meat/Poultry* –

KENSINGTON

Z NYC Icy | *Ice Cream* 29

KINGS PLAZA/ MARINE PARK

JoMart Choc. | *Candy/Nuts* 28

MIDWOOD

Hot Bagels & Bialys | *Bagels* 25
Z Orchard | *Spec. Shop* 28
Z Pickle Guys | *Spec. Shop* 27
Z Pomegranate | *Spec. Shop* 26
16 Handles | *Ice Cream* 24

MILL BASIN

Dolly's Ices | *Ice Cream* 25
Mill Basin Kosher | *Deli* 24
Z Pastosa Ravioli | *Pasta* 27

PARK SLOPE

Almondine | *Baked Gds.* 26
Back/Land | *Health* 24
Bagel Hole | *Bagels* 25
Bierkraft | *Beer* 27

Big Nose | *Wine/Liquor* 24
Z Bklyn Larder | *Spec. Shop* 27
Z Blue Apron | *Spec. Shop* 28
Blue Sky | *Baked Gds.* 27
Butter Lane Cupcakes | *Baked Gds.* 25
Chocolate Rm. | *Candy/Nuts* 25
Cocoa Bar | *Candy/Nuts* 21
Colson | *Baked Gds.* 24
Cousin John's | *Baked Gds.* 22
Crespella | *Baked Gds.* –
Z D'Vine | *Spec. Shop* 26
NEW Fleisher's Grassfed | 29
Meat/Poultry
Grab Specialty | *Spec. Shop* 26
Java Joe | *Coffee/Tea* –
La Bagel | *Bagels* 22
Z Ladybird | *Baked Gds.* 27
Movable Feast | *Caterer* 23
Picada/Vino | *Wine/Liquor* 26
Prospect Wine | *Wine/Liquor* 25
Red/White | *Wine/Liquor* 26
Russo Mozz. | *Cheese/Dairy* 26
Slope Cellars | *Wine/Liquor* 26
Sweet Melissa | *Baked Gds.* 25
Tarzian West | *Cookware* 22
Trois Pommes | *Baked Gds.* 27
Union Mkt. | *Maj. Market* 25
NEW Valley Shepherd | 28
Cheese/Dairy
Yogo Monster | *Ice Cream* 22
Z ZuZu's Petals | *Flowers* 27

PROSPECT HEIGHTS

NEW Ample Hills | *Ice Cream* 28
Blue Marble | *Ice Cream* 26
Joyce Bake | *Baked Gds.* 25

PROSPECT-LEFFERTS GARDENS

Brooklyn Beer/Soda | *Beer* 25

RED HOOK

Z Baked | *Baked Gds.* 26
Botta di Vino | *Wine/Liquor* 24
Dry Dock Wine | *Wine/Liquor* 28
Fairway | *Maj. Market* 25

Vote at zagat.com

Ɀ Red Hook Lobster | *Seafood* — 27
Steve's/Key Lime | *Baked Gds.* — 26

SHEEPSHEAD BAY

Cupcake Kings | *Baked Gds.* — 24
Edible Arrange | *Caterer* — 22
Jay/Lloyd's Kosher | *Deli* — 22
Jordan's | *Seafood* — 24

SUNSET PARK

Brooklyn Liquors | *Wine/Liquor* — 24
Costco | *Maj. Market* — 23
Li-Lac Choc. | *Candy/Nuts* — 26
Sunset Beer | *Beer* — 24

WILLIAMSBURG

Bagel Store | *Bagels* — 24
Bakeri | *Baked Gds.* — 22
Ɀ Bedford Cheese | *Cheese/Dairy* — 27
Broadway Party | *Party Rent.* — -
Brooklyn Cupcake | *Baked Gds.* — 27
Brooklyn Flea | *Spec. Items* — 22
Brooklyn Kitchen | *Cookware* — 25
Edible Arrange | *Caterer* — 22
Ɀ Fortunato | *Baked Gds.* — 27
Ice Cream House | *Ice Cream* — 24
Ɀ Marlow/Daughters | *Meat/Poultry* — 28
Ɀ Marlow/Sons | *Spec. Shop* — 27
Mast Brothers | *Candy/Nuts* — 25
Meat Hook | *Meat/Poultry* — 27
Momofuku Milk Bar | *Baked Gds.* — 25
Napoli | *Baked Gds.* — 28
Ɀ Porto Rico | *Coffee/Tea* — 27
Red Table Catering | *Caterer* — -
Whisk | *Cookware* — -
NEW Whiskey Shop | *Wine/Liquor* — 27

WINDSOR TERRACE

Terrace Bagels | *Bagels* — 25
United Meat | *Meat/Poultry* — 26

Queens

ASTORIA

Ɀ Artopolis | *Baked Gds.* — 27
Astor Bake Shop | *Baked Gds.* — 23

Berry Fresh Farm | *Spec. Shop* — 25
Best Yet Mkt. | *Spec. Shop* — 23
Cassinelli Food | *Pasta* — 29
Christos Steak | *Meat/Poultry* — 25
Costco | *Maj. Market* — 23
Edible Arrange | *Caterer* — 22
Grand Wine | *Wine/Liquor* — 22
Güllüoglu | *Baked Gds.* — 23
La Guli | *Baked Gds.* — 27
Martha's Bakery | *Baked Gds.* — 22
Med. Foods | *Spec. Shop* — 26
Red Mango | *Ice Cream* — 22
16 Handles | *Ice Cream* — 24
Titan Foods | *Spec. Shop* — 26

BAYSIDE

Ben's Kosher | *Deli* — 22
Health Nuts | *Health* — 22
Martha's Bakery | *Baked Gds.* — 22
Ralph's/Ices | *Ice Cream* — 25
Red Mango | *Ice Cream* — 22

COLLEGE POINT

Empire Mkt. | *Meat/Poultry* — 23

CORONA

Ɀ Lemon Ice | *Ice Cream* — 26

DOUGLASTON

Ceriello | *Spec. Shop* — 24
Fairway | *Maj. Market* — 25

ELMHURST

Crumbs | *Baked Gds.* — 22
Fay Da | *Baked Gds.* — 20
Godiva | *Candy/Nuts* — 23
GreatWall Supermkt. | *Spec. Shop* — 19
Hong Kong | *Spec. Shop* — 19
Party Time | *Party Rent.* — 20

FLORAL PARK

Ralph's/Ices | *Ice Cream* — 25

FLUSHING

Chung Fat | *Spec. Shop* — 22
Durso's Pasta | *Pasta* — 26
Edible Arrange | *Caterer* — 22

Fay Da | *Baked Gds.*	20
GreatWall Supermkt. | *Spec. Shop*	19
H Mart | *Spec. Shop*	22
Hong Kong | *Spec. Shop*	19
House/Spices | *Herbs/Spices*	26
Koryodang | *Baked Gds.*	22
Mauzone | *Caterer*	21
Max/Mina's | *Ice Cream*	25
🎗 Ottomanelli's Meats | *Meat/Poultry*	28
Patel Bros. | *Spec. Shop*	22
Tai Pan Bakery | *Baked Gds.*	21
Yi Mei Fung | *Baked Gds.*	19

FOREST HILLS

Andre's | *Baked Gds.*	24
Cheese/World | *Cheese/Dairy*	26
Eddie's Sweet | *Ice Cream*	25
Fay Da | *Baked Gds.*	20
Hot Bialys & Bagels | *Bagels*	23
Martha's Bakery | *Baked Gds.*	22
Yogo Monster | *Ice Cream*	22

FRESH MEADOWS

Bagel Oasis | *Bagels*	25
Red Mango | *Ice Cream*	22

HILLCREST

Bagels/Co. | *Bagels*	21

JACKSON HEIGHTS

Cannelle Patisserie | *Baked Gds.*	29
🎗 Despaña | *Spec. Shop*	27
Patel Bros. | *Spec. Shop*	22

LONG ISLAND CITY

Buttercup | *Baked Gds.*	22
FreshDirect | *Maj. Market*	23
LIC Market | *Spec. Shop*	25
Natural Frontier | *Health*	22

MASPETH

Iavarone Bros. | *Prepared*	26

OZONE PARK

🎗 Pastosa Ravioli | *Pasta*	27

REGO PARK

Ben's Best | *Deli*	25
Red Mango | *Ice Cream*	22
Trader Joe's | *Maj. Market*	23

SUNNYSIDE

Baruir's Coffee | *Coffee/Tea*	27
Butcher Block | *Spec. Shop*	27
Sugar Room | *Cookware*	-

WHITESTONE

Ralph's/Ices | *Ice Cream*	25
🎗 Stork's Pastry | *Baked Gds.*	25

WOODSIDE

🎗 Ottomanelli/Sons | *Meat/Poultry*	28
Phil-Am | *Spec. Shop*	-
Yi Mei Fung | *Baked Gds.*	19

Staten Island

Aunt Butchie's | *Baked Gds.*	26
Bari Pork | *Meat/Poultry*	26
Belfiore Meats | *Meat/Poultry*	25
Cake Chef Bakery | *Baked Gds.*	28
Cookie Jar | *Baked Gds.*	27
Costco | *Maj. Market*	23
Eggers Ice Cream | *Ice Cream*	26
Family Health Foods | *Health*	22
Mother Mousse | *Baked Gds.*	25
Bruno/Pasticceria | *Baked Gds.*	24
🎗 Pastosa Ravioli | *Pasta*	27
Pete Milano's | *Wine/Liquor*	25
Ralph's/Ices | *Ice Cream*	25

Mail Order

Listings cover the best in each category and include source names and Quality ratings.

BAGELS & BIALYS

Bagels/Co.	21
Bagel Store	24
Ess-a-Bagel	26
H & H Midtown	25
☑ Kossar's	26
La Bagel	22
Zucker's Bagels	22

BAKED GOODS

Agata/Valentina	25
Andre's	24
☑ Artopolis	27
BabyCakes	24
Baconery	25
☑ Baked	26
Baked/Melissa	24
Bee Desserts	24
Billy's Bakery	24
Bis.Co.Latte	24
☑ Black Hound	26
Blue Smoke	25
Bread Alone	25
Bruno/Pasticceria	24
Carrot Top	23
Choco Bolo	21
Cipriani	26
Citarella	26
Colson	24
Cookie Jar	27
Crumbs	22
Damascus	26
Dean/DeLuca	26
Delillo Pastry	25
De Robertis	23
Duane Pk.	25
Egidio Pastry	25
Eileen's Cheesecake	25
Eleni's Cookies	22
Eli's Manhattan	25

Eli's Vinegar	24
Empire Cake	26
Fat Witch	24
Ferrara Bakery	22
F. Monteleone	29
☑ Fortunato	27
FPB	27
Garden/Eden	23
Grace's Market	25
Güllüoglu	23
Il Cantuccio	26
Insomnia Cookies	22
Junior's	21
☑ Lady M	29
La Guli	27
☑ Levain Bakery	28
Little Brown	21
Little Pie	24
Macaron Café	24
Magnolia Bakery	21
Martin's Pretzels	26
Milk/Cookies	25
NEW Mille-Feuille	25
Moishe's	23
Momofuku Milk Bar	25
☑ Mona Lisa	24
Once Upon/Tart	25
☑ One Girl	27
Rice/Riches	24
Robicelli's	26
Rocco's Pastry	25
Ruthy's Bakery	20
☑ S&S Cheesecake	28
Sarabeth's	24
Schick's	23
☑ Soutine	27
NEW Sprinkles	26
Streit's Matzo	27
Sugar Sweet	26
Three Tarts	26

Tribeca Treats	21
Trois Pommes	27
Tu-Lu's GF	25
Veniero's	25
🅉 Villabate	27
Wafels/Dinges	24
William Greenberg	25
Yi Mei Fung	19
Yonah Schimmel	24
🅉 Zabar's	27

CANDY & NUTS

Charbonnel/Walker	23
Chocolate Bar	25
Chocolate Rm.	25
Chocolat Michel	27
Citarella	26
Dean/DeLuca	26
🅉 Dylan's Candy	23
Economy Candy	25
Eli's Manhattan	25
Eli's Vinegar	24
Fifth Ave. Choc.	25
Godiva	23
🅉 Jacques Torres	28
JoMart Choc.	28
🅉 L.A. Burdick Handmade Chocolates	28
🅉 La Maison/Choc.	29
Leonidas	26
Liddabit Sweets	25
Li-Lac Choc.	26
Lily O'Brien's	22
Lindt	25
NEW London Candy Co.	25
M&M's World	21
MarieBelle's	26
Martine's Choc.	25
Mast Brothers	25
Max Brenner	22
Minamoto	29
Mondel Choc.	24
Neuchatel Choc.	28
Neuhaus Choc.	26
Nunu Choc.	25

Nut Box	24
Papabubble	23
Roni-Sue's	24
Sweet Life	27
🅉 Teuscher Choc.	29
Varsano's	29
🅉 Vosges	27
NEW Xocolatti	22
🅉 Zabar's	27

CAVIAR & SMOKED FISH

Agata/Valentina	25
🅉 Barney Greengrass	27
Caviar Russe	26
Citarella	26
Dean/DeLuca	26
Eli's Manhattan	25
Eli's Vinegar	24
Grace's Market	25
🅉 Murray's Sturgeon	28
Petrossian	27
🅉 Russ/Daughters	29
🅉 Sable's	27
🅉 Zabar's	27

CHEESE & DAIRY

Agata/Valentina	25
🅉 Alleva Dairy	28
🅉 Artisanal	27
Barnyard Cheese	26
🅉 Bedford Cheese	27
NEW Beecher's Cheese	27
Calandra Cheese	27
🅉 Casa Della	29
Citarella	26
Dean/DeLuca	26
🅉 Di Palo Dairy	29
Eli's Manhattan	25
Eli's Vinegar	24
🅉 Formaggio	27
Garden/Eden	23
Grace's Market	25
Ideal Cheese	27
Lamazou	26

Vote at zagat.com

Lucy's Whey	29
Z Murray's Cheese	29
Ronnybrook	26
Russo Mozz.	26
Z Saxelby Cheese	29
Z Stinky Bklyn	27
Z 3-Corner Farm	27
Z Zabar's	27

COFFEE & TEA

Agata/Valentina	25
Alice's Tea/Wonderland	22
Baruir's Coffee	27
Carry On Tea	25
Citarella	26
Z D'Amico	27
NEW DavidsTea	28
Dean/DeLuca	26
Eli's Manhattan	25
Eli's Vinegar	24
Empire Coffee	24
Harney & Sons	28
In Pursuit of Tea	28
Z McNulty's	28
Z Nespresso	27
Oren's Roast	24
Z Porto Rico	27
Radiance Tea	24
Z Sahadi's	28
Sensuous Bean	25
Tea/Honey	29
Ten Ren Tea	25
Two for the Pot	26
Z Zabar's	27

COOKWARE & SUPPLIES

Alessi	26
Bari Equipment	-
Bloomingdale's	25
Bowery Kitchen	23
Broadway Pan.	26
Brooklyn Kitchen	25
Z Cook's Companion	28
Dean/DeLuca	26
Eli's Manhattan	25

Eli's Vinegar	24
Gracious Home	26
Japanese Culinary Ctr.	24
Z J.B. Prince	29
Z Korin	29
Macy's Cellar	23
New York Cake	25
S. Feldman	26
Z Sur La Table	27
Whisk	-
Z Williams-Sonoma	27
Z Zabar's	27

DELIS/CHARCUTERIE

Agata/Valentina	25
Ben's Best	25
BuonItalia	26
Z Calabria Pork	27
Carnegie Deli	23
Citarella	26
Z Despaña	27
Z Dickson's Farmstand	28
Z Di Palo Dairy	29
Z Eataly	27
Eli's Manhattan	25
Eli's Vinegar	24
Z Formaggio	27
Iavarone Bros.	26
Katz's Deli	25
Mill Basin Kosher	24
Z Murray's Cheese	29
Salumeria Biellese	26
Z Salumeria Rosi	28
Sarge's Deli	22
Z Schaller/Weber	28
Z Stinky Bklyn	27
Todaro Bros.	25
Z Zabar's	27

DRIED FRUIT

Bell Bates	24
Citarella	26
Dean/DeLuca	26
Z D'Vine	26
Economy Candy	25

Eli's Manhattan	25
Eli's Vinegar	24
Gourmet Garage	20
Gustiamo	-
Z Kalustyan's	27
Nut Box	24
Patel Bros.	22
Z Russ/Daughters	29
Z Sahadi's	28
Sweet Life	27
Z Zabar's	27

FLOWERS

Academy Floral	22
Ariston	26
Banchet Flowers	26
Belle Fleur	28
Big Apple Florist	27
Z Bloom	27
Chestnuts	-
Elizabeth Ryan	-
Flowers by Richard	-
Flowers/World	26
Z Gramercy Park Flower	27
Katrina Parris	-
L'Olivier	27
Ovando	29
Rebecca Cole	-
Rosa Rosa	24
Spruce	-
Windsor Florist	24
Z ZuZu's Petals	27

HEALTH & NATURAL FOODS
(See also Organic)

A Matter/Health	23
BabyCakes	24
Bell Bates	24
Health/Harmony	-
Health Nuts	22
NEW Heritage Meat Shop	27
Integral Yoga	23
LifeThyme Mkt.	22
One Lucky Duck	25

NEW Soft Serve Fruit	23
Tu-Lu's GF	25
Westerly Natural	23

HERBS & SPICES

Dean/DeLuca	26
House/Spices	26
Z Kalustyan's	27
La Boîte à Epice	-
NEW Spices/Tease	25
Z Zabar's	27

MEAT, POULTRY & GAME

Agata/Valentina	25
Bari Pork	26
Z Calabria Pork	27
Citarella	26
Dean/DeLuca	26
Z Dickson's Farmstand	28
Z Eataly	27
Eli's Manhattan	25
Eli's Vinegar	24
Fischer Bros.	24
Z Florence Meat	29
Z Flying Pigs	29
Garden/Eden	23
Grace's Market	25
NEW Heritage Meat Shop	27
Hudson Valley Foie Gras	29
Le Marais	23
Z Lobel's Meats	28
Malaysia Beef Jerky	25
Z Ottomanelli's Meats	28
Park E. Kosher	24
Z Schaller/Weber	28
Z Staubitz Mkt.	29
Vincent's Meat	29
Z Zabar's	27

PASTAS

Durso's Pasta	26
Z Pastosa Ravioli	27
Z Piemonte Ravioli	27
Z Raffetto's	28

PRODUCE

Red Jacket	26
Stokes Farm	26

SEAFOOD

Agata/Valentina	25
Citarella	26
Dean/DeLuca	26
Dorian's Seafood	26
Eli's Manhattan	25
Eli's Vinegar	24
Z Fish Tales	27
Grace's Market	25
Leonard's Market	26
Z Lobster Pl.	27
Pescatore	25
Slavin/Sons	28
Wild Edibles	24
Z Zabar's	27

SPECIALTY SHOPS

Bangkok Grocery	24
Z Beth's Farm	28
BuonItalia	26
Butterfield/Baked	25
Ceriello	24
Chelsea Baskets	23
Z Coluccio/Sons	27
Z Despaña	27
Z D'Vine	26
Greene Grape	27
Gustiamo	–
Internat'l Grocery	24
Z Kalustyan's	27
Kam Man	21
Katagiri	23
Z Manhattan Fruitier	25
McClure's Pickles	27
Meadow	29
Med. Foods	26
Myers/Keswick	25
Nordic Delicacies	28
O&CO.	27
Z Orchard	28
Patel Bros.	22

Z Pickle Guys	27
Z Pickles/Olives	25
Z Pomegranate	26
Rick's Picks	26
Z Sahadi's	28
Z Salumeria Rosi	28
Spoon	25
Z Teitel Bros.	27
Titan Foods	26
Todaro Bros.	25

WINES, BEER & LIQUOR

Z Acker Merrall	28
Ambassador Wine	25
Appellation	26
Astor Wines	26
Beacon Wines	23
Beekman Liquors	24
Bierkraft	27
Z Bottlerocket	25
Bowery/Vine	22
Brooklyn Brew Shop	26
Brooklyn Wine	25
Z Burgundy	28
California Wine	24
Z Chambers Wines	27
Chelsea Wine	24
Columbus Circle Wine	25
Z Crush Wine	27
Despaña Vinos	29
Z Eataly	27
Garnet Wines	26
Gotham Wines	24
Grand Wine	22
Greene Grape	22
Harlem Vintage	27
Z Heights Chateau	25
Z Italian Wine	29
K & D Wines	26
Z Le Dû's Wines	29
Martin Bros.	24
Mister Wright	25
Z Moore Bros.	28
Morrell & Co.	26

Mount Carmel	24	Rosenthal Wine	29
New York Vintners	28	⦿ Sherry-Lehmann	29
New York/Exchange	25	67 Wine & Spirits	25
⦿ Park Ave. Liquor	27	Skyview Wines	26
Penn Wine/Spirits	26	Slope Cellars	26
⦿ PJ Wine	27	Smith/Vine	25
⦿ Pour	24	Sutton Wine	22
Premier Cru	25	Union Sq. Wines	25
Prospect Wine	25	Vinyl Wine	-
Puro Chile/Wine	-	Yorkshire Wines	24
Red/White	26		

ONLINE SOURCES

Top Quality

29	Cowgirl Creamery	28	American Spoon Foods
	Upton Tea Imports		Di Bruno Bros.
	Pop's Wine		Bob's Red Mill
	Point Reyes Cheese		Zingerman's
	Maine Lobster Direct		Rancho Gordo
	D'Artagnan		King Arthur/Baker's Catalogue
	Salumi		Norman Love Confections
	Anson Mills		Pike Place Fish
	Big Island Candies		Enstrom's
	Mighty Leaf		Grafton Vill. Cheese

BY CATEGORY

BAKED GOODS

- 26 Metropolitan Bakery
- Greyston Bakery
- Boudin Bakery
- 25 Grand Traverse Pie
- 24 Dancing Deer Baking

BEANS/GRAINS/PASTAS

- 29 Anson Mills
- 28 Di Bruno Bros.
- Bob's Red Mill
- Rancho Gordo
- King Arthur/Baker's Catalogue

CANDY

- 29 Big Island Candies
- 28 Norman Love Confections
- Enstrom's
- Scharffen Berger
- Fauchon

CAVIAR/SMOKED FISH

- 28 Pike Place Fish
- 27 Browne Trading
- igourmet.com
- 25 Mackenzie Ltd.
- 24 Chefs' Warehouse

CHARCUTERIE

- 29 D'Artagnan
- Salumi
- 28 Di Bruno Bros.
- Ferrari, A.G., Foods
- Zingerman's

CHEESE/DAIRY

- 29 Cowgirl Creamery
- Point Reyes Cheese
- 28 Di Bruno Bros.
- Zingerman's
- Grafton Vill. Cheese

COFFEE

- 28 Intelligentsia Coffee
- Whole Latte Love*
- 27 Illy
- 25 Peet's Coffee
- Green Mountain Coffee

COOKWARE/SUPPLIES

- 28 Fante's Kitchen
- 27 Chef's Resource
- Bodum
- Bridge Kitchenware
- CutleryAndMore

FLOWERS

- 26 Calyx Flowers
- 22 ProFlowers
- 21 Just Flowers
- 20 1-800-flowers.com

GIFT BASKETS

- 28 Di Bruno Bros.
- Zingerman's
- Fortnum & Mason
- Fauchon
- Ferrari, A.G., Foods

HERBS/SPICES

- 27 Spice House
- 26 ChefShop.com
- 25 Melissa's
- Atlantic Spice
- 24 Earthly Delights

MEAT/POULTRY/GAME

29 D'Artagnan
28 Niman Ranch
   Nueske's Meats
27 Usinger's
   Harrington's of VT

NUTS/DRIED FRUIT

28 American Spoon Foods
27 Chukar
26 Sunnyland Farms
   Peanut Shop/Williamsburg
25 Atlantic Spice

PRODUCE

27 Frog Hollow Farm
25 Melissa's
24 Hadley Fruit
   Cushman Fruit
23 Hale Groves

SEAFOOD

29 Maine Lobster Direct
28 Pike Place Fish

   Browne Trading
27 igourmet.com
24 Lobster Gram

SPECIALTY ITEMS

28 American Spoon Foods
   Di Bruno Bros.
   Zingerman's
   Fortnum & Mason
   Fauchon

TEA

29 Upton Tea Imports
   Mighty Leaf
28 Fortnum & Mason
   Fauchon
27 Republic of Tea

WINES/LIQUOR

29 Pop's Wine
27 Zachy's
   Wine Library
26 K&L Wine
24 Wine.com

Top Display

27 Big Island Candies
   Fauchon

26 Norman Love Confections
   Di Bruno Bros.
   Mackenzie Ltd.

   Fran's Chocolates
   Calyx Flowers
   Zingerman's
   Republic of Tea
   Fortnum & Mason

Top Service

28 Maine Lobster Direct
   Big Island Candies
27 Zingerman's
   Di Bruno Bros.
   King Arthur/Baker's Catalogue

   Norman Love Confections
   Salumi*
   CutleryAndMore
   Upton Tea Imports
26 La Tienda

---

* Indicates a tie with property above

ONLINE SOURCES DIRECTORY

Online Sources

Adagio Teas *Coffee/Tea*   25 | 24 | 25 | M
www.adagio.com | 973-253-7400
Sample "many new teas without breaking the bank" via this online
brew broker, whose "diverse" lineup is a bonanza of 200 "superior"
varieties – "especially rare" and "unusual" leaves – plus "wonderful"
pots and paraphernalia, all shipped out "quick" at a "fair" price; it's
a "favorite for gifts" as well, and its site has a "unique function" that
allows "amateur" tisaners to "create their own blends and then pro-
mote them to family and friends" for sale on the site.

Allen Brothers *Meat/Poultry*   27 | 25 | 26 | VE
www.allenbrothers.com | 800-957-0111
"It doesn't get any better than this" rejoice carnivores selecting
"beautiful, restaurant-quality meats" from this venerable (since
1893) Chicago butcher's online service, which ships "the finest"
cuts of "dry- and wet-aged beef" (including Wagyu) in "superior"
style, along with game, sausage, burgers and seafood; being a "rare
indulgence" that's also served in swanky steakhouses, the stock
fetches "exorbitant prices" but "can't miss" if "you have the means
and want to impress"; P.S. the "whole-meal packages" and other assortments "make really nice gifts."

American Spoon Foods *Specialty Shop*   28 | 24 | 25 | M
www.spoon.com | 800-222-5886
Taste "the best of what Michigan has to offer" at this Great Lakes-
based online "ambassador", whose "superb" jams, preserves and
spreads are "made with locally grown fruits" and hand-processed in
small batches to yield "fresh and clean" flavors ("go for the sour
cherry spoon fruit") that also extend to its "high-quality" sauces,
salsas, relishes, dried fruits and other savories; with "pretty packaging" and "fabulous customer service", it "costs a bit more" but is
"loved by most" and rated "totally worth it."

Anson Mills *Beans/Grains*   29 | 21 | 24 | M
www.ansonmills.com | 803-467-4122
Dixiephiles give "eternal thanks" to this "wonderful" Columbia,
SC, farm's online operation for offering "real-deal" "Southern
staples" milled from all-organic heirloom grains and Carolina
Gold rice, including "the best-tasting grits on either side of the
Mason-Dixon" plus "fabulous" cornmeal, polenta, flour and
buckwheat; "the shipping's a bit pricey", but "any discerning palate" would "jump through hoops for" such "super-fresh products" –
and "in case you're a Yankee", "step-by-step cooking tips" are
posted on its "marvelous website."

Atlantic Spice Co. *Herbs/Spices*   25 | 19 | 21 | M
www.atlanticspice.com | 800-316-7965
Hard-pressed chefs "can find almost anything" "all in one place"
through the online catalog of this Cape Cod operation, whose ware-

house stores a vast hoard featuring virtually "any spice in the world" plus "quality" herbs, extracts, oils, teas, grains, beans, nuts, dried fruit and even potpourri ingredients; both "the regular stuff" and "hard-to-get" items are shipped "fresh" at "fair prices", and the service is "friendly and helpful"; P.S. check out the bulk discounts.

BevMo *Wine/Liquor*
24 | 21 | 22 | M

www.bevmo.com | 877-772-3866

When it's "party time", this California-based liquor-mart chain runs an "easy-to-navigate site" boasting a "huge selection" of wines, spirits and beers, including "hard-to-find" vintages, "the finest brews" and "stuff you never knew you needed but somehow must have"; "decent prices" (improved by frequent "deals"), "seamless service" and "perfectly packed" shipping provide even mo incentive.

Big Island Candies *Candy/Nuts*
29 | 27 | 28 | M

www.bigislandcandies.com | 800-935-5510

An "unexpected island treat", this top-drawer Hawaiian confectioner's range of "unique and delectable goodies" features "awesome cookies and candies" like "the tastiest chocolate-dipped shortbread" and "anything with macadamia nuts" ("of course") along with truffles, brownies and more exotic sweets; the "artfully packaged" boxes and baskets make "the perfect gift" or primo wedding and "party favors", and since it's "tough to find similar quality", "for what you get it's a big value."

Bob's Red Mill *Beans/Grains*
28 | 23 | 25 | M

www.bobsredmill.com | 800-349-2173

"Not just for hippies", this "trusted" "old name" in natural foods is "the online mill of choice" for an "exhaustive" selection of "outstanding" whole grains, flours, hot cereals, baking mixes and beans that incorporates "superior" "organics", a "gluten-free line" and lots of the "more obscure stuff"; besides "super service" to "fill your needs quickly", its "easy site" offers "great tips for improved health and yummy recipes", and though shipping costs "are a little steep", bulk discounts are offered.

Bodum *Cookware*
27 | 24 | 24 | M

www.bodumusa.com | 800-232-6386

"Ooh-la-la", this global appliance-maker is famed for the "unique designs" of its "stylish and functional products", notably the "wonderful" "French press" coffeemakers and tea infusers that lead an "innovative" lineup extending to cups and vessels with double-glass insulation and designer "kitchen products that last", whether cookware, servingware or gadgets; the "very clear website" is "helpful" even for ordering "replacement parts", and though the goods are "a bit pricey" the "fabulous quality" is "well worth it."

Boudin Bakery *Baked Goods*
26 | 23 | 24 | M

www.boudinbakery.com | 800-992-1849

It's "been doing it right" since 1849 with "exquisite" sourdough that's "in a class by itself", and these days this SF bakery "makes getting real bread possible" just about anywhere with "fast shipping" of its "fantastic", "fluffy" rounds and loaves ("like you got it fresh in the store"); the "distinct" goods are available seasonally themed for a "holiday" "treat", and the site also features classic accompaniments, gift baskets and bread-of-the-month clubs.

Bridge Kitchenware *Cookware* 27 | 19 | 21 | E
www.bridgekitchenware.com | 973-287-6163
The longtime Manhattan store moved to Jersey, but "everything a professional chef or an aspiring one could need" is still available through this "unsurpassed" culinary supplier's website, which lists an "overwhelming" selection of "top-quality" cookware, bakeware, appliances, knives, glassware and "gadgets", ranging "from the mundane to the esoteric" ("you name it, they have it"); "they aren't cheap", but then given the "exceptional products" that's no surprise.

Bridgewater Chocolate *Candy/Nuts* 26 | 24 | 24 | E
www.bridgewaterchocolate.com | 800-888-8742
You're hard-pressed to find "chocolate more scrumptious than" the creations of this high-end confectioner, whose "delicious little" American-style "treasures" include handmade truffles, toffees, caramels, turtles and more; the bonbons are "beautifully designed" and packaged (the signature hinged boxes make for "great gift presentation"), and though critics cry they're "too costly", the "reliable quality and dependable service" are part of the price.

Browne Trading Co. *Caviar* 28 | 24 | 26 | VE
www.brownetrading.com | 800-944-7848
A rarefied supplier of "the best" in fresh fin fare, this family-owned Maine merchant is "reliable" for pristine fish that frequently surfaces at Le Bernardin and other first-class restaurants (including imports like turbot, daurade and loup de mer), along with caviar and catch cured in their own smokehouse; it's all "very expensive", but the quality "matches the pricing."

Burgers' Smokehouse *Meat/Poultry* 23 | 21 | 24 | M
www.smokehouse.com | 800-345-5185
"Some of the best meat candy out there" can be ogled at the online adjunct of this family-owned Missouri smokehouse, a leader since 1952 for "the finest" country ham and bacon naturally aged to hickory-smoked and sweet-cured perfection, not to mention sausage, ribs, hog jowl, bacon-wrapped sirloin and other Ozark delicacies; "fast, reliable" service ensures orders arrive "when promised to the day", while the "wonderful taste" earns "nothing but raves" from recipients; P.S. the "bargain" cuts are "real values."

CajunGrocer.com *Specialty Shop* 23 | 18 | 23 | M
www.cajungrocer.com | 888-272-9347
"The only place to buy your turducken" and "so much more", this online specialty grocer is "the ultimate source for all things Cajun", shipping out the "enticing" likes of boudin sausage, crawfish, Gulf shrimp, alligator, gumbo and king cakes, along with "hard-to-find"

spices, sauces, condiments and "hurricane mix too"; since it's "fairly priced" and service is "outstanding", there's "no need to go down South" for "a memorable" New Orleans food "experience."

Calyx Flowers *Flowers*

| 26 | 26 | 25 | VE |

www.calyxflowers.com | 800-800-7788

"If you want to impress" someone special, this "excellent" website from the renowned "luxury" bloom specialist excels at "elegant", "high-end" arrangements made with "exotic" "fresh flowers", augmented by plants and "fantastic" wreaths (and you'll never "have to worry about the quality of the vases"); service is "reliable and fast" when you "positively need to get them there", and though "the prices are stratospheric", supporters who "wouldn't trust" anyone else say it's such "beautiful stuff" you'll "want to treat yourself as well."

Chefs *Cookware*

| 26 | 24 | 24 | M |

www.chefscatalog.com | 800-884-2433

Considered a "go-to" for "high-quality equipment for the home chef", this site satisfies "all your kitchen needs" with an impressively "broad range" of culinary "gear" – from cookware to cutlery to "hard-to-find" "gadgets" – listed in a "user-friendly" format that's "fun to browse" and loaded with "every bit of information you could want" to find "one more essential item"; the customer service is "excellent" and everything's "delivered promptly", and "watch for shipping specials and sales" to better the already "competitive pricing"; P.S. there's also a registry service.

ChefShop.com *Specialty Shop*

| 26 | 24 | 25 | E |

www.chefshop.com | 800-596-0885

A "wonderful resource" for the "inventive" chef, this online outlet of a Seattle specialty store proves "very useful" for an "amazing variety" of "excellent" "gourmet foods" and "harder-to-find ingredients" culled from around the world, with "interesting" and often "unique" types of truffles, seafood, herbs and spices, oils, pastas, grains, condiments and baking supplies; the site obliges epicures with videos and recipes, while "timely delivery" and "outstanding" customer service help justify prices that are upmarket but considered "fair."

Chef's Resource *Cookware*

| 27 | 24 | 25 | M |

www.chefsresource.com | 866-765-2433

"They've got the right stuff" for resourceful chefs at this online kitchenware merchant, which carries top brands of "high-quality" cookware, bakeware, tools and gadgets, cutlery, appliances, furniture like islands and racks and even a smidgen of vinegars, condiments and other gourmet pantry items; customers can expect a "quick response" and "fast" delivery, and the cost is "competitive" considering that some of the items are "otherwise hard to get."

Chefs' Warehouse *Specialty Shop*

| 24 | 22 | 22 | M |

www.chefswarehouse.com | 718-842-8700

"Chefs of all levels" scouting for specialty foods turn to this online vendor's functional site and its "wide selection" of "fabulous" condi-

	QUALITY	DISPLAY	SERVICE	COST

ments, foie gras, caviar, imported cheeses, spices and other gourmet goods, many of which make their way into restaurant kitchens; it's handy for finding "everything you need" in "one place" (especially if you "live in the boonies"), though sophisticates cite a "run-of-the-mill" inventory that, as the name suggests, is "better for volume purchases."

Chukar *Candy/Nuts*   27 | 25 | 26 | M

www.chukar.com | 800-624-9544

A "must" "if you love dried cherries", this Washington State orchard processes its sweet Bing and tart varieties in small batches to produce "wonderful" treats offered alongside "delicious" chocolate-covered renditions on its retail site; the "excellent" product variety extends to other dried berries, preserves and fruit fillings for pies, and the "well-packaged" tins and baskets make "unique gifts" that become a "big hit" at "every holiday."

Cookies By Design *Baked Goods*   22 | 25 | 24 | E

www.cookiesbydesign.com | 888-882-6654

"When sending a gift" to a "sweet tooth", this online operation offers an attractive "alternative to flowers" with its "creative and decorative" cookie "bouquets", neatly crafted into "adorable arrangements for every occasion" (choices include birthday, get well, congratulations, baby shower, etc.), with an option to personalize; prices are "steep", but those "beautiful little treasures" are always a "well-received" treat – even if a few whisper they "look better than they taste."

Cooking.com *Cookware*   24 | 22 | 23 | M

www.cooking.com | 800-663-8810

Providing "one-stop shopping" for "all the kitchen implements a cook – aspiring or experienced – could want", this mega-supplier is ever "dependable" for an "excellent" "array" of "brand-name" merchandise in "all types and styles", always delivered "in a timely manner" at "hard-to-beat" prices (frequent "free-shipping offers help"); given its "easy-to-navigate" site's wealth of consumer ratings and "reviews", "tips" and "recipes that are actually good", culinary "enthusiasts" confirm there's "very little they don't have."

Cowgirl Creamery *Cheese/Dairy*   29 | 25 | 26 | E

www.cowgirlcreamery.com | 866-433-7834

Just about the "best around" in the eyes of fromage snobs, this creamery on the coast in Port Reyes Station, CA, specializes in "superb artisanal cheeses" whether "handmade" on-site in trademark varieties like its "exquisite" Mt. Tam and "ethereal" Red Hawk or listed in its 'library of cheese', a catalog of myriad "unusual" options imported from purveyors based in Bordeaux and beyond; "great customer service" ensures the wares are "delivered in excellent condition", and while some surveyors are cowed by "prohibitive" pricing, most say it's "worth it" for "high quality" that "can be tasted."

	QUALITY	DISPLAY	SERVICE	COST

Cushman Fruit Co. *Produce*   24 | 21 | 24 | M
www.honeybell.com | 800-776-7575

Diehards "wait all year" for this "tried-and-true" Florida grower's "incredible honeybells", a "sweet and juicy" tangerine-grapefruit hybrid offered only in January that "oozes and drips" so tantalizingly "they even include a bib" with the shipment; the other fresh citrus, candy, cakes and preserves are likewise "second to none in quality", and while "not cheap", the goods "arrive as if they were just picked" – so as gifts they're "like sunshine in a box."

CutleryAndMore *Cookware*   27 | 23 | 27 | M
www.cutleryandmore.com | 800-650-9866

Besides being on "the cutting-edge of online knife merchants" with "brand-name" cutlery in every category at "fair prices", this long-running site is a boundless trove of cookware, kitchen tools and small appliances (including replacement parts), all searchable by manufacturer; "orders ship promptly", and cost-watchers who comb the inventory and "shop opportunistically" report there are "fantastic bargains to be found"; P.S. they offer "free shipping on purchases over $49."

Dancing Deer Baking Co. *Baked Goods*   24 | 22 | 23 | M
www.dancingdeer.com | 888-699-3337

"Sweet treats" from this Boston outfit put "smiles on everyone's faces", especially the "delectable" gourmet cookies "homemade" from "pure", "natural ingredients" in some "unusual flavors" (molasses-clove, cherry-almond-ginger) and "awesome brownies" that furnish a "major chocolate fix"; everything's "packaged prettily", "delivered fresh" and "well appreciated by giftees", and even somewhat "dear" prices produce "good karma" since part of the profit goes to charity.

D'Artagnan *Meat/Poultry*   29 | 24 | 25 | VE
www.dartagnan.com | 800-327-8246

The "gold standard" for "exquisite game" and other "gourmet" "indulgences" "you probably won't see at your supermarket", Ariane Daguin's "one-of-a-kind", Jersey-based site is "all it's quacked up to be" for "utterly first-class provisions" including its celebrated "rich foie gras", pâtés, "moulard duck breast" and confit, as well as "delectable poultry", heritage meats and "finer foods" like truffles and smoked specialties; it also has an "impeccable reputation" for service, so while you'll "pay top dollar", when "you want to be certain" of "exceptional quality" you're "not wasting a penny."

Di Bruno Bros. *Cheese/Dairy*   28 | 26 | 27 | E
www.dibruno.com | 888-322-4337

Bringing a famed Italian market "to your home", this online arm of a "long-respected" (since 1939) "Philly landmark" is best known as an "excellent" "purveyor of cheeses" featuring handmade mozz and imports from The Boot and "around the world"; it also earns "*amore*" with the "highest quality" in charcuterie, caviar and smoked fish,

pastas, sauces, oils and condiments, and with "outstanding customer service" that makes sending gifts "easy", most maintain it's
"worth a slight markup."

Earthy Delights *Specialty Shop* 24 | 22 | 23 | E
www.earthy.com | 800-367-4709

Like "foraging in the Garden of Eden" for "unique" tidbits, this premium
purveyor is a "go-to place online" for "seasonal" delights like "wonderful wild mushrooms" ("treats like morels" are available dried or
fresh) and "fabulous" truffles from small producers, as well as artisanal cheeses, vinegars, condiments, honeys, spices and more; the
site's replete with recipes and "good to deal with", but you may be
distracted from the "excellent quality" when you "see the price."

Enstrom's *Candy/Nuts* 28 | 25 | 26 | E
www.enstrom.com | 800-367-8766

The "best almond toffee ever" is the "main event" at this "easy-to-
navigate" site from a veteran Colorado confectioner, whose "spectacular" specialty's "wonderful, buttery" crunch is an "addictive"
"guilty pleasure"; it also turns out gourmet chocolate truffles, mints,
chews, fudge and "sugar-free" sweets if you prefer to "save a few
calories", and the "excellent service" and "quick delivery" are com-
mended by gift-givers who attest it's "worth every penny for
the exquisite taste."

Ethel M. *Candy/Nuts* 25 | 24 | 24 | E
www.ethelm.com | 800-471-0352

Possibly "the best of the commercial" chocolatiers, this "high-end
division of Mars" with a facility and stores in the Vegas area produces its "top-notch" bars, bonbons and signature brittle in small
batches presented in "beautifully packaged" boxes; when you need
an "easy-to-order" "treat" at a "reasonable price" it delivers "exactly
what you expect", though some cocoa connoisseurs appraise the offerings as "fine, not outstanding."

Fante's Kitchen *Cookware* 28 | 23 | 25 | M
www.fantes.com | 800-443-2683

"If they don't have it, you don't need it" vow boosters who deem this
online "go-to" from an "old-time" Philly cookware merchant the
"best source for kitchen equipment on the planet" given its "tons" of
"hard-to-find" necessities (especially baking tools and supplies
from Italy) and "cutesy gadgets" most "had no idea" existed;
"knowledgeable" customer service ensures items are delivered "exactly as listed" in "quick time", so few mind if the site itself is
"less than awesome."

Fauchon *Candy/Nuts* 28 | 27 | 23 | VE
www.tasteofparis.us | 305-421-9906

When you "can't get to Paris", this U.S.-based site devoted to
"unique" gourmet "nibbles" from the "traditional" (founded 1881)
French purveyor imports "exquisite" house-brand delicacies à la "incomparable" chocolates and "sweets", "wonderful preserves", teas,

mustards and other "decadent" provisions; "when only the best will do" it provides "chic" "indulgences" and gifts "delivered ASAP" with "lovely" customer service, so even if the "limit on your credit card" is stretched, you "get what you pay for."

Ferrari, A.G., Foods *Specialty Shop*

28	25	26	E

www.agferrari.com | 877-878-2783

You "don't need to go to Italy" for artisanal imports thanks to this California-based link to The Boot, which stocks a "wide assortment" of "hard-to-find" goods from small producers including "excellent dried pastas", cheeses, salumi, olive oils, wines and *autentico* groceries; "fast, efficient" shipping and a recipe-loaded site organized by product category and region help make it a "great source" for specialty cooking or gift baskets for the would-be *culiniere.*

Fortnum & Mason *Coffee/Tea*

28	26	26	VE

www.fortnumandmason.com | 877-533-2636

Proof that "the English really know how to do it properly", this "reliably marvelous" U.S. site representing the "upper-crust" Piccadilly Circus shop of nearly three centuries' standing vends its "glorious wares" – "lovely teas" bolstered by "the finest jams and preserves", biscuits and other Anglophonic "goodies" – minus the London store's "gentlemen in morning coats"; when "money is no object", their "terrific" hampers of "beautiful merchandise" make "impressive gifts" for your "British pals", though sticklers "wish one could buy their full catalog" statewide.

Fran's Chocolates *Candy/Nuts*

27	26	25	E

www.franschocolates.com | 800-422-3726

"When you're ready for heaven", "don't miss the signature sea-salt caramels" from consummate Seattle-based confectioner Fran Bigelow, whose line of "extraordinary" handmade chocolates also extends to truffles and dipped fruit, all "elegantly packaged with satin ribbons" for "gifts or personal treats" that are "always a delight"; "helpful" service rounds out a "sweet indulgence" that's "well worth the occasional investment."

Frog Hollow Farm *Produce*

27	25	24	VE

www.froghollow.com | 888-779-4511

Expect "superb quality" from this Bay Area organic farm, renowned for "beautiful" stone fruits like "the best peaches outside of Georgia", apricots, plums and cherries, along with tree fruits, homemade baked goods and "gotta-try" spreads "that burst in your mouth like manna"; "you pay for it", of course, but it's "worth whatever price they charge" and fructiferous samplers and by-the-week programs make for "a special present for yourself or others."

German Deli *Meat/Poultry*

26	22	26	M

www.germandeli.com | 877-437-6269

A "most authentic" source of "very German" goods you "can't find in the local grocery", this Dallas-area retailer's online market stocks its virtual aisles with an encyclopedic selection of Deutsch imports (with a Dutch sideline) including meats and wursts, seafood, everyday "staples", sweets, beverages and *haus*-wares; it's favored for "personal" service and "top-notch" packaging and shipping, and the themed gift boxes are sure to earn a "*danke schön.*"

Ghirardelli Chocolate *Candy/Nuts* | 25 | 24 | 23 | M |

www.ghirardelli.com | 888-402-6262

"Your mouth begins to water the minute you" arrive at the "wonderful website" of this "classic" (since 1852) SF confectioner, whose "addictive" "fine chocolate" is "consistent through and through" no matter which of the "oh-so-delicious" bars and squares you're "craving"; bakers can consult online "recipes for using their products", and "top-notch customer service" and "right-on" "shipment arrival" make it a "better-than-average" choice, even if snoots say it's "serviceable" but rather "ordinary" for "the true connoisseur."

Grafton Village Cheese *Cheese/Dairy* | 28 | 22 | 25 | M |

www.graftonvillagecheese.com | 800-472-3866

Nestled in "a Vermont hamlet" since 1892, this "fabulous" cheesemaker is a "top producer" of "excellent cheddars" that are handcrafted in small batches and "aged to perfection" to yield "melt-in-your-mouth" traditional wheels and "fantastic" flavored options (garlic, sage and its maple-smoked specialty); also furnishing syrups, jams and mustards, it's an "easy-to-use" source of "ideal gifts" for turophiles with "service that always pleases"; P.S. check out its new World Cheese Award–winning line of cave-aged fromages.

Grand Traverse Pie Co. *Baked Goods* | 25 | 23 | 26 | M |

www.gtpie.com | 866-444-7437

"If it's cherry pie you're after", this "excellent" baked-goods chain with stores traversing the Michigan region (aka the "cherry capital of the world") is famed for its "mmm" "deep-dish" babies sporting either pastry or crumb topping, as well as other fruit pies (apple, blueberry, blackberry, peach and more) and a minor lineup of cakes, brownies and cookies; the goods are moderately priced, "fresh" and "ship well", and a monthly club is available for serious sweet tooths.

Green Mountain Coffee Roasters *Coffee/Tea* | 25 | 22 | 24 | M |

www.greenmountaincoffee.com | 888-879-4627

Committed to keeping your "caffeine level stable", this "worthy" coffee colossus offers "the absolute best selection" of single-serving K-Cup "pods" to fit its Keurig brewers (also sold online), including a "range of organic and Fair Trade" options "you can feel good about buying" and a myriad "enjoyable" specialty blends; it's "convenient" for beans too, though spoilers snipe the "site's a bit clunky" and the java's "middle-of-the-road"; P.S. the "price is reduced if you join their club."

Greyston Bakery *Baked Goods* | 26 | 22 | 22 | M |

www.greystonbakery.com | 800-289-2253

"Fabulous tastes for an excellent cause" is the win-win proposition from this Yonkers baker, which produces its "awesome" Do-Goodie brownies and blondies "with a serious social purpose", as profits are used to support community development; widely available in fine markets, the squares are sold online in packaged assortments that make attractive personal or corporate gifts.

Hadley Fruit Orchards *Candy/Nuts*

24 | 24 | 22 | M

www.hadleyfruitorchards.com | 800-854-5655

While these well-established Banning, CA, orchards "can't be beat" for "an amazing variety of overlooked delicacies", their site's an especially handy way to "get fixed up" with "great dates", whether their best-selling Medjools or "less common" types like Deglet Noor or Golden Princess ("you won't regret it"); it's also a source of "delicious" "dried local fruits and nuts" as well as trail mixes, snacks and sweets, and it assembles some of the more wholesome gift packs.

Hale Groves *Gift Baskets*

23 | 22 | 24 | M

www.halegroves.com | 800-562-4502

Fruit aficionados hail this stalwart Florida grower for "superior" citrus that's "so juicy you need a bath after eating one", all shipped in season from a "luscious" lineup led by the "freshest" temple oranges and ruby-red grapefruit; the "wonderful" wares can be sampled in gift baskets or via monthly clubs, and as this is an "accommodating" outfit that "stands by its products", any order that "fails to meet quality standards is promptly replaced."

Harrington's of Vermont *Meat/Poultry*

27 | 23 | 24 | E

www.harringtonham.com | 802-434-4444

"Incredible" corn cob–smoked ham is this Vermont retailer's "delicious" claim to fame, but it's equally "excellent" for turkey, chicken, bacon and other meats as well as select cheeses and condiments, making it one of "the easiest and best choices" for entertaining "around the holidays" or any time "you have a crowd" (even "the hash from leftovers is divine"); its "reliability" extends to "easy" ordering and "on-time" delivery, and the "reasonable cost" improves with "special offers" that "really are special."

Harry & David *Gift Baskets*

23 | 24 | 24 | E

www.harryanddavid.com | 877-322-1200

"A name you can trust", this Oregon-based outfit "excels year in, year out" as "the Cadillac of online gift" options, "expertly" assembling its "justifiably famous" pears with other "lush" fruit and "scrumptious" snacks into baskets or towers that are "impressive" for "any occasion"; the site's a "delight to browse" and its customer-service staff goes "overboard to ensure satisfaction", so although you'll "pay dearly" (and a "disappointed" few claim the "quality doesn't justify the price"), most note "there's certainly value" in the "tried-and-true" performance and "thrilled" recipients.

HoneyBaked Ham Co. *Meat/Poultry*

25 | 22 | 23 | E

www.honeybaked.com | 866-492-4267

Rivals "just don't measure up" according to hog-wild fans of the "phenomenal" namesake available online from this nationwide

QUALITY DISPLAY SERVICE COST

chain, whose "sweet"-glazed and "beautifully spiral-sliced" hams are touted as "unsurpassed for quality and flavor"; since it also supplies "juicy turkey", traditional sides and desserts, the site "makes it easy" to "splurge" on a "no-fuss" spread that's a "staple for the holidays" and "a real crowd-pleaser" any time.

igourmet.com *Gift Baskets* | 27 | 24 | 25 | E |
www.igourmet.com | 877-446-8763

When you "don't know where to get it", this "dazzling" mega-site offers up a "virtual boatload" of almost any "gourmet" provision "you can imagine" – notably an "excellent" array of "artisanal cheeses" – all "smartly indexed" with the option to "create your own gift baskets"; newcomers may be daunted by "too many choices" (it "helps if you know what you're looking for"), but the "wonderful customer service", "speedy delivery" and "reasonable prices" for "first-rate" quality sustain a "great track record" that's made it an online "favorite."

Illy *Coffee/Tea* | 27 | 23 | 23 | E |
www.illyusa.com | 877-469-4559

"The closest you can get" to *genuino* "Italian-style coffee" is found on the stateside website of this Trieste-based bigwig, whose "terrific", "full-bodied" espresso and drip blend are "roasted heaven" whether purchased in whole beans, single-serving "pods" or ground; it's also "excellent" for a "beautiful assortment" of espresso machines, brewers, grinders and an ever-changing lineup of "designer cups", and if the "price is pretty steep", its subscription service for "recurring delivery" is a "good deal" for junkies who have to "have it every morning."

Intelligentsia Coffee *Coffee/Tea* | 28 | 24 | 24 | E |
www.intelligentsiacoffee.com | 888-945-9786

Wised-up brew buffs opine "it's hard to beat" this Chicago-based cafe chain–cum–java merchant for "excellent" Fair Trade and organic coffee given its lineup of "freshly roasted" beans and blends showcasing "rare and amazing" finds gathered from across the globe; it's also a smart choice for loose-leaf tea and chai, along with brewers, grinders, espresso machines and other merchandise, and "orders are sent promptly" whether "for yourself or for gifts."

Just Flowers *Flowers* | 21 | 22 | 21 | M |
www.justflowers.com | 800-777-1911

"If you need to send" flowers and can't "call a florist", this online operation is a "lifesaver" offering a vast assortment of mainstream arrangements and baskets that "really impress", with the option of same-day delivery; its site is organized by occasion and type of bloom, and those who are "surprised to see how beautiful" the buds are and "how long they last" are justly "happy with the service."

K&L Wine Merchants *Wine/Liquor* | 26 | 20 | 25 | M |
www.klwines.com | 877-559-4637

A "wine geek's dream", this "user-friendly website" of a Frisco-based vintner "caters to all tastes" with an "excellent selection" that ranges "from old world to new" (highlighting "gems" from Bordeaux and California) and "from budget to the highest-end", with descriptions and "advice" to go along with each vintage; "orders are filled quickly and accurately" with "follow-up over the phone", making it "easy to start a small collection" for "those just getting into" the game; P.S. check for online auctions and clubs too.

Karl Ehmer *Meat/Poultry*

26 | 19 | 22 | M

www.karlehmer.com | 800-487-5275

As a family-owned purveyor of "quality meat" that "reminds you of the Europe your parents know", this "old-time" German butcher (since 1932) appeals to traditionalists who "appreciate the variety" of its house-brand specialties, citing "sausages in particular", including "wonderful bratwurst"; proffering numerous "hams and pork products" plus specialty groceries like sauerkraut, pickles, spaetzle and red cabbage, it "never disappoints" *treu* fans.

King Arthur Flour/
The Baker's Catalogue *Beans/Grains*

28 | 25 | 27 | M

www.kingarthurflour.com | 800-827-6836

"Add that extra pizzazz to your baking" through this New England bicentenarian's online catalog, a "godsend" for "amateur" and "advanced" toques alike featuring a "full range" of "superb" flours, "flavorings" and "scratch ingredients" along with "exceptional" mixes and "tons" of "top-notch bakeware" and "fun gadgets" to help your efforts "rise above all the others"; priding itself on "super service" and a site studded with "great recipes" and "helpful hints", it's an "essential source" hailed as "truly the king."

La Tienda *Specialty Shop*

27 | 26 | 26 | E

www.tienda.com | 800-710-4304

"Spain's at your doorstep" thanks to this "fantastic" online pantry, a "go-to for everything Spanish" loaded with "real-deal" "imported favorites" including "many varieties" of "mouthwatering chorizo", *jamón* and *queso* plus "brilliant offerings" spanning oils and spices to wines and cookware, many "difficult or impossible to find" elsewhere; add "fair prices" (with "frequent sales"), "prompt shipping" and "personal" customer support "to back it all up", and amigos wonder "how did I live without it?"

Lobster Gram *Seafood*

24 | 22 | 23 | VE

www.livelob.com | 800-548-3562

"When you can't get to the coast", the "next best thing" for a "wonderful" "taste of Maine" may be this online leader's "sumptuous" live lobsters and frozen tails, tendered along with shrimp, scallops, shellfish and "indulgent" full-meal deals like surf 'n' turf and clambakes complete with "all the goodies"; deliveries "arrive perfectly packed" and supported by "top-notch" customer service, so though the goods are "pricey", they make the "perfect gift" for crustacean cognoscenti.

	QUALITY	DISPLAY	SERVICE	COST

Mackenzie Ltd. *Caviar/Smoked Fish*
25 | 26 | 25 | VE

www.mackenzieltd.com | 800-858-7100

You'll "want to order everything" on offer from this high-end online outfit, which expands on its original specialty, Scottish smoked salmon, with caviar and other seafood plus "scrumptious" prepared items from a "tempting" catalog of gourmet entrees, hors d'oeuvres, sides and desserts, not to mention gift samplers abrim with British sundries; the cost can run "outrageously" "high", but you can "rely" upon "excellent" service – "if you're in the mood to splurge", the goods are "all amazing."

Maine Lobster Direct *Seafood*
29 | 25 | 28 | E

www.mainelobsterdirect.com | 800-556-2783

"This is the real deal" cheer "lobster lovers" with claws to celebrate this net-based biz, which ships "excellent" live crustaceans direct from Maine "to your door", along with frozen tails, chowders and assorted "fresh" seafood and sides; the goods are also offered as dinner packages (some including a "convenient cooking vessel"), and it's a "great gift resource" for "something a little different" that "receivers rave" about.

Melissa's *Produce*
25 | 24 | 23 | M

www.melissas.com | 800-588-0151

Forage through a "cornucopia of nature's bounty" via the online service of this LA-based specialty produce vendor, a "favorite supplier" of "all sorts of interesting" fruit and veggies, ranging from high-grade seasonal staples to "unique" exotics, dried items, organics and herbs and spices; thankfully, the searchable site abounds with info and recipes "so you know what to do with all those mysterious" products.

Metropolitan Bakery *Baked Goods*
26 | 22 | 23 | E

www.metropolitanbakery.com | 877-412-7323

Breads from this Philly-based bakery/cafe chainlet are among "the closest" to European-style manna available online thanks to an ownership duo (one French-trained) who use old-world techniques to produce "excellent" artisanal loaves, including organic and "wholegrain" varieties that serve as "the perfect nutritious canvas" for a healthful repast; they also hawk house-brand granola and flavored popcorn, and the "bread-of-the-month club" is a "good gift idea" for dough nuts.

MexGrocer.com *Specialty Shop*
24 | 20 | 24 | M

www.mexgrocer.com | 877-463-9476

For "Mexican culinary" goods that "can't be accessed locally", this online *mercado* is a "reliable" "all-around resource" offering "unique" imports among its stock of packaged and canned staples (salsas and spices, beans, sweets) along with utensils and kitchen equipment (tortilla presses, tamale kits); it's a somewhat basic setup, but "when you can't find your product elsewhere" "this is the place."

	QUALITY	DISPLAY	SERVICE	COST

Mighty Leaf *Coffee/Tea*   `29` `24` `25` `E`
www.mightyleaf.com | 877-698-5323

"They really take pride" in their brews at this SF-based standout, whose "terrific" teas flaunt "top-of-the-line" "quality and appearance" with their "heavenly bouquet" and "attractive" presentation in "elegant-looking", "individually bagged" cotton pouches (whole leaves are also available); its organic-leaning line of "imaginative", handcrafted blends includes herbal, green, black, white and oolong varieties in "fabulous" flavor combinations that "really warm up your taste buds", leaving sippers mighty satisfied despite "expensive" prices; P.S. they have teaware and gift samplers too.

Mo Hotta Mo Betta *Specialty Shop*   `27` `25` `25` `M`
www.mohotta.com | 800-462-3220

It doesn't get betta for "heat addicts" than the "vast selection" from this online hot sauce specialist, whose exhaustive inventory ranges from its own house brand to small producers that pride themselves on turning up the flame; BBQ sauces, salsas and marinades are also available for "on-time delivery", and the "custom-made label" option is a "great gifting idea" for those "who like to get a burn on."

NapaStyle *Specialty Shop*   `24` `26` `23` `E`
www.napastyle.com | 866-766-1600

A "glimpse into the world" of "talented chef" Michael Chiarello, this "little bit of Napa" is an "appealing" site abounding with "interesting choices" in "first-rate" "gourmet foods" – seasonings, spreads, chocolates, oils, condiments and wines from the Chiarello Family Vineyards – and "upscale items for the kitchen and home" spanning cookware to furnishings; the "smart" selection will "fit any gift or personal need", and supporters say the "higher-caliber" products "make the higher prices not so painful."

New Braunfels Smokehouse *Meat/Poultry*   `26` `22` `25` `M`
www.nbsmokehouse.com | 800-537-6932

It's the "real Texas deal" declare disciples of this "authentic" Hill Country smokehouse, a "family business" since 1943 that's still "tops" for its "traditional preparation" of hickory-smoked meats, namely "fantastic" brisket, sausage, jerkies, poultry and "bacon that'll make you rethink breakfast"; the online inventory includes numerous samplers, and "excellent quality at reasonable prices" ("watch for the sales") means you "can't go wrong" whether you "treat yourself or others."

Niman Ranch *Meat/Poultry*   `28` `24` `25` `VE`
www.nimanranch.com

Proving "serious meat" can be "all-natural", this "top-shelf" supplier's site is a "healthy alternative" for "superb" sustainable beef, pork and lamb, all "responsibly and humanely raised" on independent family farms to produce "restaurant-quality" cuts that are "easy to love on your plate"; while the "excellence comes at a high price", principled sorts promise it's "deserving of every dollar spent."

	QUALITY	DISPLAY	SERVICE	COST

Norman Love Confections *Candy/Nuts*   28 | 26 | 27 | E

www.normanloveconfections.com | 866-515-2121

"Wow someone" with "the finest chocolates" via this "exceptional" Florida-based confectioner run by the eponymous cocoa virtuoso, whose "artisanal" bonbons are handcrafted from imported beans and intense "fresh" flavorings to yield "delicious and beautiful" collections including a premium series of single-origin darks; its online service "accommodates without any hassle", and despite the predictably "high" price tag, "once you love Norman you'll find the money for the next order"; P.S. wedding favors and cakes are a specialty.

Nueske's Applewood   28 | 25 | 26 | E
Smoked Meats *Meat/Poultry*

www.nueskes.com | 800-392-2266

"You haven't had pork until you've had" specialties from this family-owned Wisconsin operation, which casts an "applewood-smoked spell" with "the best bacon on the market" ("so fresh and flavorful you'd swear it oinks") backed up by ham, sausage, beef and poultry, plus gourmet extras and gift baskets; with "top-notch" vittles and service that goes "beyond what's needed", it keeps its faithful followers in hog "heaven."

1-800-flowers.com *Flowers*   20 | 20 | 21 | M

www.1800flowers.com | 800-462-7842

"When you need flowers in a hurry", this online outfit is a "quick-and-easy" standby for "efficient", "on-time" delivery that "comes in handy in a pinch" if you "forgot mom's birthday"; the less-impressed cite "middle-of-the-road" arrangements of "lesser-quality buds" that are "safe rather than exciting", and "you're gonna pay" for "last-minute orders", but when you "don't know of a local florist" it "gets the job done" – "it's the thought that counts."

Pampered Chef *Cookware*   24 | 23 | 23 | E

www.pamperedchef.com | 888-687-2433

"Everyone needs a little pampering", and this "wonderfully organized" online store "makes life so much easier" for the "most or least experienced chef" with its own "terrific" line of "handy-dandy" cookware, cutlery and "clever" kitchen accessories; "customer service is top-notch", and the site also features "spice mixes", gift sets and "recipes to try", though paupered types point out it's all "a bit costly"; P.S. they also sponsor "home parties."

Peanut Shop of Williamsburg *Candy/Nuts*   26 | 23 | 24 | M

www.thepeanutshop.com | 800-637-3268

"These truly are the best peanuts going" insist boosters "bowled over" by the "ultracrisp, jumbo-grade" Virginia goobers available online from this Colonial Williamsburg shop, which tins its "excellent" wares "salted, unsalted", chocolate-coated, honey-roasted or spiced up with flavors like BBQ or wasabi; also offering brittle, cashews and other snacks, it's "wonderful" for an "indulgence" or treat "for discerning guests" ("don't waste these on children").

	QUALITY	DISPLAY	SERVICE	COST

Peet's Coffee & Tea *Coffee/Tea*

| 25 | 22 | 24 | M |

www.peets.com | 800-999-2132

"If you can't get to" one of this Bay Area–based franchise's "retail stores", let them "come to you" via this "most excellent" online java junction, which "takes pride in" vending "exceptionally fresh roasts" (and "wonderful" teas) so "revelatory" they "almost demand you have a second cup"; with an "educational website" and "A-1" customer service, cheerleaders claim it runs the "conglomerate" competition "into the ground"; P.S. recurring delivery through their Peetniks club "reduces the cost of shipping."

Pike Place Fish Market *Seafood*

| 28 | 25 | 26 | E |

www.pikeplacefish.com | 800-542-7732

"Almost as good as shopping" the fishmongers' stalls in Seattle's "famous" Pike Place Market, this "wonderful" web annex supplies "the best quality" in salmon, halibut, Dungeness crab and other Pacific Northwest seafood (including seasonal rarities like Copper River king salmon), all shipped as "fresh" "as if you just caught it"; the goods are "packed with care" and "reliably delivered" so "you can't go wrong" – and it's "cheaper than a flight."

Point Reyes Cheese Co. *Cheese/Dairy*

| 29 | 24 | 25 | E |

www.pointreyescheese.com | 800-591-6878

"Oh, my!" sigh turophiles acquainted with this family dairy farm on the Northern California coast, which raises the bar with the "terrific quality" of its longtime specialty: the "creamiest, richest" handcrafted blue cheese "ever"; joining the "excellent" wheels and wedges are toma table cheese, dips and dressings, and their online outlet puts together "delicious" collections for those "lucky enough to be a recipient of a gift."

Pop's Wine & Spirits *Wine/Liquor*

| 29 | 22 | 26 | M |

www.popswine.com | 516-431-0025

"When you can't find it anywhere else", this durable LI superstore stocks a "terrific range of fine wines" (as well as harder pops) on a searchable site with thousands of vintages listed in 60-plus categories at "competitive prices" bolstered by "some of the best deals" around, including "generous" "case discounts" and the ongoing "end-bin sale"; with its "honest, accurate reviews" and "excellent customer service", it's a "staple" for imbibers in the know.

ProFlowers *Flowers*

| 22 | 21 | 23 | M |

www.proflowers.com | 800-580-2913

Proponents say this "user-friendly" online florist is "always a hit" with its "timely" delivery of "super-fresh flowers" in "pretty" arrangements that can "last so long it's scary"; maybe the "middle-of-the-road" presentation's "not the most imaginative", but with "consistent quality" and service that's "easy to work with" it "gets the job done" at a "fairly affordable" cost ("watch out for specials" and e-mail offers).

Rancho Gordo *Beans/Grains*
28 | 24 | 25 | M

www.ranchogordo.com | 707-259-1935

Owner Steve Sando's "singular passion" is the reason his Napa-based "shrine to beans" is hailed for "hands-down the finest heirloom" varieties in an "amazing" and "colorful" lineup (scarlet runner, tepary, Vallarta, Rio Zape et al.) gathered from California growers; with a sideline in dried corn, chiles, wild rice and quinoa and a site filled with "great recipes" and "interesting" info, "legume enthusiasts" know there's "nowhere else" like it.

Republic of Tea *Coffee/Tea*
27 | 26 | 25 | M

www.republicoftea.com | 800-298-4832

"Tea lovers" thirsty for "something other than the run-of-the-mill" "swear by" this premium purveyor for its "terrific choice of blends and types" showcasing "exceptional flavors" ("some rather surprising") and "seasonal selections" "from all over the world", supplemented on its site by "wonderful" sipware and steeping "accessories"; the leaves are "prettily packaged" and "orders arrive promptly", leading "discerning" sorts to deem it "well worth the cost."

Salumi *Charcuterie*
29 | 25 | 27 | E

www.salumicuredmeats.com | 877-223-0813

"If it's cured meat you're after", this salumeria run by Gina Batali (Mario's sister) "comes up with phenomenal" "balanced" flavors to create a "unique and wonderful" line of salami and cured pork and lamb that "gives Italia a run for the money"; it's "fast becoming a Seattle institution" with a national following grateful for online access to the "excellent" goods, but it's also a small, artisanal producer, so check for availability as supplies may be limited.

Scharffen Berger *Candy/Nuts*
28 | 24 | 24 | E

www.scharffenberger.com | 866-972-6879

"One of the very best" of the domestic cacao crafters, this "epicurean" outfit's "incredible dark chocolate" is made from scratch in its San Francisco factory using "old-school" artisanal methods and primo imported beans to yield bars and squares with "spectacularly rich" "nuances of flavor", including "excellent" varieties "for fine baking"; its products are sold in "better" markets and online, and "every bite's like a piece of gold" – which may explain why the cost approaches "over-the-top."

See's Candies *Candy/Nuts*
24 | 23 | 24 | M

www.sees.com | 800-347-7337

Given its standing as a "California institution", this "trustworthy" confectioner is seen as "the only way to indulge" in the "traditional" likes of "excellent chocolates", peanut brittle, lollipops and other "dependable" "diet wreckers"; the "wide selection" (with the option to "pick your own" boxes) is "reasonably priced" and "arrives fresh", making for a "sweet" "temptation" that giftees are "delighted to receive."

	QUALITY	DISPLAY	SERVICE	COST

SmithfieldHams.com *Meat/Poultry*   `25` `22` `23` `E`
www.smithfieldhams.com | 800-926-8448

"After all these years", this Virginia-based retailer is still "distinctive" with an online arm featuring its "marvelous hams" in popular varieties like dry-cured and honey-glazed that'll provide a "delish" centerpiece "for any occasion"; also known for bacon, sausage and classic sides, it's "always a favorite at family gatherings" or "around the holidays" even if antis allege it's "living on reputation"; P.S. they also carry Paula Deen's line of spices, sauces and desserts.

The Spice House *Herbs/Spices*   `27` `24` `26` `M`
www.thespicehouse.com | 800-972-8496

Make your "food sing" with "aromatic" wares from this "wonderful" Chicago-based seasoning specialist, whose "go-to site" "can't be beat" for an "unmatched" variety of "fantastic", "absolutely fresh" spices and herbs "from the usual to the exotic" (including some most "didn't even know existed"), expertly "organized online" with plentiful recipes and "tips on how to use them"; service comes courtesy of a "formidably" informed staff, and it's a "total bargain" to boot – "what more do you want?"

Stash Tea *Coffee/Tea*   `25` `23` `25` `M`
www.stashtea.com | 800-800-8327

It's "just my cup of tea" declare admirers "impressed with" this far-flung Oregon outfit's "outstanding" online stash of "first-rate", "attractively" packaged specialty blends, sold loose-leaf or bagged from a "large inventory" that includes varieties "you can't buy in most local stores"; it stocks a "wide array" of teaware too, and along with "fair prices" and "dependable" service, there's "comfort in knowing" that "what you see is what you get."

Stew Leonard's Gifts *Gift Baskets*   `24` `22` `24` `M`
www.stewleonardsgifts.com | 800-729-7839

"Just like the stores", you "can always count on" this Connecticut-based chain's website to provide "a lot for your money" with "top-notch" gift baskets, buckets and towers laden with "fresh, yummy" fruit, cheeses, brownies, popcorn and other "snack items"; its "service-oriented" team sees that shipments "deliver on time and in perfect condition", though a few stew over the "reliance on 'cute' in the presentation"; P.S. selections of wine are also available.

Stonewall Kitchen *Specialty Shop*   `27` `26` `25` `E`
www.stonewallkitchen.com | 800-826-1752

"If there's a flavor you can't find here, you're making it up" claim champions of this "esteemed" New England operation's "creative" lineup of "reliably excellent" jams, jellies, condiments, syrups and sauces, which kick off a "fabulous", ever-"growing" product line extending to "baking mixes", marinades and more; the "tempting" catalog and "superior" "ease of ordering" make it a "trusty go-to" for "beautifully packaged" gift sets, and while the goods cost "a pretty penny", they're "worth it."

Sunnyland Farms *Candy/Nuts*
26 | 23 | 25 | M

www.sunnylandfarms.com | 800-999-2488

"Simply the best" nuts "raw or roasted" are the pride of this Georgia-based merchant, whose "tender and delicious" pecans are the highlight of a "wonderfully fresh" array ranging from almonds, cashews, walnuts and peanuts to pralines, brittles, dried fruits and chocolate-dipped treats; sunny service means a "quick response to any problem", and their tins are bound to be a "well-received" gift.

Tao of Tea *Coffee/Tea*
25 | 24 | 23 | M

www.taooftea.com | 503-736-0198

Cognoscenti of steeped brews say this Portland, OR, outfit "passes the tasty tea test" with "some of the highest quality" available, proffering "amazing" loose leaves (many certified organic) imported from Far Eastern growers and hand-processed to yield a mix of exotic varietals, now augmented by chai concentrates; a site replete with teaware, a monthly club and info and tips for brewers proves beyond a taobt they "know their product inside and out."

Taza Chocolate *Candy/Nuts*
27 | 24 | 25 | E

www.tazachocolate.com | 617-623-0804

Sweet tooths craving something "different from what else is out there" turn to this artisanal manufacturer for "top-notch" "Mexican-style stone-ground chocolate", traditionally handmade in small batches from organic, sustainably sourced cacao beans to yield "wholesome", "intensely flavored" bars and disks, baking squares, extract and coated nuts; the "somewhat grainy" texture may run contrary to "your smooth and creamy" expectations, but it's acclaimed by connoisseurs as an "unusual and delicious" departure.

Upton Tea Imports *Coffee/Tea*
29 | 23 | 27 | M

www.uptontea.com | 800-234-8327

It's "just the best" attest "serious tea connoisseurs" touting this online brew "heaven", whose Massachusetts warehouse harbors 400-odd "high-quality" loose leaves that span the familiar to the exotic and "all price ranges", with "sample sizes that make it easy to try" "without making a big investment", and it also offers "wonderful teapots" and paraphernalia; "totally reliable" service and a site infused with discounts, a "historical newsletter", a best-seller list and consumer ratings ensure its devotees stay "totally converted."

Usinger's *Meat/Poultry*
27 | 22 | 25 | M

www.usinger.com | 800-558-9998

A "Milwaukee tradition" dating to 1880, this time-honored butcher's online outlet is "simply da best" source of "the finest old-world style sausages" made from family recipes "like they were 100 years ago", "especially" the "divine" bratwursts but also "excellent" beef franks, smoked meats and cold cuts ("and that's no baloney"); Midwestern expats who confirm it's "unquestionably" "the only place to get this quality" also sing the praises of the "superb" service and assortments that "make a wonderful gift."

	QUALITY	DISPLAY	SERVICE	COST

Whole Latte Love *Coffee/Tea*

| 28 | 23 | 24 | M |

www.wholelattelove.com | 888-411-5282

"Get your java on" at this online "go-to" for "everything coffee", a "convenient" way to peruse a "fantastic selection" of "upscale" espresso machines and drip brewers plus a "full complement of top" brands of beans, along with "hard-to-find components" and "all the accessories an aficionado could need or want"; throw in "fair pricing" and "on-site reviews", videos and other "useful information", and it earns a whole lotta loyalty from percolators who prefer "one-stop shopping"; P.S. teas and their trappings are available too.

Wine.com *Wine/Liquor*

| 24 | 22 | 23 | M |

www.wine.com | 800-592-5870

Considered a "breeze" to navigate for "connoisseurs and the every-man" alike, this earliest of web-based vino vendors stocks a "quite extensive" "general inventory" in a "user-friendly display" laying out "lots of reasonable bottles" and "some great finds" at "competitive prices"; shipments are "timely" and "packed properly", and even snoots who say it's "reliable" for "mass-produced" labels with less of a selection "at the top end" concede it's "a good place to start looking."

Wine Library *Wine/Liquor*

| 27 | 23 | 25 | M |

www.winelibrary.com | 888-980-9463

"Terrific" "volume and variety" qualify this online branch of a "grail"-like New Jersey retailer as a "first choice" for oenophiles eagerly checking out its "incredible" compendium of "excellent and often little-known" vintages, all "fairly priced" and scattered with "bargains"; with a "service-oriented" staff that's "incredibly knowledgeable and ready to assist", it's a "wine-lover's dream."

Zachy's *Wine/Liquor*

| 27 | 24 | 24 | E |

www.zachys.com | 866-922-4971

The "epitome" of emporiums for the fancier of "fine wines", this Westchester grog shop's site shows off an "excellent selection" of more than 5,000 "high-profile" labels that's especially "worth attention" for "rare and exceptional" varietals; the stock's curated by an "accommodating" staff to "steer you in the right direction", though for cash-strapped customers the prices "tend to be on the high side unless they're having a sale"; P.S. it also hosts online auctions.

Zingerman's *Specialty Shop*

| 28 | 26 | 27 | E |

www.zingermans.com | 888-636-8162

"It's always a blast" browsing the "humorous", "wonderfully illustrated" website of this Ann Arbor deli "institution" offering an "incomparable" lineup of "addiction-inducing" breads, cheeses, charcuterie, olive oils, vinegars and other "top-of-the-line" specialty items "not available just anywhere", including gift baskets that "everybody loves"; the "responsive", "super-helpful" service is a "joy", and though it can be "kinda pricey", if you're "an adventurer with deep pockets" this is the "gold standard"; P.S. discerning foodies "love the monthly clubs" too.

ONLINE SOURCES
INDEXES

Special Features

Listings cover the best in each category and include Quality ratings.

BAKED GOODS

Big Island Candies	29
Boudin Bakery	26
Cookies By Design	22
Cooking.com	24
Dancing Deer Baking	24
Fauchon	28
Frog Hollow Farm	27
German Deli	26
Grand Traverse Pie Co.	25
Greyston Bakery	26
igourmet.com	27
Metropolitan Bakery	26
Norman Love Confections	28
Zingerman's	28

CANDY

Big Island Candies	29
Bridgewater Chocolate	26
ChefShop.com	26
Cooking.com	24
Enstrom's	28
Ethel M.	25
Fauchon	28
Fortnum & Mason	28
Fran's Chocolates	27
German Deli	26
Ghirardelli Chocolate	25
Hadley Fruit	24
igourmet.com	27
La Tienda	27
NapaStyle	24
Norman Love Confections	28
Scharffen Berger	28
See's Candies	24
Sunnyland Farms	26
Taza Chocolate	27
Zingerman's	28

CAVIAR & SMOKED FISH

Browne Trading	28
Chefs' Warehouse	24
Cooking.com	24
Di Bruno Bros.	28
igourmet.com	27
Mackenzie Ltd.	25
Pike Place Fish	28

CHARCUTERIE

Burgers' Smokehouse	23
ChefShop.com	26
D'Artagnan	29
Di Bruno Bros.	28
Ferrari, A.G.	28
igourmet.com	27
Karl Ehmer	26
Salumi	29
Zingerman's	28

CHEESE & DAIRY

Chefs' Warehouse	24
Cooking.com	24
Cowgirl Creamery	29
Di Bruno Bros.	28
Earthy Delights	24
Ferrari, A.G.	28
Grafton Vill. Cheese	28
Harrington's of Vermont	27
igourmet.com	27
La Tienda	27
NapaStyle	24
Point Reyes Cheese	29
Stew Leonard's Gifts	24
Zingerman's	28

COFFEE & TEA

Adagio Teas	25
Atlantic Spice	25
Di Bruno Bros.	28
Fauchon	28
Ferrari, A.G.	28
Fortnum & Mason	28
Green Mountain Coffee	25
igourmet.com	27
Illy	27
Intelligentsia Coffee	28
Mighty Leaf	29
Peet's Coffee	25
Republic of Tea	27

New Braunfels Smokehouse	26
Niman Ranch	28
Nueske's Smoked Meats	28
SmithfieldHams.com	25
Usinger's	27
Zingerman's	28

NUTS & DRIED FRUIT

American Spoon	28
Atlantic Spice	25
Bob's Red Mill	28
Chukar	27
Fauchon	28
Hadley Fruit	24
igourmet.com	27
Melissa's	25
NapaStyle	24
Peanut Shop/Williamsburg	26
Sunnyland Farms	26

PASTAS

ChefShop.com	26
Di Bruno Bros.	28
Ferrari, A.G.	28
igourmet.com	27

PRODUCE

ChefShop.com	26
Cushman Fruit	24
Earthy Delights	24
Frog Hollow Farm	27
Hadley Fruit	24
Hale Groves	23
Harry & David	23
igourmet.com	27
Melissa's	25

SEAFOOD

Allen Brothers	27
Browne Trading	28
CajunGrocer.com	23
ChefShop.com	26
igourmet.com	27

Lobster Gram	24
Mackenzie Ltd.	25
Maine Lobster Direct	29
Pike Place Fish	28

SPECIALTY ITEMS

American Spoon	28
Browne Trading	28
Chefs	26
ChefShop.com	26
Chef's Resource	27
Cooking.com	24
D'Artagnan	29
Di Bruno Bros.	28
Earthy Delights	24
Fante's Kitchen	28
Fauchon	28
Ferrari, A.G.	28
Fortnum & Mason	28
Frog Hollow Farm	27
Grafton Vill. Cheese	28
Hadley Fruit	24
igourmet.com	27
La Tienda	27
Mackenzie Ltd.	25
MexGrocer.com	24
Mo Hotta Mo Betta	27
NapaStyle	24
Stonewall Kitchen	27
Wine.com	24
Zingerman's	28

WINES & LIQUOR

BevMo	24
Ferrari, A.G.	28
K&L Wine	26
La Tienda	27
NapaStyle	24
Pop's Wine	29
Stew Leonard's Gifts	24
Wine.com	24
Wine Library	27
Zachy's	27

Vote at zagat.com